BRAILLE
INTO THE NEXT
MILLENNIUM

BRAILLE
INTO THE NEXT
MILLENNIUM

National Library Service
for the Blind
and Physically Handicapped
and
Friends of Libraries for
Blind and Physically
Handicapped Individuals
in North America
Washington, D.C.
2000

Library of Congress Cataloging-in-Publication Data

Braille into the next millennium.
      p. cm.
   Includes bibliographical references.
   ISBN 0-8444-1021-7
   1. Braille. I. Library of Congress. National Library
Service for the Blind and Physically Handicapped.
II. Friends of Libraries for Blind and Physically
Handicapped Individuals in North America, Inc.

HV1672.B67 2000
411—dc21

00-055583

CONTENTS

Part III: Braille in the Future

FOREWORD

With a tactile medium such as braille comes literacy—spelling, writing, and broad communication possibilities are open and available. With literacy comes the possibility of freedom. With freedom comes the possibility of endless achievement—from pleasant living to significant social contributions. Personal and institutional commitments to braille by enthusiasts in the United States have helped advance literacy for blind individuals in North America and have therefore advanced the possibility of freedom for thousands.

The National Library Service for the Blind and Physically Handicapped of the Library of Congress (NLS) is committed to braille! Each year the NLS spends nearly eight million dollars on the training of braillists; the production of braille books, periodicals, and music materials; and the purchase of materials in all languages from many hundreds of countries around the world. In 1999, there are more than sixty-eight thousand braille titles in the NLS union catalog (a comprehensive listing of special-format materials), with many hundreds to be added every year.

Every possible effort has been and will continue to be made to maintain and expand braille services and materials to residents of the United States and citizens living abroad. With that in mind, it seemed appropriate to provide a review of braille in the United States at the turn of the millennium. From this vantage point, those involved in library matters and those concerned with the development of codes, the production of braille, and the identification of source material will ground their future efforts.

All who have contributed and brought braille to the important place it occupies in the lives of blind individuals are commended. Their work has been recognized—documented—and will be used by those in the generations ahead as a base.

Frank Kurt Cylke

PREFACE

This book on the value and history of braille symbolizes the times in which we live. It highlights the importance of braille in the life of every man, woman, and child who is blind, and points the way to the future—a future of promise and hope. It is particularly appropriate that the book be issued and circulated by NLS (the National Library Service for the Blind and Physically Handicapped of the Library of Congress), for it was NLS and its director, Frank Kurt Cylke, who nurtured braille and helped keep it alive during the bleak days of the lean years.

In recent times and in certain quarters, braille has been extremely controversial and often ignored as a means of teaching blind children to read, but it was not always so. Until after the Second World War, almost all blind children who were to be educated, as well as a great many partially sighted children, went to residential schools for blind children. Braille was a given. Everybody learned it, and the students with partial sight made a practice of reading it with their eyes, blindfolds and lectures from teachers notwithstanding.

In the 1940s, because of retrolental fibroplasia, a form of blindness caused by excess oxygen in the incubators of premature babies, and the consequent sudden increase in the number of blind children, public school education became a necessity. There wasn't anywhere else to put the increased population, and the parents were not about to permit their children to grow up illiterate.

But there was a side effect of this change, one that received relatively little comment at the time. The centrality of braille was destroyed. The public school teachers didn't know braille, and the new crop of teacher trainees in the mushrooming university programs were not much better off. It is true that the teachers received a course or two in braille, but that is not the same as concentrated use and everyday practice.

It was only a small step from not knowing braille to the rationalization that it was unimportant, outdated, and in many instances harmful. The teachers of that time took that step easily. As technology advanced, it offered the vehicle for the rationalization. Parents, of course, were not only willing but anxious to swallow the fallacy. If the child could see even the tiniest bit, the teachers, not knowing braille and feeling comfortable with print, could say:

> "Reading print is normal. You want your child to be normal. Therefore, you want your child to read print if at all possible. Never mind that magnifiers may be awkward and clumsy and that large print may be scarce. Never mind that reading print may be slow and painful. After all," they said, "braille is that way, too."

Almost without exception, the parents nodded in agreement and settled down to a life of limited expectations for their children. Mostly they didn't know any blind adults, people who could read braille at hundreds of words a minute and use it as flexibly and effectively as print is used by sighted people. The parents relied on the "professionals," the people who were trained to know and give competent advice.

I don't mean to paint a picture that condemns the professionals of the forties, fifties, and sixties. In the main, they were sincere and dedicated, and, in many instances, they coped extremely well. The problems they faced were unprecedented, and there was probably no way that a proper emphasis on braille could have been maintained or a true perspective achieved.

I attended a residential school for the blind in the thirties and forties and had a thorough grounding in braille, so

I suffered no damage and feel no resentment. The same cannot be said, however, of many of the children of the post–World War II era. For the most part, those with any sight at all swallowed the flimflam and limped along with print. When they reached high school and college, these same partially sighted people found their reading needs increased; their sight often worsened; they met blind people who were literate and competent in braille; and their anger and frustration congealed into a cold fury. They felt that they had been cheated and lied to and they were determined that blind people of future generations should not be similarly victimized.

This brings us to the eighties and nineties, but before continuing the story, I think it is only fair to say a word about the changing climate among professionals. Many (but by no means all) of today's teachers of blind people have reassessed the value and necessity of braille. Working with the organized blind, these new pioneers insist that blind children have the opportunity for true literacy and a full life. This means braille. It also means an understanding of the part public attitudes play in creating or inhibiting opportunity. It means the daily reinforcement of the concept that it is respectable to be blind and that, given adequate training and reasonable opportunity, blind people can compete on terms of equality with sighted people.

Many elements have gone into the movement for braille literacy, which has built to a crescendo and is now sweeping the nation, but few would deny that the fight has been led by the National Federation of the Blind. The Federation has introduced and continues to press for the passage of braille bills in state legislatures—laws that guarantee to blind children the right to be taught braille and to have teachers who are competent in its use.

In June 1997, the Individuals with Disabilities Education Act (IDEA) was amended and signed into law by the president of the United States, guaranteeing the right of blind and partially sighted children to be taught braille. The new amendments are clear and uncomplicated. The federal law now requires that if a blind or partially sighted child is to be taught reading and writing, braille must be part of the program unless the teachers and the parents unanimously agree that braille is inappropriate in the circumstances. If any member of the team believes that braille should be taught, then the law requires that this be done.

The new amendments also say that teachers of blind people should be competent in the use of braille. As part of this upgrading of the knowledge of the professionals, a National Literary Braille Competency Test has been developed, which is now in the process of being validated. This process has necessarily been a slow and cumbersome one, and there has been some resistance to it from a few of the teachers. But there is every reason to believe that as the years go by, taking and passing the test will be a universal requirement and standard. This is progress, indeed.

Passing a law is one thing. Getting it enforced and, more to the point, *accepted* is quite another. Laws tend to be a reflection of public opinion, not a creator of it. They give a final nudge to new reality. With respect to braille, there can be no doubt that the climate of public opinion has changed dramatically during the past decade. Once again, braille is becoming the centerpiece in the education of blind people, just as print is for sighted people. There is now real hope that blind children will again be given the opportunity for literacy and the tools that will enable them to compete on terms of equality with sighted people. As I have already said, this means braille. There is no substitute, no avoiding the issue, and no turning back.

It is in this atmosphere of renewed opportunity and hope that the current book is produced. It will make a valuable contribution to the new emphasis on braille, and it will give historical background and perspective. It will also synthesize and draw together present thinking and point the way to the future.

Kenneth Jernigan

EDITOR'S INTRODUCTION

At a period when time is much in the forefront of our thoughts and we are barraged with articles and documentaries looking back and looking forward, it seems fitting that we take a moment to look critically at braille. Braille holds a special place of honor in the lives of those of us who use it—not only as a tool for true literacy but also as a tool for personal dignity, privacy, and independence.

We owe a great debt to Louis Braille. He recognized that the raised alphabets of the day were inadequate and that blind people do not need to read in a medium that is convenient for sighted people. He created a system that allows us to read in a medium that is fast and flexible, and, most important, can be written by the individual. Louis Braille, we thank you from the bottom of our hearts!

In this volume, we will trace braille from its beginnings through the myriad of current uses and also take a peek at the future. We will discuss the effect of current technology on the production, distribution, storage, and use of braille and the need for changes in the braille code to meet the reading needs of blind persons in the English-speaking world. Both of these developments have been evolving and will continue to evolve for many years to come.

Change is healthy. It is heartening that change is at the core of what we think of as braille. This change, in whatever form it appears, will no doubt invigorate and revitalize the use of braille and the belief in braille as a way of life.

Each author represented in this volume is an expert in his or her field and has brought to this work a perspective that can be acquired only through experience and a profound closeness to the subject. Braille continues to endure as a vital tool of literacy.

Judith M. Dixon

ORIGINS OF BRAILLE

by Pamela Lorimer

Introduction

Many realize that the braille code is a means for blind people to be literate, but few know why it is called the braille code or what led to its invention and its acceptance today. Many centuries ago, when versions of the alphabet were first used by those with sight, it was accepted that blind people would not be able to take part in the normal life of their community. That acceptance constituted the reason a suitable code for reading and writing was not available until comparatively recently.

The French philosopher Denis Diderot (1712–1784) was the first to study how blind people could manage their lives without the unifying sense of sight. He talked with blind people, observed how blind people lived, and spent time with blind people, one of whom was Nicholas

Saunderson, a mathematician at Cambridge University. Diderot was editor of the great *Encyclopédie*, which "should be a compendium of all knowledge and a work of propaganda for the new ideas" (Cobban 1957). In the first edition of the *Encyclopédie*, published in 1751, Diderot included his observations on Saunderson in what was probably the first written account of some of the problems faced by people living without sight. He gave more detailed observations on Saunderson in *An Essay on Blindness: In a Letter to a Person of Distinction*, written in 1773. He also wrote articles on the subject for *Le Journal*, a Paris newspaper. These writings captured the interest of a young man named Valentin Haüy, who would come to have a great impact on the education of blind people.

The Birth of Embossed Text

Haüy lived in Paris during the second part of the eighteenth century, earning his living by helping businessmen with their foreign correspondence and by deciphering old manuscripts in French and foreign languages (Henri 1984, 25). He seems to have been interested in the writings of the times—it was the age of new thinking, when people wanted to challenge traditional ways of thinking and acting—an age of great developments in art, literature, and the scientific world. Haüy read the writings of Diderot on the plight of blind people and became interested in doing something about it. Haüy gave credit to Diderot as the inspiration for his interest in educating blind people in 1784 in a letter to *Le Journal*.

In addition to Diderot, there seem to have been at least three influences that helped to develop Haüy's determination to provide education for blind people. First, he was appalled when, during a public holiday, he saw a group of blind men mocked as entertainment (Haüy 1800, 9–10). Second, he was interested in the work carried out in a school recently opened for deaf pupils. And third, he was impressed by the abilities of a young blind Austrian lady who accompanied her own singing, played cards that had been pricked to help with their identification, and had her own printing press for correspondence (Levy 1872, 316–318). Unfortunately, we do not know anything about the construction of the press. We do know, however, that Haüy had several meetings with her and she gave him much encouragement in his desire to open a school for blind children.

In 1784, Haüy chose his first pupil in a most unusual manner (Henri 1966, 12). A blind beggar used to sit outside the church Haüy attended. When the beggar, whose name was Lesueur, returned a coin to Haüy thinking it had been dropped by mistake because of its high value, Haüy was much struck by his honesty and keen sense of touch. He offered to teach Lesueur, but the young man needed his earnings to support his parents and younger brothers and sisters. Haüy solved the problem by paying his pupil.

To teach the first stages of reading and arithmetic, Haüy came up with a slotted board into which small wooden tiles could be fitted. The upper surfaces of the tiles were embossed with individual letters or numbers.

Although these tools did help in teaching, Haüy regarded them as "gross and imperfect utensils" that "only presented to the blind the possibility of attaining and enjoying the pleasures and advantages of reading without affording them the proper means of acquiring them" (Haüy 1786, 12).

Purely by chance, however, Haüy had a moment of inspiration that led to the production of the first embossed books for reading by touch. His student, Lesueur, had picked up a funeral card from the floor of his master's study and discovered that he could understand some of the letters because they had been so strongly pressed that they could be read on the reverse side (Galliod 1829). Lesueur made such rapid progress using the embossed books that Haüy was encouraged to open a small school, known as l'Institut des Aveugles, which grew so rapidly that by 1786 it was firmly established.

Producing the embossed books was slow, exhausting work for his pupils. Regular ink-printing used to involve dies cast in the reverse position to the characters appearing on the printed page. For embossed printing, Haüy had type cast in the normal position. He placed thick, dampened paper on top, followed by a layer of soft material, then placed the whole thing in an extra strong press. When dry, the pages were stuck back to back and then sewn together between thick board covers. Book production was expensive, and reading was not as successful as Haüy had hoped, because the pupils found the alphabet letters very complicated for reading by touch.

Nevertheless, these were the first books that made literacy possible for those without sight.

At that time, education was not available for everyone. Haüy recognized the need for publicity to help the general public understand his project and encourage them to provide financial help. He had his pupils give many public demonstrations of their work, and, in addition, he wrote an essay explaining his methods (1786). Although some who watched the public demonstrations by Haüy's pupils criticized the need for such an opportunity for blind children, the publicity led to an invitation to have his students demonstrate their work before Louis XVI and his court (de la Sizeranne, trans. 1893, 66). As a consequence of that demonstration, it became the fashion to visit and support the school, and for a short while it flourished. However, with the coming of the French Revolution, when many of Haüy's supporters fled overseas or met their fate by the guillotine, he was faced with many troubles, such as a shortage of basic materials for his pupils and even constant threats to his own security. Inevitably, standards dropped, and Napoleon closed the school in 1801. The pupils were transferred to an annex of the Quinze Vingts, an asylum for blind adults, where academic subjects were dropped and craft work encouraged with a view to future employment (Dufau 1852, 7).

In spite of difficulties in France, Haüy's influence spread abroad. The tzar of Russia, Alexander I, had received reports of Haüy's teaching, and in 1806 invited Haüy to St. Petersburg to advise him on setting up an institution for young blind people (Henri 1966, 20). Haüy set out on the long journey with his wife and one of his best pupils, Fournier. On the way to St. Petersburg, he was received at the Berlin Academy of Sciences (Henri 1966, 22), where he used Fournier to demonstrate his methods to the king of Prussia; as a result, a school for the blind was inaugurated there. The future King Louis XVIII of France received him at Mittau, near Riga, and he too was impressed by Fournier's capabilities (Henri 1966, 22). In contrast, despite the royal invitation, Haüy found no preparations to welcome him at St. Petersburg. He stayed for a year without pupils before his request to start work was greeted with a smile and the words, "We have no blind people in Russia" (Henri 1966, 22). Eventually, however, Haüy was provided with a building, some pupils, and one very inefficient teacher. Haüy remained 11 years before returning home a sadly disillusioned man.

It seemed to Haüy that he had failed. Had there been no French Revolution, his school would probably have survived and he would have had time to develop his methods further. In fact, the school was reopened some years later under a new director who used much the same methods as Haüy.

Little was understood at that time about touch perception, and the relatively poor progress in reading and book production using Haüy's methods was caused by his choice of alphabet type. He believed that blind people should be enabled to be as much like sighted people as possible, which led him to think that all that was necessary was for the characters to be embossed in enlarged roman type. He did not realize that, although a person with acute touch perception could read by his method, for the majority, the shapes were too complicated to be easily recognized. Others who followed him made the same mistake. Nevertheless, Haüy was the first to show that education and literacy for blind people were both possible, and the first to encourage the opening of institutions abroad where embossed methods of reading could be fostered. The French nation honored him by calling their institution for helping blind people in all walks of life by his name, the Association Valentin Haüy.

The Progression of Embossed Text

In 1821, Charles Barbier introduced a new method of reading by means of embossed text (Pignier 1860, 101). As a retired artillery captain in the French army who was acquainted with coded messages, he became interested in many projects connected with mathematics, telegraphy, and secret codes. Above all, he seems to have been interested in methods to increase the rate of reading, believing that illiteracy was partly caused by difficulties with the use of the alphabet.

Among Barbier's artifacts was a pamphlet written in 1809 titled "The Principles of Expediency in France in Order to Write as Quickly as One Speaks" (Henri 1947, 6). It included an abbreviated process of writing by using a penknife to make puncture marks in paper. An advantage of this process was that several copies could be made at a time. This was undoubtedly the precursor to his later invention of *écriture nocturne* (night writing), a system he designed for use on the battlefield to send messages as speedily as possible without the use of a torch or lantern, which would give away positions to the enemy. Instead of using a penknife, the signs (indications of phonetic sounds) were pricked out by means of a sharp instrument, such as a marlinespike, a pointed tool generally used to separate strands of rope or wire.

We have a detailed description of the elements of the *écriture nocturne* (Berger 1909). His key to the code was a 7 × 7 grid. The rows were numbered 1 to 6 down the left column, beginning with the second square down, and the columns were numbered 1 to 6 across the top row, beginning with the second square across and thus leaving the top left square empty. The squares enclosed by the numbers each contained one of the phonetic sounds into which Barbier divided the French language (see Figure 1).

Two numbers were required for each sound, the first identifies the row; the second, the column. The letter O

Figure 1. Key to Barbier Code

	1	2	3	4	5	6
1	a	i	O	U	é	è
2	an	in	On	Un	eu	ou
3	b	d	G	J	v	z
4	p	t	Q	Ch	f	s
5	l	m	N	R	gn	ll
6	oi	oin	Ian	Ien	ion	ieu

would therefore be represented by 1-3, CH by 4-4, and ION by 6-5. The sounds could also be represented by dots arranged on a 6 × 2 matrix. For example, the letter O on Barbier's system would be identified by one dot in the left column and three dots in the right column; CH would have two columns of four dots each.

Some signs are very similar when using the dot method and might be confused if not occurring in juxtaposition. Here are three examples:

ION	LL	R

The military authorities were not interested in the invention, but members of l'Académie Royale des Sciences suggested that Barbier's system might be appropriate for use with blind children. In 1823, l'Académie appointed two adjudicators—the naturalist de Lacépède and the physicist Ampére—to test the method. Their complimentary report included the statement, "Ordinary writing is the art of speaking to the eyes; that discovered by Monsieur Barbier is the art of speaking to the fingers" (Henri 1947, 10).

In 1821, the pupils at l'Institut Royal des Jeunes Aveugles assembled for Barbier to give a demonstration of this new method of reading, and it was received with acclamation. The punctiform method was much easier to read than the old method of embossed lines and curves. In addition, Barbier provided an adequate method of writing.

This was an historic occasion, for it was the first time that writing had been practically possible for blind people.

The writing board Barbier introduced consisted of a narrow strip of wood with six horizontal parallel grooves. The wood had a moveable metal clip attached to it to hold the paper in position and to regulate the distances of the signs, and a pointed tool was used for making the signs. The writing progressed from right to left so that when the paper was turned over the words appeared in the normal reading position. Pupils were permitted to keep examples of the apparatus for practice.

The reading method was slow to use but was easier for touch recognition, and the blind pupils who used it much appreciated the fact that at last they could write. With use, however, the pupils found six basic problems that needed to be addressed before the code could be used successfully for education:

1. The use of phonetics resulted in unreliable spelling.

2. Punctuation was not included, probably because night writing was originally intended for giving short commands.

3. Barbier had not invented a way to indicate numbers.

4. Writing was slowed down because some of the signs required the inclusion of many dots.

5. The large number of dots made recognition more difficult.

6. The signs stretched beyond what lay immediately below the reading finger.

The pupils vied with one another to see who could make the best improvements to the system.

Perfecting Embossed Text

Among the pupils at Barbier's demonstration of his code was twelve-year-old Louis Braille. He was the youngest by thirteen years of a family of four children. His father was a saddler and a well-respected member of the town of Coupvray, approximately 40 kilometers east of Paris.

When Louis was three years old, he had an accident in his father's workshop (Coltat 1853, 14). He was trying to copy his father at work, but a knife he was holding slipped and cut his eye so badly that he became blind in one eye; infection spread, and by the time he was five he was totally blind. He attended the local school and his studies progressed so well that his parents were persuaded when he was ten years old to let him become a pupil at l'Institut Royale des Aveugles in Paris. Pignier, who became director of the institution soon after Braille's arrival and was to take a particular interest in the young boy, wrote, "Gifted with great ease in learning, with keen intelligence and remarkable uprightness of mind, he soon became known for the rapid strides he made and for the success in his studies" (Pignier 1859, 9).

Like the other pupils, Braille was most interested in Barbier's method of reading, finding dotted signs much easier to recognize than the lines and curves of roman characters, and with the added bonus that at last it was possible to write in class instead of having to put so much dependence on memory. However, with practice it became apparent that, for the reasons already given, Barbier's code left room for improvement. Braille spent many of his rare moments of free time, usually in bed at night, puzzling over how these improvements could be made.

He found that two major changes at once seemed necessary. First, as a touch user, Braille found the 6 × 2 matrix unwieldy. It was time-wasting and confusing to use an up-and-down movement to cover the signs when reading from left to right. Braille therefore halved the sign, making it a 3 × 2 cell that would lie immediately under the cushion of the reading finger. Second, Braille substituted the full alphabet for Barbier's phonetics.

It may have been at this stage of his radical thinking that Braille asked if he might meet Barbier in order to "make a few suggestions" (Pignier 1860, 14). Although Braille intended no disrespect, Barbier, who tended to be somewhat irascible, did not appreciate what he took as criticism from one so young (Braille was sixteen at the time). It became obvious that cooperation between them was not going to be possible. Even so, Braille acknowledged in both published versions of his work his indebtedness to Barbier for giving him the inspiration that led to the development of his own code.

Braille next had to determine the specific signs to be used and their meanings. The 3 × 2 matrix gives a possible 63 signs, and a blank cell that Braille used to separate words. It has been suggested that although most of Braille's system shows a logical sequence of signs, it is based on an arbitrary choice for the first ten letters. In fact, according to Gaudet, a teacher at the school who knew Braille well, his choice of the first ten letters was systematic (Henri 1952, 38). Fifteen patterns are possible using variations of the top four dots in the cell. He arranged these logically, then eliminated any that might cause touch confusion. All but one of the single-dotted signs were eliminated, signs with dots only on the right side of the cell were eliminated, and a two-dotted sign that had no dots in the top position was eliminated. The remaining signs were left in the same order and became the letters A through J. The rest of the alphabet and the French accented letters were formed by the addition of dots to the lower parts of the signs, as shown in Figure 2.

Figure 2. Braille's Alphabet

1st Line	A (1)	B (2)	C (3)	D (4)	E (5)	F (6)	G (7)	H (8)	I (9)	J (0)
2nd Line	K	L	M	N	O	P	Q	R	S	T
3rd Line	U	V	X	Y	Z	Ç	é	à	è	Ù
4th Line	â	ê	î	ô	û	Ë	ï	ü	œ	W

Notice that W appears to be out of order, at the end of the fourth line instead of after V. Braille was at first thinking only in terms of the writing of notes in class, but an English pupil suggested that the W should be included because of its use in foreign languages, his own included.

It did not form part of the French alphabet at that time, so Braille included it in the space left at the end of the accented letters, which were in alphabetical order (Guilbeau 1907, 47).

In the first edition of the Braille code, punctuation and numerals included the use of dashes as well as dots. These were possible because the writing frames, as mentioned before, had parallel lines etched across the board so that, where required, it was possible to slide the writing tool along to make the dashes. Braille adapted additional signs for mathematics and music.

Some have thought that because Braille was a gifted musician the music code evolved before the literary one. The reverse is true, however: the music code was a successful adaptation of the writing system and forms part of the 1829 publication. Basically, Braille used seven consecutive signs (D-J) to indicate the notes of the sol-fa system, and adapted extra signs to indicate the key; note values were indicated according to the line in which they occurred. Braille had worked out the details of the system so carefully that no changes were made to the music signs in the second edition. In America, during the long years when different codes were being considered, some institutions used the braille music code as well as a braille literary code that was still not officially accepted.

Le Grammaire de Grammaires was handwritten in the new code in 1827 and, along with the literary braille code rules and those for the music code, was bound in Braille's first manual (Braille 1829). Braille asked the director of the institution to put the descriptive parts into embossed roman type, and he provided the braille examples. This first method proved to be slow, which caused Braille to make radical changes in the second edition of his code.

In 1832, Braille hand wrote *Géographie de l'Asie* and *Géographie de la France* to show his simple solution for the elimination of dashes used in signs for numbers. He invented the numeral sign (⠼) that, when placed immediately in front of the letters A–J, converted them to the numbers 1 to 9 and 0.

By 1837, the first edition of the code had gone out of print. Braille prefaced the second edition by writing, "We are taking advantage of this fact to add some useful observations and ingenious applications which we owe to the kindness of several distinguished colleagues" (Braille 1837, 2). In the second edition of the braille code, the numeral sign, first used in 1832, was retained. In this edition, though, Braille showed that it could also be used for fractions—being followed immediately by the numerator in the regular position and then the denominator in the lower position, or by lowering all the dots in a sign down one position. Braille gave the following examples:

2/3   7/10

Dashes previously used in punctuation signs were also eliminated in the second edition by the simple method of placing signs of the first line in the lower position of the cell.

Braille wrote, "Since the methods of writing and printing take up a lot of space on paper, we must compress the thought with the fewest possible words" (Coltat 1853, 16). He showed in the second edition that words could be shortened. Nine of the accented letters and the W were given extra meanings, each representing two letters (now referred to as contractions), and a few rules were suggested for abbreviating some words by the elimination of internal vowels (called shortforms). He regarded this second edition of the braille code as definitive, and he must have hoped that his code would be used far beyond the confines of his school, for he included parts of the Lord's Prayer in several languages. Copies were sent to all the institutions then in existence. But at first there were problems accepting this means of communication.

Gradual Acceptance of the Braille Code

Also in 1837, the pupils and teachers at l'Institut Royale des Jeunes Aveugles produced in braille *Précis sur l'Histoire de France*. New type was required to print the book, but, for economic reasons, each type was made the same, showing all six dots. The teachers and pupils spent many laborious hours filing away the unnecessary dots until the required set of type remained. This was a remarkable show of support by colleagues who were inspired by Braille's invention.

It seemed that the code was now accepted both for individual use and for book production, but there were still political problems to surmount. Pignier was pensioned off before his time in 1840. Dufau, his successor, had been impressed by Alston type he had seen in Scotland, which used raised capital letters in roman type. Because the authorities of the school had looked with disfavor on the use of a type such as braille that was so different from their own, it is possible that Dufau's preferences helped him in his promotion.

In 1843, when the school moved to new buildings, Gaudet, the second master, gave a speech in which he extolled in detail the advantages of the braille code. Although this does not seem to fit in with Dufau's opinion, we gather that after initial trials (about which we know nothing), Dufau had come to recognize the superiority of braille for reading but, for political reasons, could not yet reveal his changed opinion in public. Personal use of braille by blind students had never ceased, and when printing by means of a press was invented, books began to appear without reference to the school's printing house. Eventually prizes were given for braille writing.

In 1850, Dufau wrote a critical evaluation of the historical development of all the codes then in existence in Europe and America (1850). Two years later, he wrote, "This [braille] system of writing is simple and practical, and is preferable to other means of communication being in appearance both scholarly and logical" (Dufau 1852, 33). Sadly, this was written a few months after Braille's premature death from tuberculosis in 1852. Two years later his code was officially recognized in France.

Some of the directors of institutions in mainland Europe—notably Klein of Vienna, Austria, and Knie of

Breslau, Poland, who were both respected for their work—did not favor the use of the braille code at first, because it constituted an additional barrier between blind and sighted people. Knie, who was blind, was eventually persuaded by Gaudet to change his views. In Leipzig, Germany, and in Boston, Massachusetts, adaptations were made in which the letters occurring most frequently were given signs with the fewest dots. Such changes may have saved some writing time, but in practice caused some perceptual problems. Also, because languages do not have the same letter frequencies, the new versions could not have universal application. In Britain there were six codes in use before the newly created British and Foreign Blind Association decided in 1870 in favor of an adaptation of the French version. The problem of too many versions was solved at the Congress for the Improvement of the Lot of the Blind and Deaf-mutes, held in Paris in 1878, when a large majority voted in favor of the unmodified braille system. America still had many code battles ahead but finally accepted the English version of the braille code in 1917, albeit with fewer shortforms. In 1932, unity was reached among nations, although with slight variations in rules. Languages and circumstances change, so from time to time the code is slightly altered, but Louis Braille's basic precepts remain.

Braille's remains now lie in the Pantheon in Paris, where France honors her great benefactors. Carved on the wall nearby, Braille's name is darkened by the fingers of the countless numbers of those who have come to honor him. To stand there is a poignant moment.

References

Berger, L. 1909. "L'écriture nocturne de Charles Barbier," in *Le Valentin Haüy*. Paris: Association Valentin Haüy.

Braille, L. 1829. *Procédé pour écrire les paroles, la musique et le plain chant*. Text in embossed Guillié with examples in braille. Paris: Imprimerie de l'Institution des Jeunes Aveugles.

Braille, L. 1837. *Procédé pour écrire les paroles, la musique et le plain chant*. Text in embossed Guillié with examples in braille. Paris: Imprimerie de l'Institution des Jeunes Aveugles.

Cobban, A. 1957. *A History of Modern France*. Vol. 1. Harmandsworth, Middlesex, United Kingdom: Penguin.

Coltat, H. 1853. *Notice biographique sur L. Braille*. Paris: Imprimerie de l'Institution des Jeunes Aveugles.

Diderot, D. 1751. *Encyclopédie*. Paris: Briasson.

Diderot, D. 1773. *An Essay on Blindness: In a Letter to a Person of Distinction*. London: Sampson Low, Marston and Co.

Dufau, P.-A. 1850. *Des Aveugles: Considérations sur leur état physique, moral et intellectuel*. Paris: J. Renouard.

Dufau, P.-A. 1852. *Notice historique, statistique et descriptive sur l'Institution Nationale des Jeunes Aveugles*. Paris: Chez le Concierge de l'Institution.

Galliod, M. 1829. *Notice historique sur l'établissement des Jeunes Aveugles*.

Gaudet, J. 1843. Exposé du système en points saillants à l'usage des aveugles. *Annales de l'education des sourds-muets et des aveugles,* 1843, 80-90.

Guilbeau, E. 1907. *Histoire de l'Institut National des Jeunes Aveugles.* Paris: Berlin Frères.

Guillié, D. 1894. *An Essay on the Instruction and Amusements of the Blind.* London: Sampson Low, Marston and Co.

Haüy, V. 1786. *An Essay on the Education of the Blind.* Translated by Blacklock. 1793. Reprint, London: Sampson Low, Marston and Co.

Haüy, V. 1800. *Première, seconde et troisième notes du citoyen Haüy.* Paris: Association Valentin Haüy.

Henri, P. 1947. *Charles Barbier et la genèse du système braille.* Paris: Le Valentin Haüy.

Henri, P. 1952. *The Life and Work of Louis Braille: The Inventor of the Alphabet of the Blind, (1809-1852).* Translated by Elizabeth Whitehead. 1987. Pretoria: South Africa. National Council for the Blind.

Henri, P. 1966. *Valentin Haüy: Premier instituteur des Aveugles.* Paris: Association Valentin Haüy.

Henri, P. 1984. *La vie et l'oeuvre de Valentin Haüy.* Paris: Presses Universitaires de France.

Levy, W. 1872. *Blindness and the Blind: Or a Treatise on the Science of Typhlology.* London: Chapman and Hall.

Pignier, A.-R. 1859. "Notice biographique sur Louis Braille." In *Notice biographique sur trois professeurs, anciens élèves de l'Institution des Jeunes Aveugles de Paris,* pp2-27. Paris: Imprimerie de l'Institution des Jeunes Aveugles.

Pignier, A.-R. 1860. *Essai historique sur l'Institution des Jeunes Aveugles.* Paris: Imprimerie de Vve Bouchard-Huzard.

de la Sizeranne, M. 1893. *The Blind as Seen through Blind Eyes. Translated by Lewis.* 1893. London: Putnams.

EMBOSSED PRINTING IN THE UNITED STATES

by Carol B. Tobe
Eugene and Marie Callahan Museum of the
American Printing House for the Blind

First Embossed Books for Blind People

Introduction

John T. Sibley, champion of the braille system, and superintendent of the Missouri School for the Blind during the 1880s and 1890s, held that the French became leaders in embossed printing because they relied on blind people as the inventors and the judges. He said that all the arguments during that period about which tactile system was superior "count for but little against the results obtained by the practical application of these things by the people who must use them." (Sibley 1888).

If, Sibley speculated, Samuel G. Howe had given the same attention to the work of the blind people in Paris as he gave to the methods of sighted teachers in Edinburgh, line letter would never have become popular and braille would have been universal from its introduction.

One of the French leaders so admired by Sibley was Valentin Haüy. Haüy founded the first school for the blind in the world and created the first successful work in embossed printing for blind people. Louis Braille attended Haüy's school in Paris and, in 1829, Braille created and introduced his system of raised dots. The first book in braille was a history of France produced by students and teachers at the Paris school in 1837.

Systems Based on Roman Letter Forms

The Tactile Types of Haüy, Gall, Frye, and Alston

Haüy's historic book was titled *Essai sur l'Éducation des Aveugles.* He used roman characters in italic style. James Gall of Edinburgh, Scotland, devised an angular type that combined capital and lowercase roman letters. He called it the "triangular alphabet." The introductory books using his alphabet, which Gall produced beginning in 1826, were the first embossed books published in English. Later, he formed the letters (of the triangular alphabet) with a series of punctures to make his system more tactile. Edmund Frye of London and John Alston of Glasgow devised systems using capital letters. These systems were problematic because so many capital letters are similar and indistinguishable by touch.

Snider's System and Howe's Boston Line

In the United States, the first embossed book was produced in 1834 in Philadelphia by Jacob Snider, Jr. The book, *The Gospel According to Saint Mark,* used rounded roman letters similar to Haüy's. Samuel G. Howe, America's pioneer educator of blind children, visited the European institutions and was particularly impressed with the work of James Gall. The type Howe developed was based on Gall's type, but it was closer to standard roman characters. His system was called Boston Line, or simply, "line letter," and used lowercase, angular letters.

Friedlander's Philadelphia Line and the Kneass Combined Letter

Julius Friedlander, at the Pennsylvania Institution for the Instruction of the Blind in Philadelphia, embossed in a system of all capital letters, known as Philadelphia Line, that was similar to Alston's system. William Chapin of the Pennsylvania Institution began advocating a single system of embossed letters, combining the angular, lowercase letters of Boston Line with the Philadelphia Line system's capitals. By 1868, N. B. Kneass, Jr. was printing books in what was called the "combined" system, returning the roman-based embossed system to the standard ink print configuration of capital and lowercase letters.

Systems Based on Arbitrary Signs

While some chose to use the roman alphabet as a basis for an embossed system, the logical extension of tactile record keeping with knotted string, sticks, and pins was an arbitrary system of tactile signs representing the alphabet and numbers. One of the first arbitrary systems was invented by Thomas Lucas, a London teacher of shorthand. Lucas' characters were based on shorthand and included signs for phonetic values. Another Londoner, James Hatley Frere, designed a system that was also phonetic and stenographic. It differed from Lucas' system in that it used the boustrophedonic method (ox-plowing), in which lines are read alternately from left to right and then from right to left, with the symbols reversed in the return line.

In the late 1840s, about ten years after Lucas and Frere published their systems, William Moon, who became blind as an adult, designed a tactile alphabet that combined arbitrary signs and elements of roman letters. It was also read in boustrophedon. Moon type is still produced in England and claims a small group of dedicated readers.

The system of raised dots first introduced by Louis Braille in 1829, however, represented the culmination of the arbitrary systems and was a complete departure from the linear signs used previously. The most obvious advantage of braille was that it could be produced manually with a slate and stylus, whereas producing the other systems required a press and printing plates.

In 1868, another dot system, New York Point, was introduced and was widely used in the United States through the 1920s. It was invented by William Wait, superintendent of the New York School for the Blind. Wait had originally promoted braille, but, when he was unsuccessful, he devised his own raised-dot system. The system was two dots high and of variable width. To save space, the most frequently used letters were assigned the fewest dots.

The First Embossed Printing

The first embossed printing in the United States was done by the New England Institution for the Education of the Blind, the Pennsylvania Institution for the Instruction of the Blind, and the New York Institution for the Blind. The press of the Virginia Institution for the Blind printed about 12 volumes in raised type in 1852. The North Carolina and Louisiana Institutions for the Blind also had presses and the Missouri Institution for the Blind was printing braille in the 1860s. With the exception of the New England Institution for the Blind (later called the Perkins Institution and Massachusetts Asylum for the Blind), the schools printed materials primarily for their own students.

In response to the need for a national center for producing materials for blind students, the American Printing House for the Blind (APH) was founded in 1858. Located in Louisville, Kentucky, APH continues to fulfill its original mission of providing books, educational materials, and learning aids to blind and visually impaired students nationwide. The first embossed book printed at APH was *Fables and Stories for Children,* which was printed in 1866.

The early books were produced in Boston Line, and later, in New York Point and braille.

Production greatly increased when a federal subsidy was granted to APH in 1879. In addition to printing, APH began to produce tactile maps and other educational aids for blind students at that time.

Summing up the situation in 1870, William Chapin, one of the leaders in education of blind students, noted, "In the United States, the ordinary alphabet in one or two forms is almost universally used. Arbitrary characters have not found much favor; though the braille dotted character is taught in most of our Institutions rather as an auxiliary than for general use." (Chapin 1870).

This was not true, however, at the Missouri Institution for the Blind. In the school's 1861 report, S. Pollak, a board member who researched the use of braille in his European travels, states, "Another matter...calculated to render the school more efficient, is the introduction of that system of print-writing known as the 'Braille type,' now universally adopted in the leading schools of Europe." (Fleming 1861).

Officials of the Missouri school seemed to be alone in their championing of the braille system. Other educators and leaders in the field were heavily influenced by Howe and therefore favored line type. Later, the dynamic William Wait of New York promoted his point system so effectively that it was endorsed by the American Association of Instructors of the Blind at its 1871 convention. In 1882, the APH Board of Ex Officio Trustees, national leaders in the education of blind children, who served as advisors for the administration of the federal funding allocated to APH, determined that half the federal subsidy given to APH be devoted to printing in New York Point and the rest to printing in line letter.

First Braille Books in the United States

Thus, the Missouri school led the way in producing books and music in braille. Henry Robin, music teacher at the Missouri school, was responsible for the printing and wrote a small handbook promoting the use of braille (Robyn 1867).

Even Howe, Director of Perkins, although fiercely devoted to his line type, acknowledged the advantage of writing in braille. The Perkins Institution and Massachusetts Asylum for the Blind offered "Braille's Writing Boards" for sale in 1869. After Howe's death, his successor, Michael Anagnos, asked Joel W. Smith, a Perkins instructor, to devise an improved system of braille. This new system, which Smith completed in 1878, was first called modified braille and then renamed American braille in 1892. The system retained the six-dot braille cell, but assigned the symbols on the basis of frequency of letter occurrence. Modified braille was adopted at Perkins in 1879; however, it wasn't until 1887 that Howe Press offered a braille music book followed by a braille primer in 1891.

American braille was used for the first braille books produced in 1893 at APH: the *St. Louis Readers, Davis' Second Reader* in two volumes, and two children's books.

Because most of the ex officio trustees of APH were advocates of New York Point, they made certain that the federal appropriation for printing tactile books was used to produce books in that system. In 1882 the trustees had directed that 50% of the appropriation be used to print in New York Point, and, although those favoring braille kept making proposals, very few braille books were published. It wasn't until 1910 that the braille advocates were able to win adoption of a proposal that 40% of the federal funds be used for books in American braille. New York Point was phased out as American braille was replaced by Revised braille $1\frac{1}{2}$ which was in use from 1917 until 1932 when Standard English braille grade 2 was adopted.

The Process of Embossed Printing

When Valentin Haüy created the first book in raised letters, he used a specially made, right-reading type that was the opposite of standard printing type, which is made in reverse. He set the type in a frame, placed a damp sheet of paper over it, and beat the paper over the type to make a raised impression. Later he had a special press made that would apply the pressure necessary for embossing. The sheets were then glued together back to back. In some of Haüy's books, the raised letters were inked to make it easier for sighted people to read (Harris 1986).

In 1834, Jacob Snider, Jr.'s book, *The Gospel According to Saint Mark,* was embossed in an entirely new method. Instead of the commonly used method of pressing metal type into the back of the paper, Snider pressed an engraved copper plate on the front of the page, forcing the paper into the impressions on the plate. He used a small hydrostatic press and printed on special, long-fibered paper, which produced a smooth page with even letters. Despite the fine quality of the embossing, the system was never used again, probably because the process was too complicated and expensive, requiring specialized paper and equipment not readily available.

Stereotype Plates

Printers in the late eighteenth century introduced a process called stereotypy. In this process, the type was set in a form and a mold was made from it using papier-mâché, plaster, or another material. The mold was filled with metal to make a stereotype plate, and the type was free for another use. Multiple plates could be made from the same mold.

Stereotype plates worked equally as well for embossing as for printing with ink. In the early 1870s, APH announced two improved methods of stereotype making. One process boasted low cost: "We secure a stereotype plate for ten cents of a size that by the ordinary method would cost from two to five dollars." The second method of stereotype making employed a papier-mâché, mold taken from a page of a previously embossed book. A metal stereotype plate was then cast from this mold. The advantage was in the ability to make plates directly from the page, thus avoiding typesetting (Bullock et al. 1876). In 1875, APH published the first book ever printed from brass stereotype plates. The printing was on extremely thin brass, purchased from brass manufacturers in New York, and the depressions made by the type were then filled up with hydraulic cement, a cement that hardens, or sets, under water (Bullock 1875).

Benjamin Huntoon of APH described their process of stereotyping, ca. 1874: "The tinfoil linings of two or three old tea chests from the Institution supplied us with the type metal, and a two-quart iron sauce pan, that we could put through the furnace door of our Baxter steam engine was our melting pot." (Huntoon 1913). Using the embossed sheet as matrices, they could make flexible stereotype plates.

Books in point were printed either from moveable type or from a stereotype plate cast from the type. Several interesting techniques were devised for making the braille types. The first braille book, *Précis sur l'Histoire de France,* produced in 1837, was printed from moveable type. The types were identical, each having all six braille dots of the cell. To make the different letters, the dots not used were chiseled off each type (Lorimer 1996).

In 1865, students at the Missouri Institution for the Education for the Blind were printing their own braille books. Henry Robyn, a professor at the school, designed a printing press and devised an efficient system of producing braille type. He divided the cells vertically, and the dots were arranged on five types. Arranged in pairs, the types provided the necessary combinations to form a braille cell. Blind students set the type from braille produced on a slate or from dictation. The pages were printed directly from the type on a hand press. They could set a page in an hour and print one hundred pages in an hour (Robyn 1867).

Another method of producing braille embossing plates was used in Europe. It employed hand embossing of a metal plate with a mallet, a stylus, and a frame (Rodenberg 1955).

The Braille Stereotype Machine

"The stereotyper is the silent orator whose arguments are unanswerable, and whose work will eventually make the braille absolutely universal." (Sibley 1897).

The braille stereotype machine was introduced at the Colombian Exposition in Chicago in 1893. It had been invented by Frank H. Hall, superintendent of the Illinois School for the Blind, simply by enlarging his invention of a year earlier, the braille writer, a personal writing device for blind people. The braille stereotype machine embossed or stereotyped metal sheets using a pedal, or foot power. At the time of Hall's invention, stereotype plates for embossing were made by several methods. One of the methods was to impress the dots with a mallet and punch onto copper plates. Plates were also made by handsetting braille type in the same manner as letter type and either printing from it or making a lead stereotype from a paper matrix.

Hall's braille writer embossed plates made of treated bristol board or sheets of tinfoil that had been backed by a shellac, turpentine, and litharge (an oxide of lead) mixture. He concluded that embossing on a thin metal plate worked best, and for that he would need a stronger, heavier machine than the braille writer.

From that, Seifried and Harrison, the company making the braille writer in Chicago, developed the first experimental stereotype machine in September 1892. By November of that year, Hall reported that his printer, Arthur Jewell, was printing braille music from the stiffened paper plates he made on the machine.

In January 1893, Hall had a model of the stereotype maker that could emboss metal plates. The machine was mounted on a pedestal, and had a single foot pedal in addition to the six keys he had on his braille writer. By pressing the keys and stepping on the pedal, the operator could impress the dots of the braille letters on a thin brass sheet held in an upright frame. The resulting embossed plate was put in a hand press, a dampened piece of paper was placed over the plate, pressure was applied, and the braille characters were transferred to the paper. Using this method, thousands of copies could be produced.

First to procure one of the new stereotype machines in 1893 was the Missouri School for the Education of the Blind. At the Missouri school, the operator of the stereotype-maker worked from a braille manuscript. A blind student created the braille manuscript by listening to a phonograph recording made by a teacher and transcribing it to braille on a braille writer (Sibley 1893).

Braille production increased dramatically as a result of the invention of the stereotype machine. By 1901, the Missouri school had a library of 2,500 braille volumes, many of which were printed at the school. Compare this with the fact that, in 1852, there were only about 50 embossed books in the entire country available for blind people.

It was thought that the invention of the braille writer and the stereotyper machine would make the production of braille so much more efficient than New York Point that braille would become the standard immediately. That was not to be. Wait quickly produced his own mechanical writer and stereotype machine for New York Point (Nolan 1913). Through the years, various improvements were made on the braille stereotype machine, the most notable being the change from foot power to electric power. In 1928, the American Foundation for the Blind purchased the stereotype machine production equipment from the Cooper Engineering Company of Chicago. Cooper was the original maker of the Hall Stereotyper and had given up its production of the machine. Using this equipment, the Foundation developed an improved model stereotyper in its experimental print shop. APH, which had agreed to adopt and manufacture the most promising new stereotyper, tested the Foundation model and other machines under actual production conditions. One of the machines tested was the Improved Braille Stereotyper introduced by J. Robert Atkinson of the Universal Braille Press in 1923 (Atkinson 1923). However, the Foundation model was selected. In 1932, a contract was signed under which APH would manufacture the stereotyper and the Foundation would market it. Sixteen of the machines were produced and put into use in the United States and abroad (Koestler 1976).

In 1936, APH developed a duplicating stereotype machine that could make two plates simultaneously. The idea was to enable APH to share plates with the Royal National Institute for the Blind print shop in England. This project, however, did not last more than a few years. APH also developed a new model stereotype machine in its own shop in 1948, which was produced for a number of years.

It was not until 1960 that automation was introduced in the plate-making process. The process, introduced at APH, used a keypunch computer program to translate print to braille. Then, a metal plate was embossed by means of magnetic tape. Its use was limited, however, and, until recently basic stereotype makers were used exclusively for production of braille plates. Even today, they are used occasionally for specialized plates.

Printing Presses

While the invention of the stereotype maker was a creative invention of revolutionary importance to the field of braille production, presses for embossed printing—at least in the early years—followed closely the development of the printing industry. The presses that were said to be "invented" for embossed printing were, in effect, adaptations of contemporary printing presses.

In 1836, the New England Institution for the Education of the Blind (later, Perkins Institution and Massachusetts Asylum for the Blind) obtained its first press. The press was touted as having been "invented and manufactured expressly for the purpose of printing for the blind." Books were embossed in raised letters in "Boston Line." Stephen Preston Ruggles of Boston is credited with developing the press for the Institution, even though Howe later claimed that "Ruggles was the hand of my brain." (Howe 1873).

Describing his development of the press, Ruggles wrote that he broke two of the most powerful iron presses available in his attempts to produce sharp relief printing. He had to build the press himself in order to obtain the desired results. The press Ruggles built for the Perkins Institution (formerly New England Institution for the Education of the Blind) was, Ruggles boasted, "a very powerful press of an entirely new construction, which could be actuated either by hand, steam, or other power." He reproduced the press for the institutes in Philadelphia and Virginia. Ruggles described it as a flat pressure press. When the original press at Perkins wore out, it was replaced by a Hoe cylinder press without the inking apparatus. Richard Hoe patented the first rotary press in 1844. The Hoe press consisted of a large cylinder with the columns of type attached and several small cylinders. The small cylinders provided the pressure and were hand-fed the sheets of paper. Later the composed typeforms were replaced by curved stereotype plates which fit around the cylinder.

In 1863, Ruggles invented a cylinder press especially for the APH. He claimed that it was superior to the Hoe cylinder press. Before he sent the press to Louisville, he had it on exhibit at the Massachusetts Institute of Technology. In 1872, APH attached a Baxter steam engine to the press. The steam engine was a gift from the Colt Arms Manufacturing Company. APH took great pride in being the first printer of books for blind people to use steam power for printing.

In 1879, John Spencer of McHenry, Illinois, built a double cylinder embossing press for APH. This press was believed to be the first of its kind in printing. The press employed the flexible stereotype plates that had been developed at APH for use in their line letter printing.

At APH, the adapted platen job press became the standard for braille books. A platen press has two flat-surfaced jaws which open and close to press the paper. One side holds the type form, the other, the paper on the standard ink-print press. For embossing, the inking mechanism is removed and paper is inserted between the two surfaces of a stereotype plate which is then pressed by the jaws of the press.

In 1933, APH experimented with improvements in printing methods and adapted a Kelly Press for printing braille. Modifications made by the APH machinist allowed the press to be quickly adapted to produce either print or braille. It was thought to be the first time a press had been modified for this dual purpose. Later, rotary presses (which print from a continuous roll of paper) were used for magazines and larger runs. Platen presses are still in use for customized braille printing.

Various adaptations were made to the presses, but generally progress has been parallel with the printing industry, from the change from steam to electricity to the change from printing from plates to electronic input. Because of limited production demands, braille printers have not needed the high-speed presses used in today's large-volume printing.

Interpoint, Two-Sided Braille Embossing

From the beginning of tactile book production, there was concern that the backs of the sheets were not used. Valentin Haüy glued two sheets together to form a back and front of the page. The pages of Louis Braille's first book in his system were glued together in the same fashion.

The size and bulk of tactile books was a concern of producers and readers alike. When the point systems replaced the old line letter systems, ways were found to emboss on both sides of the page. The first method tried was called "Interlining" in which the lines of dots on one side of the page are inserted in the spaces between the lines of the other side. This used the backs of the pages, but did not save much space.

Because the indented or reverse side of braille is not recognized by touch, printing what is known as "interpoint" braille was developed. Interpoint braille is embossed on both sides of the page, with the dots slightly offset. The dots on the reverse side do not interfere with reading the page. Early attempts at interpoint printing failed because the machinery was not precise enough to maintain the registration of the dots.

A press for producing of New York Point on opposite sides of the same sheet (interlining) was patented in 1909 by B. B. Huntoon and Owen McCann of APH. Because of its varying configuration, New York Point could not be produced in interpoint.

Even though technology made interpointing possible in the early 1900s, there was resistance to the idea. Sighted teachers objected to interpoint in school books because it was harder to read by sight, although tests of braille readers proved that high-quality interpointing would not affect reading speed or accuracy. Since embossing on both sides of the page saved 40% in bulk and about that much in cost, the savings made up for any inconvenience to sighted teachers.

The *Matilda Ziegler Magazine* for the Blind led the way in interpoint; printing two-sided pages on a rotary press in 1912. Walter G. Holmes, then editor of the braille magazine, is credited with introducing interpoint into the United States. The first interpoint books were produced in the mid-1920s by the Howe Memorial Press and the Universal Braille Press of America; however, there was no rush by the schools to embrace interpoint for all braille printing.

In 1923, the research department of the American Foundation for the Blind (established in 1921) took on the study of interpoint printing as its first project. The Foundation sent several leaders in braille printing—Edgar E. Bramlette, superintendent of APH, and Frank C. Bryan, superintendent of the Howe Memorial Press—to the leading printing houses in Europe. They found no equipment in Europe capable of producing quality interpoint.

Bramlette had begun preparing for interpoint printing at APH even before his European research. In 1922, he had installed two new braille stereotypers that made two-sided plates and purchased a press that could be adjusted for two-sided plates. However, interpoint printing at APH would have to wait.

Opposition to two-sided embossing continued. The APH Board of Ex Officio Trustees stated in its 1926 report that interpoint printing was still in the experimental stage in the United States. The Board supported the concept but felt that it could not yet be adopted for general use. APH was encouraged to continue experimentation, and in 1927, *Our Own*, an interpoint braille magazine, was published on a trial basis. Finally, in a 1931 survey of educators, APH received enthusiastic approval for its interpoint printing. The educators recommended that all non-technical books above fifth grade level be printed in interpoint.

Three methods of two-sided printing were used before one was chosen:

1. Printing from a single plate, which was embossed on both sides and attached to a corrugated roller.

2. Embossing on both sides of a single plate and printing with a soft rubber roller that would not only permit the paper to be embossed by the raised dots but would also force the moist paper into the pits in the metal sheet. This method, patented by Bramlette in 1927 (patent no. 1,726,803, United States Patent Office) did not work because air became trapped in the pits, preventing the paper from filling the entire cavity.

3. Folding the thin metal plates on which the original embossing was done so that both sides printed at the same time. This is the method that was finally adopted.

The American Foundation for the Blind, the Universal Braille Press, and the American Printing House for the Blind all developed presses that do quality interpointing without additional spacing between the lines or dots.

The Braille Printing Establishments

Although many of the pioneer presses at schools for the blind continued limited printing for their own uses, APH, with the 1879 federal subsidy, took over production of embossed school books. The print shop at the Perkins School for the Blind also remained active, offering a selection of books and music in its catalogue. Because of these printers' association with schools and educators, the production of titles for adults was limited and arbitrary. Most of the books produced were children's books, textbooks for children, and religious or inspirational works.

By the early 1920s, four presses besides APH were large enough to provide materials on a national level:

1. Howe Memorial Press in Boston, which was the original print shop of the Perkins School for the Blind. Howe Press provided space and equipment to the National Braille Press, which was founded in 1927 by a Perkins graduate. It soon acquired its own facilities and was so successful that Howe Press transferred its printing operation to the National Braille Press, which has become one of the country's leading braille producers. Howe Press continued as a manufacturer of the many appliances including the Perkins Brailler, a device designed in 1951 by David Abraham which

continues to be the "classic" device for brailling by individuals for school and general use (Waterhouse 1975).

2. The Clovernook Printing House for the Blind in Cincinnati, which began as a residence for blind women in 1903 and began printing braille in 1914. Its braille printing department continues as a leading braille producer.

3. The Universal Braille Press in Los Angeles, which was founded in 1919 by J. Robert Atkinson, a blind man. This was the first braille press in the western United States. After examining braille presses in the East, Atkinson decided to build his own, which he patented and named the Atkinson Press. He also designed the Atkinson model stereotype machine to produce interpoint plates. The first project of the Atkinson Press was the printing of the Bible in revised braille, which Atkinson completed in 1924. After experimenting with interpoint, Atkinson printed one of the first books in interpoint braille, *The Dawn of Tomorrow,* by Frances Hodgson Burnett (Westrate 1964).

4. The Matilda Ziegler Magazine Press in New York. *Matilda Ziegler Magazine* for the Blind, a national monthly magazine for blind people, began publication in 1907.

While it was not a major producer of books in this country, the American Braille Press, founded in New York in

1916 to benefit blinded veterans, was instrumental in establishing braille printing houses throughout the world. In order to meet the need for braille reading materials, the American Braille Press established a printing house in Paris. The first book was printed in 1924, and its books, periodicals, and musical compositions were distributed worldwide. In 1931, the organization transferred printing activities to presses all over the world, which it established and supplied. The American Braille Press affiliated with the American Foundation for the Blind to become the American Foundation for Overseas Blind.

The next challenge for major braille printers in the United States was to meet the needs of blind adults when, in 1931, Congress passed the Pratt-Smoot Act. This act provided funding for the Library of Congress to purchase and distribute braille books for blind adults. Books were selected and the braille printers bid on them competitively. The books were distributed to regional libraries for blind people nationwide.

Braille production was practically non-existent in the United States until the last quarter of the nineteenth century. Books for blind readers were produced in raised letters and New York Point. In keeping with the times, production of tactile books utilized the mechanical inventions and improvements of the nineteenth century adapted for embossed printing. The Hall Stereotype Machine revolutionized plate making, and, because it made braille easy to produce, turned the tide of opinion in favor of the exclusive use of braille in the United States. Only in the last third of the twentieth century has braille production moved beyond the mechanical stereotype machines and hand-fed printing presses that served so well for so many years.

Personal Braille Writing Devices

The Slate and Stylus

Embossed books and the process of embossed printing were a large part of the development of literacy for blind people. Most of the early tactile codes developed for blind people used characters that could only be produced by a printing press and an embossed plate. Only the codes that were made up of dots could be easily written by an individual. Braille won out over its competitors because it was easier to read and could be easily "written." In fact, the braille system enabled blind people to be completely literate: not only could they read, but they could also write.

Charles Barbier, who in 1808 introduced the dot system that was later modified by Louis Braille, also invented a frame for embossing his code. Braille simplified the writing frame to comply with his own code. The braille slate, with its stylus for punching the dots, is basically the same today as it was when it was invented.

The braille slate and stylus is the traditional device for writing braille by hand. All slates manufactured in the United States have a metal or plastic guide. Slates designed to be mounted on a solid board are called board or desk slates. The two parts of the guide are joined by a hinge. The bottom section is pitted with a series of six small round depressions corresponding to the shape and spacing of dots in the braille cell, and the top section has lines of holes outlining the individual braille cells and corresponding to the arrangement of pits in the bottom of the guide.

To write in braille, paper is inserted between the top and bottom of the guide and the stylus is used to punch the braille dots in the paper. The stylus is a pointed steel punch with a handle. Because the stylus punches the dots downward into depressions, the paper must be turned over to be read. This means that braille is written from right to left on the slate so that written symbols are the mirror image of those used in reading. For finger readers, this is a readily acquired skill, although it may seem difficult to sighted people.

The first writing frames, the kind used by Louis Braille, had horizontal grooves all down the page instead of the pitted cells. These continued to be used and were sometimes called "washboard" slates. Because there were grooves instead of cells, these boards could be used with either braille or New York Point guides. Upward writing slates, which enabled the writer to emboss the braille dots on the face of the paper with a hollow stylus, were produced, but were not generally successful.

Through the years, improvements and adaptations were made to slates and styli. The number of lines on a slate may vary as well as the number of cells in a line. Styli are designed for more comfortable and longer use. Slates, such as the postcard slate, are made for specialized uses. The Brown Slate was designed with an extra frame to allow the bottom of the slate to drop open so that the braille can be read without removing the paper. Interpoint slates have holes for registration to allow writing on both sides of the page.

Mechanical Writing

Just as the typewriter replaced many uses of pens and pencils, mechanical writing devices for tactile type were easier to use, faster, and more accurate than the slate and stylus. One of the first mechanical writing devices was invented about 1850 by Joel Wight. It has nine pearl button keys that produce pin-prick dots. Joel Smith, who created American, or modified, braille, developed a mechanical writer to produce his system. Called the Daisy or Star Point writer, its keys radiate from a central point.

In the last half of the nineteenth century, several writing devices were introduced that could write both braille and New York Point. One of these was the Seifried Midget Braille and New York Point writer, made in Chicago about 1890. It had only three keys and a cell spacer that moved the carriage at half spaces. All three keys were used to write braille and just two of the keys were used for New York Point.

James F. McElroy of Lansing, Michigan, patented his writing machine for the blind in 1888. McElroy's point writer was made in Louisville, Kentucky, for APH. This writer produced New York Point by means of two hollow styli, which forced paper into the formed dots of the matrix. It was one of the first upward writing devices.

Frank Haven Hall and
the Invention of the Braille Writer

Before Frank H. Hall, Superintendent of the Illinois Institution for Education of the Blind, invented the stereotype machine, he had decided to try his hand at inventing a point writer. At that time, he was familiar with previous attempts to make a machine to produce embossed letters, and he recognized his students' need for a faster, more efficient method of writing than the slate and stylus.

The first commercial typewriter had been manufactured by Remington in 1876, and this served as a model for Hall. He chose to work with braille rather than New York Point because each letter would be a uniform width. Like a typewriter, the carriage of Hall's writer moved one space to the left as the keys were released. The styli in the embossing heads were activated by the keys in the same way bars on a typewriter were activated. The styli operated from the back so that letters appeared in the normal position for reading, rather than the right-to-left method of the slate and stylus.

To work out the technical details, Hall enlisted the help of Gustav Sieber, a gunsmith and skilled metal worker. Sieber produced a working model, which Hall took to the Munson Typewriter Company in Chicago, where patterns and dies for production were developed. The first five pilot models were completed in May 1892, and by the next month, Hall had his students demonstrating the machines in a speed competition. The winner wrote eighty-five words a minute from memory and thirty-one from dictation.

The production cost of the first 100 models was so low that Hall was able to offer them to blind people for twelve dollars each. Hall was proud of the fact that no one involved with the development and production of the writer made a profit from the invention. Because he had strong feelings against making a personal profit, Hall did not seek a patent on his inventions.

The braille writers that followed the original Hall were generally variations on his machine. The Kleidograph, for New York Point, was designed to be operated with one hand, leaving the other free for reading. Efforts were made to make the writers more portable by making them smaller, lighter, and equipped with carrying cases.

Tape writers were developed for braille note taking. The best known of the tape writers was the Banks Pocket Writer. It was invented by Alfred Banks about 1928 and produced by IBM. The writer used a one-half-inch-wide tape and was made available nationwide through Lions Clubs.

The Stainsby Berridge Braillewriter is one of the models that is sometimes called "crab writers" for their sideways movement and three keys that extend from each side of the carriage. In the original design, the carriage moved from right to left along a track and the braille was formed downward, just as on a slate. A Japanese braille writer, called the Light Brailler, operates in the same way.

Atkinson of the Braille Institute came up with an unusual design in the Atkinson Model Portable Braillewriter. Introduced in 1945, this machine was designed so that the paper would remain flat during brailling. The paper table moves under a stationary embossing head. Its appearance is quite different from other braille writers, with the keys and space bar mounted at the top of a rectangular case.

The Foundation Writer was developed in the experimental shop of the American Foundation for the Blind in 1932. It was manufactured by L. C. Smith & Corona Typewriters, Inc., between 1933 and 1947.

APH produced the New Hall Braille Writer from 1940 to 1972. The New Hall was a modernized version of the original 1892 Hall Braille Writer. Research proved that the original Hall Braille Writer had great merit and APH engineers decided to simply update the original Hall design with additional features. Designed to be rugged, light and simple, and suitable for school use, the New Hall was the result of APH research that tested existing writers for durability, simplicity, and cost. Many standard, commercial typewriter parts were used to keep costs low and to simplify repairs.

Beginning about 1900, the Perkins School for the Blind produced a series of braille writers. Various models of the Perkins Braillewriter, later called the Boston Braille Writer, were manufactured. The current, "classic" model for school and general use, the Perkins Brailler, was designed in 1951 by David Abraham and produced by the Howe Press of the Perkins School for the Blind. Abraham designed the writer so that it would be easy to use for children as well as adults. Its features are lightness of touch, quiet operation, and a locking device that prevents the paper from falling out of the machine when it reaches the end. The fixed carriage with moveable punch and die box prevented the accidents and damage caused by a movable carriage. Entirely enclosed in aluminum plates, with keys projecting only slightly, the braille writers are very sturdy and not easily damaged.

Because braille—as opposed to line letter and other systems—could be written, its use enabled blind people to be fully literate. Just as the production of braille was mechanized, the slate and stylus evolved into the mechanical braille writer. Even though great strides have been made in personal braille writing, the mechanical braille writer, because of its simplicity and practicality, is still in wide use today.

References

Atkinson, J. Robert. "Improved Braille Stereotyper." *Outlook for the Blind, XVIII,* no. 3: 38–39. (December 1923)

Bullock, William F. 1875. "Trustees' Report." Seventh report of the Board of Trustees of the American Printing House for the Blind, Frankfort, Kentucky, adopted January 11, 1875, for the year ending December 31, 1874.

Bullock, William F., T. S. Bell, Z. M. Sherley, William Kendrick, John G. Barrett, John P. Morton, and W. N. Haldeman. 1876. "Trustees' Report." Eighth report of the Board of Trustees of the American Printing House for the Blind, Frankfort, Kentucky, for the year ending December 24, 1875.

Chapin, William. 1870. "Printing in the Raised Type." In *Thirty-Eighth Annual Report of the Managers of the Pennsylvania Institution for the Instruction of the Blind.*

Presented to the corporators at their annual meeting, December 15.

Fleming, J. "Report of the Principal," Ninth Annual Report for the Year Ending October 9, 1860. Biennial report to (of) the trustees of Asylum for the Blind of the State of Missouri. Presented (printed) in Jefferson City, Missouri, 1861.

Harris, Elizabeth M. 1986. "Inventing Printing for the Blind." *Printing History VIII*, no. 2: 15–25.

Howe, Samuel G. 1873. *Forty-First Annual Report of the Trustees of the Perkins Institution and Massachusetts Asylum for the Blind.* Presented in Boston, for the year ending October 1872.

Huntoon, B. B. January 1913. "Printing for the Blind as Developed by the American Printing House for the Blind, Louisville, Kentucky." *Outlook for the Blind*, Vol. VI, no. 4: 97–104.

Koestler, Frances A. 1976. *The Unseen Minority: A Social History of Blindness in the United States.* New York: David McKay Company, Inc.

Lorimer, Pamela. December 1996. *A Critical Evaluation of the Historical Development of the Tactile Modes of Reading and an Analysis and Evaluation of Researches Carried Out in Endeavours to Make the Braille Code Easier to Read and Write.* Ph.D. thesis, University of Birmingham.

Nolan, E. J. 1913. "The Late Samuel J. Seifried." *Outlook for the Blind*, Vol. VII (spring), no. 1: 19–20.

Robyn, Henry. 1867. *Thorough Description of the Braille System for Reading and Writing of Music.* St. Louis, Missouri: August Wiebusch & Son.

Rodenberg, Louis W. 1955. *The Story of Embossed Books for the Blind.* New York: American Foundation for the Blind.

Sibley, John T. 1888. "Systems of Embossed Printing." Paper presented at the annual meeting of the American Association of Instructors of the Blind, *Proceedings of the Twelfth Biennial Meeting of the American Association of Instructors of the Blind,* July 5, 1892, Brantford, Ontario, Canada: 62.

Sibley, John T. 1893. "Stereotyping for Embossed Printing." *The Mentor,* Issue no. 10, December 1893: 385–9.

Sibley, John T. 1897. Superintendent's Report. Twentieth Biennial Report of the Missouri School for the Blind to the Thirty-Ninth General Assembly, St. Louis, Mo.

Waterhouse, Edward J. 1975. *History of the Howe Press of Perkins School for the Blind.* Watertown, MA: Howe Press of the Perkins School for the Blind.

Westrate, Edwin J. 1964. *Beacon in the Night.* New York: Vantage Press.

LA MAISON NATALE DE LOUIS BRAILLE

by Euclid J. Herie, C.M.

In this house
on January 4, 1809 was born
Louis Braille
inventor of writing
in raised dots
for use of the blind.
He opened the doors of
knowledge to those
who cannot see.
(Marble plaque affixed in 1952 to the external wall of
La Maison Louis Braille. Text is in print and braille)

I have come to Coupvray France to visit and to restore myself at La Maison Natale de Louis Braille, the birthplace of Louis Braille, the blind inventor of the braille alphabet. This is a place of pilgrimage for those without sight who seek liberation through literacy. While many have sought liberty through battle, those of us who are blind seek our liberation through the ability to read and write. La Maison Natale de Louis Braille is the enduring symbol of that liberation.

Treasures and authentic artifacts from Braille's life and work can be discovered in countless museums around the world. What compels this article and my journey to Coupvray is the house itself—the birthplace.

My first visit to Coupvray was in 1984 accompanied by André Nicole of France. It was André Nicole and the Canadian, Edwin Baker (co-founder of the Canadian

National Institute for the Blind), who in the mid-1950s were instrumental in initiating the preservation and the restoration of this humble little house for all the blind people of the world, now and in the future.

André Nicole impressed and inspired me to carry out the work that he and Baker had started. Until his failing health limited his work, Nicole's dedication and support deepened my personal resolve to preserve and restore this humble home. I could not have anticipated the opposition both inside and outside the World Blind Union. I have often thought that this fifteen-year struggle required all the persistence and determination on my part and I resolved to remember Braille's patient struggle to gain universal acceptance of his embossed reading and writing system.

On this fine May morning, I am sitting on a simple bench in the back garden awaiting the arrival of Mme. Calvarin, the curator of this magical and beloved place. The birds sing, and a gentle breeze is blowing. The air is redolent of fresh hay, roses, lilacs, and the bright orange poppies that grow along the hedgerows and in the fields. There is an argument amongst some schoolchildren on the street down below, now named rue Louis Braille. The argument is a friendly one with laughter and ends as suddenly as it began. Peace returns except for the birds.

Coupvray

The view from this garden, which is on a slight hill, over-looks farms and woodlands. It is remarkably unchanged over the centuries and since the day when the Braille family lived and worked here as is Coupvray itself, a rural village of 3,000 inhabitants situated twenty-five miles northeast of Paris. The historic character of Coupvray has been preserved intact, thanks in large part to the efforts of its Mayor. The village stands in stark contrast to the very artificial world of nearby EuroDisney where on a clear day, Sleeping Beauty's pastel castle spirals heavenward over the picturesque Marne Valley.

Coupvray is not simply the birthplace of Louis Braille. It is very much a memorial to his life and work. If you walk through this ancient town, you will encounter the little cemetery where he was originally interred and where his hands ("the most precious relics") remain entombed in a small urn. The town affixed a plaque to the urn with these words, "The Commune of Coupvray keep religiously in this urn the hands of this inventor genius."

Another plaque was mounted on his tomb by the state and on this is written:

The 20th June 1952
the Body of Louis Braille
Has Been Exhumed
and Transferred
to the Pantheon
the 22nd June 1952
in National Homage

Next, on your walk through town, you will find L'Eglise St. Pierre (St. Peter's Church) where Braille was baptised on the 6th of January 1809 and where the last honours were accorded him before his ultimate journey to the Pantheon in Paris. The baptismal font where he was baptized stands in the center of the church.

The Louis Braille Monument is the focal point of the village square. It is comprised of a bust mounted on a white stone plinth and underneath, a bas-relief of Louis Braille seated, teaching braille to a blind child. This monument is the work of the sculptor, Etienne Leroux. Funded by international subscription, it was erected in 1887.

Nearby is one of my favourite places in Coupvray, although one that has very little direct relation to the life and work of Louis Braille. It is the "Lavoir des Mesdisances" (the Gossips' Wash House) and it dates to Roman times. It is the place where the women of the town did their laundry and gossiped. While the wash house is a very beautiful and tranquil place now, I like to think that it is these determined, relentless, and slightly mischievous whisperings which keep the teachings of Louis Braille alive in Coupvray and around the world.

Any discussion, therefore, on the birthplace of Louis Braille must include not only La Maison Natale but also the Village of Coupvray and these specific sites which perpetuate the memory of the man who "...opened the doors of knowledge to those who cannot see."

La Maison Natale

(Before starting this descriptive tour of the house, the reader is urged to carefully examine the architect's drawings included in this article.)

The Braille family home is in the lower part of Coupvray on "rue Louis Braille" (Louis Braille Street) (formerly Le Chemin des Buttes). Originally, the Braille family farm consisted of a number of stone buildings on both sides of the street. On one side of the street were the farm buildings and a small vineyard, as well as the work-shop, or "atelier," of Louis' father, Simon Rene Braille, a harness maker (saddler); on the opposite side was the family home. It is the family home, including a reconstruction of Simon Braille's atelier, that has become a museum to Louis Braille's memory. While the façades of the other farm buildings remain, they have not been restored and are not part of the museum.

Built in the latter half of the eighteenth century, the house has been restored a number of times. Although owned by the Braille family, it originally consisted of two separate properties back to back that shared an adjoining wall. By the time of Louis Braille, the two houses had become one, created by cutting a door through the common wall on the stairway at the level of the third floor landing. It remains the same today: each half of the house has its own staircase and these steep and narrow stairways meet at the third floor landing. Visitors to the house must navigate from one staircase to the other in order to see both sides of the house. While such manœuvring can be

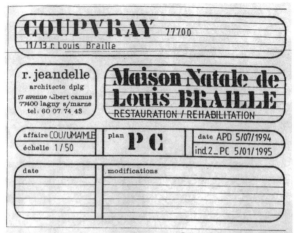

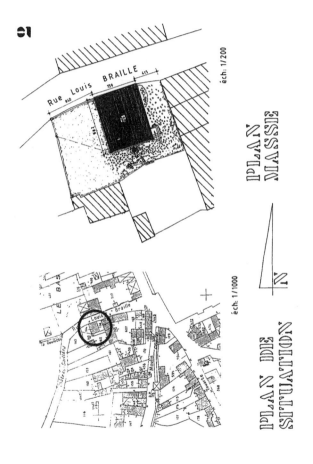

éch. 1/200

PLAN
MASSE

N

éch. 1/1000

PLAN DE
SITUATION

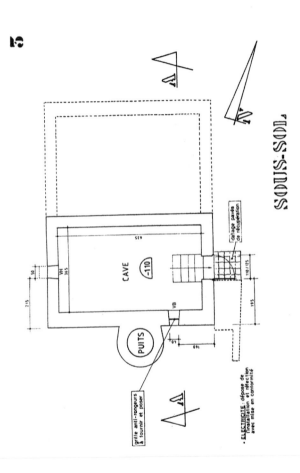

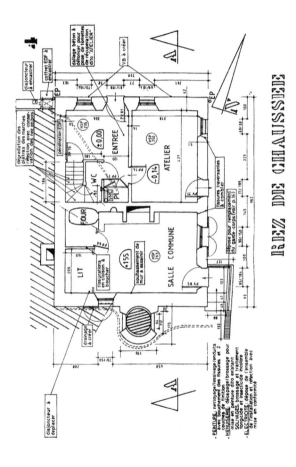

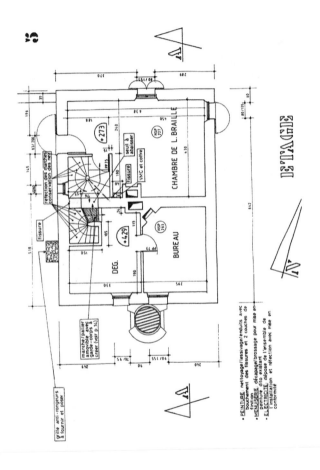

82

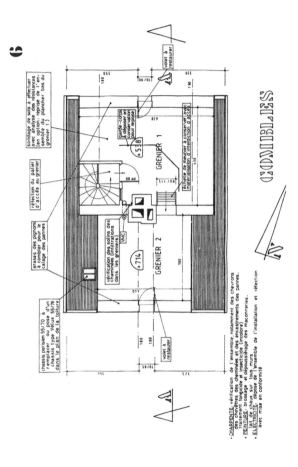

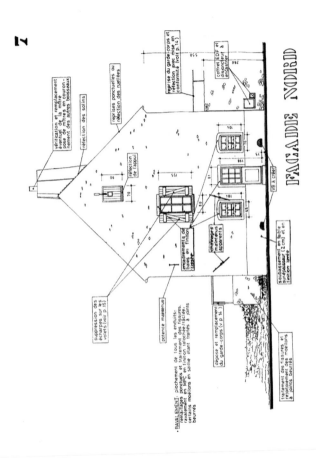

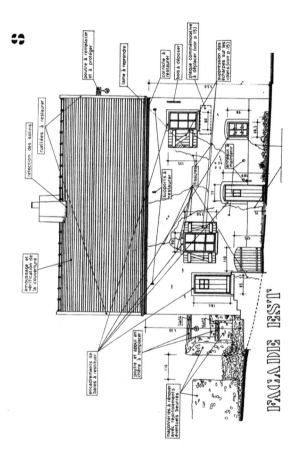

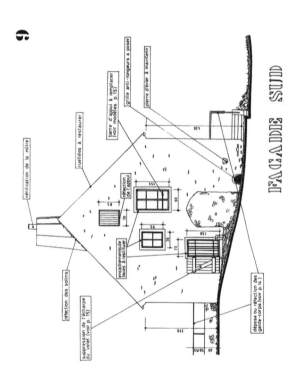

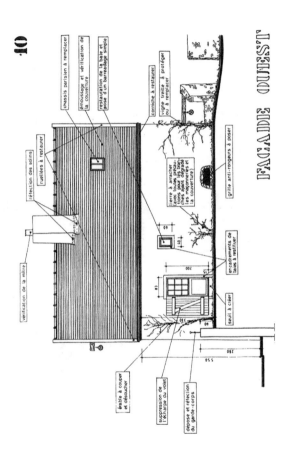

10.

FAÇADE OUEST

chassis parisien à remplacer

démoussage et vérification de la couverture

restauration de la baie et pose d'un barreaudage simple

corniche à restaurer

vigne treille à protéger ou à remplacer

réfection des soins

ruellées à restaurer

lierre à arracher avec toutes précautions pour les branches ayant dégradé les maçonneries et la couverture)

grille anti-rongeurs à poser

vérification de la mître

encadrements de baies à restituer

seuil à créer

établi à couper et dérouler

suppression de l'écharpe du volet

dépose et réfection du garde-corps

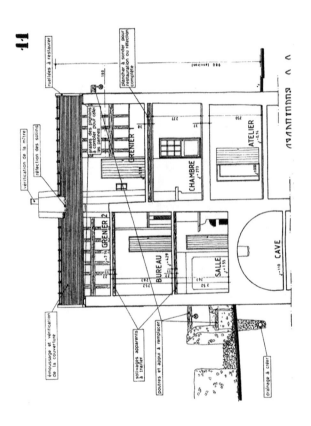

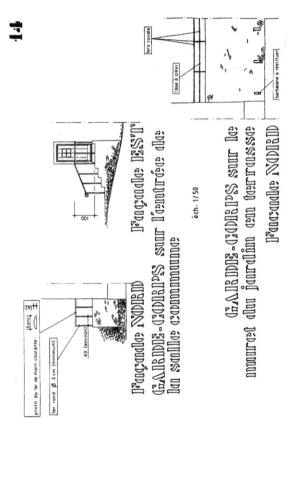

iii

fers ronds

lisse à créer

barbacane à restituer

Façade EST

GARDE-CORPS sur l'entrée de
la salle commune

éch. 1/50

GARDE-CORPS sur le
muret du jardin en terrasse

Façade NORD

100

profil du fer de main-courante :

fer rond ⌀ 2 cm (minimum)

40 (environ)

16 env.

zett

Façade NORD

GARDE-CORPS sur l'entrée de
la salle commune

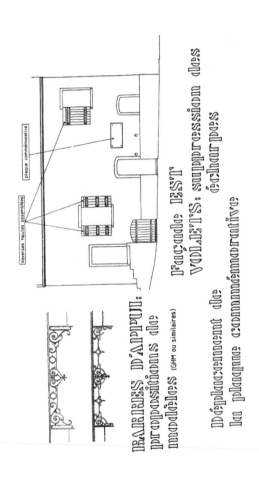

treacherous for both sighted and blind visitors, this authentic feature of the house has been retained.

One half of the house faces onto a courtyard and the other onto rue Louis Braille. The half facing the courtyard contains four floors; the "cave," which you enter from the courtyard; the "*salle commune*," or living room, on the main floor; and what is now called the library on the second floor. "*Grenier 2*," or the second loft, is on the top floor.

The half of the house that faces rue Louis Braille has three floors; on the bottom is a reconstruction of Simon Braille's workshop called the *Atelier du bourellier;* on the second floor is the bedroom of Louis Braille; and the top floor is the loft or *"grenier 1."*

La Salle Commune

The two days I am here are hot sleepy days—only the odd other visitor. I have been given full access to the house which is very cool thanks to the thick stone walls. The lovely oak-beamed room where Louis Braille was born— La Salle Commune is the room where all the important activities of family life would take place—the conception and birth of the four Braille children in the beautiful oak framed "*alcove lit*" (alcove bed); the family meals prepared with the use of a wood burning bread oven and eaten at the rectangular oak table in the centre of the room; a cheese recess next to the oven which provided sufficient warmth for the making of Brie cheese. The room would have been heated by the large fireplace; washing done in the stone sink—a large flat stone from which the water drained away through the wall into the back yard. The room has a simple cozy charm that belies all that would have happened here—cooking smells, family work and family play, conversation and learning. Today it is peaceful, but the room resonates with the life that once inhabited it.

L'Atelier

The workshop of Simon Rene Braille, although a reconstruction of the original, is, without a doubt, the most important room in this house for those of us who are blind. Were it not for the tragedy that cost Louis Braille his sight at the age of three, blind people may not have found the liberation we sought. It is difficult to imagine what genius, if any, would have invented a way for blind people to read and write. For it was Braille's loss of sight, caused in his father's workshop, which provided him with the inspiration to create the braille system.

For more than a century, the Braille family had worked at the craft of harness making, passing on the skills from father to son. Sitting in front of the worn wooden workbench in the low-slung chair of crossed leather thongs I think about the day in 1812, when a curious three-year-old crept into his father's workshop to play with the tools that he watched his father use so ably everyday. Above the workbench is mounted a "serpette" (awl) with a plaque inscribed with the following words: "Cette serpette a ete trouvee par M. Charpentier dans un lot d'outils provenant de la cession du fonds de bourellerie de Louis Simon Braille. Cest en jouent avec un outil sembable que vers l'age 3 ans, Louis Braille se blessa a l'oeil." (This awl was found by Mr. Charpentier in a lot of tools removed from Simon

Braille's workshop. It was when playing with a similar tool, when he was aged 3, that Louis Braille injured his eye.)

In attempting to use his father's awl on a piece of leather, Braille's hand slipped and he was blinded in one eye. The eye became infected and the infection spread to his other eye causing him to become totally blind. To give readers a sense of the power present even today in this small room, I would like to quote from Dr. Kenneth Jernigan who wrote these words following a visit in 1995:

> I was as thorough and careful as I knew how to be, and of course I was moved by the spirit of the place. I sat in a chair with a leathern strap seat by the workbench in the saddleshop and felt the worn surface. I looked at the tools of the saddle maker's trade and held in my hands an awl (curved narrow blade) of the type that blinded Louis Braille…at that very bench. (Jernigan 1995)

And so begins our story the various chapters of which are told in the remaining rooms of this house.

The Bedroom of Louis Braille

Louis Braille prepared this room for his own use when, as a young adult, he returned to Coupvray. It is the room where he rested and attempted to recuperate from the respiratory illness which eventually took his life. It is the room where he studied and, on visits home, spent time evolving his embossed alphabet. And so today, his bedroom is devoted both to his work and to personal and family mementos.

Various pieces of equipment as well as documents have been assembled here to illustrate the origins, development, and use of the braille system. Historical antecedents such as the Barbier rule and slate, and the Raphigraph, invented by Braille and Foucault, to enable the shape of normal handwriting to be reproduced by means of a succession of raised dots, are also represented. Included as well are books written in linear relief following Valentin Haüy's method, and books printed in Braille such as one of the first books published in raised dots, *The Imitation of Christ*.

In addition, several personal and family mementos are displayed in this room. There are Braille family portraits and letters handwritten by Louis Braille to his mother and other family members. His deep attachment to his native village is illustrated in one such letter to his mother that says in part: "I do so long to see you. Staying in the big town bores me and I shall be happy to breathe the air of our countryside and to wander with you through the vineyards…"

This room also includes an arithmetic prize awarded to Braille by the Royal Institution for the Young Blind and some dominoes that he once possessed.

It contains many of the gifts and honors received by the museum. Notable among these are the Commemorative Medal struck by the Paris Mint to mark the occasion of the transfer of Braille's remains to the Pantheon in 1952; a sculpture of Louis Braille done by Raika in 1954; and a miniature of him on ivory done by Lucienne Filippi (1966).

The Library

The library contains all the gifts and memorabilia donated to the museum over the years by organizations for the blind around the world. The room is an enduring testimony to the significance of Louis Braille and his alphabet to blind people everywhere.

Rooms Representing Daily Life in Coupvray in Louis Braille's Time

The remaining rooms, the passageway (*le degagement*) that links the two houses and their separate stairways, the cellar (*la cave*), and the two lofts (*les greniers*), while not devoted specifically to the life of Louis Braille, present various aspects of life in Coupvray at the turn of the seventeenth century.

The passageway contains objects of daily life such as children's games, books, and clothing; household tableware and furnishings, as well as religious articles of the period.

The two lofts contain the tools and implements used for harvesting grain and other agricultural work, and those used by women for laundry, butter and cheese making. The cramped cellar (*cave*) contains implements associated with winemaking—the growing and harvesting of grapes, the tools for the making of wine barrels and casks, and old wine bottles from the period.

These rooms depict an agrarian society where a family, whatever its occupation, would grow and harvest its own grain for bread and grapes for wine. These objects reveal, as Jean Roblin states in his excellent publication *Louis Braille and Coupvray: His Birthplace,* "...clearly another way of life." (Roblin 1986)

The Birth and Stewardship of a Museum

Since its inception, La Maison Natale de Louis Braille has struggled to survive with less-than-adequate resources. Although it is a small museum in terms of both its scope and its public (it receives about 3,000 visitors a year), it remains an exceedingly important destination for blind people. Thanks to the support of the world blind community under the auspices of the World Blind Union and the Commune of Coupvray, the physical property as well as a variety of programs and services to the public have been maintained. However, repeated efforts by leaders of the blind community over the years have failed to identify a source of sustained funding either as a national museum of France or as a World Heritage Site under UNESCO (United Nations Educational, Scientific, and Cultural Organization).

Following the death of Louis Braille and his direct heirs, the property was administered jointly until 1878 by his nieces and nephews—the Maurice, Marinesse, and Braille families—after which the two separate properties were purchased outside of the family. In 1898, the property again became one entity. In March 1952, the property was sold to the association: "Les Amis de Louis Braille" (The Friends of Louis Braille) under the leadership of M. Pierre Henri Monnet, the mayor of Coupvray. In this same year, it was converted into a museum and opened to the public.

In 1956, Les Amis de Louis Braille donated all of its assets to the Commune with the intent of acquiring the fledgling museum the status of a municipal museum, to be administered and funded by the government. The association also recommended that the museum be administered by an international organization. On July 27, 1957, the Deed and Covenant articulating the agreement between the World Council for the Welfare of the Blind (now the World Blind Union) and Coupvray was signed. At the same time, the property was endowed in perpetuity to the Commune of Coupvray.

Since then, the World Blind Union has been instrumental in caring for and promoting this single most important shrine of the blind people of the world. Early on, the Union established the "Louis Braille Committee," which was responsible for managing the birthplace; raising the necessary funds for operating, maintaining, and ensuring the conservation of the site and its artifacts, as well as for directing and coordinating its services and programs with the museum's curator. The "Louis Braille Committee" of the World Blind Union raises funds worldwide. The activities of this Committee have been coordinated first by André Nicole and then by Marcel Herb.

Throughout its lifetime, "La Maison Louis Braille" has been managed by three highly qualified and dedicated conservators/curators, as required by the French Directorate of Museums (La Direction des Musées de France). Consequently, although La Maison Natale de Louis Braille has not achieved museum status as defined by the Directorate, it has been developed and maintained to the greatest extent possible in accordance with the criteria and standards set by that body. The first and longest serving conservator was Jean Roblin, who struggled to maintain the museum and develop its programs on the limited operating budget provided by the World Blind Union and the Commune of Coupvray. Roblin, who died in 1993, is commemorated on a plaque in the reception area of the museum.

Roblin was followed by Christian LaPointe who was next followed by curator Margaret Calvarin. Both of Roblin's successors were and are passionate in their mission to promote and preserve the memory of Louis Braille and his birthplace. Because of a lack of resources, however, all three individuals have been employed only on a part time basis and have had to provide their own office space elsewhere, most often in their homes.

By 1993, the museum was in a sad state of disrepair. As treasurer of the World Blind Union, I wrote in an article for the *International Yearbook of Library Service for Blind and Physically Handicapped Individuals* regarding my concern:

> Currently, the house is in serious peril of disintegrating because adequate funds have not been available to ensure its proper maintenance and security. Like the memorial itself, there are cultural and educational elements which threaten the integrity and the future of the braille system. Once abandoned and lost, this permanent memorial will vanish, and with that loss, literacy for the blind will lose its spirit, its focus, and its destination. (Herie 1993, 10)

During the 1990s, the Louis Braille Committee undertook a number of initiatives aimed at gaining a source of sustained funding for the museum to cover the cost of not only ongoing operations, but also badly needed renovations and restoration of the property. Since its inception in 1952, the Museum had not charged an entrance fee to visitors. Recently, the Committee decided that a nominal entrance fee would be charged and agreed to accept donations as well.

Raising the profile of the museum worldwide was an important goal of the Committee. In conjunction with that, the Committee examined the possibility of expanding the very small museum through the acquisition of the buildings across the street which would serve as a visitors centre. Originally owned by the Braille family, these buildings had at one time housed Braille's father's workshop. These buildings were in serious disrepair, and their purchase from the Commune of Coupvray and their restoration would require significant resources in addition to those monies required for the restoration of the house.

In 1990, the committee, with the support of the leadership of the World Blind Union, approached UNESCO to have La Maison Natale de Louis Braille declared a World Heritage Site. UNESCO protects both cultural and natural sites that are in peril as a result of destruction or degradation and that are deemed to be of universal and irreplaceable value to the world's citizens. Generally, a site is considered endangered when it is determined to lack adequate protection within its country. Although UNESCO affirmed the importance of the Louis Braille Museum as the home of the inventor of the braille system of writing, it turned down the Committee's proposal stating that it did not meet all the criteria that UNESCO uses to determine "...*un patrimoine mondiale*," or a World Heritage Site. While this decision was appealed by the committee and other approaches were made at my recommendations to higher level UNESCO officials, the original decision remained.

In 1994, the committee applied to the French Directorate of Museums to have the museum classified as a national museum and to have financial support both for the renovations of the house itself and the proposed expansion project across the street. In May 1994, the officers of the World Blind Union met with the Directorate to discuss the proposal. Representing the World Blind Union were: David Blyth, president; Mr. Pedro Zurita, secretary general; Rodolfo Cattani, vice president; the late Kenneth Jernigan, president of the North American/Caribbean region; Mr. Marcel Herb, secretary treasurer of the International Louis Braille Committee; Pierre Paul Belanger (representing me, Euclid Herie, Treasurer of the WBU); and Christian LaPointe, conservator of the Louis Braille Museum. Many members of the delegation had travelled a significant distance (Australia, Canada/USA, Italy, and Spain) for what was regarded by the leadership of the World Blind Union as a meeting of the greatest significance. Jernigan emphasized to the Directorate the importance of Louis Braille in transforming the lives of blind people in all countries.

The Directorate, however, refused the Committee's requests for financial support for the renovations and for ongoing operational support. The reason given was that Braille's birthplace did not meet the criteria of scientific research and authentication for a national museum in the same class as the Louvre or Château de Versailles. It recommended that the museum be reclassified as a historic site which was in fact done in 1995 when the name was officially changed from Le Musée Louis Braille to La Maison Natale de Louis Braille.

Restoration

By now, the renovations to the house had become the Committee's most urgent priority. Kenneth Jernigan, president emeritus of the National Federation of the Blind, detailed the extent of the work that needed to be done:

> The house…is basically in sound condition. However, certain things need to be done. The roof is made of clay tiles. Some of these have deteriorated, and others are missing. Water is coming through. Where necessary the roof must be re-tiled. There is leakage around the base of the chimney, which must be repaired. Below ground, the walls and foundation must have a layer of waterproofing material; and above ground, plastering and repair must be done as required. Original exterior shutters have been replaced by more modern ones. There is nothing wrong with these modern shutters, but a return

to the original style will be made. Inside the house, the walls must be thoroughly dried, scraped and painted, and the doors and windows must also be painted and refurbished.

As to other inside repairs, all stairways will be removed, reinforced, and then reinstalled. There is a fairly good-sized hole in the floor of one of the rooms at the third floor level, and there may be other less obvious damage. All floors must be examined and, where needed, repaired. At the first floor level, the entry room and adjoining workshop...were originally floored with brick. Later, the bricks were removed and replaced with concrete. It is planned to remove the concrete and replace it with brick. (Jernigan 1995)

Various fund-raising efforts were attempted, but in the end the World Blind Union and its membership together with the Commune of Coupvray provided the major funding for the renovations. Private donors provided the balance of the funding—a total of approximately 1,000,000 French francs ($250,000 US).

The funding provided for a total restoration of both the exterior and the interior of the house. All the repairs recommended by Jernigan were made, including the exterior stone walls, the tile roof, the chimneys, the windows, and the doors. Equally extensive was the internal restoration. The electrical wiring was upgraded; the internal stairwells were improved; the walls were cleaned, replastered, and painted. Security systems were installed. A comparison of photographs, available at the museum, of the house before and after the renovations illustrates how extensive the restoration work has been.

Following the restoration, a rededication ceremony for La Maison Natale de Louis Braille was held on February 8, 1997. The ceremony was organized jointly by the Comité International de la Maison Natale de Louis Braille and the Commune of Coupvray under the devoted and energetic leadership of Coupvray's mayor, François Benz. I attended this important event as president of the World Blind Union along with my colleagues from around the world who have joined me in the battle to preserve this historic site and cultural symbol for the 150,000,000 blind people worldwide. Kenneth Jernigan wrote most eloquently about the importance of Louis Braille's birthplace to the blind community:

> The visit to Louis Braille's home and the reading of his letters caused me to wonder what he thought as he was growing up and how he felt, but it also caused me to think about my own childhood and how I felt and thought. It strengthened my determination to do all I can to preserve and continue the Louis Braille heritage, for except for him I might still be living as a virtual prisoner on the farm where I grew up in Tennessee, hungering to know and longing for freedom. Instead, I escaped to a broader world of books and achievement, to a life of opportunity and hope, and to a distant day in France when I stood at the birthplace of my benefactor and

reached across the years to a common bond. Yes,
the home of Louis Braille will survive. The blind
of today will make it happen, and the blind of
future generations will keep the commitment.
(Jernigan 1995)

We must give recognition to this important partnership
between the commune of Coupvray and the World Blind
Union, for without their dedication and work, it is doubt-
ful that the home of Louis Braille would have survived as
the vibrant memorial to Louis Braille that it is today.

In December 1999, Mayor Benz announced publicly
that a visitors' reception area and gift shop would be established in the house adjacent to La Maison Natale de Louis
Braille. When restoration is complete the Center will be
available to the World Blind Union indefinitely. Further
interest in the birthplace itself is anticipated with another
project conceived by Mayor Benz: the building of a park in
Coupvray which will be designed specifically for the enjoyment and accessibility of blind people.

Although my renewal is complete and my visit to
Coupvray has come to an end, this is not the end of my
story. The work continues. To truly transform La Maison
Natale de Louis Braille into a World Heritage Site, more
development and promotion is required. A CD-ROM has
been developed and a web site is planned. We now have a
wonderful photographic archive of the house and of the
other monuments in Coupvray. These can be made into
postcards for distribution amongst all the member countries of the World Blind Union. Certainly, we will be meeting again at some future date with UNESCO and the

French Directorate of Museums. And who knows what plans the mayor has up his sleeve. You can rest assured that the spirit of Louis Braille will continue to thrive in Coupvray, France, for all time.

References

Herie, Euclid. "The Dawn of the Information Age for the Blind of the World: Reflections on the Eighteenth-Century Memorial to Louis Braille at Coupvray, France." In *International Yearbook of Library Service for Blind and Physically Handicapped Individuals.* Volume 1/1993, edited by Barbara Freeze, p. 10, Munich: K.G. Saur, 1993.

Jernigan, Kenneth. *A Visit to Louis Braille's Birthplace.* National Federation of the Blind, 1995.

Roblin, Jean. *Louis Braille and Coupvray: His Birthplace.* World Blind Union, 1986.

THE LITERARY CODE

by Darleen E. Bogart

The current English literary braille code (*English Braille—American Edition*, 1994) is the result of evolution, compromise between British and U.S. developers, and a struggle in the United States known as "the war of the dots." The developers of the tactile reading system have long desired a single system for the English language. The various agreements reached through U.S.-British cooperation are separated by many years, but they have provided the basis for changes in the standardized code and are an integral part of the code as we know it today.

The Move to One Code

The tactile reading system took a century to move from various systems of raised print letters and symbols to one system of raised dots. Originally, there were several raised dot systems, and two major ones—braille and New York Point—were in a tug-of-war for many years in the United States. From 1903 through 1917, the Uniform Type Committee of the American Association of Workers for the Blind (AAWB) conducted several research projects to determine which system was the best: New York Point, British braille, or American braille. As part of this research, American and Canadian readers were tested on capitalization, position and density of dots within a cell, word signs, and partword signs.

In an attempt to devise a new code that emphasized readability, elements of the competing systems were brought together in the Standard Dot Code (grade $1^1/_2$). In 1915, the AAWB accepted this code, and the AAIB (American Association of Instructors of the Blind) accepted it on condition of British approval. But the British rejected it, because they wanted to retain the code they had adopted in 1905, which had more contractions and thus saved space. (The British contracted code used 189 contractions, word signs, and shortform words at that time.) The American Commission on Uniform Type adopted grade $1^1/_2$ braille as the standard dot system for U.S. schools, publishers, and libraries in 1918—the first standard code in the United States.

The Move to Standard English Braille

The Commission continued to work with the British toward agreement on a standard code. More and more American braille readers read the more highly contracted system that had been put aside, along with New York Point, when grade 1$\frac{1}{2}$ braille was adopted. The American Foundation for the Blind (AFB) conducted a study on the differences between the grade 2 braille used in Britain and the grade 1$\frac{1}{2}$ braille used in the United States. American braille bridged syllables with contractions far less than British braille did; it denoted capital letters; and it used many fewer contractions (only 44 compared with the 189 used by the British code, with no two-cell, lower, or double-letter contractions). The study figured the space saving of grade 2 braille at 11.9 percent over grade 1$\frac{1}{2}$.

After a meeting in 1929 in Britain to consider a proposal by Robert Irwin (AFB) to minimize the differences between grades 1$\frac{1}{2}$ and 2, some American publications began to use the new signs to familiarize their readers with the more highly contracted braille code. The London Conference in 1932 was a milestone. The United States and the United Kingdom adopted standard English braille (grade 2). The United States accepted the signs in British braille not found in grade 1$\frac{1}{2}$; the code deleted nine religious word signs that were in British braille; and the capital and italic signs from American braille were adopted. In spite of its name—standard English braille—differences remained in the two countries' versions of the code. The

British did not adopt capitalization. To try to lessen the different practices in syllable bridging, Rule 34 was inserted in standard English braille, grades 1 and 2, as a compromise. It stated:

> The contractions forming parts of words should not be used when they are likely to lead to obscurity in recognition of pronunciation, and therefore they should not overlap well-defined syllable divisions. Word signs should be used sparingly in the middle of words unless they form distinct syllables. Special care should be taken to avoid words of relatively infrequent occurrence (Lorimer 1996).

The participants left the London conference with a feeling of cooperation that would enable them to work together on future changes to the braille code.

U.S. and British Cooperation

The next significant date in the development of the literary code is 1956. The British Uniform Type Committee (UTC) completed a study on the frequency and space saving of grade 2 contractions, which formed the basis for the UTC's recommendations to the U.S. Joint Uniform Braille Committee (JUBC). The UTC also registered a change in its primary emphasis, from space saving to ease of reading and learning. Meanwhile, the JUBC, formed in 1950 to replace the Commission on Uniform Type, had undertaken the study of problems it perceived with the braille code, such as usage, addition and deletion of signs that would enhance reading, and production of braille materials. When they met in 1956 in London, the representatives of the two countries reached some decisions for their "braille authorities" to consider: the introduction of new shortform words (afternoon, afterwards, besides, first, friend) and the sequencing of lower signs.

These changes were adopted by the JUBC, which revised and published *English Braille—American Edition*, 1959. In the foreword, the case is made for separate codes: "...braille readers on both sides of the Atlantic could best be served with separate, though basically similar, codes designed to apply to the English language as practiced in each country" (Joint Uniform Braille Committee, 1959). The British assessment of the situation is described by Pamela Lorimer: "Many of the suggestions were accepted in Britain, but in America, not only were the deletions suggested in 1956 approved, but further deletions had been approved since, thus breaking the 'gentleman's agreement' between the two countries" (Lorimer 1996).

Twenty-six years passed before the next international conference on English braille was held. The long hiatuses between agreements allowed divergent, separate codes to develop as each country tried, independently, to deal with the presentation of technical materials in braille.

Braille Authorities

In 1959, the JUBC became the AAIB-AAWB Braille Authority. When the AAIB became the Association for the Education of the Visually Handicapped, the authority's name changed to the AAWB-AEVH Braille Authority. In 1975 it changed again, to the AAWB-AEVH-NBA Braille Authority, to acknowledge a third sponsor, the National Braille Association. And in 1976 a new authority, the Braille Authority of North America (BANA), was established that included braille publishers, national consumer organizations, the Library of Congress Division for the Blind and Physically Handicapped, other national organizations, and the Canadian National Institute for the Blind.

American Code Development

English Braille—American Edition, 1959, was revised in 1962. Three new signs were added: the ditto and two signs required for the pronunciation of words in dictionaries. A further revision in 1968 changed the method of brailling footnotes to that devised for textbook transcription (many more textbook transcription formats would be adopted as well). More liberal use of contractions within words was permitted—for example, in common terms in botany, music, and so on, if they were explained in the text or glossary; in coined words in science fiction; and in dialect.

The Code Accommodates the Computer

The AFB hosted a meeting in New York City in 1976 to bring together braille and computer experts to discuss the literary braille code. Many aspects of the braille code presented difficulties for automatic translation software programs for computer-assisted braille production. This subject was addressed by the newly formed BANA, and fairly extensive code changes were approved for use effective October 1, 1980. Most of these changes moved braille practice closer to print practice. The concept of following the quotation marks used in print was adopted whereas previously the prevalent quotes in print were always the one-cell quotes in braille. The natural pause rule was removed for to, into, by, a, for, of, the, and with. The contractions to, into, and by could now be both preceded and followed by a capital sign and an italic sign. No longer would punctuation be inserted in braille to recognize a change of typeface. The italic sign would be used in braille. Sports scores and results of votes would use a hyphen between the components. A hyphen would be inserted after an oblique stroke at the end of a braille line when necessary to divide a word group. Computer translation software was not required to fill the braille line by dividing a word.

Transcribers, educators, proofreaders, and consumers field-tested these changes. There were no adverse responses and the children who were tested accepted the changes quickly and easily.

The Move to International Consultation on Code Standardization

A comparison of British and American braille found more differences than expected. BANA reestablished communication with the British Uniform Type Committee, and the International Conference on English Braille Grade 2 was held in Washington, D.C., in September 1982. This historic meeting was chaired by Richard Evensen of the United States and included delegations from Australia, Canada, Hong Kong, New Zealand, South Africa, the United Kingdom, and the United States.

Resolution 12 made recommendations for specific code changes, which were incorporated into the American code in July 1987. The rules for the use of the italic sign dropped the concept of "series of names." For consistency, the letter sign would always be inserted before any letter following a number, regardless of capitalization. There was a change in the method used to determine when word(s) in an English context were to be brailled as foreign words. The author's intent, by a change of typeface, was the new criterion. The "ar" contraction would be used in the "ear" letter groupings, which was not a change for American braille.

Agreement was reached in 1982 that wording for these code changes would be circulated for comment to the conference participants, and that further code changes should not be undertaken unilaterally. The International Coordinating Committee on English Literary Braille

(ICCOELB) was established, with William Poole of the United Kingdom as chairman.

The ICCOELB conference was held in London in September 1988 with delegations from Australia, Canada, New Zealand, Nigeria, South Africa, Sri Lanka, the United Kingdom, the United States, and Zambia. A group from Ireland was present as observers. More specific changes were recommended, continuing the standardization of the two codes. The conference also voted to form a permanent body made up of the braille authorities of countries in which English was the predominant or a significant language. The founding meeting of the International Council on English Braille (ICEB) was held at Lake Joseph, Canada, in June 1991.

BANA's draft of the wording for the code changes approved at the 1988 London conference was circulated to the international group and approved by BANA in October 1991. A provision was made to use the single-cell quotation mark for the predominant print quote. A line sign was adopted to represent the print mark that indicates the end of a print line. The same sign would be used to mark the end of a poetic line when poetry was written as prose. A Special Symbols page was incorporated in the code to provide a reference for the reader for unfamiliar symbols, including those from other braille codes. The braille convention for writing abbreviations of weights, measures, and coinage before the quantity was dropped in favor of following the print order, spelling, capitalization, punctuation, and spacing. The braille symbols for cent, percent, and inches were altered to begin with dot 4, the newly adopted print symbol indicator. A symbol for the yen was introduced.

One of the study groups formed in London was reviewing the whole question of braille equivalents for print symbols. BANA postponed the implementation of the dot locator and changes in the shortform words in order to proceed with the other code changes in a timely fashion.

The BANA Literary Technical Committee

BANA's Literary Technical Committee (LTC) was established in 1979 with responsibility for clarification, interpretation, and recommendations for any code changes to the literary code. A new group of braille experts came to the fore who would provide consistency through the end of the century: Richard Evensen, Maxine Dorf, Darleen Bogart, and Martha Pamperin chaired the committee during this period. Long-serving committee members included Jill Cooter, Constance Risjord, Norma Schecter, Joseph Sullivan, and John Wilkinson.

After the code changes were adopted in 1980, the BANA board of directors charged the LTC to begin a complete revision of *English Braille—American Edition* (EBAE). However, this revision was put aside after considerable work by the committee because of the successful acceptance of code changes at the 1982 Washington and

1988 London conferences. The committee's new task was to incorporate the 1980, 1987, and 1991 addenda into a reprinting/clarification of EBAE, which was approved in 1994. The 1994 revision also included a number of format additions borrowed from those used for textbook transcription. They included rules for the use of cell-5 headings and a Transcriber's Notes page which contained decisions made by the transcriber which would affect that braille volume.

In 1991, BANA undertook the Unified Braille Code Research Project (UBC); in 1993, ICEB took over the project, and the LTC forwarded a list of suggestions that had been part of its earlier work on the literary code revision. Those suggestions are included here to illustrate how similar the LTC's ideas were to those contained in the 1995 draft of the UBC. The suggestions included a method to show underlining and to show a switch from one special typeface to another within a special typeface, for example boldface type within italics; the effects of the elimination of lower signs on the efficacy of teaching and reading braille; adherence to print spacing between words; foreign words in uncontracted braille with the proper accented symbols; a new symbol for the slash; termination of the italic and double capital signs by the hyphen; examination of termination by the slash, number, and letter signs; one symbol for the print dot regardless of meaning; consistent terminology; and rule simplification.

Standardized Formats

BANA continued to work on standardized formats for its codes. The first, published in 1987, was the *Provisional Guidelines for Literary Linear Braille Format,* which could be used with most subjects but not with mathematics. The second, *Flowchart Design for Applicable Braille Codes,* was published in 1991. The third, *Braille Code for Columned Materials and Tables,* 1995, provided one format for the presentation of tabular material where at least three methods had existed previously.

In 1997 the long-awaited revision to the *Code of Braille Textbook Formats and Techniques,* 1977, was published as *Braille Formats: Principles of Print to Braille Transcription.* BANA decided with its publication to make a division between format and code in its future publications. The LTC was charged with removing most format rules from EBAE and with adopting, where possible, the code suggestions contained in Braille Formats.

One Code for the Future

Should the Unified Braille Code become a reality, it will supercede the LTC's current work on code changes. Regardless of the outcome of the UBC Project, there is a strong resolve within BANA that changes to English braille in the future must be made in concert and with the approval of the other ICEB members, so that the outcome will be one code for all English-speaking countries.

References

Braille Authority of North America (BANA). 1994. *English Braille—American Edition,* 1994. Louisville, KY: American Printing House for the Blind.

Joint Uniform Braille Committee (JUBC). 1959. *English Braille—American Edition,* 1959. Louisville, KY: American Printing House for the Blind.

Lorimer, P. 1996. "A Critical Evaluation of the Historical Development of the Tactile Modes of Reading and an Analysis and Evaluation of Researches Carried Out in Endeavours to Make the Braille Code Easier to Read and to Write." Unpublished Ph.D. dissertation, University of Birmingham, United Kingdom.

THE NEMETH CODE

by Abraham Nemeth, Ph.D.

History

I was born congenitally blind, and I have always had a fascination for mathematics. As I progressed from one math course to the next in each of the eight semesters of high school, however, I found that the standard mathematics braille code of the time was increasingly inadequate. When I attempted math courses at the college level, that code was useless.

My counselors persuaded me that my dream of becoming a mathematician was entirely unrealistic. They strongly suggested that I declare a more attainable major, which I did, and I eventually earned an M.A. degree in psychology from Columbia University. In so doing, however, I lost about six valuable years in my profession of choice.

But I never really abandoned my first love. I began improvising a private braille code, and I returned with it to my local college as an unmatriculated student and took all the undergraduate math courses in the catalog. Through a combination of networking and good fortune, my private code was brought to the attention of the Joint Uniform Type Committee, a cooperative effort between the United States and Great Britain to resolve the disparities between their two braille codes. This committee adopted my code as the national standard on the same day that I presented it. Over time the code, called the Nemeth Code, went through three revisions: in 1956, in 1965, and in 1972; the last revision is today the official standard.

Demographics

As of 1999, the Nemeth Code has been official in the United States for forty-seven years. In that time, several generations of blind students have studied arithmetic and high school math using the code. The Braille Book Bank of the National Braille Association (NBA) has a large library of college-level and professional math books transcribed in the Nemeth Code. The NBA and the California Transcribers and Educators of the Visually Handicapped (CTEVH) are the two largest volunteer organizations in this country providing reading material in braille to the blind and visually handicapped. The two organizations run annual national and regional conferences in which Nemeth Code workshops are regularly scheduled features, and both organizations publish journals in which the Nemeth Code is a regular feature of their skills columns.

Hundreds of transcribers in this country transcribe in the Nemeth Code, dozens of whom are certified in the Nemeth

Code by the Library of Congress. The Nemeth Code is also official in Canada and in New Zealand. It has been translated into French and now has official status in the French-speaking provinces of Canada. Both the Duxbury and the Megadots braille translation systems have added modules to deal with the Nemeth Code.

Basic Philosophy

In creating the Nemeth Code, I first formulated a set of principles to which the code must adhere. Many of these principles were motivated by my use of other mathematics codes in which these principles were observed mostly in the breach, making those codes unusable for my purpose. Here, in no particular order, are what I found to be the most important principles I employed in creating the Nemeth Code.

The Prefix-Root Principle

Each symbol in the code is either a one-cell root, a one-cell or multicell prefix, or a one-cell or multicell prefix followed by a one-cell root. No symbol is a multicell root. The problem with a multicell root is the difficulty in determining where one symbol ends and the next begins. Adherence to this principle makes the parsing of a braille expression into its component symbols unambiguous, which was not the case in previous codes. The 1972 official code does not strictly adhere to this principle, but the one that I have enhanced and expanded and which I now use privately does.

The Principle of
Just-in-Time Information

When the braille I am reading represents a fraction, I want to know that I am dealing with a fraction from the very outset. I do not want to read an expression that requires thirty-six cells for its representation only to find from the last two or three cells that it is a fraction with a denominator of two. Similarly, if it is a complex fraction, I want to know from the very outset about the degree of its complexity. The Nemeth Code provides a set of symmetrically shaped fraction indicators, the first of which tells the reader that a fraction is about to begin and the second of which tells the reader that the fraction has ended. In addition, a prefix which precedes these indicators and also precedes the fraction bar indicates the level of complexity of the fraction at hand. The same is true about radicals. I don't want to be surprised to find that there is an inner radical lurking in the notation associated with the one I am already reading.

The Preservation-of-Orthography
Principle

In standard English braille, there are rules that require the transcriber to replace a slash with a hyphen when writing a date. Other rules in braille require the insertion of an apostrophe where none exists in print or, conversely, the omission of an apostrophe where one is present in print. I regard this as unnecessary tampering with the orthography of the English language. The Nemeth Code, accordingly, does not include any such tampering. For example, in the older Taylor code, there were symbols for squared, cubed, and fourth power but no symbols existed for higher powers.

The Non-Enclosure Principle

As a major corollary to the preceding principle, the Nemeth Code does not supply enclosure symbols (such as parentheses or brackets) in braille when none are present in print. Other codes employ such enclosure symbols for various purposes, which I have found to be completely unnecessary. In some codes, these enclosures are necessary for accurate interpretation in the absence of just-in-time indicators. I refer to these as "phantom enclosures."

The Principle of Good Mnemonics

A code that undertakes to represent dozens and even hundreds of symbols must be based on good mnemonics or it becomes too unwieldy to use efficiently. The Nemeth Code, therefore, groups related symbols into families, and the assigned braille representations of these symbols are related in such a way as to be easily memorized. As a corollary to this principle, symbols that are symmetric in print are also symmetric in the Nemeth Code.

The Spacing-Is-Irrelevant Principle

The meaning of a braille symbol should be independent of the spaces or lack of spaces that surround it. In the Nemeth

Code, spaces may be inserted or omitted to improve readability, or to imitate print practice, but not to alter the meaning of any braille symbol.

The Continuous Notation Principle

Once the reader is processing notation, his attention should not be diverted by braille indicators (the number sign and the letter sign) that tell him how to interpret the braille. That is why the Nemeth Code is based on the dropped-number system. In that system, if a number sign or a letter sign is required at all (frequently it is not), it occurs only at the beginning of a word or phrase and never in its interior. Thus, once the reader begins to read notation, he is not distracted from that task by intervening braille indicators.

The Principle of Meaning Versus Notation

In my view, it is the transcriber's function to supply only notation, not meaning, in an accessible form (speech or braille). It is the reader's function to extract the meaning from the notation the transcriber supplies. Consider the common notation: (x, y). That notation can mean many things: the ordered pair whose first component is x and whose second component is y; the point in the cartesian plane with abscissa x and ordinate y; the open interval on the real line with left endpoint x and right endpoint y; or the greatest common divisor of x and y. The transcriber's function, however, is only to convey this five-symbol expression to the reader. It is the reader's function to extract whatever meaning his experience and the context of the text permit. To this end, the Nemeth Code does not require the transcriber to be concerned with meaning.

The cumulative effect of applying these principles is that when a braille notational expression is translated into print, the print that results, apart from format and spacing, coincides exactly with the print from which the braille was produced.

Concluding Remarks

When I first devised the Nemeth Code, it was my intention that it should be used primarily for mathematics and other natural sciences. In fact, its official name is the Nemeth Braille Code for Mathematics and Science Notation. I have found, however, that I use it for every writing activity. Dozens of transcribers have told me that except for the dropped numbers, the Nemeth Code is already the uniform braille code for which the braille-using community has been striving. There is nothing that could not be transcribed in the Nemeth Code.

A Nemeth Code transcriber need not be proficient in mathematics; all that is required is to look up the symbols and follow the rules. That is what has attracted so many transcribers and what accounts for such a large collection of braille books in math and other natural sciences.

You now have an overview of the history, the demographics, and the philosophy of the Nemeth Code without having become involved in its operation. Should you desire to know about its operation, print and braille codebooks containing the official version of the Nemeth Code are available from the American Printing House for the Blind.

THE
BRAILLE
MUSIC CODE

by Harvey Horatio Miller

Braille music has become the worldwide code for blind and partially sighted musicians. It evolved to what it is today through the work and imagination of many musicians and educators, both blind and sighted, interested in assisting the blind student in learning music. It is surprising to many people that blind musicians actually have a system of reading music and are not forced to rely on learning music aurally. While a good ear is important and improvisation is an excellent talent, a printed score is crucial if a musician, blind or sighted, wishes to adhere strictly to what a composer has written. Obviously, if any musician also wishes to compose music, the ability to create a written score is necessary. In schools of music the ability to read music is a required skill. The answer to this need for music literacy for the blind musician is a score written in a form that can be felt by the fingertips rather than seen by the eyes. The person responsible for creating a viable method whereby blind musicians are able to read and write music independently was Louis Braille, who was at an early age also an accomplished musician and teacher.

Since Louis Braille first published his music code in the 1800s, dedicated teachers have worked together to share and standardize this code for use throughout the world. The most up-to-date, universally accepted revision of the braille music code is the *New International Manual of Braille Music Notation* (Krolick 1996). This most recent international manual was published in 1996 in Zurich under the auspices of the Braille Music Subcommittee of the World Blind Union (WBU), which was chaired by Ulrich Mayer-Uhma of Germany. This manual came about after years of work by the subcommittee and was a continuation of the work done on previous manuals of the Braille music code. According to the manual, it "summarizes the resolutions and decisions of the WBU subcommittee's conferences and workshops held between 1982 and 1994."

These meetings, conferences, and workshops, sponsored by the WBU, were first held in Moscow in 1982, where Dr. Jan Drtina was elected chairman of the subcommittee; and subsequently in Prague in 1985; in Marburg, Germany, in 1987; and in Saanen, Switzerland, in 1992. Their purpose was to create a unified braille music code for all countries and blind musicians in the world. This manual was written not so much to revise the basic braille music code as it appears in earlier manuals, but to work on and incorporate divergent ideas, rules, and symbols that recently had appeared in various countries and braille music publications. As the preface states, "As with most agreements, results could not be reached without compromise…some traditional signs of one country or the other were not accepted in the voting." Unification was reached in regard to clef signs, figured bass, guitar music, chord symbols, modern music, and many other single signs. The revised manual also added material from eastern European countries.

The delegate from North America, Bettye Krolick, was active throughout this decade-long project and was instrumental in drawing together the many deliberations and agreements into its final form. The New International Manual of Braille Music Notation is available in braille from the Braille Press in Zurich, in ink print from SVB Studie—Amsterdam, and in a multimedia Windows CD-ROM version from Opus Technologies in San Diego, California. This is the first time a manual of this type has been available in an electronic format.

Mrs. Krolick is also the editor of an earlier publication, *Dictionary of Braille Music Signs,* which was produced and published in 1979 by the National Library Service for the Blind and Physically Handicapped of the Library of Congress (NLS). It has proven to be extremely valuable to students and teachers, and because it is published both in braille and ink print, it is a practical working manual for use in the classroom or studio. Mrs. Krolick, most recently serving as chairman of the music subcommittee of the Braille Authority of North America (BANA), has also worked on the revision of the *North American Manual of*

Braille Music of 1988, to make sure it conforms with the *New International Manual of Braille Music Notation*. The title of this manual is *Braille Music Code 1997* and it was published in September 1999 in braille and ink print at the American Printing House for the Blind in Louisville, Kentucky.

The worldwide activity to consolidate and unify the braille music code is focused on a system created more than a century and a half ago by a blind teenager. That creator, of course, was Louis Braille. His system had many precursors which were not truly adequate or suitable for the blind musician because they were created by sighted teachers and musicians. Thus the sighted musician was, in essence, blinded by his own sight in that he was working with music designed for sight-reading. Musical notation for the blind musician, however, must be easily read with the fingers and designed and set on the page for ease of memorization. Because the fingers and ears are the eyes for the blind, it is virtually impossible for the blind instrumentalist to read and play music simultaneously. When musical notation was first developed in the late middle ages for the sighted, and there was no notation system for those without sight, the blind musician's option was to play mainly folk music and to become a street musician. In fact, this option was protected by law in Spain, where only blind musicians were permitted to perform in the streets of that country until the mid-nineteenth century (Reuss 1935).

Through the centuries, there were notable exceptions to the folk and street blind musician in the art music world. Francesco Landini, 1325–1397, was well known as an organist, teacher, and organ builder in the fourteenth century. He was organist at the Church of St. Lorenzo in Florence, Italy, for many years and was extolled by his contemporaries for his musicianship and the great beauty of his compositions. His musical works, numbering more than 150, are particularly important because they represent approximately a quarter of extant Italian fourteenth century music (Zlonimsky 1992).

It is not known how Landini managed to get his music transcribed into print, or how the fifteenth-century German composer Conrad Paumann, circa 1410–1473, developed the notation for his "Fundamentum Organisandi," or how the sixteenth-century Spanish composer, Francesco de Salinas, 1513–1590, was able to independently write his theoretical treatise, "De Musica Libri Septern." These blind musicians were, however, able to contribute to the art music world, and it is conjectured that they had assistance from sighted persons. We do know that in the eighteenth century an English musician, John Stanley, 1712–1786, employed a copyist to transcribe his vocal and keyboard compositions. Stanley was also one of the first blind musicians to memorize major works of other composers in order to conduct them. He was noted for his annual performance of Handel's "Messiah" in London (Zlonimsky 1992).

At this point in history, unfortunately, there was still no useable system for the blind musician to learn or compose music independently. One of several attempts to create readable music notation for the blind musician was the work of French Baroque composer and theoretician Jean-

Philippe Rameau, 1683–1764. In his work, *Code de Musique Pratique*, he describes a method of using wood and metal type as notation for the blind musician. There are no examples of this mechanism today, supporting the thought that it may have been only theoretical and not put to practical use (Groves 1980).

Another famous blind musician, keyboardist, vocalist, and composer was Maria Terisa von Paradis, 1759–1834. Because her father was quite wealthy and influential at the imperial court, she received an excellent education in Vienna, Austria. Von Paradis studied with the court composer Leopold Kozeluch, and studied singing and dramatic composition with Antonio Salieri. She created her own compositions with traditional print musical notation with the help of a composition board invented by her teacher and biographer, Johann Riedinger. The composition board was not truly successful in that it was meant only to assist her transcriber when copying her compositions or as a memorization aid.

Von Paradis concertized throughout Europe and became a protégée of the Queen of France, Marie Antoinette. In 1784, von Paradis presented fourteen concerts in Paris, eleven of which were in the Concert Spirituel. This was a series of concerts founded in 1725 to provide entertainment on religious holidays when opera was prohibited. These concerts included instrumental and sacred vocal music (Randel 1986). On tours throughout Europe and at the Concert Spirituel, she performed many of her own compositions for piano and voice and was accompanied by Antonio Salieri. It was said her performances were truly astonishing and that she was a gifted vocalist and keyboard performer. Listeners declared that she could not be praised too highly. Her abilities were not only recognized by the concertgoer but also by contemporary artists and musicians such as W. A. Mozart, who wrote a concerto (K. 456) for Mademoiselle von Paradis (Groves 1980).

It was perhaps the stunning performances of von Paradis that inspired King Louis XVI to invite a well known philanthropist and teacher, Valentin Haüy, and his blind students to the Parisian court. There they displayed their method of reading literature with their fingers. Haüy was the first to produce embossed books for blind students at his school, L'Institut des Aveugles. The students' visit prompted the King to rename the school L'Institut Royal des Jeunes Aveugles. It was only eleven years prior to this auspicious visit that Valentin Haüy founded his institute in Paris in 1773. He was inspired to create the world's first boarding school for blind children after taking on the education of a blind beggar boy in 1771. Haüy designed a program of education that included the study of literature and history as well as other subjects, such as math and music. Through the use of embossed letters, which he had invented, he taught the students in his school to read. For the singing of plain chant and simple melodies, the music of the sighted musician was embossed on paper. The latter proved less than satisfactory because of the confusing jumble of lines and strange shapes that appeared under the fingers. It is thought that most of the musical training at the school was done by rote learning rather than by reading the embossed music (Bickel 1988).

Louis Braille was enrolled by his father at age ten to study at the L'Institut Royal des Jeunes Aveugles in 1819. He was introduced to the embossed Roman letters used for literature and embossed music with the lined staff, clef signs, and notes familiar to all sighted musicians. Even with the limited resources and clumsy method of reading literature and music, Braille received an excellent education, which is a tribute to his instructors and his keen, receptive mind. During his second year in school, Braille won prizes for his outstanding abilities in several subjects including music. In fact, he won top prize for solo cello, defeating his best friend and rival, Gabriel Gauthier.

That same year, Captain Charles Barbier introduced his "*Écriture Nocturne*," or night writing, to the director of the institute, Dr. André Pignier. Dr. Pignier had the task of evaluating this new system of reading text with the fingers. He subsequently engaged the help of his blind students to evaluate this system. Because of his outstanding record, Louis Braille was among the few students selected to test the usefulness of this system of raised dots and lines. Braille spent his summer vacation in 1821 and the next three years with the new dot system and a writing device, which consisted of a metal grid, or ruler, and a stylus. These tools were used to emboss dots onto heavy paper, which could then be read by the fingers.

When Captain Barbier introduced his dot literary system for the blind, he also created a method of writing music using dots placed on a five-line staff. During Braille's three years of studying and working with Barbier's dot system, he modified it by reducing the number of dots in the cell from twelve to six and discarding the use of staff lines for the music code. Through his own new system, Braille created a completely different arrangement of dots and a reading method that was more suitable for the blind student.

Louis Braille's new six-dot system was formally introduced to the world in 1829 in his small thirty-two-page volume, *Procédé pour Ecrire les Paroles, la Musique et la Plain-Chant au Moyen de Points (Method of Writing Language, Plain Chant, and Music By Means of Raised Points for the Use of Blind Persons)*. He based his initial music system on one that had been published by the eighteenth-century composer, Jean-Jacques Rousseau, 1712–1778. This type of music notation had been used for several years at the institute, replacing the Haüy embossed print music. Rousseau's system used twenty-five letters of the French alphabet plus five accented vowels. This thirty-note scale extended over the grand staff, including ledger lines.

Even though there were symbols for sharps, flats, and naturals, this system fell short in that there was no way to indicate note values. Because the letters were embossed on paper, and for those used to reading embossed books, this system was a decided improvement over the complicated and confusing embossed scores that Haüy used.

Braille improved on Rousseau's method in his 1829 publication by substituting his new six-dot alphabet code for the print letters while retaining the essence of the Rousseau method. In his constant quest to improve and simplify reading and writing systems for the blind, Braille spent the next five years completely revising his music code. In 1834, Braille published a thirty-seven-page document which included a simplified version of the music code (Krolick 1979, Bickel 1988). Braille set out on a new path with this system, resolutely breaking away from the traditional method of symbolizing the pitch of a note using a lined staff, embossed or implied. Rather, his principle was based on the layout of the keyboard with repeating octaves, and on a system created by an eleventh-century teacher, Guido of Arezzo, which is known as "Solfège." Guido's system assigned syllables to each of the seven notes of the musical scale, that is, starting with "C" on the keyboard as Do, followed by "D" as Re, "E" as Mi, and on up the scale.

Braille took seven consecutive letters from his literary code to represent the seven notes in the scale, beginning with Do, or "C", on the keyboard. He did not use the first three letters of his literary alphabet but began with the fourth letter, or letter "D" (see Table 1). Braille also devised a system of "octave signs" to be inserted when a note or a group of notes changed octaves.

Table 1: Pitch Notation		
Do	C	dots 1 4 5
Re	D	dots 1 5
Mi	E	dots 1 2 4
Fa	F	dots 1 2 4 5
So	G	dots 1 2 5
La	A	dots 2 4
Ti	B	dots 2 4 5

By using only dots 1, 2, 4, and 5 in his six-dot cell to represent the seven letters of the musical alphabet, dots 3 and 6 remained available to indicate note values (see Table 2).

Table 2: Note Values

(use "C", dots 1 4 5 as sample note)

whole note, sixteenth note	dots 3 6
half note, thirty-second note	dot 3
quarter note, sixty-fourth note	dot 6
eighth note, 128th note	no dot

As indicated in Table 2, dots 3 and 6 are used for both the whole note and the sixteenth note, dot 3 for the half and thirty-second notes, dot 6 for the quarter and sixty-fourth notes, and no dots indicate eighth and one hundred twenty-eighth notes. Even though different note values share the same configuration of dots, the reader would have no problem determining the note value within the context of a measure of music.

Braille's decision to use the literary code for "D" as the music code for "C" is open to speculation as he did not keep a journal on his thought process. However, the Braille literary symbols for "A," "B," and "C" are utilized to show fingerings and slurs. They also indicate rests, natural, flat, and sharp signs, when combined with the lower two dots of the cell. *The Dictionary of Braille Music Signs* (1979), published by the Library of Congress Music Section, explains in further detail the many signs found in braille music.

By the year 1834, Louis Braille had developed his basic music code as we know it today (Krolick 1979). Unfortunately, Braille did not live to see the general acceptance of the principles of his six-dot system. In fact, even though it was continuously used in the Paris school from the time it was introduced, his method was not officially adopted until about the time of his death in 1852. Shortly after his death, other schools for the blind throughout Europe and Great Britain and several of the schools in the United States enthusiastically began using the braille system. Daniel Wilkinson, a music teacher at the Missouri School for the Blind, one of the first schools in the United States to use the braille system, is quoted:

> Many methods have been devised by which the blind are enabled to commit their thoughts to paper, and each has its merits; but in my opinion, none possesses as many advantages as the Braille one. The most attractive feature of this system is its simplicity...in music this system is invaluable, it is in fact the only practical one ever adopted, by which we can write music. When its merits are fully appreciated, it will undoubtedly supersede every other system.

> —Daniel Wilkinson, St. Louis, November 1862 (Robyn 1867).

The museum at the American Printing House for the Blind in Louisville, Kentucky, has within its holdings an 1863 music publication using the braille system containing works composed by professors from the l'Institut Royal des Jeunes Aveugles. They are all written for organ, most of which were composed by Gabriel Gauthier, one of Louis Braille's closest friends in school and later a fellow professor at the Paris School. The music in this publication is easily read and has all of the essential signs of the braille music code. The format for these compositions is one known as "paragraph form." In other words, there are a number of measures for the right hand, followed by a "paragraph" for the left hand, and then a third paragraph for the pedal. This format is still being used today, along with other formats, such as bar-over-bar, which is similar to ink-print music, and the bar-by-bar format, in which one measure of the left hand is written followed immediately by a measure of the right hand on the same line.

Shortly after the braille system was brought to England by Dr. T. R. Armitage, 1824–91, the British and Foreign Blind Association, currently known as the Royal National Institute for the Blind, published the first full explanation of the braille music code in 1871. It was called *A Key to the Braille Alphabet and Musical Notation.* After this initial publication, statements of the braille code were published in Germany (1879) and France (1885). Minor modifications and discrepancies appeared among these publications, making it clear to educators that chaos was approaching with the music code and must be avoided. This recognition spurred teachers and educators to form a commission, called the Society of Teachers of the Blind, with the purpose of unifying the braille music code. The commission's report was presented and accepted by the Sixth Congress of the Society of Teachers of the Blind in 1888. This conference, held in Cologne, Germany, brought together representatives from Germany, Austria, France, England, and Denmark. This agreement led to the standardization of the braille music code for the countries participating in the conference and became known as the "Cologne Key." The agreement also was adopted by other countries including many schools in the United States that were using the braille system.

At this time, the United States also experienced a brief period of controversy between the users of braille and those using New York Point. Because the braille system was easier to understand and was less cumbersome, the braille system predominated and was eventually accepted by all schools in the United States.

For the next several years, the basic signs that were agreed upon in Cologne remained unchanged. However, new problems began to appear, especially in the transcription of scores of twentieth-century music. New signs and formats were introduced, such as clef signs, which were not necessary in braille music. This made braille music more closely resemble the ink print editions, especially helpful for blind teachers of sighted students. These new signs were being developed independently in various countries of Europe and in the United States. By the turn of the century, there were many publishers of braille and braille music on both continents perpetuating these differences.

In the year 1900, the British and Foreign Blind Association published a series of graduated lessons in braille music compiled by Edward J. Watson, who was director of music at the Liverpool School for the Blind. Novello and Company published an ink print version of Watson's book in 1902 for sighted readers. This work was subsequently published by the Royal National Institute for the Blind as a companion to the revised version of the

1871 publication, *Key to Braille Music Notation.* The result of this and various other publications was that the unity of the braille code formed in Cologne was short-lived. By 1912, the Society of Teachers of the Blind came to the realization that the agreement of 1888 needed to be reworked and strengthened.

Because of the advent of World War I, a new conference was put on hold. Consequently, during the 1920s, publishing houses continued to produce large quantities of braille music using a diversity of symbols. This posed great difficulty for the interchange of braille music from country to country and continent to continent. By 1926, the necessity for action became clear to educators throughout the world. The foreign secretary of the American Braille Press in Paris, George L. Raverat, began working at this time to bring together experts in the field of braille music. In the year 1927, Raverat began a pilgrimage throughout Europe and America, seeking support for his crusade to unify the music code. After two years of work, he announced that a conference would take place in Paris in the spring of that year.

The conference was scheduled for April, 1929 under the auspices of the American Braille Press with representatives from France, Germany, Italy, the United States, and Great Britain. Other countries in Europe and the Americas that were not present also agreed to abide by the decisions of the Paris conference. In honor of a prior agreement to avoid controversy, the conference withheld discussion of the variety of formats found in braille music. Instead, the conferees concentrated on specific signs, such as ties, rests, and octave signs. A significant action of the conferees was the adoption of clef signs, page turns in the print score, and other signs, all of which showed a progression toward facsimile transcription of ink print music. This gave blind musicians more information about the print score. As stated in the final report presented by the British secretary, Mr. Watson, "The work of the congress was happily crowned with success. We succeeded in carrying out our difficult task with harmony and broad-mindedness, all being united in a common effort...."

Less than thirty years after the 1929 Paris conference set the standards for publishing, it was found that the various countries of the world differed in their interpretation of how these rules were to be applied. As a result, UNESCO (United Nations Educational, Scientific, and Cultural Organizations) took the initiative and joined with the World Council for the Welfare of the Blind and the World Braille Council to plan a conference to work once more on the braille music code. Paris again was the venue for the 1954 conference; however, this time all the major countries of Europe were represented, along with Canada, the United States, Argentina, Brazil, Mexico, Yugoslavia, Egypt, Greece, India, and Japan.

Louis Rodenberg of the United States was given the responsibility of preparing plans and documents for this conference. With his assistance, great strides were made in creating uniformity in both format and signs. A majority of the delegates approved the use of bar-over-bar format; however, there were many to whom the paragraph, or section-by-section, format was still preferable. An important decision involved how right-hand chords in keyboard music would be published. For many years, the United States had been printing the chords to read upward. At this conference, all delegates, including the United States, agreed to the downward reading of chords for the right hand for keyboard music.

Another important focus of the conference was on facsimile transcription, which put as much detail as possible from the print score into the braille music. New signs were then introduced at the conference to facilitate this type of transcription. H. V. Spanner of Great Britain was appointed secretary to compile and edit the recommendations of the conference. This led to the publication of the *Revised International Manual of Braille Music Notation* of 1956.

Since the Paris conference of 1954, there have been many publications and pamphlets intended to assist transcribers of braille music, such as *Lessons in Braille Music,* published by American Printing House for the Blind (1956) and *Introduction to Braille Music Transcription,* published by the Library of Congress (1970). Pamphlets have also been published to clarify questions about the code, such as the variety of signs used in guitar music, figured bass, and the explanation of shortform scoring developed primarily for popular music.

The *Manual of Braille Music Notation American Edition,* 1988, included corrections, alterations of the 1956 manual, and previously unpublished material dealing with special signs in twentieth-century scores, percussion music, and vocal ensemble music. The main difference between this book and the 1956 manual is the emphasis it places on non-facsimile publications. As cited in the manual's preface, "this Addendum champions the right of the majority of braille music readers...to be provided with a copy which...is unencumbered with extraneous and...extra signs." In addition, the manual instructs printing houses and transcribers of braille music in the United States to leave out all extraneous signs unless a facsimile score is specifically requested (Bennette 1988).

George Bennette, appointed by the Braille Authority of North America (BANA) as chairman of its Braille Music Technical Committee, writes in the forward of this 1988 manual, "No doubt, some day this book will be superseded by yet another revised manual of braille notation...in the meantime, we trust this volume will be serviceable to the transcribers and readers of braille music for at least a generation." Indeed, Mr. Bennette was correct in his prediction of the replacement of the volume for which he was responsible. It was replaced by the *Braille Music Code 1997*, discussed earlier in this chapter.

One of the most recent developments in the field of music for sighted people is in the area of music programs for the computer. Educators are using these programs for teaching note names, note values, intervals, and the many aspects of music theory. What is perhaps even more valuable is that the students can use MIDI (musical instrument digital interface) programs to create and print their own theory assignments and original compositions. Many of these programs are not available to blind musicians because the programs depend on the use of a mouse and graphics on the screen. Computer programmers are working, however, to increase the number and variety of music programs accessible to the blind music student and musician.

A breakthrough in this field has recently come from the work and persistence of William R. McCann, a blind computer programmer and musician. He states that he has waited for years for someone to develop a program that would produce braille music, and when one did not appear, he took up the challenge (McCann 1999). His "GOOD-FEEL" program is designed to translate a MIDI file into braille music code. It has been developed to address the global shortage of material available in the braille format. "GOODFEEL" uses the same computer files used by sighted musicians when printing scores in staff notation to produce the equivalent music in braille. To quote Mr. McCann, "Using our system, any sighted musician who can use a computer can learn to produce braille music scores without necessarily needing to be able to read braille music. This facility addresses the global shortage of braille music transcribers." Many public schools and most colleges and universities use computers for producing scores and music parts for their ensembles. Now, when an instructor produces ink print parts for sighted students, he can also produce braille music parts with "GOODFEEL" for both instrumental and vocal blind music students. "GOODFEEL" opens a whole new world for the blind musician and may possibly promote braille music literacy throughout the world.

The World Wide Web also makes available a new resource to the reader of braille music. Since the adoption of the *New International Manual of Braille Music Notation*, and because of the universal acceptance of the braille music code, the European Economic Community (EEC) is funding a database of braille music on the World Wide Web. The EEC is inviting any interested country, library, or organization to join in the development of this project, known as MIRACLE. These other organizations can assist the EEC with the program by loaning, selling, or donating music to the database. There will not only be a list of the library's holdings on the web site, but there will also be a digital copy of the braille music that can be downloaded to a personal computer. The person or organization that orders the music can then either have the score displayed on a refreshable braille output device attached to a computer or print it with a braille embosser. This means that braille music can be in the hands of the blind musician almost instantaneously. They can be reached at www.svb.nl/project/Miracle.

After Louis Braille introduced his music code in 1834, braille music evolved and diverged in many directions. His work ultimately led to the need for unification through conferences of musicians and educators to standardize the braille music code. The current high standard of music education for the blind has grown from the dedication of hundreds of individuals, starting with Louis Braille's thirty-two-page publication, which included the music code. As a comparison, the most recent international publication, *New International Manual of Braille Music Notation*, is a three-volume, 356-page tome. There is no doubt that the braille music code will continue to evolve as the language of music also evolves. However, it is conceivable, with our shrinking world and our worldwide communication network, that there will be no isolated development of the braille music code as has occurred in the past. Any developments will be swiftly carried to the world community for rejection or acceptance, and, of the latter, made immediately available universally.

There is currently much interest and concern by educators regarding the future evolution of braille music. One concern is regarding the education of blind students and, more specifically, blind music students. With many of the American residential schools for the blind students losing their students to public schools, the music education of blind children is at risk. This problem could be averted by making the public and private school and private music teachers aware of the many publications, resources, and services available to assist them in caring for the needs of the blind music student. These publications are available from many sources, including the American Printing House for the Blind, the Library of Congress, and the Royal National Institute for the Blind.

The future of braille music relies, as it always has, on its promotion and use by both sighted and blind music teachers. As with literary braille, the teacher must be aware of and use the many books and educational materials that will help the student to learn and utilize the braille code. This requires concerned teachers with a spirit of dedication that was manifest in the founder of the first school for the blind, Valentin Haüy. He made it possible for his students to get a well-rounded education, including training in the musical arts. Louis Braille was educated in this program and saw the need for a better system for the blind student to read music as well as literature. It was not only because of the intelligence and persistence of this young man but because of the encouragement and support he received from his fellow teachers and the director of the school, Dr. André Pignier, that he was able to do what he did for blind people. The blind students of today also need encouragement and support that will allow them independence in the field of music. With the many resources available, beginning with the braille music code, and the resources of today's electronic age, the blind music students can find themselves well prepared to compete in the professional music world.

References

Bennette, George. 1991. *Manual of Braille Music Notation American Edition,* 1988. Louisville, Kentucky: American Printing House for the Blind, 1991.

Bickel, Lenard. 1995. *Triumph Over Darkness: The Life of Louis Braille* (Braille Edition). Stockport, England: National Library for the Blind, 1995.

Krolick, Bettye. 1979. *Dictionary of Braille Music Signs.* Washington, D.C.: Library of Congress, National Library Service for the Blind and Physically Handicapped produced in braille by Volunteer Services for the Blind, 1979.

Krolick, Bettye., ed. 1996. *New International Manual of Braille Music Notation.* Zurich: Braille Press, 1996.

Krolick, Bettye., ed. 1997. *Braille Music Code 1997.* Louisville, Kentucky: American Printing House for the Blind, 1999.

Randel, Don Michael., ed. 1986. *The New Harvard Dictionary of Music.* Cambridge, Massachusetts, London England: The Belknap Press of Harvard University Press, 1986.

Reuss, Alexander., Translated by Ellen Kerney and Merle E. Frampton. 1935. *Development and Problems of the Musical Notation for the Blind.* New York, New York: The New York Institute for the Education of the Blind, 1935.

Sadie, Stanley., ed. 1980. *The New Grove Dictionary of Music and Musicians.* London: MacMillan Limited, and Washington, D.C.: Grove's Dictionary of Music, Inc., 1980.

Slonimsky, Nicolas., ed. 1958. *Baker's Biographical Dictionary of Musicians,* Eighth Edition. New York, New York: G. Schirmer, Inc., 1992.

CODE FOR COMPUTER BRAILLE NOTATION

by Tim V. Cranmer

The advent of computers in the 1960s brought with it a new "alphabet." The American Standard Code for Information Interchange (ASCII) was used by computers all over the world and would eventually make it possible for people to communicate via computers over the Internet. As of this writing, the ASCII symbol set still dominates the computer world.

Although this fact is only an interesting footnote in the mainstream computing world, the original ASCII character set was composed of 64 symbols, just like braille. These symbols included only uppercase letters, numbers, and a few extra symbols for common punctuation marks such as period, comma, and parentheses. It was this symbol set that enabled the embossing of braille directly from a computer and may, in part, have inspired a few blind pioneers to seek employment in the computer field.

By the mid-1970s, the burgeoning computer industry offered many opportunities for blind persons as IBM, Honeywell, and other large manufacturers installed multi-million-dollar mainframes throughout government, academe, and corporate America.

With the expansion of computer frontiers came an accompanying increase in the number of characters in the ASCII character set. The set first expanded from 64 to 128 characters, 95 of which are printable. (Since then, additional "upper" character sets have been added; however, these sets are beyond the scope of this work.)

Despite the expansion of the printed computer character set, the braille code, a six-dot code, remained at 64 characters until braille embossers became available through Triformation Systems, Inc., in the early 1970s. These embossers were based in part on the Braille-Emboss developed at the Massachusetts Institute of Technology, probably the first truly successful, computer-based braille embosser.

To accommodate an expanded version of ASCII, the Triformation embossers added a seventh and eighth dot to the braille cell, thus expanding the braille code into an eight-bit code that could display 256 combinations and thus conform once again to standard ASCII.

Even though embossers of the day were capable of brailling an eight-dot braille character set, the characters written in books continued to be displayed only in a six-dot representation. The disparity between the standard six-dot braille system and the machine-based eight-dot system seems not to have been a serious problem to technically savvy blind computer programmers. This was, after all, their work, and familiarity with the subject matter enabled them to resolve the growing differences between their eight-dot machine code and the six-dot representations they saw in books brailled on computer-related topics.

But as blind people began using computers to create and edit work outside the scope of pure computer programming and data processing, it became apparent that a more sophisticated merging of braille and computer code would be necessary for the blind community to fully benefit from this powerful new communications tool. Machine versus paper encoding was a particularly difficult problem for students coming into the increasingly sophisticated computer environment. Most of the symbols a student would read in a braille book embossed on paper were entirely changed when presented on a braille computer terminal. Besides having different dot patterns in the paper versions of computer learning texts, many symbols might be made up of two or three characters, although the actual computer terminal symbol would be composed of only one character.

Simply stated, what was needed was a one-to-one correspondence between the symbols of braille and ASCII. Without such a computer braille code on paper, the blind community would certainly suffer from a new form of illiteracy. By 1975, the problem was evident, with all paper books using the Provisional Braille Code for Computer Notation of 1972 and all braille terminals using the eight-dot code, often referred to as the MIT code. In June 1976, the American Foundation for the Blind concluded that "computer-compatible" grade 2 literary braille was essential. Teachers of the visually impaired, their students, and other blind consumers of braille were voicing the need for change. Computer technology was being developed for braille transcription; this breakthrough was already affecting the way future generations of braille transcribers would produce the tactile language.

Three months later, leaders of the American Association of Workers for the Blind, the Association for Education of the Visually Handicapped, and the National Braille Association convened. Their meeting was the first of what was to become the Braille Authority of North America (BANA), the body that ultimately became responsible for setting standards for a computer braille code as well as for braille in general.

It wasn't until late 1979 that the first mention of a computer braille code appeared in BANA's minutes, and not until November 1982 that BANA's Mathematics Technical Committee was asked to report on the status of computer braille encoding with recommendations for actions to be taken. In 1984, an ad hoc committee was formed with the assignment of developing a braille code for computer notation, with this author as chairman.

Extending the Braille Code

The challenge was clear: Computer programming code was intolerant of ambiguity. Could a braille code be created that would be precise enough to reproduce the exactness of language required? The committee quickly accepted

ASCII (or MIT) as the foundation on which to build a computer braille code.

The committee began by determining which characters of the ASCII code had already been unambiguously represented in braille, then moved on to the problem of creating a one-to-one braille representation of the characters that remained. After letters and numbers, only a few symbols could ever have a single character to represent them, so a preferred list had to be agreed upon as well.

For those characters not on the preferred list, the committee had to design reasonable two-cell symbols. In addition, the committee had to work out a mechanism by which readers could know when they were reading computer text and when literary text was being used. (For a list of those characters, please refer to the appendix, Computer Braille Code Symbols, in the back of this book.)

The 26 letters of the alphabet would be the same in the computer braille code as in literary braille, but the characters would stand only for the letters themselves. The letters would be used to spell words, not to represent entire words or parts of words, as they are in the literary braille code. No contractions would be used—every letter, number, and punctuation mark would have its own separate meaning so that there would be no ambiguity, precisely as intended in ASCII.

The resulting computer braille code uses all 64 combinations of dots that are possible in a standard six-dot braille cell (64 with the blank space) and assigns the same meanings to them as in literary braille, insofar as possible. All letters, numbers, and Common punctuation marks were assigned single-cell representations.

To represent the remaining characters of the ASCII code and the additional symbols necessary for transcription, the committee assigned two meanings to a very few braille symbols. This was accomplished by using a prefix of dots 4-5-6, which appears as the first cell in all of the computer braille code's two-cell symbols.

Finally, the committee had to devise techniques to show on paper what could be obvious on a computer screen. In addition, print formatting had to be accommodated in this code.

The solution worked. In November 1986, BANA approved the Code for Computer Braille Notation for publication, and it was officially adopted in 1987. The goal was to "make the Code for Computer Braille Notation a realistic code, capable of unambiguous representation of current computer notation but flexible enough to respond to changing and demanding needs." (Braille Authority of North America 1987). An addendum that delineated the representation of flowcharted materials was added in 1991.

The Code is Successful

By the end of 1988, personal computers were being used extensively by producers and transcribers of braille, and braille computer-related materials were regularly being transcribed with the new code. Computer braille had enhanced communication among operators, computers, and braille output devices worldwide, and BANA was assured by braille programmers that all the rules and formats it had developed and approved were being used.

For the broader market of blind consumers, today's English braille publishing industry has successfully adopted the computer braille code, incorporating it into publications that use the literary braille code and switching to computer braille whenever e-mail, web site addresses, or computer notations are encountered. To help braille readers become familiar with the code, the National Braille Press has published simple training materials (Dixon and Gray 1991). Computer braille code is used when absolute precision is necessary; it is transcribed character for character, with no abbreviations or contractions. It is used interchangeably with English literary braille, textbook format, the more complex Nemeth code for mathematical material, and braille music code.

The system is not without its difficulties, but if the unified braille code that is under development is successful, perhaps one day there will be no need for separate braille codes for literature, math, computers, and scientific disciplines. As things stand, the computer braille code has at least contributed to meeting the needs of blind people in today's society, allowing documents that pass between them to be translated from print to braille and back again with the ease and speed that only modern computers can provide.

References

Braille Authority of North America. 1987. *Code for Computer Braille Notation.* Louisville, Ky.: American Printing House for the Blind.

Dixon, Judith M., and Chris Gray. 1991. *The Computer Braille Code Made Easy.* Boston, Mass.: National Braille Press.

UNIFYING THE BRAILLE CODES

by Darleen Bogart, Tim V. Cranmer,
and Joseph E. Sullivan

Background and Overview

In 1990, the braille codes used for English materials in North America were well established and documented, but they were essentially divided by subject. The general, or basic, code (also called the "literary" code) was used for most literature; a specific code was used for mathematics; another for computer notation; another for music; and there were special conventions for textbooks that, although intended to be extensions of the literary code, were in conflict with that code in some respects.

While this situation had come about for good reasons and as the result of good work by many people over the years, four main developments, especially in the 1970s and 1980s, had set the stage for change:

1. Blind children were increasingly integrated into the regular school system, especially in the United States, and laws and tax incentives created improved employment opportunities for blind persons in the general workforce.

2. Corresponding to moves toward integration, there was a swing to the philosophy that braille should reflect print notation faithfully rather than only conveying print meaning.

3. The Braille Authority was reorganized into the Braille Authority of North America (BANA), with a greatly expanded membership, for the first time including major braille production houses.

4. Technological advances made the automatic production of braille possible through the use of braille translation software, often from electronic files that had originally been created for other purposes, such as publishing a print document.

These developments were the background for a growing awareness that multiple braille codes that differed by subject were in many ways a hindrance to overall literacy. For students especially, a different braille code for each new subject added another learning task to that already presented by the subject. Moreover, the different codes greatly complicated the transcription process, thereby driving up the cost of producing braille and, as an inevitable consequence, reducing its availability overall.

Taking Action

This general awareness of the problem of multiple codes was brought into focus in a letter to the chair of the board of directors of BANA from T. V. ("Tim") Cranmer, chair of the BANA committee that had developed the code for computer notation (Computer Braille Code, or CBC), and Abraham Nemeth, the original author of the math code (Nemeth Code for Mathematics and Science Notation) approved by BANA. In the letter, Cranmer and Nemeth outlined the reasons for unifying the codes into one basic code and suggested that a BANA project be launched to attempt to develop such a code. The letter was particularly significant in that the two authors were, respectively, the two people most involved in the development of the two separate technical codes then officially approved by BANA.

In response, the BANA board voted in November 1990 to invite Cranmer and Nemeth to its next meeting in May 1991 to present their views. Although they were unable to attend, they produced a seminal paper, "A Uniform Braille Code," which the board discussed in their absence. The board requested clarification of, expansion of, and supporting examples for Cranmer and Nemeth's proposal in order to report to BANA in greater detail. Hilda Caton, representative to BANA from the Association for Education and Rehabilitation of the Blind and Visually Impaired (AER), was the BANA resource person named to work with Cranmer and Nemeth.

The Right Time

At the next BANA board meeting—October 1991 in Albuquerque, New Mexico—Cranmer and Nemeth made their presentation. After a private session, the board made its unanimous and historic decision to embark on a research project to unify the braille codes (except music). The project was called the Unified Braille Code (UBC) Research Project.

The Right People

Guidelines, a budget, and an action plan were approved in May 1992 at the next BANA board meeting. Every member wanted to participate, so the entire BANA board became the Ad Hoc UBC Project Committee. Darleen Bogart, BANA chair, agreed to direct the project. Cranmer and Nemeth were named to the main working group, Committee II—Extension of the Base Code (literary braille), because they had the experience of having developed the codes for computer notation and mathematics, and they were both avid users of braille and promoters of the concept of one code. Joseph Sullivan, a mathematician and computer programmer, was selected to lead the Committee II working group because he had experience as a developer of braille translation software for many languages as well as for mathematics, was involved in the development of CBC, and was a long-standing member of the BANA Literary Braille Technical Committee. Emerson Foulke, also involved with the development of CBC, was named to the working group because of his experience as a researcher in haptic perception and because he was an avid braille reader. Cranmer, Foulke, Nemeth, and Sullivan were named to the Ad Hoc UBC Project Committee. The selection of the team was made solely on the qualifications of the members and their abilities in braille code-writing. Gender and politics were not considered. The team couldn't be better—these were the right people.

Internationalization of the Project

It has long been recognized that much would be gained if only the various braille codes used by English speakers around the world could be standardized. Not necessarily that there would be just one code for all purposes, but that, for each purpose, there would be just one code used everywhere. Clearly, that would simplify production and allow braille to be shared among countries more freely. Yet, as of 1990, only one English code—the general literary code—could be said to be used internationally, and even in that case there were small regional differences. The BANA codes for mathematics and computer notation, used mainly in North America and New Zealand, were both matched by codes, utterly different in design, used in the United Kingdom and among many other English-speaking populations in Africa, Australia, and elsewhere (sometimes with notable local variations). Not surprisingly, these two main systems for technical notation differed not only from each other but also from the codes that had been adopted by speakers of other languages for the same purposes—even though the print notation for mathematics and computer material is essentially the same across language boundaries.

Standardization of the English braille codes was proving to be, however noble, a difficult goal. But if standardization was to be remotely possible, communication and cooperation among the various national braille standard-setting bodies had to be established. That communication and cooperation crystallized around the same time that the BANA board was considering Cranmer and Nemeth's paper, "A Uniform Braille Code."

In May 1991, in Canada, the International Council on English Braille (ICEB) was created. ICEB had been developing over the previous decade as the result of two international conferences: the International Conference on English Braille Grade 2, held in Washington, D.C., September 13–17, 1982, and the International Conference on English Literary Braille, held in London September 18–24, 1988. The founding members of ICEB were Australia, Canada, Ireland, New Zealand, Nigeria, South Africa, Sri Lanka, the United Kingdom, the United States, and Zambia. However Ireland, Sri Lanka, and Zambia did not choose to become participating members in 1991.

Although the UBC project was a BANA initiative, extending it to include the ICEB was a major goal of the BANA board from the beginning of the project. After all of BANA's hard work in fostering international cooperation and communication, it was important that these actions were regarded by the ICEB members as a constructive, forward-moving step towards standardization. As a result, in December 1991, very soon after BANA made the decision to proceed with UBC, Bogart, BANA chairman and project director, and Fred Schroeder, BANA board member and ICEB chairman, telephoned William Poole, the chairman of the Braille Authority of the United Kingdom (BAUK), as the other major code development body, to advise him of BANA's venture and to invite BAUK's participation. BAUK agreed that Bill Poole should accept designation as ICEB's official liaison to the UBC project.

BANA requested in a memo to Fred Schroeder in January 1992 that the ICEB members be invited to participate in the BANA UBC project. In June 1992, shortly after the May 1992 BANA meeting, Schroeder wrote to the ICEB members inviting each of them to name a participant to Committee II as it began its deliberations. Poole, as the official ICEB representative, and Terry Small, chairman of the Braille Authority of New Zealand, attended the November 1992 BANA meeting and were granted voting rights at the Ad Hoc UBC Project Committee meeting that followed. Bogart, already a voting member because of her representation of the Canadian National Institute for the Blind (CNIB) on the BANA board, brought the official participation of the Canadian Braille Authority to the project. The next month, December 1992, Schroeder and Sullivan attended BAUK's meeting in London to discuss the UBC Research Project. BAUK designated Stephen Phippen a member of Committee II, whose task remained the unification of the BANA codes.

With the interest shown by other ICEB members, Canada, New Zealand, and U.K. braille authorities, the Ad Hoc UBC Project Committee developed a plan for the internationalization of the project. The BANA board approved the plan at its spring meeting in 1993 for subsequent circulation to ICEB members for action at the Executive Committee meeting, June 15–17, 1993, in Sydney, Australia. ICEB accepted the plan with only a few minor changes. That meant that as of June 1993, the UBC project was no longer only a BANA project but was officially under the direction of ICEB.

As a result of the approved plan, BANA committed its resources designated for UBC to the international project. Bogart was confirmed as the chairman of the Project Committee on the Unified Braille Code. Voting at the now expanded Project Committee would be on the basis of one country, one vote. Representatives from the ICEB participating countries—Connie Aucamp (South Africa), Joan Ledermann (Australia), Raeleen Smith (New Zealand), and William Poole (U.K.)—were approved as members of the Project Committee, as were all members of the original BANA Ad Hoc Project Committee. Darleen Bogart (Canada) and BANA chair Hilda Caton (U.S.) would cast the votes for their respective countries. Everyone was aware that the task had just become even more difficult, but also that the rewards of success would justify the efforts.

Final Organization

Committee II membership was expanded to include a representative from each additional participating country. Canada declined membership on the committee because Bogart was project chair.

Other working committees were formed, and each ICEB participating country named at least one member to each of the four new committees:

1. Committee III—Contractions

2. Committee IV—Interface with Foreign Language Codes

3. Committee V—Format Guidelines

4. Committee VI—Rules (transcriber rules)

A due date of 1996 was approved for completion of the tasks. As of early 2000, however, all of the tasks had not been completed. Many reasons could be cited, but three stand out:

1. All the committee chairs and members have undertaken these tasks, which constitute a huge amount of work, as volunteers, in addition to their regular professional activities.

2. All communication has been by e-mail, which, although effective, is not nearly as efficient as face-to-face meetings, for which funds are lacking.

3. The evaluation process has been much slower than expected.

In November 1999 the ICEB Second General Assembly convened in Baltimore, Maryland. The UBC Research Project was a major part of the agenda, with reports from UBC Committees II through VI. Resolutions unanimously passed gave time lines for required face-to-face meetings, and for the completion of work by the five working committees and their final reports to the Project Committee. The final report on the UBC research project is to be completed in time for consideration by the ICEB Executive Committee at its meeting early in 2002.

Funding of the Project

BANA member organizations contributed financial and in-kind donations in the early stages, including a long-term yearly pledge in one case. These monies were transferred to a separate organization, the Braille Research Center (BRC), in November 1992 when it became BANA's partner in the UBC Project, responsible for approved research for the working groups, facilitation, and fund-raising.

After the internationalization of the project, expenses were paid for those ICEB representatives on the Project Committee whose braille authorities or agencies were not able to contribute financially to their attendance at meetings.

The BRC became the International Braille Research Center (IBRC) with United Kingdom (and later, Canadian) representation on the board. This move did not have the anticipated results in fund-raising. ICEB's fund-raising committee was unable to provide any funds at all for the project.

Writing the Code—The Work of Committee II

As mentioned earlier, the BANA board approved the original UBC Project Committee in May 1992 and immediately launched the project by appointing several working committees, including one called Committee II—Extension of the Base Code. The name was intended to emphasize that UBC was not to be a completely new code but rather would be based firmly on English braille—that is, the literary code—with minimal changes. Committee II was charged with defining the rules of UBC so that it would not only preserve the English braille foundation for literary material but also seamlessly go beyond it to encompass technical notation, such as math and computer science, in a consistent way. The carefully worded guidelines called for UBC to be just about the perfect braille code: usable both by beginning and advanced readers, fully convertible in either direction between print and braille by computer, comfortably readable by people, and unambiguous.

Because all four of the original members of Committee II had attended the May 1992 BANA meeting and thus were present when they were appointed, they took the opportunity to have an informal meeting on procedural preliminaries and also to get a quick feel for the substantive issues that would need to be addressed. The atmosphere was friendly and lively, with the sense that an important new beginning was at hand. It also quickly became clear, however, that the guidelines needed to be interpreted and that there might not be complete consensus on certain important questions, such as how to represent numbers.

As with any new committee, Committee II first had to figure out what it had really been asked to do, and within what limitations. The guidelines sometimes overlapped, and they sometimes conflicted in the sense that it would be impossible to realize all of them perfectly. The committee also found it difficult to discern priorities. To cope with these difficulties, the committee adopted a constructive approach to the guiding principles: they were all to be considered as a group and balanced as necessary; and although each principle was important, none would be considered as absolute. This approach, involving balance and sometimes compromise, was deemed essential for any progress at all to be possible.

Other important enablers of progress were the adoption of electronic means for communication—first a bulletin board system (BBS) and later e-mail—and of suitably adapted Robert's Rules of Order for procedure. The former permitted the geographically scattered committee members to hold an essentially continuous electronic meeting, during which most of the work and certainly some of the most important and drawn-out debates took place. The latter ensured that when the time came, there was an accepted way of making each decision and moving on to the next subject.

As the process evolved, it seemed that some guidelines did take priority on the basis of the committee's judgment as to the main purposes of UBC. Given the need to represent technical notation and the dire consequences if such notation is not precisely understood, the need for the braille to be unambiguous to the reader was considered paramount. A few exceptions were made even here, but not in any instance that would adversely affect the reader's exact knowledge of significant symbols and their sequence. The committee wished to eliminate the kind of ambiguity that can arise because braille symbols sometimes include two or more braille characters and, especially in older codes, it might not be clear how the characters are grouped, that is, where the implied boundaries are between the individual symbols. For perhaps the first time ever in the formulation of any general-purpose braille code, the committee took the time to establish symbol formation rules so that readers would always be sure where each symbol begins and ends, even in a sequence of symbols whose meanings are not yet known to the reader. In general, the committee always considered the reading process first, and the writing or transcribing process second, a defining principle that came to be known as "reader rules."

What became clear in retrospect was that these priorities amounted to an overall implied bias in the design of UBC toward the beginning and occasional user of technical notation as opposed to the advanced technical expert, to the extent that it was not always possible to satisfy both groups. The beginner needs precision (lack of ambiguity), consistency, and a minimum of unnecessary new nomenclature in order to grasp the meaning of technical notation most easily, especially in new subjects. Efficiency—that is, minimizing braille cells or dots—is also usually desirable, but it is definitely less important. On the other hand, for the advanced and constant user of some specific branch of technical notation, efficiency may be judged to be more important as a way of maintaining mental concentration without added "noise." Even some ambiguity may be preferable to inefficiency for those who are already so familiar with the subject matter that context suffices to decide among several possible meanings. Of course, for basic usability, both groups need UBC to give them a way to represent the needed symbols in braille. In that sense, UBC is equally usable by both beginners and experts. But as to nonambiguity versus efficiency, UBC most definitely leans toward nonambiguity, and hence toward general readers rather than technical experts. (It should be mentioned, though, that technical experts will also have the option of writing UBC in informal or extended ways, to achieve the desired efficiency for their own use or that of other experts. Such a development would not be a violation of the UBC principle, nor would it affect general readers; rather, it would be akin to the shortcuts normally taken when jotting notes for one's own use, or where the context is otherwise presumed to be well understood.)

The committee had many symbol assignments and other kinds of design decisions to make, some easy and some not, but it was the question of numbers that required the most time and thought. In Louis Braille's original system for French, and in the basic codes for virtually all languages ever since, the ten digits do not have their own braille character assignments but rather share the characters that are also used for the letters "a" through "j." This way of representing numbers is sometimes called "upper numbers," because each digit consists of some combination of the four uppermost dots within the six-dot (three high by two wide) configuration. Of course, with upper numbers, the reader must have some way of knowing whether a given braille character is a letter or a digit; for example, whether a particular series means "dab" or "412" or even "41b." The distinction is accomplished by having special separate indicator characters in the braille. One such indicator, called the "number sign" or more formally the "numeric indicator," precedes any series of digits to announce that the numeric meaning is understood up to the next character that cannot be numeric, such as a space. Another indicator, often called the "letter sign," is interposed whenever the normal letter meaning must be resumed before the natural end of the number; for example, just before the "b" in the case of "41b."

These indicators consume space and reading time, arguably contributing to a certain awkwardness when digits and letters are frequently juxtaposed, as would generally be the case in algebra and other technical notations. One approach to this problem is to use "lower numbers," where the dot combinations are kept in the same geometric pattern but moved to the lowermost four dots. In that position, the dot combinations for digits are no longer the same as for any letter, but they do correspond to assignments typically used for punctuation marks. That way, at least in certain circumstances, one may still need indicators before or after a number.

In their earlier work designing technical braille codes, all four committee members had opted for lower numbers. Because of that, many people expected Committee II to quickly adopt lower numbers and move on. However, because UBC was to serve as a general code and not just a technical code, three of the four Committee II members (Nemeth being the exception) came to believe that upper numbers were more suitable. There were three main reasons for their thinking:

1. Numbers and punctuation marks are more commonly juxtaposed than numbers and letters (even, surprisingly, in material with heavy technical content), and so upper numbers require fewer indicators than lower numbers overall.

2. Upper configurations are more easily read and, in terms of Louis Braille's evident design intent, more suitable for principal information, such as numbers, than for auxiliary information, such as punctuation marks.

3. Upper numbers are the traditional form and are most familiar to most readers.

The committee also briefly considered a third approach to braille numbers, in which dot six (the lower-right dot of the of the six-dot pattern) is added to the traditional upper-dot configuration. Such "dot-six" digits do not clash with either ordinary letters or punctuation marks in customary English assignments, except that zero would clash with w, which is circumvented simply by giving zero a special assignment. In the original French, Louis Braille used these same dot patterns for accented letters. In English, they are used for contractions. Use of these patterns for digits began with a mathematics code devised by a Professor Antoine in France around 1920 (hence they are sometimes called "Antoine numbers"). Such use is now common in some of the European technical codes, including the British code for computer notation, but they had never been used in any American code. Because of that history and the consequent assumption that American readers would find them too radical a departure, these numbers were not considered further by the committee during this first, BANA-only, phase.

The committee submitted its report in November 1992. It was well received overall, although the unexpected choice of upper numbers, together with some other assignments, made for some critical comment within the intended American audience. The rigorous and reader-oriented basis of the UBC also drew encouraging interest from overseas. As mentioned previously, BAUK appointed Stephen Phippen to join the committee in December 1992. In June 1993, ICEB formally adopted the UBC as its project, and seats were created on Committee II for three additional countries. Australia appointed Bruce Maguire. South Africa, after appointing a pro tem, permanently appointed Christo de Klerk. New Zealand appointed Terry Small, whose untimely death a few months later was a deep loss for the project and the cause of braille in general. Raeleen Smith pro tem, and later Margaret Salt permanently, were assigned in his place. Nigeria did not appoint members.

At this point, some of the UBC design work was moved to other committees, notably those matters related to English contractions and the treatment of other languages within English context. Committee II was asked to carry on with a primary focus on technical subjects such as mathematics, computer notation, chemistry, and science generally.

It could be said that this expanded committee now had an expanded unification task: to unify not only three American codes (for literary, mathematics, and computer notation) but also the corresponding British codes, two of which (those for mathematics and computer notation) were very different from the corresponding American codes. In other words, five different codes, not including special conventions and extensions such as for textbooks and chemistry nor regional variations, were to be unified. While the essential work remained the same, the international aspect was more pervasive with the other ICEB members involved in the project. Consideration of international issues and codes, including languages other than English, which had been present but of lower priority in the earlier BANA-only phase, now intensified.

Taking into account the reactions to the earlier report and also the expansion of both the committee's role and the geography represented, Committee II revisited many assignments and other matters, including numbers. The second debate on the subject of numbers was as spirited as the first and even more protracted. It included a much more in-depth consideration of the dot-six forms. In the end, the dot-six numbers were not adopted, mainly because they have a relatively high dot density that was judged problematic for reading efficiency. The upper numbers were confirmed for general use over other forms by vote of seven to one, thus putting the matter to rest and solidly reaffirming one of Louis Braille's original design decisions.

Committee II presented its second report in March 1995. From that time until early 1999, the UBC project was mainly engaged in a process of evaluation by users of braille. That process has resulted in a few minor changes to the code, but in the main has confirmed that the UBC is on the right track. It is this evaluation process that has delayed the project from its original deadline of 1996.

Evaluation of UBC

The first report, "Extension of the Base Code," had been received by the Ad Hoc UBC Research Project Committee from the BANA working group on schedule in November 1992. It was a technical report, not envisaged as one for general circulation. But the interest from the braille community—readers, educators, and producers—was so great that there was not time to produce a more easily understood document. The original report was widely distributed with a brief evaluation requested of all who wanted to respond. This survey, in addition to giving valuable feedback, allowed a wider involvement in the project. The next evaluation, though, was to be scientifically constructed and conducted.

The expanded Committee II, with full ICEB international participation as of June 1993 and with the earlier feedback in hand, produced a revised and extended report in March 1995. The IBRC and ICEB signed a letter of agreement whereby the IBRC would prepare the evaluation of that report, make it available to all participating countries, analyze the results for each country, and prepare a consolidated report. The IBRC agreed to conduct the evaluation in North America. But once again, people involved in braille wanted to participate, so the evaluation went to everyone who signed up.

Foulke, an original member of the working committee, had been named to oversee the production, distribution, and tabulation of the evaluation results, but his illness and untimely death prevented him from doing so. The project was thus further delayed.

The CNIB undertook the tasks and designed and presented a database with tabulations of all the responses of the participating countries for the IBRC. The IBRC has engaged Edwin Vaughan of the University of Missouri in the United States to analyze the results and write the reports, the last of which was completed in February 2000.

There is still some work to be done, mainly in contractions and foreign-language treatment, in formatting, and in chemistry as well as some less-common technical notation areas. Of course, as anticipated in its basic design,

UBC will never be finished per se. Its eventual acceptance as an official code is still not certain, but it has been authorized by ICEB, BAUK, and BANA for experimental and other unofficial uses, such as for immediate rendering of World Wide Web documents into braille. Considering the explosive growth of the Web, and the fact that UBC was designed very consciously for just such purposes, all signs for eventual adoption remain very positive.

THE BRAILLE AUTHORITY OF NORTH AMERICA AND ITS CONTRIBUTION TO BRAILLE PRODUCTION

by Dolores Ferrara-Godzieba

The Founding of BANA

During the 1970s, computer technology was being developed for braille transcription; this breakthrough would change the way future generations of braille transcribers would produce braille. In June 1976, the American Foundation for the Blind (AFB) sponsored a workshop in New York City, where it was suggested that creating a computer-compatible grade 2 literary braille code was essential. In September of the same year, in response to the development of computer technology for braille transcription, the first informal meeting of the Braille Authority of North America (BANA) took place. The meeting was convened by the leaders of the American Association of Workers for the Blind, the Association for Education of the Visually Handicapped, and the National Braille

Association (NBA). These groups represented organizations of braille consumers, teachers of visually handicapped people, and braille transcribers.

One goal of the September 1976 meeting was to restructure the former Braille Authority of the United States, which had disbanded and had its responsibilities taken over by a department of Florida State University. The other goal was to increase the number of sponsoring groups that would constitute a new braille authority. The aim of this newly united group would be to strengthen the mechanism for the development of new braille codes, to adopt changes to existing codes, to be responsive to the needs of braille producers and readers, and to keep abreast of the new technology that would benefit the production of braille materials. The invited organizations were asked to consider becoming members in the restructured braille authority.

An historic meeting was held on December 2, 1976, in Rosemont, Illinois, with eleven organizations from the United States and Canada present, including government agencies that served blind people, advocacy groups for blind people, braille producers, braille computer programmers, teachers of the visually handicapped, researchers, and braille transcribers. The organizations, which joined together at this meeting to form the Braille Authority of North America, were the Library of Congress, National Library Service for the Blind and Physically Handicapped (NLS); the Canadian National Institute for the Blind (CNIB); the American Association of Workers for the Blind (AAWB); the American Council of the Blind (ACB); the National Federation of the Blind (NFB); the

American Printing House for the Blind (APH); the Clovernook Home and School for the Blind; the Association for Computing Machinery (ACM); the Association for Education of the Visually Handicapped (AEVH); the American Foundation for the Blind (AFB); and the National Braille Association (NBA). Those organizations then formed a committee to write the BANA articles of incorporation and bylaws. BANA thus became the recognized authority for approving and adopting changes in all existing braille codes in use both in the United States and Canada (Minutes 1976).

Prior to the establishment of the Braille Authority of North America, Florida State University had received a grant from the United States Office of Education for a project called the Braille Codes Standardization Project. The grant was made to Florida State University because the former Braille Authority of the United States had not been active, but it included the provision that the code changes be approved by the Braille Authority of the United States before they went into effect. At its formation, BANA took over the responsibility of reviewing and revising all braille codes. The grant was used to establish technical advisory committees for mathematics and science braille, music braille, and computer braille. The textbook formats for braille codes—the *Code of Braille Textbook Formats and Techniques, 1976*—was in the process of being published, so at this time there was no immediate need for the establishment of a textbook formats committee. In addition, in response to the recommendation of the June 1976 AFB workshop, the founding BANA agencies created a committee whose purpose was to discuss the computer compatibility of grade 2 literary braille (Minutes 1977).

On November 9, 1977, the Articles of Incorporation of the Braille Authority of North America were signed and filed. This corporation was organized to fulfill a two-fold purpose:

1. To promulgate rules, make interpretations, and render opinions pertaining to all provisions of literary and technical braille codes and related forms and formats of embossed materials for blind persons.

2. To perform its function and authority relative to embossed materials including but not limited to literary braille codes, mathematics and scientific notation, music braille codes, computer notation, textbook formats and techniques, diagrams, maps, and tables; to consider the effects on production of such materials by stereograph machine and press, computer translation and processing, and hand transcription; and to gauge their acceptability to readers (Articles of Incorporation 1977).

Soon after BANA was established, Florida State University made an agreement to include BANA members on the technical committees of the Braille Codes Standardization Project, to submit proposed code revisions to BANA for consideration and action, and to agree that BANA had the sole responsibility for reviewing and revising all braille codes.

At an April 1978 meeting of BANA, technical committees were formed for music braille, mathematics and scientific notation, textbook formats, and literary braille. Additional committees would later be formed as the need arose.

The Beginning of International Dialogue

At its formation, the BANA board decided it would be open to a dialogue with agencies throughout the world that were similar to itself, such as the National Uniform Type Committee (NUTC) of Great Britain and the World Council for the Welfare of the Blind (WCWB). The board also decided that it would not necessarily limit BANA's scope to English braille. In a letter the board reviewed at the April 1978 meeting, the director of NLS suggested that the presence of two codes—namely, English braille American edition and standard English braille—created confusion and had the effect of reducing the supply of books in braille for both the British and American braille-reading public. A resolution was proposed at that meeting that BANA join with the NUTC of Great Britain to explore the possibility of devising a common literary braille code for the English language, focusing on both readability and computer implementation.

At a meeting in November 1979, the BANA board decided that a liaison committee of BANA/NUTC members should meet in London to determine the differences in the basic literary codes of both countries. The board also recommended that the primary function of the negotiating team be to establish a common code of literary braille (Minutes 1979).

One year later, at a November 1980 meeting, the BANA members of the liaison committee reported that the NUTC members of the committee, along with the Braille Authority of the United Kingdom (BAUK), had proposed an international conference to discuss the unification of the braille codes. The board agreed with the proposal and established a planning committee of technical experts to promote an international conference on standardizing braille for all English-speaking countries. Also at this meeting, it was agreed that BANA should make public the fact that it was indeed the recognized authority for approving changes in all existing braille codes in use in the United States and Canada. The statement BANA released pointed out that BANA was actively working with BAUK to achieve the uniformity of braille codes.

The result of that November 1980 meeting was the International Conference on English Braille Grade 2, sponsored by BANA and BAUK, and held in September 1982 at the NLS in Washington, D.C. Papers were presented by both countries on the themes of unifying English braille grade 2, researching contracted braille, and international cooperation. A new committee was formed from members of BANA and BAUK; it was called the International Coordinating Committee on English Literary Braille (ICCOELB).

At a June 1985 BANA meeting in Canada, representatives of the United Kingdom, South Africa, and New Zealand were present and plans for a 1988 meeting in London, England, were discussed. The ICCOELB suggested that there should be up to four delegates per country at the 1988 meeting, with each country having only one vote, and that a simple majority of 51 percent should pass a resolution. During the London Conference the delegates resolved that ICCOELB shall remain in existence with the original seven member countries to continue the work of identifying differences in braille codes and to seek agreement on measures designed to eliminate them; also a resolution was adopted calling for the establishment of an International Council on English Braille to coordinate the work of various braille authorities throughout the English-speaking world (Minutes 1988).

BANA and BAUK, in order to continue the process of code unification, made the ICCOELB a permanent committee in 1988 with responsibility for English literary braille grade 2.

At the September 1988 meeting in London the need for a unified braille code was officially recognized. This decision for unification was a monumental step, the effects of which are still being felt. At a November 1991 BANA meeting, and in response to a suggestion from the creator of the mathematics code and one of the developers of computer braille notation, BANA approved the development of an ad hoc committee to develop guidelines for the establishment of a Unified Braille Code (UBC). At the November 1992 BANA meeting, a motion was passed that the chair of BANA be a member of ICCOELB and represent BANA at ICCOELB's organizational meeting. It was resolved that the countries that would permanently be represented in ICCOELB were Australia, Canada, New

Zealand, South Africa, the United Kingdom, and the United States.

BANA, BAUK, and braille authorities of all English-speaking countries now make up the International Council on English Braille (ICEB), which became the successor to ICCOELB. The ICEB so far has spent almost a decade researching the UBC.

BANA's Growing Mission in the Braille Community

The stated official purpose of BANA was expanded at its November 1981 meeting to include the promotion of the teaching, use, and production of braille. At the same meeting, the board moved to accept Volunteer Services for the Blind, later renamed Associated Services for the Blind, as a new member of the BANA board.

At the April 1983 board meeting, a rewording of BANA's mission was adopted. It now read:

> The purpose of BANA is to promote and facilitate the uses, teaching and production of braille. Pursuant to this purpose, BANA will promulgate rules, make interpretations and render opinions pertaining to all provisions of literary and technical braille codes and related forms and formats of embossed materials now in existence or to be developed in the future for the use of blind persons in those countries served by BANA.

At this meeting, the board also approved the Guidelines for Mathematical Diagrams and the distribution of this volume by NBA.

In January 1984, the American Association of Workers for the Blind and the Association for Education of the Visually Handicapped formed an alliance called the Association of Education and Rehabilitation of the Blind and Visually Handicapped. Because of this consolidation, BANA now had one fewer board member. In the same year, an ad hoc subcommittee on linear braille was formed. Linear braille provides format information for braille presented on a one-line refreshable braille display.

At a BANA meeting in November 1986, the computer braille code was approved for publication. BANA also approved the development of a provisional braille code for chemical notation at this meeting. The Association for Computing Machinery left the BANA board.

In 1987, BANA agreed to publish *Learning the Nemeth Braille Code: A Manual for Teachers and Students; Code for Computer Braille Notation;* and *The Provisional Guidelines for Literary Linear Braille.* Format changes were made to English Braille American Edition, 1972, and distributed. All these publications represented important steps in BANA's goal of promulgating rules, making interpretations, and rendering opinions on braille codes.

By the end of 1988, personal computers were being used extensively by producers and transcribers of braille. BANA was assured by the braille programmers that all rules and formats developed and approved by BANA were being used.

In order to establish standards of competency in braille among teachers of blind people (because competent and confident teaching ensures that children acquire excellent braille skills), BANA supported the efforts of NLS to develop a teacher certification procedure for teachers of blind students. This effort began in the early 1990s and activities to validate the test continue today.

In 1990, National Braille Press and the California Teachers and Educators of the Visually Handicapped were approved as new member organizations of BANA, and the Royal New Zealand Foundation for the Blind was accepted as the first Associate Member. During the 1990s, BANA has approved the following technical books used by transcribers and proofreaders: *English Braille American Edition, 1994; Braille Code for Columned Materials and Tables, 1995; Braille Code for Chemical Notation, 1997; Braille Code for Music, 1997; and Braille Formats: Principles of Print to Braille Transcription, 1997.* The publishing of these books also shows BANA's attempt to achieve its stated goals.

In 1998, in order to educate teachers, transcribers, consumers, and the interested public about the work of BANA, a brochure, outlining BANA's purpose and publications was printed, a traveling exhibit was established, and a BANA web site (www.brailleauthority.org) was created. These tools made BANA more visible and accessible by both the sighted and blind populations.

Today, BANA continues expanding its mission of service to the braille community. For example, because the Americans with Disabilities Act (ADA) requires signage for blind people, BANA is developing a pamphlet of guidelines for sign makers. Graphics have become so important in the production of textbooks that a committee has been formed to prepare guidelines for transcribers and teachers to help them in the preparation of tactile graphics.

For almost a quarter of a century, BANA has worked to promote the use of braille and has helped transcribers produce valuable products for the visually impaired. Braille literacy has been BANA's goal from the beginning, and BANA will continue to devote itself to this goal in the new millennium.

References

Articles of Incorporation. 1977.

Minutes. 1976.

Minutes. 1977.

Minutes. 1979.

Minutes. 1988.

ALTERNATIVE METHODS OF BRAILLE PRODUCTION

by Geoffrey Bull

Introduction

In this chapter, we will discuss alternative methods of braille production. To understand these methods, we must consider them in light of the history of braille production, its present status, and even some "best guesses" for the future. We will consider braille production under two main headings: transcription/proofreading and braille output (the production of copies).

Transcribing and Proofreading

Until the mid-1970s, transcription was done by a braillist familiar with the rules of braille who directly input braille either on paper (for single copies) or on plates (for multiple copies). Various computer programs were developed during the 1970s and 1980s whereby text with the addition of formatting characters was input, and contracted grade 2 (normally) braille was output.

During the 1970s and early 1980s, text needed to be keyed manually, but during the later 1980s and the 1990s, as optical character recognition (OCR) became cheaper and more available, text could be scanned. Scanned input thus rapidly superseded manual input, particularly in the larger braille printing houses.

Scanning, in its turn, has been toppled as the number one choice for data capture. With the increasing availability of data in digital form, either through the Internet or on CD-ROM and floppy disk, further advances in speed and accuracy of data capture have been achieved. The increased accuracy offers an extremely significant benefit at the proofreading stage, where the much cleaner initial proofs lead to more timely and accurate finished products.

The evolution of transcription processes during the past twenty-five years has had a dramatic effect on both the speed and cost of production. In real terms, the cost of transcription and proofreading has been cut in half during the past two decades.

Have braille translation programs replaced the skilled braillist? For the individual producing his or her own work and for material that will not be used for any professional purpose, perhaps the answer is a qualified yes. But for professionally produced braille, braille distributed to a large readership and subject to strict quality control, the complexity of the exceptions and anomalies in the braille rules still create an environment that requires skilled transcribers and proofreaders. The complex and often contradictory braille rules frequently require the transcriber to study context as part of the decision-making process, a process well beyond the scope of current translation programs. Despite recent cost savings, these front-end processes of braille production remain by far the most expensive stages of the production process.

The Future

Two developments are likely to have the most impact on the speed, accuracy, and cost of braille translation: 1. Easy access to and conversion of digital data. 2. The simplification of the braille code and thereby the rules governing that code.

Reference has already been made to the availability of digital data and the fact that more and more braille printing houses and individuals are taking advantage of it, but it is almost exclusively the text, not the format, of that material that is being downloaded. In many instances, formatting strings denoting paragraphs, headings, italics, and the like are linked to the text, but because of the nonstandard application of formatting strings and markup languages (sets of codes that specify a wide variety of document characteristics including the format of a particular word, line, or paragraph) a separate conversion program would be needed for each producer of source material in order to take advantage of these formatting codes. Computer programs have been written for specific applications that can take the text and the formatting codes and produce a very acceptable and clean formatted braille document, but we are still a long way from being able to create a standard, multipurpose program capable of producing formatted grade 2 braille from multisource digital files.

The complexity of grade 2 braille will continue to inhibit the automatic conversion of text to braille without the need for painstaking and costly proofreading. Even the most sophisticated computer program is unlikely to meet the demands of the purist with respect to braille letter-signs, restrictions on the use of braille contractions, and context-based decisions.

Fortunately, both of these areas that currently inhibit the virtually automatic production of formatted and translated braille are being addressed. Organizations of and for the blind are meeting with publishers and producers regarding the standardization of markup languages and well-defined data type descriptions (DTDs). At the same time, national and international groups concerned with the definition of English braille grade 2 are meeting in attempts to simplify braille code(s). Success in these two areas would mark a major step forward in the production of inexpensive and accurate braille products.

Braille Output

We will discuss this aspect of production-braille output under three headings: 1. Embossed braille (dots produced on paper by distorting the surface, normally by mechanical pressure). 2. Superimposed braille (raised characters or lines produced by superimposing one material on another).

3. Refreshable braille displays (braille produced by electro-mechanical means, and of a transient nature, often called paperless braille).

Embossed Braille

Since its inception, braille has been produced by distorting paper by mechanical means. In the early days of embossed braille, this was done with a sharp instrument, or stylus, that poked indentations into paper, producing dots—laboriously, one dot at a time—on the opposite surface. Mechanical devices, capable of producing up to six dots with each impression (one braille character), slowly replaced the stylus. Embossers capable of producing braille on one side of the page were succeeded by those capable of producing braille on both sides (interpoint braille), by offsetting the dots on the second side. As the demand for braille increased, braille was embossed onto master plates (brass, zinc, and later plastic) so that multiple copies could be made by using the masters to emboss paper. Plates were initially embossed using manually operated stereotype equipment, embossing up to three or four characters per second, but with the advent of the computer, automatic plate embossers arrived with speeds up to ten times that of the stereotypists.

The computer also heralded the paper embosser. Very similar in concept to the plate embosser, the paper embosser, capable of embossing several hundred characters per second directly onto paper, is proving a great boon to individuals producing their own braille and, for limited runs, to those in professional production environments. Whether paper or plate embossers are more appropriate for a particular situation tends to be determined by the number of copies required (as of June 1999, fewer than fifty copies tend to be produced with paper embossers and more than a hundred copies with the intermediate step of plate embossing) and the speed and cost of the embossing device.

In writing about embossed braille, mention must be made of thermoform. In contrast to embossed braille produced by mechanical distortion, thermoform braille is produced by heating a plastic-based material that, in its heated state, accepts the impression from a previously embossed master (paper) page. Thermoform production has in large part been replaced by paper embossers, particularly for straightforward text, but it still plays a significant role in the reproduction of graphic material. The widespread use of thermoform products has always been limited by the cost of the raw materials used and a somewhat reluctant acceptance of plastic braille by the user.

Superimposed Braille

The word "superimposed" (not a widely recognized term) is used here to describe the process of producing raised dots and lines by superimposing one material upon another. The first significant attempt at producing braille by means of superimposition was in England in the 1970s. The Royal National Institute for the Blind in London circulated several of its magazines using what was called "solid dot" braille. The braille was produced by projecting onto a plastic-base material an ink-like substance that, after cooling, was left as a dot on the surface. The process was discontinued in the late 1970s after research showed that the ink was toxic in its liquid state. It should also be mentioned, however, that solid-dot braille did not receive a high approval rating from braille readers, because, as with thermoform braille, readers did not like the sticky feel of the dried ink on plastic.

The rationale for developing the process of superimposition was that thinner paper could be used, making braille volumes less bulky, and the dot would be more durable. The braille volumes were indeed thinner, but there is a question as to the durability of the braille, because it was easy to remove dots from the page with a fingernail.

Interest in this field has resurfaced in the past year or so. Experimental work is being done in Texas, Canada, and Japan, using ultraviolet curable lacquer or thick film silk screen on a substrate to produce raised characters and images. None of these development centers are in full production mode to my knowledge, but many samples have been widely circulated. The superimposed process seems to lend itself very readily to the reproduction of diagrams, charts, maps, and other material not readily represented by the braille cell. The embossing process has never quite solved the problem of reproducing diagrammatic material, whereas this would appear to be the tour de force of the superimposition process. It is probable therefore that superimposition will play a major role in the reproduction of graphic material at some point in the future, but there must be a big question mark regarding whether it will replace embossed braille in the production of hard copy braille text.

Refreshable Braille Displays

Refreshable braille displays provide a means for accessing electronically stored data and displaying it in braille (a more detailed description of their operation is found in Chapter 17). Their versatility can best be demonstrated by the fact that, despite their extremely high cost, thousands of individuals have purchased them during the past two decades. Refreshable braille displays are currently used more for accessing digital data that is not necessarily in braille format and may or may not have been passed through a translation program. To date, braille printing houses produce very little braille output in digital form, but as more and more devices come into the hands of readers, this output option, with all its advantages, will certainly play a large part in braille production.

The typical cost for a braille display in the United States today is one hundred dollars per braille cell plus the cost of any additional features the device may have; in general, a display costs no less than three thousand four hundred dollars and as much as fifteen thousand dollars. Despite the growing number of braille readers with braille displays, the very high cost will prevent the vast majority of braille readers from having personal devices in the near future, and it may be some time, therefore, before a significant number of books and magazines are produced and distributed to the braille display market. But the rationale for a major change is there: data (braille or otherwise) distributed in digital form has enormous advantages in terms of shipping and handling costs, production costs, speed of production, bulk, storage, and portability.

These advantages might influence and lead to change in the current production methods. In many countries, for example, it is customary to distribute braille magazines to individuals but to store hardcover books in central state, provincial, or national lending libraries and circulate them to readers on request. For hardcover books in particular, the costs of production (in small quantities), initial distribution, storage (including space and manpower), circulation to and from persons, and product wear and tear are enormous. If the debate has not already been triggered, then let it start here: Is the time fast approaching when it will be more cost-effective for the Government to issue all braille readers a braille display and provide all of them with their own copies of books and magazines in digital format?

Even faced with the current cost of refreshable braille displays, this debate merits serious consideration. The potential benefits to the users are immeasurable in terms of access to massive data banks of current material, building a library, and running shoulder to shoulder with their sighted peers. Bring the cost of a forty-character braille display in the United States to less than one thousand dollars—or, even better, make a full braille page display (twenty-five lines of forty characters) available and affordable—and a revolution in the approach to braille production and distribution will take place!

Collating and Binding

The introduction of automatic collating and binding of braille materials lagged well behind this development in the print world. It was commonly believed that the interlocking of the dots between one braille page and the next would interfere with collation and that most folding and stitching equipment would damage the braille by compressing it between rollers. The high cost of performing these activities manually, however, has prompted more research into this area. More and more producers have now found that with careful selection of collating equipment, and with the development of modified folding and stitching units, the automatic processing of this stage of production has been successful and very cost-effective.

Summary

During the first hundred years or so in the life of the braille system, changes in the alternative methods of braille production occurred very slowly, with minor modifications taking place with each passing decade. In the last quarter of the twentieth century, major changes have evolved every two or three years—the introduction of computers, OCR replacing keyboard input, braille translation programs, one-sided followed by interpoint computer-driven paper embossers, faster and faster plate embossers, automated collating and binding, refreshable braille displays, and availability of data in digital form. All these changes have played their part in making more braille available more quickly and at a dramatically reduced cost.

Faced with this escalating rate of progress, it is difficult to anticipate what might transpire during the first decade of the twenty-first century, but events most likely to affect braille production methods in the next few years are the cost of refreshable braille displays, standardization of markup codes used by publishing houses, and simplification of the braille code. We look forward to a time when braille production becomes as quick, efficient, and accurate as print production.

TANGIBLE
APPARATUS

by Carol B. Tobe

Reading, Spelling, Writing, and Music

In the early years of educating blind children, the early to mid-1800s, the recognition and use of Roman letterforms were the basic skills learned for reading and writing. Tactile aids—either handmade or manufactured—presented the letters of the alphabet in tactile form on practice sheets or individual letter cards that could be arranged to form words. Guides were designed to help blind people write Roman letters on paper to be read by sighted people.

Reading and Spelling Aids

Teachers taught Roman-letter recognition using alphabet cards embossed in the Boston line system. The American Printing House for the Blind (APH) produced alphabet cards embossed with upper- and lowercase letters in alphabetical as well as random order. And blind people or teachers of blind children could buy spelling frames with words and letters sold separately.

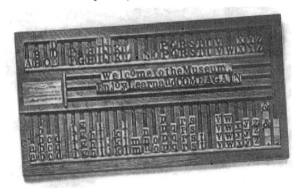

Some of the same kinds of aids were used to teach braille as it gained in acceptance in the early 1900s. The spelling frame with words—a slotted frame, plus two separate sets of words, one in braille and one in large type—was used as an aid in teaching spelling, sight recognition of words, and sentence building. In 1884 the Braillette board was used to form braille characters by inserting round-headed metal pegs in holes in a drilled baseboard. When the lid was closed and the box turned over, characters appeared as they were written on a braille slate. The De Braille Instructional Device, also from 1884, was designed as a braille teaching device. It was made of three sections of wood that rotated around a common axis; by turning the sections independently, a student could form any braille letter.

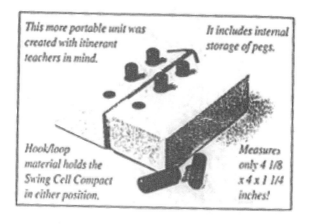

This more portable unit was created with itinerant teachers in mind.

It includes internal storage of pegs.

Hook/loop material holds the Swing Cell Compact in either position.

Measures only 4 1/8 x 4 x 1 1/4 inches!

Braille pegboard devices are still used today. A modern version of the Braillette board is the Peg Slate produced by APH. The plastic frame of the Peg Slate has ten braille cells with plastic pegs. Blind children use their fingers to push the pegs down from right to left as in slate writing. The board can then be turned over and the letters read on the other side from left to right.

The Swing Cell, also developed at APH, introduces the braille cell to beginning braille students. Three holes in each of two rectangular blocks, which can be placed vertically or horizontally, represent the spaces for the dots in a braille cell. Pegs are inserted in the holes to represent braille dots. In the vertical position, with the blocks next to each other, the pegs form the braille cell. In the horizontal position, the pegs show how braille is written on a braillewriter.

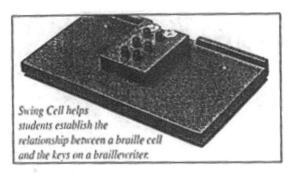

Swing Cell helps students establish the relationship between a braille cell and the keys on a braillewriter.

Swing Cell ▲

Reading Readiness Devices

The first kindergarten for blind children was opened at Perkins Institution and Massachusetts School for the Blind in Watertown, Massachusetts, in 1887. In his appeal for funding this endeavor, director Michael Anagnos said, "Experiments with the blind have shown that through the delicacy of touch the highest results in science and thought can be reached, and the kindergarten early in life trains this sense of feeling." The kindergarten children of the day modeled with clay and made designs with pins on a board. In more recent times, devices for braille reading readiness have been designed to develop specific skills. A wide range of aids is available for reading readiness that promotes textural discrimination with textured cards, blocks, and other objects. Also, there are many devices available for teaching young blind children basic concepts, such as size discrimination, shape recognition, texture, and position.

Writing Guides

In his 1874 report, Samuel Gridley Howe, director of the Perkins Institution, described the French writing board as "the most simple, most effective, and cheapest method ever yet invented." This apparatus has grooved lines, or channels, running an inch apart across the pasteboard plate. The pasteboard is inserted between two pages of letter-sized paper, and the first leaf is pressed with the forefinger into the grooves, which leaves depressions that can be felt by the pencil point. The guide was sold at the Perkins shop for fifteen to twenty-five cents, depending on the quality.

The Pennsylvania Institution for the Instruction of the Blind sold "Writing Cards, Grooved and Beveled" for thirty-five to fifty cents in 1878, and APH was producing writing guides as early as 1875, when a report from APH trustees stated, "As for cheap writing-guides, our printing-house for the blind makes one of superior finish at eight cents, and an article inferior in finish at four cents." The product was improved, and in 1883 the APH catalog offered writing cards that were "narrow, wide, and beveled grooved." The flexible version was five dollars per hundred and the pasteboard—oiled and varnished—was eight dollars.

The 1884 *A Guide to the Institutions & Charities for the Blind in the United Kingdom* listed aids that had been produced for blind people. Among them were a machine enabling blind people to write in raised letters without types; a machine to write with a pen or pencil in skeleton Roman capitals; an apparatus for embossing Lucas characters; tangible ink; a number of writing machines and instruments for teaching writing and drawing; and an apparatus to enable blind people to write in tactile Roman letters.

There has been a great variety of styles of writing guides over the years: they may be cardboard with raised lines or boards with a hinged metal frame and parallel wires for guiding the pencil; they may have a movable metal bar that can be lowered to the next line; and today some guides are specialized for signature and check writing. In the end, however, they are all based on the same concept.

When learning to write Roman letters, blind students are taught to follow the pencil point with the index finger of their left hand to help with letter spacing, dotting i's, and crossing t's. For learning the formation of letters in script writing, nineteenth-century students could use script letter sheets with letters raised or depressed. Script letter sheets of embossed letters and script letter boards with incised letters are still in use today.

The Hebold Writing Frame, or Heboldtafel, which was used for writing Roman letters as well, dates to the mid-1800s. This method of writing was developed by a German teacher, Ernst Eduard Hebold, who also published a book on writing for blind people, *School for Writing for the Blind*, in Berlin in 1859. The Hebold Writing Frame has a notched frame attached to a base. A metal bar, with a line of rectangular openings at regular intervals, fits into the notches in the frame. Angular capital letters are formed in the openings using the outside edge as a guide. The bars were available with different-sized openings so that writing could be large or small.

The Astrand Machine, with frames for both handwriting and braille, was invented by Otto Astrand, a teacher at the Manilla School for the Deaf and Blind in Stockholm, Sweden, from 1846 to 1870. His writer has a rectangular opening in the movable slide into which the user places a pencil, which then forms angular characters as the slide is moved along the frame. Two hinged flaps also allow for ascenders and descenders. It was used in Sweden until the 1920s.

In the Perkins Institution 1874 report of the director, Howe described how he taught his first deaf/blind student, Laura Bridgman. One of the devices he used was pin type. The types, instead of having the form of the letter cast in metal, have the outline of the letters made with projecting pinpoints. When the points are pressed into paper, a dotted outline of the letter is made on the reverse. Invented by John W. Klein of Vienna, Austria, the Pin-type Printing Box was made available in the United States by the Pennsylvania Institution for the Instruction of the Blind for many years beginning in about 1840.

Music Apparatus

Louis Braille first worked out his system of music notation and later adapted and expanded the same principles to create literary braille, both of which were published for the first time in 1829. He was the first to abandon entirely any attempt to simulate staff notation in printing music for blind people. Perhaps in music, more than other subjects, teaching methods are very close to those used for sighted students.

An 1893 volume of *The Mentor* carried an article announcing a "music-writer" for blind people, which was a machine on which blind people could write music in ordinary notation. It was complicated to operate and probably was not ever produced.

Because it was most practical to write music in braille—or, at one time, New York point—the only reason for a blind student to learn nonbraille music notation was to be able to teach sighted students. A well-known music educator at the New York School for the Blind, Hannah Babcock, suggested in 1882 that students use a cushion or board on which movable characters could be placed to construct the forms of the staff notation.

The Beetz Notation-Graph is simply a more elaborate form of Babcock's cushion. It is a model of the print grand staff, mounted on a cloth-covered cork base set in a wooden frame. The various musical symbols can be mounted on the graph at will, making it possible for blind students to express musical phrases in standard musical notation. The device was designed not only to familiarize blind students with print music notation, but also to enable a blind music teacher to teach sighted pupils to read music.

Charles B. Beetz, a blind piano teacher in Brooklyn, New York, who invented the device, gave the rights to his invention to APH, where it was first produced in 1934. In 1956, an updated version was manufactured and was available for many years. At this time, no mechanical music writing devices are available. They have largely been replaced by electronic methods.

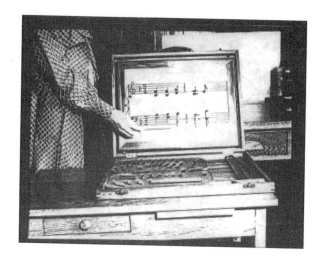

Geography Aids

The challenge of presenting the information on a print map to blind students lies in the basic difference between receiving information with the eyes and with the fingertips. While the eye moves from the whole to the part, the finger can achieve the whole only through a synthesis of the parts. Charles W. Holmes, a former director of the Canadian National Institute for the Blind (CNIB), expressed it this way: "The eye cannot help seeing much that it is not looking for, but the finger finds only what it actually touches."

Because they are designed to convey information through touch, tactile maps are simplified and contain less information than printed maps. Also, some devices found in print have no counterpart in embossing; colors and shading, for example, are difficult or impossible to duplicate in tactile form.

Like other tactile aids, maps were first handmade by teachers and students from materials close at hand. They were made with clay, papier-mâché, muslin, wood, or metal, and cities were marked with nails and boundaries with string. The 1880 Perkins *List of Appliances and Tangible Apparatus* listed cushions for pin maps and diagrams for school use. In 1878 John T. Sibley of the Missouri School for the Blind described how he made tactile maps for his students by placing an outline map on a stack of paper and stitching around it with an unthreaded sewing machine. In this way, he could make multiple copies of tactile maps.

Sometimes large maps were made especially for a school. For example, it was reported in 1845 in the *Third Annual Report* of the New York Institution for the Blind that "during the past year a terrestrial globe of 18 in. in diameter has been constructed, showing the most prominent features of the earth, with the parallels of Latitude, Longitude &c. in relief; a map of the two hemispheres upon a plane surface, showing many Geographical features in more detail, and a large map of the United States in raised lines, covering a surface of thirty square feet."

The Perkins Institution has a well-known tactile globe that is dated 1837. Made by Charles Ruggles, it was the first large globe made for blind students in this country.

Howe, of Perkins, was the first in this country to make and sell maps embossed on paper. *Howe's Geography,*

Howe's General Atlas, and *Howe's Atlas of the United States* were published in 1836, followed by *Howe's Atlas of the Islands* in 1838. APH offered its first cardboard maps in 1885, selling them separately and in atlas form, and began printing embossed paper maps with New York point text in 1895.

In 1875 APH announced that it had "brought out the most complete dissected maps of physical geography yet known." The maps were handmade by Benjamin B. Huntoon, superintendent of APH. Huntoon cut the topographic shapes from thin layers of wood using a foot-powered jigsaw. He applied the wood in layers and then hand carved the details. Models were made first and, after ten subscriptions were received, the maps were produced. Maps were produced by practically the same process into the 1930s.

The Works Progress Administration (WPA) and the Perkins Institution launched a cooperative project of making embossed geographical and historical maps in 1935. WPA funded thirty thousand dollars worth of free maps for all the schools for blind people in America. Each geographical unit was represented by three maps—outline, physical, and political. Blind editors were employed for the project, which was headed by CNIB director Holmes. The plates were embossed by hand, one symbol at a time, and a special embossing machine was designed and used for the project. The 22-by-28-inch maps were organized in folders containing 237 geographical maps, 108 historical maps, and 5 maps showing the chief air routes of the world.

In the early 1940s, APH made a dissected map of the United States cast in hard rubber from an original wood model. The states were painted in bright colors. Plastic dissected maps were introduced by APH in 1950; vacuum-formed relief maps in 1960. Working with the Panoramic Studios of Philadelphia, APH also developed a large (36-

inch diameter) globe that was produced in 1955. The large globes were offered until the early 1980s.

Experiments have continued in tactile map production. Plastics continue to be used for classroom maps. In addition to the use of embossing, paper maps are produced using ink-bonded and heat-bonded texturing materials. Some of the texturing materials, which function in the same way as color in maps for sighted users, are thermo-engraving resin, flocking, fine glass beads, and sand. An ink containing a foaming agent is currently in use; the ink becomes raised when heat is applied, creating the relief sections of the map.

Science Apparatus

The study of science by blind students requires, as it does with sighted students, as much direct experience as possible. In 1948 William T. Heisler, a science teacher at Overbrook School for the Blind, in Philadelphia wrote:

> We must realize that the degree of pupil comprehension…is directly proportional to the contact experience with the subject studied. The experience may be direct or indirect and vary in intensity; but it must be present! Most of the public school experience is visual; ours must be tactual and auditory.

Throughout history, science teachers used natural specimens for their blind students to observe. They collected and mounted minerals, animals, bones, and plants for classroom use, and some schools had a museum, where specimens were kept for study. Students were also taken on field trips for experiences outside the classroom.

The teachers would also construct models of objects that were very large or otherwise untouchable, or models would be constructed as a class project. Some models were produced and sold for use in other classrooms. Small-scale models represented buildings, furniture, and animals, while large-scale models could represent microscopic structures.

In the last half of the nineteenth century, American schools imported science models from European manufacturers. There were three-dimensional models of animals and plants embossed in high relief on heavy paper and highly detailed models in cast metal. In 1872, a collection of natural history models manufactured by M. Auzoux in Paris could be purchased for about 300 dollars. The collection included a model of the eye magnified twenty-five times and models of the digestive, circulatory, and respiratory organs. The collection also included models of the honeycomb, mammals, birds, fish, mollusks, and both the interior and exterior of flowers and seeds.

A series of embossed paper botanical and zoological illustrations, called *Pictures for the Blind*, was made by Martin Kunz, director of a school for blind children in Germany. The series was produced in the late 1800s and was purchased by schools in the United States. In the 1880 report of the Perkins Institution director Michael Anagnos reported that the most valuable new addition to the collection of models, specimens, and tangible objects was a complete set of the Schaufuss anatomical preparations purchased from W. L. Schaufuss of Germany.

In 1907, United States educators A. B. Norwood and H. W. P. Pine visited European schools and described the educational aids in use there for teaching blind students. They were impressed by the "wonderful provision for teaching by means of objects and models, the quantity and variety of which were indeed surprising." They described specimens of a wide variety of animal and bird life, a German modern battleship, a submarine boat and torpedo, a windmill, a mole's subterranean home, and models of mechanical appliances and tools. "It is difficult to imagine," they wrote, "any objects likely to be named in the school instruction which could not be illustrated by means of a specimen or model from the school museum."

Physical science classes generally could use the same apparatus used in classes for sighted students. It was reported in the 1845 annual report of the New York Institution for the Blind that, "Of Philosophical [physical science] apparatus we have very little, except an air pump and its usual accompaniments." The 1844 report from the Ohio Institution for the Education of the Blind reported that an appropriation of $150 was made by the legislature and used to purchase a set of physical science apparatus. Instruments, "neatly and beautifully constructed by Mr. Mason, of Philadelphia," included a galvanic battery; Magdeburgh hemispheres; Guinea and feather apparatus; an electrical machine with such various appendages as chiming bells, lightning jar, and electrical fly; self-generating hydrogen apparatus; thunder house and pistol; and working model steam engine. Superintendent William Chapin wrote, "Experiments with these are all readily comprehended by the pupils, and will be a source of much interest, especially to the class in natural philosophy [physical science]."

Instruments of measurement were the primary physical science apparatus adapted for blind students. APH introduced its first science aid in 1969, when Carson Nolan announced that the Educational Materials Research and Development Department had tested and refined the *Science Measurements Kit*. The kit was designed to provide equipment needed to illustrate basic operations of measurement, such as temperature and weight, to blind students.

Mathematics Apparatus

Small objects that were readily available and easy to manipulate, such as shells, pebbles, and sticks, were the first aids that blind people used for numerical calculation. For recording numbers, they made knotted cords and notched sticks. The blind person's fingers, however, were the most convenient counting tools. In the past, most blind people devised their own counting and recording systems from common materials. James Gall of Scotland, for example, an early nineteenth-century advocate of literacy for blind people, published a system for calculation that used pins inserted into clothing in various positions.

The first known calculating device for blind people was created by an Englishman, Nicholas Saunderson, in the early eighteenth century. Saunderson, who was blind, was a brilliant mathematician and gifted teacher. He called his method of calculation Palpable Arithmetic, probably to distinguish it from mental arithmetic. Saunderson's calculating board was about one square foot and it was divided into nine small squares, each of which was divided into four equal parts by perpendicular lines. The intersections of the lines formed nine points, one in each square, where a pin could be placed. The heads of the pins were two different sizes, and numbers were represented by the placement of the pins. Problems were worked on the board in the same way numerals are arranged on paper, vertically. Saunderson also created geometric figures with thread strung around the pins on the board.

The mathematics devices following Saunderson's replaced the pins in his system with pegs that fit into holes in a board. In the early 1800s, efforts were focused on ways to represent numbers in the simplest way, that is, with the fewest pegs. The most attention was given to devices that were thought to relieve mental exertion because they were more direct substitutes for pencil and paper, which is better understood by sighted people.

Henry Moyes (1750–1807) was born in Scotland and became blind at an early age. He was highly educated and became a respected lecturer. He was the first blind person to lecture on chemistry. Moyes devised a system of a board with pegs that had three different heads—a right triangle, a right triangle with a notch in the hypotenuse, and a square. The round bases of the pegs fit tightly into round holes in the base. The pegs are rotated into different positions so that each head in a specific position represented a numeral.

A device with square pegs that fit into square holes was invented by David McBeath of Scotland. Two different pegs represented the numbers. The first peg had a projection at one corner and at the center of the opposite side. This peg, depending on the position of the projection, could represent 1, 3, 7, and 9 or 2, 4, 6, and 8. The second peg, which had no projection represented 0 and 5.

In 1829, William Lang, a teacher at the Glasgow Asylum, found a way to represent all ten figures on one peg by changing the shape of the peg from a square to a pentagon. The projection was positioned at the angle of the pentagon on one end; on the other end, it was at a side. The board had pentagonal holes and problems were set up as they are written on paper.

The Reverend William Taylor, first superintendent of the Wilberforce Memorial School, York, England, introduced his arithmetic board in the early 1850s. By this time, these boards were being called arithmetic slates, the holes were referred to as cells, and the pegs or pins became known as types, probably because of the resemblance to printing types, or in some cases, the type itself. With the Taylor Slate, the student could make signs and letters as well as numbers—thirty-two different symbols in all. This was accomplished by using octagonal-shaped cells in which square types were positioned. The zinc frame measuring $7^1/2$ by 12 inches contained twenty-four rows of eighteen cells. There were two different square types: the first, with its two different ends, could represent sixteen numbers and signs; the second represented sixteen signs and letters. The Taylor Slate was the only device to get as many different positions from one piece of type. It was the first arithmetic device to gain widespread acceptance.

Howe reviewed the state of mathematical study at the Perkins Institution in 1874. He noted that the school's original ciphering boards, which were made of lead and difficult to use, were imported from Europe in 1832. A graduate of Perkins, George Eaton, made a wooden board with square holes that was praised by Howe. The wooden types of the Eaton Slate, however, were too light and easily lost. Howe experimented with porcelain types, but they proved to be too expensive. Glass types turned out to be the most satisfactory. The Boston Slate was also developed at the Perkins Institution. Its brass frame had twenty-four by twenty-eight cells and was known as a type slate.

For a number of years, the New York point tactile reading system was dominant in the United States. A system for mathematics calculation called TVL was devised to accompany the New York point system. The name derived from the numeral indicators on the three square types: a T, a V, and an L, which, by their various placements in the cells, represented the numbers.

Because mental calculation was the basic method of mathematics problem solving taught to blind students, there was fear among some educators that students would come to rely on mathematical devices at the expense of mental arithmetic. At the 1902 American Association of Instructors of the Blind (AAIB) convention, J. S. Graves of Alabama spoke on The Use and Abuse of Arithmetic Slates. He cautioned, "We should endeavor to impress upon the mind of the pupil the importance of mental arithmetic and the insignificance of the slate. To do this, he should never be required to solve a problem with the use of the slate that he could not readily do without it."

Nonetheless, slates and other devices continued to be used in schools for the blind up to the present. In a paper delivered at the 1924 AAIB convention, George F. Meyer, supervisor of the Sight Saving Department of the Minneapolis Public Schools, listed four ways that mathematical devices helped the blind student:

1. They could relieve the student of the mental exertion of mental calculations.

2. They could assist in the development of proper mathematical concepts.

3. They could facilitate mathematical expression.

4. They could serve a purely utilitarian and social end.

Other twentieth-century slates were the Bertha Shepard Arithmetic Slate and the Texas Slate. The Bertha Shepard Arithmetic Slate was metal and had pentagonal cells and pegs. It was listed under "New Appliances" in the 1936 AAIB convention literature. The Texas Slate had Arabic numerals and used Philadelphia Great Primer ink-print lead type. The cells were square, and it was used primarily to familiarize blind people with the shape of the numerals used by sighted people.

Braille Mathematics Devices

As braille became more widely used, the devices that required memorization of a special code for mathematics were replaced by devices that used the braille code. In his 1867 book *Thorough Description of the Braille System for the Reading and Writing of Music* Henry Robyn, champion of braille at the Missouri School for the Blind, pictured an "Apparatus for Writing, Cyphering and Music for the Blind of Prof. L. Braille, of Paris." Pictured was a braille board slate, which could be used for writing literary braille and music braille as well as using braille mathematics.

The invention of the Hall Braille Writer in 1892 enabled blind people to produce braille efficiently and quickly and could be used to write numbers as well as words. The Perkins Brailler, introduced in 1951, offered more flexibility in moving the paper to different positions and made writing math problems somewhat easier.

Writing a problem with numbers vertically aligned still involved a number of manipulations of the keys and paper, and some math teachers had their students write the problems horizontally. Braillewriters do not generally offer the most efficient means of working math problems. Their primary advantage is the ability to write literary material as well as numbers.

Paul W. Hoff, a teacher at the Minnesota Braille and Sight Saving School, wrote that the challenge of teaching mathematics to braille students led him to develop a pocket-sized braille slate. Patented in 1946, the Hoff Aid produces braille with a single, movable braille cell that makes it possible to write braille characters on the observed side of the paper. It is an upward writing device with hollow rods that are pressed with a stylus to press the paper over raised dots on the frame.

The Cubarithm and the Brannen math slates, which are nearly identical, use braille. The slates consist of plastic frames with square cells arranged in a sixteen-by-sixteen grid for a total of 256 cells. Five sides of the cube represent ten digits, the sixth side usually contained a symbol of some kind. Because braille is symmetrical and digits can be formed from only four dots, The numerals are formed by rotating the characters. The placement of the numerals in the computation process is according to the paper-and-pencil format.

Several other mechanical braille devices were introduced in the last half of the century. The Kine Multiply Vizr, also known as "Are You Bright as a Bunny?" is a plastic disc mounted behind a cardboard rabbit face. The braille numerals on the disc are positioned between the ears of the rabbit to show multiplication quotients, squares, and cubes.

Around 1950, the Model 4A Slide Rule was offered by the American Foundation for the Blind (AFB). It was compact compared to the enlarged slide rules produced for blind students that preceded it. Raised dots and Arabic numerals marked both sides of a twelve-inch vinyl disc. Pointers, both fixed and free-moving on both sides of the disc, were rotated to solve problems.

The Abacus

Writing in *The New Outlook* in 1965, Fred Gissoni, author of *Using the Cranmer Abacus for the Blind*, described the frustrations of a blind person trying to calculate as quickly as a sighted person:

This is not because blind people cannot think abstractly. Instead it is due to the cumbersome, awkward, inefficient calculation methods in general use. While a sighted person zips through a set of calculations with a pencil and paper, slide rule or electric calculating machine, the blind student either strains over a set of mental calculations, busies himself with one of the peg-board arithmetic slates, or struggles with the forward writing, back-spacing and line spacing of a braillewriter.

What did enable blind students to compete in their calculations was the use of the abacus. For most students, the abacus was the fastest device for solving math problems. It allowed blind people to calculate with greater speed and accuracy than they could with other devices and without the need for mental arithmetic.

Although Newell Perry, a blind mathematics scholar and teacher, advocated mental arithmetic over the use of any mathematical device, he approved of the abacus. Perry suggested that the abacus be used as a recording device so that pupils could refer to their last results, thus reducing the memory strain of mental calculations.

The original Japanese abacus consists of a frame in which are mounted variable numbers of parallel rods. Movable beads or counters are mounted on the rods. Each rod with sliding counters represents one place in the decimal system. In 1963, APH produced an adaptation of the Japanese abacus especially for blind people. It was called the Cranmer Abacus for its inventor, Terrance V. (Tim)

Cranmer, who designed it so that the beads stay in place where they are set and do not move accidentally. The Cranmer Abacus was so successful that in just more than a year from its introduction, APH had received orders for more than 5,000 abacuses.

Geometry Aids

In 1886, Henry Snyder, an Ohio teacher, described teaching plane geometry to blind students at an AAIB convention. The students, he told the conventioneers, constructed their figures on a lapboard using large-headed tacks and common cord. Letters or numbers marked the position of angles and the direction of lines. Snyder said, "The pupils held the very name of geometry to be synonymous with sore thumbs and stinging fingers."

Snyder solved the problem of constructing geometrical drawings for his students. He made the drawings, then stitched over them with a sewing machine. The advantage of this method was that Snyder could sew a number of drawings at once. Snyder was also able to convince the Ohio legislature to provide for educational models to be produced by inmates at the Ohio Penitentiary. They made complete sets of figures for solid geometry as well as models of crystals.

In addition to the boards and tacks used to create geometric figures, students could use a tracing wheel with a compass and ruler. Menzel's disc, a German device, was a disc about six inches in diameter with notches at regular intervals on the circumference. It had a hole in the center and a series of holes in a circle about midway between the circumference and center. Passing string through the holes and notches forms a series of figures.

There was very little change in the pin and stringboard method of plane geometry. A 1960s device, the Graphic Aid for Mathematics, was a corkboard on which a synthetic molded rubber mat was mounted. The mat was embossed with graph lines, and pins, rubber bands, and wires were used to construct plane geometric figures and graphs. Although it had some new features, it was really not much different from the other devices.

In response to the need for a practical means of producing drawings in raised lines, AFB developed the Sewell-Embossing set in the late 1940s. The set consists of a drawing board covered with a sheet of resilient gum rubber, two screw-type clips for holding a sheet of cellophane, and a modified version of a ballpoint pen that is used to make the impression. The device eliminated the need to draw a diagram in reverse.

Solid geometry models have been produced since the middle of the nineteenth century. A geometric model used at the Kentucky School for the Blind is now displayed in the Callahan Museum of APH. It is a wooden sphere cut into sections that are attached with leather hinges so that the sphere can be opened to show the sections. This model may have been one of those made at Cornell University that was mentioned in the *1872 Kentucky School for the Blind Annual Report*. The report described a set of models of all mathematical figures made in France and purchased by New York state for twenty thousand dollars. The mechanical department of Cornell University then copied the set, manufactured it, and sold it for 800 dollars.

A century later, similar models were offered. *The Geometric Area and Volume Aid* is a kit of geometric blocks used to construct three-dimensional models. APH offered Mitchell Wire Forms with Matched Planes and Volumes, which are used to illustrate geometric outline forms, planes, and solids. The figures are to the same scale so the frames fit over planes and solid figures. The planes and their corresponding volumes are painted in matching bright colors.

Basic Concepts

A selection of arithmetic materials for use in the primary grades was developed by Catherine Stern in the early 1950s. The materials are blocks in unit measures and counting and pattern boards with square holes to arrange the blocks in different configurations. Cuisenaire Rods are similar to the Stern materials, using a basic unit and various rods representing numbers two to ten. They are used to teach basic number concepts.

The Master Cube, designed by G. Gilbert Scott, was first produced by APH in 1961. It is an aid to the development of the mathematical concepts of area and volume. Made of polished hardwood, it is a four-inch cube cut into eight pieces that can be used for addition, subtraction, multiplication, and division. The larger blocks are grooved so that units of length, area, and volume can be easily recognized by sight or touch.

In the early 1960s, the Individualized Mathematics Curriculum, which was introduced by Andrew Shott in 1957, was adapted for use by blind students in the United States. Study and development of this modern mathematics curriculum began in 1960 at APH under the direction of Carson Nolan, director of educational research.

The devices that accompanied the Individualized Mathematics Curriculum for beginners were the Numberaid, an adapted abacus, and the Calulaid, a braille numerical recording device. Higher levels of the curriculum required use of the Fractionaid, a slide rule-like device; the Geometraid, eight sets of structural parts and plane figures, which form solids; and the Measuraid, consisting of a short rule and a protractor.

Practical Aids

Practical mathematical devices for everyday life have always been a part of the education of blind students. Devices of this nature include rulers, tape measures, calipers, wet and dry measures, and weights and scales. Linking mathematical instruction to life activities are adaptations of the barometer and thermometer, as well as aids for money handling and banking.

Creativity has been and continues to be the watchword for designing and adapting instructional aids for blind students. Technology has eliminated the need for some, but by no means all, of these apparatus. Today, technology helps produce better tactile graphics for maps, and modern materials make it possible to create aids that are more detailed, durable, and attractive than ever before.

In his opening address at the 1910 convention of the AAIB, Benjamin Huntoon, superintendent of the Kentucky School for the Blind and of APH, expressed sentiments that are as true today as they were at the beginning of the twentieth century:

> We who are engaged in the education of the blind know that it is not a light task. We know that we need special appliances, special departments, if we would make a blind person a self-supporting citizen. All of his faculties are to be trained. Our experience of over fourscore years has not been in vain, nor have our results been intangible. From the beginning, the problems involved have received the attention of the best minds that have been engaged in this work.

BRAILLE LIBRARY SERVICE

by Kim Charlson

To fully examine braille library services, we must begin in the 1800s and work our way to the present. In this chapter, we will do that, as well as review current trends in the provision of braille library services and offer some speculation about the direction future braille library services will take.

The modern record of the development of library services for blind people in the United States begins with formal programs being established in 1868. Before that, services were being provided to a very limited degree on a more informal basis by a number of schools for blind students for some of their graduates. For example, the Perkins School for the Blind then located in Boston, Massachusetts, which opened in 1829 as the first school for blind people to be chartered in the United States, provided lending library services in Massachusetts and throughout New England as early as 1835. In 1837, Samuel Gridley Howe, the first director of Perkins, unsuccessfully attempted to garner congressional funding for a centralized national library service for blind people. His recommendation was completely rejected by Congress, and further progress in library services for blind people before 1868 was minimal (Kuiper 1963).

In 1868, however, eight embossed books were donated to the collection of the Boston Public Library for the use of blind people, and the library thus established a department for blind people (Ham 1968, 4). These eight books were the first circulating books publicly available to any blind person requesting them, and the program was the first of its sort to be supported by government funding. In the latter part of the nineteenth century, many other public libraries followed the Boston Public Library in establishing reading rooms where blind patrons could come in and borrow braille books.

In the early days of reading rooms for the blind, it quickly became clear that librarians were going to have to assume new and expanded responsibilities if they were to continue to serve their customers effectively. Home-based instruction and classes in braille were needed, primarily because of the various braille codes used in the late nineteenth and early twentieth centuries. Librarians were relied upon heavily to fill this need. There was also a need for home teachers (Neisser 1908, 219), because no organized program of rehabilitation for those who had lost their sight was available for nonmilitary adults until after World War II. Even for veterans of World War I, only limited rehabilitation services existed, and, on a much smaller scale, private philanthropic organizations offered rehabilitation services to blind non-military individuals. The most consistent sources of services in braille instruction were schools for blind students, highlighting the need for good braille library services.

In 1897, a reading room for blind people was opened at the Library of Congress in Washington, D.C., with approximately 500 titles. It was originally intended to serve as a meeting place for those who were blind to enjoy entertainment and read in private. At that time, the Library of Congress was not particularly interested in expanding the Washington, D.C., local area reading room into a national library program for the blind (Library of Congress 1898, 39).

Over the next decade, though, staff at the Library of Congress began to debate whether it was appropriate to be involved in a national library program. In the meantime, what ultimately would make a big difference in the effort to consolidate braille resources and was probably the most significant contribution to the advancement of braille library services was made in 1904, with the "free matter for the blind and handicapped" postal classification amendment to the postal regulations (St. John 1957, 8). These postal regulations were originally adopted in 1899 and covered only letters written in braille and raised characters, but now books, pamphlets, and other reading matter in braille and raised characters could be mailed on loan without charge by agencies serving people who were blind, by public libraries, and by blind people themselves. The return of the materials was also covered. These materials

BRAILLE INTO THE NEXT MILLENNIUM

were the first items of any type that could be mailed free of charge. For the first time, major distances became a nonissue in the dissemination of braille materials. This development was truly the first step toward equalizing access to the limited braille materials available during this era.

In 1910, after a decade of debate, the Library of Congress acknowledged responsibility for library services to those who are blind, but it was to be a short-lived decision. In his 1910 annual report, Herbert Putnam, then librarian of congress, stated that the program for the blind was not the responsibility of the Library of Congress but of a public library, because the service was not focused on research or scholarship but rather on recreational reading. He stated, "The books are used chiefly at home, and it is the public library rather than the Library of Congress which is the lending library of and for the District" (Library of Congress 1911, 73).

So in 1911, the reading room materials from the Library of Congress were transferred to the District of Columbia Public Library. It was thus apparent to all that the Library of Congress did not view the provision of these services as its function. The Library of Congress did, however, continue to provide reference services to blind individuals nationwide. Continuation of reference services was justified by the fact that the staff assistant who had been responsible for the reading room was not transferred to the public library when the collection was moved. Later in 1911, however, that position was also transferred. Putnam indicated that he would be willing to recall the collection only if it "could be provided for on a scale which would so enlarge and diversify it, as to make it really worthy of the federal government and a national library" (Library of Congress 1911, 73).

In response to a petition filed by dissatisfied braille readers with four U.S. senators, their intervention was successful in persuading Dr. Putnam to reinstate the entire collection and reading room services were again transferred back into the domain of the Library of Congress in 1912. This was done with the provision that the service would become national in scope and be funded by Congress. Unfortunately, only $1,200 was initially appropriated instead of the $7,500 requested to get the national program started. (Library of Congress Annual Report 1912, 106–108).

It was clear by this time because of demand that access to braille materials and library services were needed by blind people across the country. The availability of such services was still scattered and limited to highly populated parts of the nation, and the quality of services, when they were available, was inconsistent. The idea of consolidating or centralizing collection resources began to emerge as a component of library service delivery. In 1896, New York became the first state to establish a department for blind people within the state library agency (Bray 1965, 94), and many other states followed New York's example. People began to realize that regionalized consolidation of braille collections within a given state would allow for more efficient use of financial and collection resources.

Because of the controversy during the early part of the twentieth century over the perceived role of the Library of Congress in the provision of a national library program, and

the fact that most blind people across the nation still needed access to reliable library services, the Library of Congress
and advocates for access to information for blind people
were compelled to convince elected officials and members of
Congress to introduce the Pratt-Smoot Act in 1930.

The Pratt-Smoot Act was signed into law by President
Herbert Hoover on March 3, 1931, marking a new direction and philosophy in the provision of library services to
the blind population by publicly funding production and
distribution of braille materials to designated libraries for
use by blind adults. With the passage of this law and the
$100,000 appropriation for "manufacture and purchase of
specially selected braille books for the adult blind," the program was on its way (St. John 1957, 8). Also because of this
act and its far-reaching ramifications, a completely new and
organized picture of braille library services was beginning
to emerge. For the first time in the development of library
services for the blind, order and organization became the
operative practices. Under this new scenario, the Library of
Congress had a dual role—it acted as a regional lending
library for its internal services and it served as the key starting point in managing the flow of book selection and production and distribution of materials to regional libraries.
Without the Pratt-Smoot Act, it is likely that library services today for blind and visually impaired individuals would
still be inequitable and inconsistent.

The Library of Congress handled circulation of materials through a cooperative network of nineteen designated
regional libraries located in various parts of the country
(Haycraft 1932). These were the California State Library in

Sacramento; the Carnegie Library of Pittsburgh in Pennsylvania; the Cincinnati Public Library in Ohio; the Cleveland Public Library in Ohio; the Denver Public Library in Colorado; the Detroit Public Library in Michigan; the Free Public Library of Philadelphia in Pennsylvania; the Georgia Library Commission in Atlanta; the Library of Congress in Washington, D.C.; the Library of Hawaii in Honolulu; the Michigan State Library for the Blind in Saginaw; the National Library for the Blind in Washington, D.C.; the New York Public Library in New York City; the New York State Library in Albany; the Perkins School for the Blind in Watertown, Massachusetts; the St. Louis Public Library in Missouri; the Seattle Public Library in Washington; and the Texas State Library in Austin.

The strategy to circulate braille materials through a centralized network of libraries, while at variance with the popular library theory of decentralized distribution, was in keeping with the philosophy held by those who worked on behalf of blind people at the time. Scarce resources, the expense of purchasing braille materials, the technical nature of such a specialized library field, and the limited readership were all limitations that could be minimized with centralization to provide a more organized and equitable service to readers, regardless of geographic location. Generally, financing of library services for blind and handicapped people has been funded by state and municipal dollars through a state library agency, a public library system, or private contributions.

Initially, as the centralized library network became established, public librarians were relied upon to refer blind individuals to the centralized braille libraries. Braille reading library patrons who had always borrowed books from anywhere they could find them now had to conform to the borrowing conditions of each of the regional libraries. Direct borrowing by the regional library on behalf of patrons became a standard practice, rather than patrons having to contact each library directly for materials.

Libraries obtained braille materials for their collections from braille printing presses or printing houses. Except for the Universal Braille Press (later incorporated into the Braille Institute of America of Los Angeles, California). These printing houses were closely affiliated with a specific school for the blind, as with the American Printing House for the Blind in Louisville, Kentucky located adjacent to the Kentucky School for the Blind; Howe Memorial Press of the Perkins School for the Blind in Watertown, Massachusetts; and the Clovernook Home and School for the Blind in Cincinnati, Ohio (Haycraft 1932). All these producers of braille materials were sources for libraries to purchase braille materials, although those materials were somewhat limited in subject matter and diversity. Because of the expense of producing braille, materials tended to be concentrated in the subject areas of textbooks, classic literature, religion and inspirational materials, and books for children. Each cooperating regional library was provided with copies of every title purchased through the national program, so every library was able to offer the same materials to all their patrons.

It was primarily through the volunteer braille transcription activities of the American Red Cross and numerous

women's and religious organizations that the subject availability of braille materials began to expand. The volunteer
braille transcribers' contribution to library collections was
significant and continues today to be a valuable resource in
the availability of braille throughout the country. These
limited-copy, volunteer-produced and -donated braille
titles are circulated to readers through the Library of
Congress Multistate Centers, which were established in
1974 (National Library Service for the Blind and
Physically Handicapped 1983, 199) as backup sources for
borrowing materials for patrons and to provide circulation
services for the specialized volunteer-produced and
-donated braille collections.

With more centralized braille collections came the need
to be able to communicate what titles were available to
borrowers. In 1934, the Books for the Adult Blind program of the Library of Congress began publishing Braille
Book Review: A Guide to Braille Publications, a braille
and print monthly periodical that had been published
since 1931 by the New York Public Library through the
Henry F. Homes Fund and the American Braille Press in
Paris, where the braille edition was produced (Haycraft
1932). The publication listed new braille books, both press
braille and hand-transcribed, volunteer-produced braille,
and until 1934 listed the library location of each specific
book and provided an annotation describing the title.

As readers' demands for braille materials continued to
grow, other sources for braille began to emerge. Many of the
major religious denominations began providing braille lending library services. These private libraries established their

own service areas, lending conditions, and other terms of eligibility. Examples of these private libraries are the Christian Record Services (formerly Christian Record Braille Foundation), the Braille Circulating Library, the Jewish Braille Institute of America, the Lutheran Library for the Blind, and the Xavier Society for the Blind. Other private specialized libraries also developed to meet very specific borrower needs, such as large-cell braille, children's print/braille books, cookbooks, and other types of specialized materials.

Another component of braille library services in this country, begun in the early 1970s, has been the instructional materials resource centers (IMRCs), which are found in most states today. These centers are generally affiliated with a given state's department of education or a major metropolitan school district and are responsible for the acquisition, production, dissemination, storage, and loan of textbook materials in braille for students ages three to twenty-two who are receiving services through a local school district under special education and the federal Individuals with Disabilities Education Act. These IMRCs conduct exhaustive bibliographic searches to try to locate a specific textbook in braille. If the book is available, the IMRC will purchase it on behalf of the braille student and ship it directly to the student for class use. If the book is not available in braille, the IMRC will contact a braille transcribing organization and arrange for the title to be converted into braille.

Transcription of an entire textbook into braille is a long and involved process, often taking many months to complete. Many groups produce braille materials using volunteers and so do not charge for transcription services. As nonprofit organizations, these groups often conduct fund-raising activities to meet the group's expenses. Other brailling groups may charge a fee for transcription services to cover basic expenses of production. After the textbook is complete and has been used by the student, it is returned to the IMRC where it is housed until another student requests it. These IMRCs across the country cooperate extensively with one another to maximize collection resources and reduce duplication of effort. They provide an extremely valuable service to blind and visually impaired students, making it possible for them to meet their educational goals.

Two relevant legislative changes affected the Library of Congress's national Books for the Blind program by expanding library service eligibility and collection resources. The first change took place on July 5, 1952, when legislation was passed that allowed for the inclusion of blind children in the program to receive braille services from the Library of Congress (Koestler 1976, 112).

The second change was on October 9, 1962, when President John F. Kennedy signed legislation that created a music section for blind people in the Library of Congress. The Library of Congress was authorized to collect music scores and other instructional music materials for people who were blind; however, the legislation did not include music for listening pleasure. Because this collection was completely centralized in the Library of Congress, it soon grew to be one of the largest braille music collections in the world. It continues today to serve the needs of blind musicians.

For the next two decades, braille library services were carried on smoothly and without any major changes. In the late 1980s, however, a trend toward further centralization of braille lending library services began. Space limitations for housing braille materials, rising occupancy costs, and declining numbers of braille reading patrons made some states look at the feasibility of contracting braille library services out to other nearby states with larger populations of braille readers and more established braille collections. Examples of this type of successful regionalization of braille services include the braille library service in Massachusetts, which also provides braille lending services to Maine, New Hampshire, Rhode Island, and Vermont, and the braille library service in Utah, which also provides services to Alaska, Arizona, Colorado, Idaho, Kansas, Mississippi, Montana, Nebraska, Nevada, New Mexico, North Dakota, Oklahoma, South Dakota, Wisconsin and Wyoming (National Library Service for the Blind and Physically Handicapped 1999).

The National Library Service for the Blind and Physically Handicapped (NLS) began research in the late 1980s on the feasibility of consolidating braille lending library services nationally into one or two regional centers. After studying many factors, including staff and space costs, braille storage strategies, delivery time, postal distribution factors, and even weather conditions, NLS recommended that two regional centers could meet national braille distribution needs. After considering access to a post office bulk mailing center, geographic location, transportation resources, and average delivery time to other states within the proposed area, NLS proposed Salt Lake City, Utah, and Cincinnati, Ohio, as the sites of these centers. Having just two centers was also viewed favorably in terms of disaster management and risk diversification for such a specialized collection (ManTech 1990).

Some librarians and many patrons felt that this step toward possible national centralization of all braille materials was too far-reaching and represented a fundamental change in the basic concept of receiving library services from a state-based regional library with staff who were familiar with an individual patron's reading preferences. As it turned out, the recommendations from the study were not implemented by NLS, primarily because of lack of congressional funding for the concept. In 1999, thirty-two regional libraries provide braille lending services to readers across the country.

A major barrier that has contributed to the decline in braille readership and was identified both by borrowers and NLS as an obstacle to fully utilizing library services is the issue of getting braille materials to the post office for return to the lending library. Braille book-mailing containers typically hold two braille volumes, although some hold only one, but they were too large to fit into a curbside mailbox. After considerable research, staff at NLS designed and field tested a single-volume braille mailing container that could fit into a standard mailbox. These containers, which open and close with Velcro fastenings, also flatten when empty for easy and convenient storage by both libraries and patrons. Response from braille readers to this new mailing container design has been extremely positive, and readers have indicated that they would borrow more braille materials with this type of mailing container. This new container design is in production now (in 1999), and over the course of the next few years will be incorporated into the library network for more convenient shipping of braille.

The bulkiness of braille materials has always been one of the factors detracting from overall utilization. With the advent of refreshable braille technology in the 1980s, the storage of electronic files and access to this type of adaptive technology became the only limitations to what might be read in braille. Any computer electronic file could now be translated by braille translation software into a file that could be read with a refreshable braille display. Braille readers and other advocates for braille access were tremendously excited when refreshable braille came onto the scene. Being able to store computer disks instead of hard copy braille volumes was the solution to many a library's space limitations. The cost of refreshable braille technology, however, was not low enough to justify NLS in attempting to have a braille display as a component of the national equipment loan program. The cost of braille displays has not dropped significantly over the past twenty years, but it is hoped that revolutionary new designs in electronic braille cell technology will make this extremely valuable technology more affordable in the future.

The newest development in the increased availability of electronic braille comes from NLS. For the past decade, as braille producers have transcribed books for NLS, there has been a contract requirement that two copies of the file on disk, including the braille-translated file used to produce the hard copy volumes, be provided to NLS. These disks have been cataloged and housed, but, until recently, nothing else was done with them. In 1998, NLS conducted a pilot project in which these braille-translated files of completed books were made available on the Internet for downloading. The response was overwhelmingly positive. Braille readers enthusiastically praised the ease of downloading materials and the convenience of being able to read them with their own personal braille notetakers and refreshable braille displays. The project has been expanded, and more than 3,000 titles are now available for downloading (with a password) from Web-Braille, the NLS-sponsored Web site. Other organizations and agencies, such as the Texas School for the Blind and Visually Impaired and the American Printing House for the Blind, are making books available electronically for braille readers. This trend will continue to grow over the next few years, and readers will continue to advocate expanded materials and more availability.

As we approach the end of the twentieth century, another element that will have an impact on braille library services is the research being conducted by NLS in partnership with the National Information Standards Organization (NISO) into the development of the next-generation talking book. Why would the development of the digital talking book affect braille library services? Because of the nature of digital information storage. In a digital talking book, you have a disk with both a digital human voice recording and a single-source electronic text file. This text file could give greater access, via computer, to the more serious reader who wishes, for example, to take a quote from the book or check the spelling of a name. In addition to being accessible by computer, the same text file could be read with a refreshable braille display.

This and future developments in digital talking books could make thousands of new materials available every year in an electronic format. Other possibilities might include having a braille-translated file on the disk, along with the human voice file and the single-source electronic text file. This would make a digital talking book universally accessible, including to braille readers, and would significantly expand the number of titles produced in braille each year from a few hundred to a few thousand.

A political development that has had an impact on library services for people who are blind and visually impaired was the passage of the Americans with Disabilities Act in 1990. The ADA has made the library community more aware of the needs of people with visual impairments. Many libraries have expanded to provide services to people who are blind through small collections of braille and talking books, adaptive technology, large print materials, and descriptive videos. Other major metropolitan libraries have established access centers that consolidate services for people with disabilities, collection materials, new technology, and staff in a specific department to provide services to the disabled community. Arguments have run both ways regarding services based in public libraries, from the positive commentary that these services allow people with visual impairments to participate in mainstream library activities and use the resources the local public library offers to the concern that centralized library services specifically for people with disabilities isolate the very population that was intended to be integrated into the library's programs and services. If there is a demonstrated need in a given community to provide specialized library services—whether that be print/braille books for a six-year-old braille reader or a reading machine for reading aloud printed materials for adults with visual impairments in the community—the library must determine the extent of the specialized services it can provide. Educating blind and visually impaired individuals that the public library can be a resource for them for materials, programming, and entertainment will be a challenge for many years to come.

When braille library services were centralized away from the public libraries into regional braille lending libraries in the early 1900s, borrowers had to be educated about how the process would work. Over the years, most blind patrons became convinced that the public library really had nothing to offer them. Now we must convince patrons that public libraries do have a great deal to offer people who are blind and visually impaired, and that it is their right to have their community-based library provide braille materials for them. In its access guidelines, the ADA is very specific about physical access issues, such as the requirement for braille and large-print signage. It is less specific about programmatic access regarding braille materials. Certainly, it is clear that braille readers have the right to request materials produced by the library—such as brochures or event programs—in accessible formats, and if that means braille, the request should be fulfilled. The library receiving the request has an obligation to meet the request if it does not create an undue burden. We would hope a library would not consider a request for braille an undue burden, but rather a request for access. The ADA has allowed for major strides forward in the overall relationship between public librarians and the blind community. How that relationship continues to grow will be up to braille readers. Reasonable requests and information on how libraries can comply will go far in making greater access a reality for braille readers.

As we enter the twenty-first century, braille lending libraries are truly in a state of transition. Readers at an ever-increasing rate are demanding braille materials in an electronic format to read on their personal refreshable braille displays. The level of sophistication of most braille readers is high, and they want braille materials when they need them, not months later. Internet access to braille-translated files that can be immediately downloaded into a borrower's own braille display is certainly a positive step to increasing the availability, accessibility, and desirability of reading braille materials. As the complexion of braille lending library services evolves, whether it be in hard copy volumes or electronic files, it appears that braille materials and the demand for them is on the rise, and we hope it will continue in that direction.

References

Braille Centralization Study, Executive Summary. 1990. Man-Tech Technical Services Corporation. Fairfax, Virginia.

Bray, R. S. 1965. "Library Services for the Blind." *Blindness,* Annual.

Ham, C. W. Jr. 1968. *Development of Library Service for the Blind in the United States of America.* University of Rhode Island. Unpublished thesis.

Haycraft, H. 1932. "The New Status of Library Work with the Blind." *The Wilson Bulletin for Librarians 6,* (February), no. 6, 410–415.

Koestler, F. A. 1976. *The Unseen Minority: A Social History of Blindness in America.* New York: David McKay.

Kuiper, M. S. 1963. "Perkins Libraries." *The Lantern* 32, (March) no. 3: 12.

Library of Congress. 1898. *Annual Report of the Librarian of Congress,* 1897. Washington, D.C.: Government Printing Office.

Library of Congress. 1911. *Annual Report of the Librarian of Congress:* 1910. Washington, D.C.: Government Printing Office.

National Library Service for the Blind and Physically Handicapped. 1983. *That All May Read: Library Service for Blind and Physically Handicapped People.* Washington, D.C.: National Library Service for the Blind and Physically Handicapped, Library of Congress.

National Library Service for the Blind and Physically Handicapped. 1999. *Library Resources for the Blind and Physically Handicapped: A Directory with FY1998 Statistics on Readership, Circulation, Budget, Staff, and Collections.* Washington, D.C.: Library of Congress.

Neisser, E. R. 1908. *Report of the Committee on Library Work with the Blind.* Bulletin of the American Library Association 2, no. 5: 219.

St. John, F. R. 1957. *Survey of Library Service for the Blind: 1956.* New York: American Foundation for the Blind.

BRAILLE TRANSCRIBING IN THE UNITED STATES: PAST, PRESENT, AND FUTURE

by Mary Lou Stark

Braille, as codified by the Braille Authority of North America, is the primary embossed code used by blind persons in the United States. The people who translate print into braille are called braille transcribers or braillists, and, in the United States, these transcribers work in the literary braille code, the Nemeth code for mathematics and science, the music braille code, and the computer braille code, using *Braille Formats: Principles of Print to Braille Transcription* as a guideline for formatting all documents. A variety of print documents are brailled, ranging from books to agendas and from policy statements to recipes. Books in braille range from novels and best-sellers to cookbooks, English literature and law textbooks. All types of classroom handouts and business papers are brailled, as well as menus and utility bills. An examination of the history of braille transcribing in the United States, especially in relation to the Library of Congress, can help us understand the present and get a glimpse of what the future may hold.

The Early Days of Braille Transcription

Braille transcribing at the Library of Congress began in 1897 with patrons who had graduated from schools for blind people transcribing embossed books from dictation, often being paid six cents a page from donated funds. About 300 books were added to the collection by 1912 in this way.

In 1918 the United States ended the "war of the dots"— or the controversy over which embossed system to use— and adopted as its uniform embossed code revised braille grade 1½. At the same time Gertrude Rider, assistant in charge of the "Reading Room for the Blind" at the Library of Congress, started a volunteer braille transcribing service to provide the recreational reading materials needed to maintain the morale of U.S. servicemen blinded in World War I.

In 1921, Rider's volunteer transcription project became an official program of the National Headquarters of the American Red Cross (ARC), which recruited volunteers throughout the country to work under Rider's direction. That year the ARC published a braille transcribing manual "designed to teach sighted volunteers by correspondence to write accurate Braille" that had been prepared jointly by the Library of Congress and the ARC. Volunteers were also taught in small classes under the instruction of a qualified local teacher.

By August 1925, about 900 volunteer braille transcribers had been certified and volunteers were brailling for their local libraries as well as for the Library of Congress. In 1928 Adelia M. Hoyt, became the first acting director of the braille transcribing section, which administered the Braille Transcribing Service. The Braille Transcribing Section was initially under the Division of Services for the Blind. Later it was moved under the Project, Books for the Adult Blind.

The Braille Transcribing Section had many name changes through-out the years, as has the National Library Service for the Blind and Physically Handicapped. Table 1 includes names and approximate dates they were instituted. Table 2 contains a chronological list of section heads. It was not possible to confirm all dates, but it is believed that all section heads have been included. The objective of the Braille Transcribing Service was to formulate and execute a program for the transcription of single-copy books to supplement and complement the supply of multi-copy books. This included

1. organizing volunteers to transcribe, shellac and bind books,

2. instruct and certify transcribers and proofreaders,

3. compile and publish manuals of transcription,

4. serve as a clearinghouse for volunteer braille transcriptions to avoid duplication of effort,

5. devise means to make products of braille transcription known and available to braille readers throughout the country,

6. direct, as may be necessary and desirable, the transcription of special materials for students, professional people, and other individuals.

Many of these activities continue to be addressed by the current Braille Development Section.

Through correspondence courses, Ms. Hoyt taught sighted volunteers to transcribe accurate braille and blind volunteers to proofread. By March 1935, nearly 3000 certified volunteers who had completed a ten-week course, and there were 132 blind proofreaders.

Standard English braille grade 2 was adopted in July 1932 by a conference of American and British organizations. For many years, however, volunteer transcribers continued to braille books primarily in grade $1^1/_2$. *Braille Transcribing, Standard English Braille, Grade Two, A Manual* was written by the American Red Cross in 1937 for use by transcribers who are certified in grade $1^1/_2$ "and have had considerable practice in the latter system."

At the close of 1942, the ARC discontinued its formal association with braille transcribing and the Library of Congress, to focus its attention on support of the troops in World War II. Alice Rohrback became head of the Braille Transcribing Section of the Library of Congress, with the objectives of maintaining the transcription program, instructing by correspondence and certifying sighted students in the transcription program, (according to

Table 1. Various Names of the Braille Transcribing Section and Services for the Blind Library of Congress

Year	Name
1897	Name not known—Blind patrons did transcribing under auspices of Reading Room for the Blind
1918	Name not known—Library of Congress began training volunteers under auspices of Reading Room for the Blind
1921	Braille Transcribing Service initiated with American Red Cross as co-sponsor
1943	Braille Transcribing Section established in the Division of Books for the Adult Blind, the Library of Congress, administered Braille Transcribing Service
1946	Division of Books for the Adult Blind, Library of Congress, and Services for the Blind, Library of Congress, consolidated with the National Library for the Blind, Inc. to become the Division for the Blind, Library of Congress
	Braille Transcribing Section became Braille Training Section
1965	Braille Training Section became Volunteer Services Section
1966	Division for the Blind became Division for the Blind and Physically Handicapped (DBPH)
	Volunteer Services Section became Volunteer Training Section
1978	DBPH became the National Library Service for the Blind and Physically Handicapped (NLS)
1980	Volunteer Training Section became Braille Codes Section
1984	Braille Codes Section became Braille Development Section

Table 2. Section Heads (Some dates approximate)	
Dates	**Name**
1897–1912	Etta Josselyn Griffin (Reading Room for the Blind)
1912–1925	Gertrude Rider (Reading Room for the Blind)
1928–1941	Adelia Hoyt (first acting head of Braille Transcribing Section)
1942–1962	Alice Rohrback
1963–1965	Ruth L. Keyes
1966–1983	Maxine Dorf
1984–1987	Richard "Dick" Evensen
1989–1991	Claudell Stocker
1991–1998	Mary Lou Stark (acting head)
1998–	Mary Lou Stark

the uniform standard of grade 2), instructing blind students in braille proofreading, acting as a clearinghouse of braille transcriptions, and compiling and publishing manuals of transcription. At this time the braille transcribing section was a part of the Books for the Adult Blind project.

Early certificates for braille transcribers were signed by the President of the United States, the chairman of the ARC central committee, the ARC director of volunteer special projects, and the Library of Congress director of braille transcribing. Currently they are signed by the

librarian of congress and the director of the National
Library Service for the Blind and Physically Handicapped
(NLS).

Although the library has been through several reorgani-
zations since 1942, the Braille Transcribing Section has
always been a part of the services to the blind. A detailed
account of the early days of the program can be found in
That All May Read, a 1983 publication of the NLS.

Changes in the
Braille Transcribing Section

In 1946, three units serving blind people were merged to
form the Division for the Blind, Library of Congress:
Division of Books for the Adult Blind (including the
Braille Transcribing Section), Library of Congress;
Services for the Blind, Library of Congress; and the
National Library for the Blind, Inc. (a separate lending
library for blind persons). The Braille Transcribing Section
eventually was renamed the Braille Training Section. In
1965, the Braille Training Section of the Library of
Congress acquired a new name—the Volunteer Services
Section with Ruth L. Keyes as section head. In 1966 the
Division for the Blind expanded its services and was
renamed the Division for the Blind and Physically
Handicapped (DBPH). In February 1967, the NLS
moved from the main Library of Congress buildings to
1291 Taylor Street N.W., which brought the various parts
of NLS together in the same building.

In August 1966, Maxine Dorf was promoted from braille advisor to head of the Volunteer Services Section, and she remained in that position until she retired October 1983. During her tenure, the name changed to the Volunteer Training Section and then to the Braille Codes Section. In 1978 DBPH became the National Library Service for the Blind and Physically Handicapped (NLS).

Richard "Dick" Evensen, after working for NLS in several capacities, became head of the Braille Development Section, formed by combining the activities of the Braille Codes Section with braille research and development, in 1984; but his tenure was sadly cut short when he died in January 1987. Miriam Pace, assistant chief, Materials Development Division, provided oversight to the section until Claudell Stocker became head in July 1989, retiring in September 1992. Mary Lou Stark became acting head in 1992, and then head of the section in November 1998.

The First Transcription Publications

While the first instruction manuals for literary transcribers and proofreaders were written by the ARC and the Library of Congress, since 1943 all manuals have been written by Library of Congress staff and consultants. The literary braille instruction manual underwent major revisions by Alice Rohrback and Marjorie S. Hooper in 1950 and 1953, by Maxine B. Dorf and Earl R. Scharry in 1962 and 1971, by Dorf in collaboration with Barbara H. Tate in 1984 and 1987, and by Constance Risjord, John H.

Wilkinson and Mary Lou Stark in 2000. [See Table 3.] All the revisions were triggered by changes in the literary braille code and comments by students, teachers, and transcribers.

An instruction manual for transcribing music braille—*Introduction to Braille Music Transcription,* by Mary Turner De Garmo—was published in 1974 and an instruction manual for transcribing the Nemeth code for mathematics and science—*An Introduction to Braille Mathematics* by Helen Roberts, Bernard M. Krebs, and Barbara Taffet—was published in 1978.

Additional publications of NLS included an irregular series of publications known as *Braille Circulars.* Having an emphasis on technical matters regarding braille transcribing, such as additions and changes to codes, Braille Authority decisions, and related matters, they were distributed for many years. They varied in size and had no regular publication schedule. These circulars were supplemented by, and gradually replaced by, *Volunteer News.* The first issue of *Volunteer News* came out July 20, 1965, introducing itself as "a new series of circulars with features and information of interest to volunteers active in transcribing, proofreading, binding, recording, Thermoforming, large print, and processing, as well as information for the visually handicapped." Early issues came out monthly. They presented detailed information on handling braille transcribing problems as well as suggestions for tapists—volunteers who were doing taping (recording books on magnetic tape—first reel-to-reel tape and later cassette tapes.) The

Table 3. Instruction Manuals
Published by the Library of Congress

Dates	Title, authors from cover and/or title page
1937	*Braille Transcribing, Standard English Braille, Grade Two, A Manual;* The American National Red Cross
1950	*A Manual of Standard English Braille For the Guidance of Transcribers and Other Embossers,* By Alice Rohrback, Braillist, Division for the Blind, The Library of Congress and Marjorie S. Hooper, Braille Editor, American Printing House for the Blind, Louisville, Kentucky
1953	*A Manual of Standard English Braille For the Guidance of Transcribers and Other Embossers, Second Edition,* By Alice Rohrback, Braillist, Division for the Blind, The Library of Congress and Marjorie S. Hooper, Braille Editor, American Printing House for the Blind, Louisville, Kentucky
1962	*Instruction Manual for Braille Transcribing, Third Edition,* By Maxine B. Dorf, Senior Braille Specialist, and Earl R. Scharry, Braille Instructor
1971, 1973	*Instruction Manual for Braille Transcribing, Revised 1971, 1973,* By Maxine B. Dorf, Head, Volunteer Services Section, and Earl R. Scharry, Braille Advisor
1984, 1987	*Instruction Manual for Braille Transcribing, Third Edition, 1984,* Maxine B. Dorf In Collaboration with Barbara H. Tate
2000* projected release date	*Instruction Manual for Braille Transcribing, Fourth Edition, 2000;* Constance Risjord, Literary Braille Transcriber; John Wilkinson, Literary Braille Advisor; Mary Lou Stark, Head, Braille Development Section

newsletter also published lists of visitors to NLS and of newly certified transcribers.

In 1975, *Volunteer News* became a part of DBPH News in response to comments from its readership desiring information about other aspects of the NLS program. (In 1958, the *Division for the Blind Newsletter* began publication with the regional libraries and machine distribution agencies as its primary audience. In 1966 with issue No. 25, the name was shortened to the *DBPH News.*) In 1977 the newsletter for volunteers became a separate document once again, with a new name, *Update.*

In addition to the Library of Congress manuals, other books have been used to teach braille transcribers. The best known of these are *Lessons in Braille Transcribing* by Bernard M. Krebs, first published in 1967; and *Programmed Instruction in Braille* by S.C. Ashcroft and Freda Henderson, first published in 1963 and revised by Henderson and others in 1991.

Sources of Instruction

From the outset of the braille transcribing program, instruction has been available through correspondence. Early on, instruction was also available from local groups of transcribers. The 1996 edition of *Volunteers Who Produce Books* lists 242 groups of volunteer braille transcribers and tapists, many of whom offer local instruction. Many universities now offer initial braille instruction in their preparation programs for special education teachers of visually impaired children and rehabilitation teachers of visually impaired adults.

In recent years, technology has been incorporated in braille instruction. From April through September 1994, the Region IV Education Service Center in Houston, Texas, offered nationwide classes in literary braille transcribing via satellite television. William Dickerman presented the course materials for each two-hour class, once a week for twenty weeks. When they had completed the class, students were encouraged to submit a trial manuscript to NLS for certification.

In the late 1990s, an interactive course was introduced over the Internet from the Shodor Education Foundation, located in North Carolina. There are three levels to this course—the last includes an introduction to the specialized codes. Robert Gotwals, Jr., computational science educator and braille transcriber, was the primary developer of this project, under a Braille Literacy Program grant awarded by the U.S. Department of Education. Computerized tutorials were developed by Gaylen Kapperman, coordinator of the programs in vision, faculty of special education; and others at Northern Illinois University; to teach literary and Nemeth braille. Neither of these projects teaches all of the braille transcribing rules, but they do give a thorough introduction to the codes.

Transcription Certifications

The initial certifications given by the Library of Congress certified volunteers in literary braille transcribing and proofreading. People had been transcribing music and mathematics as well as foreign languages long before certifications were offered, but persons receiving music certificates were first recognized in *Volunteer News* in November 1965. Nemeth code transcription certificates were first issued in August 1980, and a Nemeth code proofreading certification program began in 1991. For a number of years people have been able to use six-key entry software to prepare their class exercises and certification tests. When using this software, six keys on the computer keyboard correspond to the six keys of the Perkins brailler.

Discussion of a course leading to certification of persons using braille translation software began in 1996. Using this type of software, information is entered into a word processing program in the usual manner and then translated into braille. Questions raised included how thoroughly a person using translation software should know the actual dot assignments for the various braille symbols. Also, should the certificate read the same for a person using translation software as that received by a person using six-key input on a computer or Perkins brailler, or using a slate and stylus. Two advisory committee meetings were held, one in 1996 and one in 1999. Upon resolution of certification criteria it is anticipated that the first persons to take the course will begin during late 2000.

Changes in Transcription Equipment

Early transcribers learned braille using a slate and stylus. The development in 1892 of the first braillewriter, a mechanical device for braille production, contributed to braille's becoming the dominant embossed system in the United States. Until the 1980s, the braillewriter was the main production tool used by volunteers.

In April 1968, IBM introduced the Braille Electric Typewriter. This machine had the same speed and ease of operation and the same standard keyboard as the regular electric typewriter. All sixty-three possible braille characters were provided, and thus the machine could be adapted to producing any system of braille, such as music, mathematics or foreign language. In an article by Maxine Dorf in the April 1968 *Volunteer News,* she states:

> "Many braillists have expressed the fear that this new typewriter will render their services obsolescent. I feel that such a fear is wholly groundless. The braille typewriter is supplementary to rather than competitive with existing methods of producing braille. The production of braille books will always require the skills and technical know-how of trained braillists. In fact, there is a strong possibility that more braille can be produced in less time and with much less physical effort."

The April-June 1986 issue of *Update* contained the first of several articles about computer-assisted braille transcription. This article, by Diann Smith, listed the following advantages in the use of the computer for the transcription of braille:

- Individual transcribers increase their output with far less effort.

- Groups no longer need large storage areas for masters, and back-up copies provide insurance.

- Braille readers benefit from paper copies with no erasures.

In May 1986, NLS began accepting trial manuscripts, the certification examination, produced with direct-entry software.

The most recent advance in braille transcribing has been the increased use of translation software for braille production. The first working braille translator in the United States was developed at the American Printing House for the Blind (APH) during the early 1960's by IBM and APH. The earliest braille translators to be implemented on a microcomputer were released in the late 1970's.

The information to be transcribed is entered into a word processing program in one of three ways:

- Copying the material from a computer disc containing the file.

- Scanning the material and cleaning it up.

- Typing the material.

Once the document is in the program, it is marked up for formatting purposes before being processed by the translation software. The code has some ambiguities in it, so, while the software can do a very good job of converting print letters to braille symbols, there are still some choices that require human intervention. While translation is used primarily with literary and textbook materials, new programs are being developed for use with mathematics, science, and music.

Exciting developments in the realm of publishing indicate that in the future it will be viable to use publishers' files as source data for transcribing.

Organizations of Transcribers

In the early days of braille transcribing, transcribing was one of the formal programs of the American Red Cross (ARC), and there was a network through which new transcribers could learn more about their new skills and gain support in their efforts. Although many ARC chapters continue to have braille units, the ARC is no longer a primary support system for transcribers. Two international organizations and a growing number of statewide organizations provide training and individual support.

The oldest of these organizations is the National Braille Association, organized in 1945. The California Transcribers and Educators of the Visually Handicapped was formed in 1959. Both organizations sponsor workshops, have technical committees teaching the various codes, and publish quarterly magazines to support their members in being more effective transcribers. Statewide organizations include Visual Aid Volunteers of Florida, organized in the mid-1970s, and Wisconsin Braille, organized in 1999.

Current Role of Transcribers

While the focus of the braille transcribing program of the NLS has been on people who have volunteered their services, in as early as 1970, individuals requested certificates that did not contain the word "volunteer," because they were seeking paid employment using their skills.

Early transcribers were women who gave back to their communities through volunteer work. Today's transcribers are a mix of volunteers and employed transcribers, and many of the volunteers hold jobs unrelated to their volunteer contributions. In metropolitan areas, many of the transcribers are associated with local volunteer groups in addition to being members of the international organizations. They meet on a regular basis to discuss assignments and problems encountered in brailling books. Volunteers in more isolated areas may belong only to organizations such as the National Braille Association or California Transcribers and Educators of the Visually Handicapped.

Providing braille and other special media as a profession is an expanding area for transcribers. Many transcribers work directly for school districts and state instructional material centers, and some work for major braille producers, either in-house as regular employees, or as piecework contractors. With the implementation of the Americans with Disabilities Act and its requirement that businesses and agencies provide materials to their customers in special media, more and more transcribers, blind and sighted are setting up small businesses.

Future Role of Transcribers

In the 1931 Annual Report of the Librarian of Congress, in a reference to many private contributions for the embossing of books, the question is raised "What is the future of braille transcribing?" The response was that all agreed that it will still be needed. In 1935, with the advent of talking books, the question was asked, "Is braille transcribing any longer needed?" In 1968, transcribers feared the electric braille typewriter would make their services obsolete. In an article by Richard Evensen in 1974 in the *Iowa Transcriber*, he stated, "So often one hears the question: 'Will I be replaced by a computer?'" In 1999, at meetings and conferences, the question is again raised, "Will computer software replace the skilled transcriber?" As translation software becomes more sophisticated, the role of the transcriber will change. There will be less focus on the "dots"—the actual composition of the braille symbols—and more time invested in structuring the computer files that will then be translated.

Circumstances have changed in the past. The code will continue to be modified and changed to accommodate the changes in the print world. The future may bring new and different methods of producing braille; however, the limitations inherent in a code with a finite number of symbols ensure that there will always be a need for human intervention to produce a final product that fully conveys the meaning of the print author.

References

American National Red Cross. *Braille Transcribing, Standard English Braille, Grade Two, A Manual.* Washington, D.C.: American National Red Cross. 1937

Braille Authority of North America (BANA) code books (as of 2000): *English Braille, American Edition, 1994* [literary braille code]*; *Braille Formats: Principles of Print to Braille Transcription, 1997*; *Nemeth Code for Mathematics & Science Notation, 1972 Revision*; *Addendum 1 to the Nemeth Code for Mathematics & Science Notation, 1972; Revision: Ancient Numeration Systems*; *Braille Code for Chemical Notation, 1997*; *Code for Computer Braille Notation, 1987*; *Computer Braille Code: Flowchart Design for Applicable Braille Codes, Supplement, 1992*; *Guidelines for Linear Braille Format, 1987*; *Music Braille Code, 1999*; *Guidelines for Mathematical Drawings, 1983***; *Addendum: Number Lines, 1990***.

* Louisville, KY: American Printing House for the Blind, Inc.

** Rochester, NY: National Braille Association, Inc.

Ashcroft, S.C. and F. Henderson. *Programmed Instruction in Braille.* Pittsburg, PA: Stanwix House, Inc. 1963

DeGarmo, M.T. *Introduction to Braille Music Transcription.* Washington, D.C.: Division for the Blind and Physically Handicapped, Library of Congress. 1974

Evensen, Richard, in *Iowa Transcriber*. Vol. 10, No. 2, 1974.

Koestler, Frances A. *The Unseen Minority*. New York: David McKay Company, Inc. 1976

Krebs, Bernard M. *Lessons in Braille Transcribing*. New York: The Jewish Guild for the Blind. 1978.

National Library Service for the Blind and Physically Handicapped. *That All May Read*. Washington, D.C.: Library of Congress. 1983

Roberts, Helen, Bernard M,. Krebs and Barbara Taffet. *An Introduction to Braille Mathematics*. Washington, D.C.: Library of Congress. 1978.

Rohrback, Alice. *Volunteer Braille Transcribing, A Service for the Adult Blind*. Washington, D.C.: Library of Congress. 1944.

Smith, Diann. "Computer-assisted Braille Transcription," *Update*. Vol. 9, No. 2. Washington, D.C.: Library of Congress. 1986.

Sullivan, Joe. "Early History of Braille Translators and Embossers." http://www.duxburysystems.com/bthist. html. 1998.

U.S. Library of Congress. *Report of the Librarian of Congress, 1931*. Washington, D.C.: Government Printing Office. 1932.

Volunteer News. No. 1. Washington, D.C.: Library of
Congress. 1965.

Volunteer News. No. 11. Washington, D.C.: Library of
Congress. 1968.

BRAILLE
IN THE LAW

by Marc Maurer

When Louis Braille devised the six-dot reading and writing system for blind people, he may have thought that he was merely introducing a communication method. However, even though braille is recognized today as the most useful and versatile way for blind people to read, it has been controversial from its beginning. Even now, more than a century and a half since its invention, the acceptance and use of braille in many areas inspire contention and conflict.

The Law and Library Services

To say the least, the braille system has had an interesting legal history—a history still in the making today. It began when Louis Braille invented his tactile reading and writing system in the 1820s. At the time of his death in 1852, the braille system was not officially a part of the curriculum being taught at the Paris school for the blind Braille had attended, l'Institution Nationale des Jeunes Aveugles. Only by 1854 was this tactile medium given official sanction in France (Mellor 1998). In the United States, Braille was not introduced until the 1860s, and did not have universal recognition until well into the twentieth century.

In 1879 the legal crusade began to make braille available to all blind people in the United States. In that year, the American Association of Instructors of the Blind, an organization composed of the leaders of schools for blind people in the United States, petitioned Congress for an act to provide funding for a printing house to create embossed materials that could be used by students at schools for blind people. This became the first federal statute adopted to promote reading for individuals who are blind. However, because other tactile reading systems were still dominant, the federal appropriation for embossing books was not used by the American Printing House for the Blind to create braille until 1892.

In 1904, the necessary service of making literature and other written materials readily available for those who cannot see was provided when a law was adopted to permit the mailing of books for blind people without cost. Books for blind people were scarce and bulky, and without the free-mailing privilege, almost no blind people would have been able to get them. This law is currently part of the United States Code at 39 U.S.C. section 3403 (b)(5). The budget of the postal service includes a federal appropriation to pay the costs of delivering free matter for those who are blind. This service is among the most vital provided to blind people.

In 1931, the Pratt-Smoot Act authorized $100,000 for the Library of Congress "to provide books for the adult blind." The law was amended in 1952 to include children, in 1962 to include music materials, and in 1966 to include people with physical handicaps. The original purpose of the law was for embossed books to be distributed to blind people through a network of libraries. Within a very few years, recorded books were also included in the collection. For almost seventy years, the Library has produced books and magazines in braille. The national collection currently holds approximately 50,000 braille titles. In 1999, braille-related expenditures by the National Library Service for the Blind and Physically Handicapped (part of the Library of Congress) were more than $7.2 million.

The Books for the Blind program of the Library of Congress has been the most prominent and successful national effort to promote literacy and reading for blind people. It is one of the most popular services for blind people in the nation, and it has probably served more people than any other single program for those who are blind.

In 1932, the year after the Pratt-Smoot Act was passed, representatives of organizations of blind people in the United States and Great Britain adopted braille as the standard reading medium for those who are visually impaired. The agreement among entities dealing with blindness was of great importance because competing systems of embossed type for blind people had been in existence for more than 100 years, and the competition among these systems of reading created animosity, lack of cooperation, and wasted effort. The delegates who brought the argument to a conclusion named the document declaring that braille was the reading medium for those who were visually impaired the Treaty of London. This agreement remains in effect in all material respects today.

The Law and Rehabilitation

Schools and libraries for blind people placed a major emphasis on braille. In a number of rehabilitation programs for people with visual impairments, braille was taught to blind adults. During World War II, the Rehabilitation Act, which had originally been adopted in 1920 to provide rehabilitation services to disabled veterans injured in World War I, was amended to permit blind adults to participate in rehabilitation programs. Before the amendments to the Rehabilitation Act in 1943, it had been thought that blind people were too severely disabled to be rehabilitated. In 1954, the Rehabilitation Act was again amended to encourage blind people to seek training in the alternative skills and techniques employed by those who are blind. By 1973, when the Rehabilitation Act was again substantially altered and reenacted, rehabilitation of blind individuals had become an accepted objective of the federal law. Training in the use of braille was one of the fundamental activities of rehabilitation.

The Law and Education

Training in braille for blind children, however, ran into problems shortly after World War II. Around that time, advances in medicine permitted low-birth-weight babies to survive, and the incubation techniques used for preserving life in these tiny infants also damaged their capacity to see. Consequently, an increased population of blind children came to be a part of the educational system in the late 1940s and 1950s.

Schools for blind children had been established in a number of states, beginning in the 1830s and continuing into the twentieth century. In many states, these schools are still in operation. The early schools had produced tactile writing for their blind students, and braille was among the forms of raised printing. Much of the innovation and research regarding braille was conducted at these schools for blind children. The Illinois School for the Blind and the Perkins School for the Blind, for example, created embossing facilities to produce maps, books, and other materials. By the 1940s, schools for blind children were placing heavy emphasis on braille. Until then, the majority of blind students who received an education got it from schools for blind people. With the increase of the population of blind students, however, schools for blind children were inadequate to meet the need. In ever-growing numbers, blind children began to be given education in public schools. In 1975, Public Law 94-142 was adopted, which declared that all handicapped children were entitled to a free, appropriate public education within the least restrictive environment. With amendments passed in 1990, this law became known as the Individuals with Disabilities Education Act (IDEA).

Under this act, each handicapped student receives an Individualized Education Plan (IEP) that is developed by the child's IEP team. The IEP team, is composed of parents, teachers, administrators and any other persons involved in the child's education. The IEP team is to consider the potential of the student and the educational needs in drafting the plan. The problem is that most blind students did not receive training in braille under this act. This deplorable state of education for blind children, which existed until very recently, caused hardship and frustration for them. The shift in the educational pattern for blind students placed demands on the public schools that they found difficult to meet. With the emphasis on education in integrated settings, blind students were removed from schools specifically designed for them, where specialized tools and materials were used.

The change in responsibility from state schools to local schools is said to have many positive consequences, but it has been accompanied by a dramatic deemphasis on the use of braille in the classroom. In fact, as of 1994, fewer than 10 percent of the blind students in elementary and secondary education were receiving their instruction in braille.

In the past, students at schools for blind children received instruction from teachers trained specifically to meet their particular needs. In the public schools, however, many teachers do not know braille, and, consequently, they cannot teach it to their blind students. Moreover, some teachers believe that using braille is clumsy and slow.

As a result, blind students have been taught that braille is inferior to print.

As a further complication, uninformed school officials have even asserted that teaching braille to blind students with residual vision is tantamount to child abuse. In one case, officials from the state school for blind children even testified in support of a school district that was advancing this proposition. The parents of the blind child felt particularly abused, because the school for blind children had never been asked to provide educational services, did not know the student, and had never performed an evaluation of the student's educational needs.

With attitudes such as those, it is not surprising that the percentage of blind students learning braille had dropped so much by 1993. However, it is a testimony to the robustness of this medium of communication, as well as to the tenacity of those who use it, that it has survived and that it has generated substantial sustained support.

Because of the problems faced by parents of blind children in having their children receive braille instruction in the public schools, legislative efforts were commenced in Maryland and Louisiana to mandate that braille be available to blind students who want to learn it. The first legislation mentioning braille as a mechanism of communication to be taught in schools was adopted in Louisiana in 1988. In the same year, the National Federation of the Blind adopted a resolution calling for legislation to support the right of blind people to learn braille. A National Braille Literacy campaign was launched by the National Federation of the Blind on November 16, 1990, the fiftieth anniversary of the founding of the Federation. Coupled with this campaign was the establishment of the International Braille and Technology Center for the Blind, which includes at least one of all computerized devices known to the Federation and was designed to provide information to blind people in speech and in both embossed and refreshable braille. It was declared at that time that literacy in braille is a right for all blind people.

One of the principal objectives of the campaign was the enactment of braille literacy laws in all fifty states. A model state statute, arising from the work to create legislation in Maryland and Louisiana and titled "The Blind Person's Literacy Rights and Education Act," was composed and distributed. This model legislation included seven major provisions:

1. A presumption that proficiency in reading and writing braille is essential for each blind student.

2. A requirement that each blind student be given an assessment in an inventory of braille skills.

3. A provision that braille instruction be included in the blind student's educational programs unless all members of the planning team agree that reading and writing performance cannot be affected by the use of braille.

4. A provision that braille is to be used in the educational program of the student in combination with other media of education.

5. A declaration that braille instruction may not be withheld from a blind student on the basis that the

student has sufficient remaining vision to read some materials in print.

6. A declaration that the blind student's level of proficiency in reading is expected to be comparable to that of sighted students at the same grade level.

7. A provision requiring textbook publishers to provide electronic copies of textbooks suitable for translation into braille.

As of the summer of 1999, thirty states had adopted legislation drafted in whole or in part from the provisions of this model bill.

With the adoption of state braille literacy bills, parents of blind children began to face the argument that federal law (specifically IDEA) preempted legislation by the states regarding educational programs for disabled persons. Consequently, parents were told that blind children could not receive braille instruction because federal law prohibited it. Blind adults and parents of blind children continued to give strong support for braille. On June 4, 1997, President Clinton signed into law amendments to IDEA. Section 614 (d)(3)(B)(iii) [20 U.S.C. Section 1414 (d)(3)(B)(iii)] of this amended legislation contains a provision declaring that blind children shall receive instruction in braille unless the IEP team finds such instruction for the child's present or future needs to be not appropriate. This requirement is reiterated in regulations adopted by the Department of Education. For the first time, braille has been recognized in federal law as a medium both appropriate and essential for the education of those who are blind.

The Braille System and Federal Law

Although it was not until quite recently that braille was declared by federal law to be an appropriate reading medium for blind people, it has been the subject of numerous legislative and regulatory provisions. The most recent consideration of braille in federal legislation is contained in the proposed Patient's Bill of Rights Act, which was debated in Congress in the summer of 1999. Section 111 would require health plans to disclose certain information about costs, benefits, and restrictions imposed on choosing physicians. Braille is one of the methods for disclosing this information.

Grants are available for independent living services to older individuals who are blind. A number of federal grant programs, authorized by federal law, have provisions regarding the production of braille. Training provided under these grants may include instruction in braille. Training in braille is one of the numerous factors to be considered in granting funds under this program. Such training may be for blind individuals, for teachers of blind children, or for persons who teach blind adults. Also, it may include training to promote knowledge in the use of braille.

The Copyright Act

The Books for the Blind program of the Library of Congress has been in existence since 1931. Until recently, copyright law required permission to be given by the author of a book before it could be embossed. This was changed in 1996 with amendments to the Copyright Act that provide authorized entities the right to reproduce nondramatic literary works in specialized formats, such as braille, for use by the blind. Authorized entities include schools, governmental agencies, libraries, and other agencies or nonprofit organizations that provide education and training to blind people. This change in the law has significantly increased the speed with which books for those who are blind are prepared and distributed.

Future changes in the copyright law will undoubtedly take account of advancing technology. Electronic files can now be used to produce books in hard copy or refreshable braille. It is likely that advances in methods of handling electronic text will make it possible to use this medium to create spoken-word editions of published material. Thus, the Copyright Act may be further amended to ensure that electronic copies of texts, which can be used to create books for the blind, are filed along with copyright applications. This change would make it possible for enormous quantities of material to be used by blind people.

Civil Rights Laws

From this analysis, it is clear that both braille instruction and the use of braille have received official sanction under the laws pertaining to library services, rehabilitation, and education for blind people. Recognition of braille in the context of civil rights laws has added strength to this sanction. In 1973, Congress passed a sweeping declaration of nondiscrimination for the "handicapped." This was done in section 504 of the Rehabilitation Act of 1973. Regulations to implement section 504 were first adopted in 1977. All agencies of the federal government that are responsible for distributing federal financial assistance were also made responsible for issuing regulations for compliance with section 504.

Further amendments to the Rehabilitation Act passed in 1978 now require all federal agencies to apply their policies regarding nondiscrimination to the programs they conduct as well as to the programs they assist through grants. As a result, the Code of Federal Regulations contains a number of sections citing requirements to use braille. Policies or regulations to require provision of braille materials at public or employee meetings have been adopted by virtually all federal agencies. The Department of Agriculture specifies that all commonly used program materials shall be readily available in braille and that other materials shall be produced in braille upon request. Grants offered by the Department of Agriculture to community facilities are to include methods for individuals needing information in braille to get it through the department.

The Department of Energy requires program information that will affect a substantial number of blind people to be available in braille. Those receiving grants from this department must make their policy documents regarding nondiscrimination available in braille if a number of blind people will be affected.

Some departments have regulations with respect to auxiliary aids or services that may be used by those with sensory impairments. For example, the Federal Reserve Board specifies that braille may be required to assist the blind population who participate in or enjoy the benefits of programs affected by the Board. The Department of Commerce regulations state that funding recipients (except small recipients) shall ensure that no one is denied the benefits of, denied participation in, or otherwise subjected to discrimination in a program because of the absence of auxiliary aids. One of these auxiliary aids is braille material. Braille materials are also required by regulations of the State Department and for recipients of funds provided through the State Department. Part of the regulations say that reasonable accommodations for otherwise qualified handicapped employees or applicants shall be made, unless doing so would be an undue hardship. Braille material is one such accommodation.

The Department of Housing and Urban Development, the Department of Defense, and the Department of Education specify that braille may be required as a method of communication with blind people. Even the Panama Canal Commission includes braille among the auxiliary aids listed in its regulations. A number of other regulatory provisions are set forth in the code. The Internal Revenue Service states that expenses for training in school to learn braille are deductible from personal income tax. The Central Intelligence Agency has written an exemption into its regulations declaring that material need not be put into braille for accommodating blind individuals if to do so would create a potential security risk.

In 1990, Congress passed the Americans with Disabilities Act (ADA). This act extends the principles of section 504 of the Rehabilitation Act of 1973 to private sector entities that may not receive or benefit from federal financial assistance. As a result, the impetus to promote the provision of information in braille has been expanded significantly. Under the ADA, the Department of Justice has adopted extensive regulations addressing the requirements for access to commercial and other public facilities, including the specification of requirements for construction or alteration of buildings and facilities. For example, elevators must be marked in braille and the doorjambs of elevator hoistways must have braille characters to identify the floors. The regulations are quite specific about braille, declaring that dots should be .059 inches in diameter, with spaces between the dots being 0.90 inches and the horizontal distance between cells being .241 inches. The vertical distance from one line of braille to another is .395 inches. The regulations acknowledge that signs describing public buildings, monuments, and objects of cultural interest may not give sufficient detail for blind people. Therefore, interpretive guides or audiotapes may be used as an alternative. The National Park Service has adopted similar regulations for its buildings and facilities, and the Department of Transportation employs similar provisions for over-the-road buses and accessible transportation facilities. Braille is also specified as one method for giving information to blind persons who may be eligible for paratransit assistance.

These are only a few examples of requirements for braille as a right of access to information expressed in civil rights laws or regulations. The result has been a growing recognition that information provided in a printed format, designed for persons who can see, must also be provided in an alternative format for persons who cannot see. Provision of materials in braille is almost always specified as an appropriate (and sometimes necessary) alternative format.

The following are some further examples.

- The Department of Labor administers minimum wage laws. Certain of these laws permit wages below the generally accepted minimum to be paid to disabled workers. Employers paying these special subminimum wages must have posters explaining the conditions under which these wages may be paid. Upon request, these posters must be made available in braille.

- The Labor Department has also issued a guidance statement to those administering tests to job applicants. Written tests must be made available in braille, unless the use of that format is inadequate for the nature of the test being given.

- The Department of Education administers the Randolph Sheppard Program, which authorizes blind vendors to operate vending facilities on federal property. Each of the vendors is entitled to receive financial data regarding the program maintained by the state agency charged with licensing vendors. Braille is one method for providing this information.

- The Department of Veterans Affairs provides vocational and rehabilitative training for veterans, veterans' survivors, and their dependents. Part of the training may include teaching the skills of reading and writing braille.

The Law and the Future of the Braille System

The substantial number of references in the United States Code and in the Code of Federal Regulations to braille indicates that it is the policy of our country to encourage and promote the use of braille. Despite this clearly evident policy, arguments are frequently made that braille is a dying system without adherents or proponents. These arguments fail to recognize the urgent need for blind people to communicate by as many methods as possible. They also contain a fundamental underlying misconception: that blind people are incapable of the most demanding intellectual pursuits. Under that misconception, an emphasis on braille is unimportant, because a system of reading and writing for blind people cannot give individuals who are blind the same level of independence, initiative, and self-reliance that is expected of others. If the people who use braille are not expected to employ it to achieve any worthwhile objectives, the system itself loses significance.

If those who will be reading and writing braille, however, are confidently predicted to be scientists and engineers and leaders in their communities, the reading and writing of braille becomes dramatically more important. The people who will be doing the leading and the engineering and the inventing of new products must have a reliable method for communication—and that method is braille. The outcome depends on the expectations of the people who are doing the teaching. The blind people who rely on braille are thoroughly convinced that it is essential. Indeed, blind people have determined that an emphasis on braille will be written into law, and the legislative provisions are now in the code.

In the past, blind adults were not expected to be able to make substantial contributions to society. The blind people themselves, however, have proven those expectations to be false; they have changed and continue to change the laws in this country, and, in doing so, have contributed substantially to society.

Problems with literacy for those who are blind remain, and these problems will not go away until expectations for blind students change to the extent that they are expected to achieve as much as sighted students. Part of the result of that change will be a greater capacity for blind people to make significant contributions to society and culture. It is less a matter for prediction than for decision, and blind people have made up their minds to make this decision a reality.

Reference

Mellor, C. Michael. 1998. *Making a Point: The Crusade for a Universally Embossed Code in the United States.* Address delivered at the second international conference on the history of the blind and the blind in history on June 22–24 in Paris, France.

BRAILLE IN THE WORKPLACE

by Fredric Schroeder

M any successfully employed blind people rely heavily on their braille skills and attribute a large measure of their competitive abilities to these skills. For them, using braille is the difference between adequately performing on the job and truly competing with their sighted peers. Yet, since the 1980s, membership organizations of blind people, parents of blind children, professionals in the field, and producers of braille materials have decried the nationwide decline in the use of braille and in braille literacy (Jernigan 1988; Spungin 1989; Stephens 1989; Pierce 1991; and Wittenstein 1994).

Although there are no national data on illiteracy among blind people, the American Printing House for the Blind's (APH's) annual registry of legally blind students has noted a consistent decrease in the percentage of legally blind students who use braille (Kirchner 1988). Specifically, in 1963, according to APH data, 51 percent of legally blind school-children in graded programs in public and residential schools combined used braille as their primary reading medium, and another 4 percent read both braille and print. APH data show that the percentages of braille-reading schoolchildren in the United States have declined steadily, reaching a low of 9.45 percent in 1994. The 1995 data record the percentage of braille users at 9.62 percent. An early study (1979) by the National Library Service (cited in Skilbeck 1990) similarly noted the rapid downward trend in braille usage from 52 percent in 1963 to 18 percent in 1978. Although these statistics show a severe decline in the proportion of visually impaired people who are braille readers, few empirical studies have been conducted to examine the relationship between braille literacy and successful employment.

Selected Research Findings

"…In the postindustrial era, when the majority of people in the workforce make a living with their minds, not their hands, it is education—more than coal or steel or even capital—that is the key to our economic future" (Spungin 1989, 1). In our culture we have come to expect a positive correlation between literacy and successful employment—the more education one has, the more money one is likely to make. Conversely, persons with little education on average probably earn less than more highly educated workers and are more apt to be unemployed and living in poverty.

One definition of literacy is the ability to read and write at a level appropriate to an individual's academic potential and to accomplish other functional tasks that require reading and writing (Zambone and Sanspree 1997). Academic achievement levels in reading and mathematics are among the most common measures of literacy.

Among working Americans with disabilities, academic achievement correlates positively with hourly wages. According to preliminary findings of a five-year longitudinal study of individuals with disabilities who became competitively employed after receiving vocational rehabilitation services, those with less than a high school diploma or GED (General Equivalency Diploma) earned an average of $6.30 per hour (Research Triangle Institute 1998). Individuals with more than a high school education averaged more than $9 per hour, or more than 40 percent greater earnings, apparently largely because of higher academic achievement.

Achievement levels in reading and mathematics also correlate strongly with earnings. Competitively employed workers with disabilities who read at less than the fourth-grade level barely earned the federal minimum wage, while those who read above the twelfth-grade level averaged more than 36 percent more than the poor readers (Research Triangle Institute 1998). The disparity in earnings by math achievement levels was even more dramatic. People with math achievement levels at less than the fourth-grade level earned an average of $5.56 per hour; those with achievement levels above the twelfth-grade level earned $8.54 per hour, more than 50 percent more.

The literacy skills of individuals with visual impairments significant enough to limit their ability to read print usually depend on their proficiency in reading braille and their access to braille materials (Zambone and Sanspree 1997). While higher reading levels among competitively employed persons in the general disabled population are related to higher earnings, a causal relationship between reading medium alone (either braille or print) and the economic success of blind adults is more difficult to establish (Ryles 1996).

Much of the research on blind adults and braille literacy has been based on self-reported surveys and interviews. Bauman (1963, cited in Zambone and Sanspree 1997) interviewed 434 employed blind adults and found that 58.3 percent of men and 71.4 percent of women used braille as their reading medium in the workplace. More than half used braille for taking notes, maintaining records, and identifying files.

Ryles (1996) conducted telephone interviews with 74 volunteers, ages eighteen to fifty-five, who were congenitally or legally blind and had no concomitant disabilities. Information was obtained on their visual history, education, current employment, income, occupation, and reading habits. Participants were also categorized according to their reading preferences (braille or print), which proved to be an important variable in employment rates. Participants who reported extensive personal or professional use of braille had far lower unemployment rates (33 percent) than did the total sample (58 percent).

Overall differences in the education levels of the braille reading group and the print reading group were not statistically significant, but there were marked differences at the higher education levels. Thirteen (30 percent) of the forty-three braille readers but only four (13 percent) of the thirty-one print readers had obtained graduate degrees. Only two of the subjects had doctoral degrees, and both were in the braille reading group (Ryles 1996).

Finally, the Ryles study established that while "a knowledge of braille, even as a primary reading medium, did not increase a subject's chances of employment, those who had learned to read braille as their original reading medium and used it extensively were employed at a significantly higher rate. Thus, the extensive and early acquisition of braille reading skills were the two factors that had a strong impact on employment rates" (Ryles 1996, 224).

Both the Ryles study and a 1996 in-depth analysis of the meaning of braille in the lives of eight legally blind adults (Schroeder 1996) concluded that individuals who used braille as a primary reading medium had higher perceptions of their abilities than those who relied on print reading. One of the implications of the latter study is that not only did braille have positive emotional connotations for braille readers, but their emotional attachment to braille went beyond its utility as a communications tool: Braille was tied to their self-esteem, independence, and feelings of competence.

Efficiencies of Braille as a Workplace Tool

Innovative applications of braille in the workplace are limited only by the creativity and imagination of the braille user. Braille is frequently used for labeling, note taking, document creation, and reading work-related information.

Braille labels are practical tools for identifying everything from controls on equipment and the contents of containers used by factory workers to buttons on appliances and boxes of ingredients used by professional chefs. Labels are particularly helpful in locating and identifying controls on equipment such as microwaves, audiovisual devices, and other instruments that have no tactually detectable buttons. Ellen Waechtler, a braille instructor in the rehabilitation program at the Blind Industries and Services of Maryland, suggests making notes on the layout of controls and procedures when labels do not provide adequate information to operate more complex equipment (Waechtler 1998).

Curtis Chong, director of technology for the National Federation of the Blind, primarily uses braille as a proofreading tool (Chong 1999). He creates letters and memoranda on his computer and then converts them into braille letters so he can more easily find and correct errors in punctuation, word use, syntax, and spacing. Chong also converts lengthy reports and manuals that require extended concentration to braille so that he can study them both in and out of the office.

For many blind people, a slate and stylus is a preferred method of note taking because it is more portable and efficient than audiotaping information or using an electronic note taker in meetings and classes (Halverson 1999; Hastalis 1999; LaBarre 1999). Some opt for an electronic note taker, such as the BrailleLite or the Braille 'n Speak, for long periods of extensive note taking (Chong 1999; Salas 1999). Tools typically used on a regular basis for producing work materials in braille include a four-line metal slate with slots for labeling tape, an interpoint card slate, a reversible-point metal stylus, a Braille 'n Speak, and a Juliet interpoint braille embosser.

Geerat Vermeij, a scholar and scientist at the University of California at Davis, asserts that while audio recordings and voice-recognition systems that translate print into sound are indeed useful, "the medium of sound sacrifices accuracy and efficiency due to the listener's inability to detect specifics of formatting, spelling, etc. to the point where audio is adequate only for the most routine tasks and for recreational reading" (Vermeij 1999). Braille also offers the kind of privacy in reading and creating that the audio devices do not. Vermeij concludes that braille is the medium that provides opportunities for blind people to achieve independence and equality, and its mastery is as fundamental to them as reading and writing print is to everyone else.

Value of Braille in Organizing Information

In most work environments, braille is indispensable to blind people in recording, identifying, storing, organizing, and retrieving information. Blind or visually impaired office workers use braille to label filing cabinet drawers, file folders, floppy computer disks, CD-ROMs, manuals, and other references. A single line of braille on the top or bottom of a page allows for easy identification and retrieval of printed material.

Sandy Halverson credits her versatility with braille as a primary factor in her competitive employment in a wide range of occupations in which she has had to manage large amounts of information (Halverson 1999). While earning a bachelor's degree in psychology, she worked part-time as the first blind telemarketer for a photography studio. Her fluency in reading and writing braille resulted in her earning as much in commissions as her sighted colleagues earned. Each day the office manager or a coworker read her twenty to thirty names, addresses, and telephone numbers, which she brailled. She also brailled a script that she read to potential customers. On a separate sheet of paper, she recorded pertinent information on successful sales and appointment times for photography sessions. At the end of her shift, she read the accumulated sales information to her office manager, who recorded it in print.

Halverson also worked as a rehabilitation teacher and used a slate and stylus to simultaneously interview clients and take notes on service needs, financial data, and other pertinent information. She also used different-size note cards to manage client and agency data. On three-by-five cards she developed travel itineraries for visits to clients' homes. She used four-by-six cards to maintain client names, addresses, telephone numbers, and counties of residence in a file near her telephone so she could quickly locate information in order to contact clients or respond to incoming calls. And she used five-by-eight cards with labeled dividers to track the movement of client cases through the service process. Grouping the cards according to service status enabled Halverson to manage a caseload of more than 125 clients and meet various agency deadlines. While being driven throughout her eight-county territory, she used her

Braille 'n Speak to generate service plans, file notes, and correspondence, and uploaded the documents to her computer for printing and filing when she returned to her office.

Halverson also used braille for an assortment of purposes during her employment as a court reporter. She used a slate and stylus in court to keep track of prosecution and defense exhibits and to keep her own docket of cases, because they were often heard in a sequence that was different from the printed court calendar. Dockets were prepared on thermofax sheets with a Perkins brailler and wrapped around print stenographic notes so the braille dots would not be erased after the notes were archived. Transcripts were created from the notes on computer disks and labeled with braille. She used a slate and index cards to record pertinent information on orders for transcripts from attorneys.

Today, Halverson works as an at-home medical transcriptionist, and she continues to use her BrailleLite and slate and stylus, employing many of the skills she first honed as a court reporter.

As an attorney and solo practitioner, Scott LaBarre also is no stranger to court. Although he uses several nonvisual techniques for obtaining and managing information, such as human readers, recorded text, and the like, he cites his ability to read and write braille as the one skill that allows him to function on a par with his sighted colleagues (LaBarre 1999). He uses a slate and stylus to jot down notes when he is on the move and doesn't want to be burdened with extra equipment. In the office, he uses braille labels on files, cassette tapes, and computer disks. With an embosser, he produces braille documents for depositions, client meetings, legal hearings, and other court appearances. He also uses a BrailleLite for taking notes in meetings and formal proceedings. He then uploads the notes to his personal computer and, conversely, downloads files from his computer to his BrailleLite for use at later times. Braille documents, either in hard copy or on his BrailleLite, allow him to look at the material at the same time his sighted peers review it. Listening to a recorded copy or having a reader whisper into his ear does not afford him the same freedom and immediate, independent access to information that braille gives him.

At times, LaBarre says, his use of braille gives him an advantage over other attorneys. He uses braille notes in closing arguments while continuing to face the jury, a feat sighted attorneys seldom accomplish because of their need to look down frequently at their notes. Regardless of how much technology changes people's lives, LaBarre is confident that blind people will continue to rely on braille, whether written with the slate and stylus or embossed by a high-speed, computer-driven printer.

Steve Hastalis, a twenty-four-year veteran of the Chicago Transit Authority's community relations department, relies on braille notes to make presentations to community organizations and to conduct tours of transit facilities (Hastalis 1999). He finds it easier and more efficient to write with a slate and stylus than to record meetings where there is often considerable ambient noise. He now works on ADA (Americans with Disabilities Act) compliance, attending meetings, making presentations, monitoring bus and train service, and producing braille publications. He has produced braille rail guides, fare brochures, night-service brochures, and service-change announcements. With increasing frequency, he is managing information more with his personal computer and Braille 'n Speak, but his electronic technology supplements rather than replaces the basic essential skills of reading and writing braille.

While there are innumerable examples of how people use braille to manage information, Abraham Nemeth had to invent a braille code to make it possible for him to conduct research and teach effectively as a professor of mathematics and computer science at the University of Detroit (Nemeth 1999). He created the Nemeth Braille Code for Mathematics and Science Notation as a means of accessing and comprehending the special symbols and the two-dimensional disposition of the symbols that characterize standard mathematical notation. He was fortunate in having a certified braille transcriber who worked for him exclusively. She set a goal of producing one braille volume per week and, over the course of approximately twenty years, assisted Nemeth in accumulating a library of more than 1,000 volumes covering all the main areas of mathematics and computer science. Because he had textbooks in braille, he could easily communicate with students during class sessions, making assignments and discussing formulas.

Because refreshable braille devices were not available for most of his career, Nemeth used IBM punchcards for keeping student records and for recording complicated formulas. He arranged the card file of formulas in the order in which they would be presented, and he kept the file in his jacket pocket where, while lecturing in class, he could read the braille formulas with his left hand and write them on the blackboard with his right hand, using print symbols. As he explained one formula, he would move its card to the back of the file and expose the card containing the next braille formula for presentation to the class. His students were mystified by the accuracy of his presentations, and he never enlightened them about his strategy for presenting the mathematical material. Without braille, says Nemeth, he could never have kept his job and certainly could not have advanced to the rank of full professor long before his retirement.

Advances in computer technology will no doubt enhance the abilities of blind workers to manage information. There is ample evidence, however, that fluency in reading and writing braille will remain a skill that is crucial for blind workers to achieve independence and equality in the workplace.

Implications for Special Education and Rehabilitation Personnel

If fluency in braille is vital to building successful careers, why does the widely recognized decline in braille literacy continue? Spungin (1989) suggests five reasons:

1. Medical advances have saved many infants who previously would not have survived, causing the population of people with multiple disabilities to grow tremendously. Of those with visual disabilities, many are nonreaders who also have retardation or learning disabilities.

2. Educators and parents encourage visually handicapped children to use any remaining vision at all costs, regardless of individual need or visual acuity.

3. Positive attitudes toward the use of braille have diminished, and university training programs have produced less-than-proficient braille instructors as teachers.

4. Dependence on computers, audiotapes, and other devices has reduced the perceived necessity for braille.

5. Special educators and administrators have, through the concept of least restrictive environment, resorted to itinerant and teacher-consultant models of service, limiting the time spent with students because of large caseloads and large geographic service areas.

All these factors and others, according to Spungin, have contributed to the decline in the use of braille.

The print-versus-braille question may also be a subset of a broader issue of self-identity. Braille is more than a means of literacy for the legally blind people who use it: it is also a part of their identities as competent persons with disabilities. Thus, the policy issue for special educators, administrators, and rehabilitation personnel is not simply a choice between braille and print. More complex considerations come into play, such as braille as a symbol of independence, of competence, and of career success, and braille as a means of self-acceptance and group identity.

In many respects, the issue of braille versus print hinges on an acceptance of a particular paradigm of disability. The medical model, which emphasizes deviation from the norm, casts the issue in terms of the practical benefit that either medium may have for making an individual more "normal." In contrast, the disability-rights or independent-living model poses the print-braille question in terms of the self-esteem and overall self-identification of legally blind individuals as members of a minority group. The medical model, based on the assumption that it is desirable for disabled people to perform more like nondisabled people, is the model that people without disabilities most readily understand and accept (Shapiro 1993, and Wright 1983). The disability-rights model, initiated by blind people in the 1940s, embodies the assumption that to be different is to be no less competent or valuable.

Administrators of special education and rehabilitation programs for blind people need to be watchful that their programs are not limited by professionals' reactions to the stigma of disability. On the contrary, administrators, teachers, and rehabilitation professionals may be well advised to try to understand their personal conceptions of disability and how these concepts may lead them to promote particular education or service strategies. They should be alert to the emergence of any hierarchy in their programs that promotes the idea that the more "normal" an individual is, the better off that individual is. By viewing the education and career preparation of blind people from the minority perspective, rather than from the medical model—that is, by viewing the disability as a social issue, not as a medical issue—special education and rehabilitation personnel may facilitate individuals' adjustment to and acceptance of their blindness.

One analysis has concluded that a legally blind individual's self-identity as a blind person is crucial to whether that legally blind individual will seek to learn braille (Schroeder 1996). Those who regard themselves as blind may find that braille expedites and intensifies group identification and thus leads to the development of self-confidence and self-esteem. As a symbol of blindness, braille may strengthen a sense of normalcy, despite different means of functioning. Individuals who do not regard themselves as blind may reject braille because of its relationship to blindness. Because they view themselves as sighted people with visual problems, the introduction of braille may assault the very fabric of their identities. Therefore, the issue of identification with the group may need to take precedence over the issue of the appropriate learning medium, at least at first.

The findings of several studies, which have been cited in this chapter, suggest that legally blind braille readers are employed at disproportionately higher rates than the legally blind population as a whole. It is also likely that an individual who self-identifies as a blind person is more likely to seek to learn braille. Consequently, special educators, administrators, and rehabilitation professionals have a moral responsibility to consider the effects of their educational practices and services strategies on people's perceptions of themselves as whole blind persons or as defective sighted persons. If professionals help individuals identify themselves as competent blind people, they will help guide them to a first-class role in society as highly trained and productive members of our workforce.

References

Chong, C. 1999. Letter to author, March 5.

Halverson, S. 1999. Letter to author, February 27.

Hastalis, S. 1999. Letter to author, March 10.

Jernigan, K. 1988. "A Thought-Provoking Resolution and an Issue That May Not Yet Be Settled." *Braille Monitor,* 31 7: 462–465.

Kirchner, C. 1988. *Data on Blindness and Visual Impairment in the U.S.: A Resource Manual on Social Demographic Characteristics, Education, Employment and Income, and Service Delivery,* 2d ed. New York: American Foundation for the Blind.

LaBarre, S. 1999. Letter to author, March 12.

Nemeth, A. 1999. Letter to author, March 11.

Pierce, B. 1991. "APH Figures Show Braille Still Declining." *Braille Monitor,* 34 7: 390–391.

Research Triangle Institute. 1998. *A Longitudinal Study of the Vocational Rehabilitation Service Program: Third Interim Report.* Research Triangle Park: Research Triangle Institute.

Ryles, R. 1996. "The Impact of Braille Reading Skills on Employment, Income, Education, and Reading Habits." *Journal of Visual Impairment & Blindness,* 90, no. 3: 219–226.

Salas, J. 1999. Letter to author, March 1.

Schroeder, F. 1996. "Perceptions of Braille Usage by Legally Blind Adults." *Journal of Visual Impairment & Blindness,* 90, No. 3: 210–218.

Shapiro, J. P. 1993. *No Pity: People With Disabilities Forging a New Civil Rights Movement.* New York: Times Books.

Skilbeck, M. 1990. *Braille Literacy. DORS Openers.* Springfield: Illinois Department of Rehabilitation Services.

Spungin, S. 1989. *Braille Literacy: Issues for Blind Persons, Families, Professionals, and Producers of Braille.* New York: American Foundation for the Blind.

Stephens, O. 1989. "Braille—Implications for Living." *Journal of Visual Impairment & Blindness,* 83, no. 6: 288–289.

Vermeij, G. J. 1999. Letter to author, March 4.

Waechtler, E. 1998. "101 Ways to Use Braille." *Braille Spectator.* Baltimore: National Federation of the Blind of Maryland, Summer.

Wittenstein, S. H. 1994. "Braille Literacy: Pre-Service Training and Teachers' Attitudes." *Journal of Visual Impairment & Blindness,* 88, no. 6: 516–524.

Wright, B. A. 1983. *Physical Disability: A Psychosocial Approach,* 2d ed. New York: Harper & Row.

Zambone, A. and Sanspree, M. 1997. "The Relationship Between Literacy and Employment for Persons with Visual Impairments: A Review of the Literature." *In Increasing Literacy Levels: Final Report.* Mississippi State, Mississippi: Mississippi State University Rehabilitation Research and Training Center on Blindness and Low Vision.

BRAILLE IN THE ENVIRONMENT

by Freddie L. Peaco

Introduction

The type and severity of an individual's visual impairments directly affect how that individual functions in and adjusts to the environment. Many severely visually impaired people function as if they were totally blind and receive significant benefit from tactile information. French philosopher and encyclopedist Denis Diderot said, "I found that of the senses the eye is the most superficial, the ear the most arrogant, smell the most voluptuous, taste the most superstitious and fickle, touch the most profound and philosophical." If this quotation has any validity, then the merit and advantages to blind persons of accessible tactile information in the environment are indisputable.

The twentieth century witnessed the introduction of a wide and varied assortment of braille and other tactile information into the general environment for the use and enlightenment of blind and visually impaired persons in the United States, Canada, Europe, and other countries. This chapter explores braille and other tactile media resources that enhance the environment for blind persons in areas that affect daily living, use of public facilities, education, and the workplace.

The goal of the chapter is not to rate these resources, but to create an awareness of their availability and usefulness. Although braille writing and tactile illustration tools are among these resources, they will not be covered in this chapter. The tools discussed here are easily available for use in our general surroundings. This is by no means an exhaustive survey of the braille and tactile material available in our day-to-day existence, but it illustrates the strong presence of such information in society.

Blind people, like sighted people, wish to acquire information and enjoy entertainment and beauty in their communities, only for blind people, this must be done through the sense of touch and the presence of braille. Over the years, more and more braille and other tactile information—both basic and sophisticated—continues to emerge in our surroundings. In the United States, the American Printing House for the Blind in Louisville, Kentucky; Howe Press of the Perkins School for the Blind in Watertown, Massachusetts; and the American Foundation for the Blind in New York pioneered the introduction of tactile devices and services. In Europe, the Royal National Institute for the Blind in London took the lead. These agencies lead the way in adapting, developing, and marketing products for people who are visually impaired.

Daily Living Activities

Blind and visually impaired persons rely on numerous braille and other tactile products and services for daily living activities. Some of the more generic items they rely on are braille watches and clocks, braille playing cards and board games of all types, braille greeting cards, braille clothing identification tags, and braille measuring devices. Calendars of all kinds, such as desk, wall, pocket, and art, are also available in braille for children and adults.

Major utility companies (gas, electric, and telephone) accommodate visually impaired consumers with braille bills. At least two telephone companies have enhanced the independence and privacy of visually impaired persons by offering telephone calling cards embossed with braille account numbers. Braille is also available on automated teller machines (ATMs), and it is possible to receive braille bank statements and other pertinent documents as well as braille check templates from many primary financial institutions.

Braille overlays for household appliances and thermostats can be obtained from some manufacturers to assist in one's daily and personal life. A limited number of commercially available children's toys have braille lettering; one toy displays the alphabet and shows the corresponding braille letter. Vendors of public Laundromats are offering braille overlays on laundry equipment in a few urban areas in the United States.

Michel Chapoutier, a maker and shipper of Rhone wines, has put braille labels on all of his premium wines including appellations like Hermitage, Crozes-Hermitage,

Condrieu, St. Joseph, Cote Rotie, and Chateauneuf-du-Pape. The braille labels give the type and name of the wine, the vintage date, the name of the winery, the town where the wine was made, and the color of the wine. Braille characters are stamped into the aluminum can tops of most brands of beer in Japan. In Sweden, a cookie manufacturer uses packages embossed with braille.

Visually impaired and blind people can now have braille labels affixed to medications and can purchase some Glaxton dermatology medicines packaged with braille labeling. Blind people who need to use insulin can purchase bottles with tactile markings on the caps, arranged to denote the insulin type.

During World War II, Howe Press introduced a map-of-the-month program in which each month a different map of the war zone area was produced with accompanying braille leaflets. Today, tactile maps make learning geography easier and aid in mobility on city streets and college campuses, and in national parks.

Tactile flags help convey to visually impaired persons the majesty of their country's symbol. The flags can be shown as tactile illustrations in books or created from textured fabrics or as textured models.

City transit systems in most major cities provide accessible route and schedule information, maps, and raised diagrams. And transit fare-card machines bear braille identification labels. The following are two examples of notably accessible transit systems:

- Tokyo's transit system has large tactile maps on the walls in the train stations, and braille information about platform locations and trains mounted on the handrails of the stairs. Directional tactile tiles are on the floors of the stations, and outside on the streets, railings or grooves identify the walking area.

- New York City's Penn Station provides a braille diagram and map describing the layout of that station.

This type of braille information can also be found in other major transit stations in the United States and in other countries.

In several major U.S. cities, such as Chicago and New York, taxicabs display their company name, number, and other information in braille. Major airlines provide visually impaired passengers with safety information in braille.

Manufacturers of accessible pedestrian signals (APSs) have introduced braille street names that are placed below an arrow pointing to the identified street. This system is usually placed where there is a pedestrian button to push for street crossing and combined with a locator tone to find the button. Some APSs provide tactile graphics that explain features of the street, such as its width and the presence of median strips.

Blind theatergoers find that braille opera schedules and playbills immensely reinforce their enjoyment of these performances. Restaurant menus in braille are often a welcome complement to dining out for blind people, and at least one fast-food facility (McDonald's) has braille-embossed beverage lids to identify the type of beverage (decaffeinated, diet, and the like). Entrepreneurs now prepare fortune cookies with braille fortune messages inside and chocolate bars bearing messages such as "Happy Birthday," "Congratulations," and "Get Well." Braille-embossed items for decoration, souvenirs, and accessories are now a part of society. These may include table place-mats, ashtrays, T-shirts, mugs, key rings, and jewelry. The jewelry comes in a variety of pieces and can be custom ordered (Dunham, K. J. "Fashion: The Latest Trend in Newfangled Bangles." *Wall Street Journal* B, 1:3 (September 2, 1999): sec. B, col. 1, p. 3). On rare occasions, braille labels are found on print books and record albums. If braille is found on a print book, it is usually decorative, but it still provides information to a visually impaired person. One example is the book *Beauty for the Sighted and the Blind,* by Allen Eaton, and one such album, *Talking Book,* was recorded by Stevie Wonder. Unfortunately, the case material of compact discs does not lend itself well to brailling so such commercial labeling has not been seen in recent years.

Blind sports enthusiasts can collect braille football cards, and braille inserts are sometimes included in programs for sports events. Sports schedules are also often available in braille. Blind visitors to Disney World in Florida and Disneyland in California, will find a guidebook available in braille.

Places of worship frequently make sacred books, hymnals, and other books of worship available in braille for blind worshipers. The School of Education, University of Birmingham, England, has initiated a project constructing "Touch and Hearing Centres" in the cathedrals in many of the cities in England, including Birmingham, Exeter,

Oxford, Durham, and London. These centers include wooden models, tactile floor plans, and illustrated braille guidebooks with tactile pictures of the cathedrals labeled in braille for blind visitors to examine. The National Cathedral in Washington, D.C., offers a braille guidebook and displays a model of the cathedral labeled in braille, along with other models to illustrate its relative size, such as a bus, a 747 jet, and a football field.

Education

Some braille and other tactile items chiefly dedicated to educational pursuits may be more sophisticated than those used in daily life, such as graphic aids for mathematics, which are used to construct geometric and other mathematical figures related to basic arithmetic, algebra, geometry, and higher level mathematics. Also available to the general public are math drill cards; Brain Quest™, a line of science quiz games; braille and otherwise tactile globes; braille protractors; braille relief and outline maps; and braille geographical and anatomical atlases. Tack-Tiles™ are small building blocks much like Legos™ that are embossed with braille and corresponding print letters or numbers and are used to teach braille reading or math skills, to build objects, or as an educational game. They snap together or can be placed on a slate board.

Tactile Access to Education for Visually Impaired Students, a service at Purdue University in Indiana, produces braille and other tactile materials for blind students. The program creates tactile diagrams and provides access to visual information in college-level science textbooks. Braille provides the user, particularly in educational endeavors, with greater control over the material and allows easier scanning, reviewing, and formatting of information. Developing technology has assisted tremendously in making braille material more readily available and more easily stored and retrieved. Consequently, braille text material, including standardized tests at all levels, is more readily found in academic settings. In addition, commercially available print/braille preschool books make learning and leisure activities more constructive and enjoyable for young blind children.

Government and Public Facilities

Today, as blind persons visit public facilities such as office buildings, hospitals, and hotels, they are likely to encounter braille elevator panels, braille room door plates, and tactile directories. These and other similar features enhance accessibility to public facilities for blind people. In the United States and abroad, laws, such as the Americans with Disabilities Act (ADA), have mandated this signage in most public buildings. However, many facilities have gone beyond braille signage and provide building maps, models, and directories.

Another example is the use of tactile floor plans with braille text and raised symbols for emergency evacuation, which are available in many public buildings.

Many state and national capitol buildings have braille and other tactile materials available that include braille descriptions of the buildings, raised illustrations, and models. The United States Capitol, in Washington, D.C., offers these resources, and other national landmarks in Washington also include various kinds of tactile information. Another way for blind people to get to know the national landmarks is at the National Building Museum, which hosts a hands-on permanent exhibit titled "Washington: Symbol and City," featuring tactile models of the White House, the Capitol, the Lincoln Memorial, and the Washington Monument. Braille descriptions accompany the models.

The following is a sampling of state buildings with similar tactile information:

- The Texas state capitol and other Texas state landmarks, such as the Alamo and the Lyndon Baines Johnson Memorial Library and Museum.

- The Louisiana state capitol, which provides braille descriptions of a folklife exhibit on display in the building.

- The California state capitol, which offers a directory in braille of all the state legislators as well as the standard braille signage.

This kind of information exists in many forms in many other states and foreign countries as well. The Czech Republic, for example, has prepared a book of tactile symbols and braille text describing such national treasures as the flag, the Republic's coat of arms, the Saint Wenceslaus Crown, and the Coronation Cross.

Museums and Aquariums

Museum administrators have shown commitment and creativity in helping visually impaired people experience museum treasures since before the turn of the century. The International Council of Museums (ICOM) has for many years promoted opening up museums to an ever-wider public. In 1977, the ICOM gave strong support for initiatives in favor of disabled people and recommended that museums take active steps to ensure maximum accessibility and to expand adaptive programs.

In 1986 the Institute of Museum Services (IMS) and the National Endowment for the Arts (NEA) in the United States agreed to work together to advance the Federal agencies' common goal—to encourage and assists museums in making their collections and activities available to disabled people. They assisted in composing and distributing the National Survey of Accessibility in Museums which was sent to 2,000 museums throughout the country. Results of the survey revealed a wide range of projects and resources in museums dealing with accessibility. The efforts of the groups also influenced the publication of the book, *The Accessible Museum: Model Programs of Accessibility for Disabled and Older People,* compiled by The American Association of Museums in 1992. The book exists to encourage and assist in making museum facilities and programs accessible to all.

Studies indicate that museums can be beneficial in the education of blind children and adults; tactile experiences have proven to be an important supplement to textbook and verbal instruction. The originator of the museum movement for the blind was Johann Wilhelm Klein, who, from 1804 to 1809 in Vienna, prepared a collection of teaching models. The museum he founded grew continuously until it became a museum of some 5,000 specimens devoted to all phases of the education and history of blind people. The collection was unfortunately lost in World War I.

In 1898, a museum for the blind in Steglitz, Germany, issued a catalog listing and describing the objects that were available for the teaching of blind people in that city. The Perkins School for the Blind has a museum dating back to 1881 that contains animal skeletons; stuffed skins; Indian relics; dissectible human mannequins with models of various parts of the body; detailed, to-scale, dissectible models ranging from a great temple to a skyscraper and a medieval castle; dolls from various countries; and Greek pottery. These items represent all aspects of life and nature, have appropriate braille text, and are regularly used in classroom work.

Michael Anagnus, second director of the Perkins School for the Blind, noted in 1879 that "this mode of instruction, tactual observation, is of inestimable value. It bridges over the chasm from the known to the unknown, from the concrete to the abstract, and lays a solid foundation for the mind to work upon." By 1931, thirty-nine museums in Great Britain had arranged special facilities for showing collections to blind persons for study and pleasure.

In the mid-1900s, the London Science Museum featured special exhibitions for blind adults that were displayed in a separate room for "hand-viewing" only. The models were arranged in a large room near the entrance of the museum on tables with a tactile layout of the exhibition, and braille narratives were placed by each model.

The Metropolitan Museum of Art in New York was among the first museums in the United States to offer special services and exhibits to blind and visually impaired visitors. The museum's Touch Collection, established around 1980, represents 3,000 years of art. Objects in the collection were selected from the museum's permanent collections and augmented with some casts and reproductions. Among the touchable and labeled pieces in the collection are reproductions of pre-Columbian art, classical civilizations, King Tutankhamen, American art, and medieval art. Some brochures are also available in braille.

The Smithsonian Institution in Washington, D.C., is a complex of museums that includes the National Zoological Park and two affiliate organizations, the John F. Kennedy Center for the Performing Arts and the National Gallery of Art. Each facility offers brochures and other information in braille and other tactile formats for visually impaired visitors. The various facilities also offer permanent and temporary touch exhibits, braille labeling on exhibits, braille brochures, braille guidebooks, braille programs, and even special announcements in braille. Prominent among its tactile exhibit experiences was In Touch: Printing and Writing for the Blind in the Nineteenth Century, which was presented in conjunction with an exhibit in the Hall of Printing and Graphic Arts at the National Museum of American History. An inclusive pamphlet was produced in braille to describe the items in the exhibit through text and illustrations. In addition, the museum maintains the Hands-on History Room, which presents an opportunity for visually impaired visitors to experience history in a new way and encounter numerous objects found in the environment. The chance to climb on a highwheeler and pedal, send a message by telegraph, or gin cotton on an old cotton gin are just some of the ways to get your hands on history in this tactually accessible experience.

The Philadelphia Museum of Art offers guided Touch Tours of the museum's permanent collection, its Rodin Museum, and selected historic houses. The museum also offers a studio program called Form-in-Art, which is a class that combines sculpture and art history for blind and visually impaired residents of the area. It is a three-year course, with twelve-week semesters. The museum supplies all materials in accessible formats, and an exhibit of the students' work is held at the museum as well as at sites throughout Philadelphia each year of the class. Some students become professional artists, and their work is shown in galleries nationwide. For several years, this museum has exchanged ideas and resources on art education for blind people with the Gallery Tom in Tokyo, which has exhibited works by the Philadelphia students.

In the mid-sixties, the Mary Duke Biddle Gallery for the Blind opened in the North Carolina Museum of Art in Raleigh, North Carolina. This gallery aspires to integrate art into human life, making it a teacher of all human life and history. It was designed to present great works of art to blind individuals in a way they could appreciate it—by touch—and to enhance their appreciation of art and humanity and broaden their knowledge and sense of human history. The collections contain original sculpture, such as Bourdelle's Mask of Beethoven; African masks, instruments, utensils, and figures; Renoir's Head of Venus; Houdon's bust of George Washington; and the Head of Janus from around 400 BC. The exhibit covers pieces from the Stone Age, the Greek epoch, the Gothic era, and the Renaissance through the modern age. The gallery provides braille instructions on how to explore and use it independently, a relief map of the gallery's layout, braille labels, and a braille catalog. Both sighted and blind persons are encouraged to visit the gallery.

The Hall of Ideas at the Midland Center for the Arts in Midland, Michigan, is a four-level hands-on science, art, and history museum committed to being accessible to everyone. All permanent exhibits are labeled in braille. Other tactile devices for the visually impaired include braille maps and notebooks of text giving descriptions of the collections. The first exhibit the museum offered with braille labels was called Tough First and consisted of soapstone sculptures created by a group of children at the Art Education Camp for Visually Impaired Children.

Museums in almost every major city have provided some tactile and braille exhibit materials. The following is a small sampling of these museums:

- The National Gallery of Art in Ottawa, Canada, which has a tactile art program.

- An exhibition of Sculpture for the Sighted and Blind called "Dimension" is part of a touring Art Gallery for the Sighted and Blind sponsored by the California Arts Commission. It has visited San Francisco, Los Angeles, Sacramento, San Diego, Fresno, and Long Beach.

- The Nordisk Museet in Stockholm, which has a tactile exhibit on the works of painter Carl Larsson.

- The Flint (Michigan) Museum of Arts, invites visitors to reach out and touch through its Access to Art: All Creatures Great and Small, a special exhibit that features folk art carvings and life-like animal sculptures. Some of the works in this exhibit feature simulations of the real animal's texture, such as the soft wooliness of a ram or the bristly hair of a wild boar, and each carving or sculpture is accompanied by descriptions in large print and braille.

There are other special museums for the visually impaired, such as the Gloria Barron Touch Museum at the Colorado School for the Deaf and Blind, in Colorado Springs which contains more than 150 mammals, birds, and reptiles prepared and mounted by taxidermists and categorized by ecosystem. Other artifacts labeled in braille in the museum's collection are fossils, crystals, rocks, and other minerals; reproductions of period clothing and historic statuary; and models, such as the Statue of Liberty, the Taj Mahal, and the cliff dweller ruins. The collection provides visually impaired students and adults with the opportunity to handle these items, thus learning more exact information, such as size in some cases, shape, and texture. The museum is frequently used for classroom activities, and public school groups of sighted students also visit. The Touch Museum was inspired by benefactor Gloria Barron and a visually impaired teacher at the Colorado School for the Deaf and Blind, Bambi Venetucci, and established in the mid-1970s. Other such museums have been established in France, Austria, Germany, England, and Japan.

Aquariums also offer tactile and braille information to blind visitors. The National Aquarium in Baltimore, Maryland, offers a braille script of the aquarium tour; and a "touch bag," which contains smaller bags of tactile items pertaining to each exhibit, may be borrowed by blind and visually impaired visitors.

The New England Aquarium in Boston, Massachusetts, houses a touch tank and includes some braille labeling for its exhibits. The Shedd Aquarium in Chicago, Illinois has raised thermoform (tactile) fish pictures with braille worksheets and braille labeling. The aquarium also has a Touch Cart which contains dried animal parts, freshly thawed fish and squid and hermit crabs and more.

These and many other museum and aquarium facilities present braille or other tactile information for visually impaired people. New ways to make these facilities accessible to all are continually being discovered.

Monuments, Parks, and Gardens

Monuments and landmarks in the United States and in other countries often include braille descriptions and booklets with raised diagrams. The following examples represent a very small sampling of these landmarks:

- The Franklin Delano Roosevelt Memorial in Washington, D.C., has several braille plaques, some ornamental braille signage, and several touchable objects.

- Mount Rushmore National Monument in Keystone, South Dakota, includes a braille brochure and map.

- Drayton Hall in Charleston, South Carolina, is a national historic landmark that has remained virtually in its original condition—it has no electricity, running water, central heating, or air conditioning, and some walls are still covered by the original paint. It is not a typical museum, and it has no furniture, no exhibits, no signage. Its architecture and landscape are used to shed light on the history and culture of the area, and visitors learn by hearing this interpretation. Because of the way it is set up, visually impaired visitors can learn and can also explore a model of the house, where there are some features they can touch.

For the convenience of blind visitors, many zoos offer braille maps, brochures, and plaques identifying the various animals and exhibitions. These zoos include the following popular ones:

- Chicago Zoological Park

- National Zoological Park in Washington, D.C.

- San Diego Zoo in California

- Bronx Zoo in New York

- London Zoo

Botanical gardens, sensory gardens, and nature trails bearing braille information and fragrances, textures, and statuary are routinely available to visually impaired people. It is difficult to select specific ones to mention because they are so numerous. Each has generally the same kind of braille and other tactile information, but each has a unique approach:

The Oklahoma Library for the Blind and Physically Handicapped has created a sensory garden on its grounds called The Hill. The garden contains fragrant and textured plants, braille directional map and signs, and statuary with braille labels.

The Canadian National Institute for the Blind in Toronto has a sensory garden created and designed by several garden clubs. In addition to its accessibility to visually impaired people, ceremonial activities are held in the garden.

Israel has three botanical gardens for blind people.

The Maryland School for the Blind has just opened a sensory garden that was designed by staff from the school's recreation department and volunteers, including students of the University of Maryland. In addition to the plants and trees already growing, the students are encouraged to select and plant their own plants.

St. Louis Botanical Gardens in Missouri.

Lake County Parks in Florida.

Lancaster County Park in Pennsylvania.

Full Inclusion in the Workplace

Braille and other tactile resources have expanded notably over the past two or three decades, from a few braille books and work manuals to an abundance of workplace resources. The increase of resources is significant, and blind persons in the workplace are benefiting.

Workplace accommodations include braille memorandums, announcements, and other office reading material. Braille business cards and tactile money identifiers have also made an appearance in the workplace. And braille/print keyboard labels for computer keys and musical instruments, while small, are prominent aids that may be used in almost all life activities. The sustained increase in availability of these braille and other tactile materials in this century is due in some measure to the passage of the Americans with Disabilities Act of 1990 and Section 504 of the Rehabilitation Act of 1973. However, the advancement in technology is another factor that cannot be underestimated. Although the quantity of braille in the environment is not excessive, its widespread presence in every aspect of life is astounding and profound. Blind people have sought over the past century and a half to assimilate to their environment—to learn, to enjoy themselves, and to work with their communities—and it is the presence of braille and other tactile information in the general environment that is making that possible.

References

Dunham, K. J. "Fashion: The Latest Trend in Newfangled Bangles." *Wall Street Journal* B, 1:3 (September 2, 1999): sec. B, col. 1, p. 3.

COMPUTER
ACCESS WITH
BRAILLE

by Curtis Chong

A blind person uses braille to access the computer in very much the same way a sighted person uses print. For example, braille is either embossed (printed) on paper or displayed using refreshable braille, which can be likened to the information that is displayed on a computer monitor. Paper or hard-copy braille from a computer is analogous to paper or hard-copy print.

Computer Access with Hard-Copy Braille

Information stored in a computer, whether it is the source code of a computer program or the contents of a text file, can be converted into hard-copy braille using a braille embosser, which serves the same purpose as a printer. The braille embosser is a device designed to receive electronic information from the computer and convert it into braille dots embossed on paper. Braille embossers receive information through either a parallel or a serial interface. The parallel interface is typically used by computers to communicate with printers; the term parallel is derived from the fact that the electronic bits which constitute each character are sent to the printer side by side or in parallel. The serial interface has traditionally been used to connect the computer to a modem; the term serial comes from the fact that the electronic bits of each character are transmitted one after the other or serially. Some braille embossers can also produce simplified tactile line drawings if you have the proper software running on your computer. Integrating embossers with graphically oriented software, however, is still not as simple as installing a printer driver into Windows and telling your drawing program to print. So, as a rule, embossers today are used for the purpose of brailling text.

In a cooperative venture during the early 1960s, the IBM Corporation and the American Printing House for the Blind (APH) developed the software and hardware necessary to emboss braille from data stored on an IBM mainframe. At the same time, it was discovered that a piece of elastic taped across the hammers of a commercial impact printer could be used to produce braille dots of a sort; this, combined with a program on the mainframe to convert text into a combination of periods printed in a braille cell pattern, made it possible for blind computer programmers to read the source code without sighted assistance. During the late 1960s and early 1970s, therefore, hard-copy braille was a principal means for blind people to extract information from the computer without assistance from sighted people. Refreshable braille displays and speech synthesizers had not been developed yet.

In those early days, whether a blind person was using the software and hardware from IBM or the crude but effective system involving the elastic, the information flowed from the computer in a "batch" mode, which means the computer would be asked to braille the files, and, ultimately, a braille listing would be generated. In other words, the information flowed in one direction—from the computer to the computer programmer—and there was no conversation or interaction between the programmer and the system. For example, the operator could not sit down at the keyboard and type a command such as "list * 2" and have the following result brailled immediately:

10 MOVE LAST – ENTERED – DATE TO REPORT – FIELD ONE.

20 PRINT REPORT-LINE.

The ability to interact (carry on a conversation) with a computer using hard-copy braille came in the early 1970s when the Triformation Company marketed a device that generated braille on a paper tape. This, combined with a keyboard, could be used by a blind person to interact with a mainframe computer; the blind person would type a command such as "TIME" and the braille paper tape writer would print out the results of those commands:

TIME—16:21:55 CPU-UTILIZATION-00:01:00].

The problem with the paper tape embossers was that it was incredibly difficult to receive vast quantities of information from the computer in a way which was convenient for storage. Blind programmers quickly discovered that storing an entire program on paper tape was not a convenient way to learn how the program worked. More often than not the rolls of paper tape quickly fell apart, and what was left was a disorganized mess. Nevertheless, paper tape braille embossers were extremely useful when conversations with the computer were concise.

Ultimately, when a braille embosser capable of printing on whole sheets of paper became available (some time around the mid- to late 1970s), the use of braille paper tape as a means of receiving data from the computer was virtually eliminated. The use of braille embossers to communicate with mainframe computers remained viable until the proliferation, in the mid 1980s, of synthetic speech, personal computers, and screen-access technology for the blind. The popularity of these devices, combined with improvements in refreshable braille technology, removed the embosser as the principal tool for computer access, although it remains a necessary device that provides braille on demand. So while computer access with hard-copy braille is indeed possible today, it is by no means the preferred way to communicate in a conversational way with computers. While hard-copy braille technology continues to provide valuable access to documents and other information stored in electronic form, it has largely been supplanted by synthetic speech and refreshable braille as a means of interacting with computer systems.

Computer Access Using Refreshable Braille

True interactive access to the computer using braille became possible with the invention of the refreshable braille display, which seems to have made its first appearance in the late 1970s A typical refreshable braille display consists of twenty, forty, sixty, or more braille cells with dots that appear and disappear almost instantaneously. The braille cells are arranged in a single line that blind people can read as they would read a line of hard-copy braille. Just as characters and images on the sighted person's screen appear and disappear, so can the characters on a refreshable braille display, hence the term "refreshable." Unlike the video monitor, which is capable of displaying pictures as well as text, a refreshable braille display shows only braille text. It is not possible using such a display to show drawings and other nontextual representations.

The braille displays on the market today can present information only one line at a time. Some displays have additional braille cells that are used to convey status information (for example, whether the text on the display represents all or a part of the line of data on the screen). Braille displays are typically equipped with navigational controls that provide a way to move the braille view up, down, to the left, or to the right. Some displays have cursor routing buttons, which, when pressed, move the system cursor (or insertion caret) to the braille cell being read. Some displays have controls that can be programmed by screen-access technology to accomplish some functions that are otherwise executed from the keyboard.

Early versions of refreshable braille displays used individual solenoids (electromagnetically activated plungers) to raise and lower each braille dot in a cell. The solenoids had to be extremely small and were quite costly. Ultimately, piezoelectric crystals (crystals that move when an electric current is applied) have become the mainstay technology used in refreshable braille displays. Although refreshable braille cells based on this technology are less costly than cells using individual solenoids, the price to manufacture each cell is sufficiently high to discourage their use by individuals who have to pay for them with personal funds.

Despite the relatively high cost of these displays (approximately three thousand four hundred to fifteen thousand dollars, depending on the number of braille cells), refreshable braille displays are essential for certain tasks and activities, such as the following:

- They provide quick and efficient access to information containing strings of text that would be mispronounced by synthetic speech systems.

- They provide a way for a good braille reader literally to feel the information being studied.

- They lend themselves very well to detailed examination of data—as in the proofreading of documents.

- They are often the best choice in employment situations, where information has to be provided to a customer in a matter of a few seconds. In this case, the display's relatively high cost can be justified in light of the greater efficiency and productivity that immediate access to braille information brings to the job.

The International Braille and Technology Center for the Blind

Braille displays today are generally used with programs running under the Windows operating system. In this environment, braille displays require a specific display model that is supported by the screen-access program that the blind person must use to run Windows-based applications. Some screen-access programs for Windows have built-in support for specific braille display models. Others have no support at all. It is important, therefore, to learn early on if a braille display will be needed for a specific application, because that will determine what screen-access program is purchased. The best possible course of action one can take before purchasing a refreshable braille display is to check with a reliable and objective source of information. One such source is the International Braille and Technology Center for the Blind (IBTC), operated by the National Federation of the Blind (NFB).

Established in the fall of 1990, on the fiftieth anniversary of the founding of the NFB, the IBTC represents a unique resource for blind people throughout the world. It is located at the National Center for the Blind, 1800 Johnson Street, Baltimore, Maryland 21230 (telephone: (410) 659-9314). The IBTC serves as a nerve center and laboratory to stimulate the use and development of technology for blind people, facilitates comparative evaluation of state-of-the-art technological devices, provides a test site for innovative techniques, and functions as a hands-on training center for individuals and other interested persons and groups.

The IBTC houses a continually changing collection of hardware and software worth more than two million dollars. In addition to hard-copy braille embossers, braille note takers, and refreshable braille displays, the IBTC has an extensive selection of braille translation programs (software that converts print into grade 2 braille), speech synthesizers, audible screen-review programs, reading machines (devices that scan a printed page and translate text into spoken words), scanners, optical character recognition systems, raised-line drawing equipment, and much more.

Computer-controlled braille embossers and refreshable braille displays represent a significant portion of the IBTC's holdings. The IBTC also has all the known English-speaking screen-access programs for Microsoft Windows, as well as some for other operating systems. IBTC staff routinely evaluate these programs. One of the key factors the staff evaluates is the ability of screen-access programs to work with refreshable braille displays. The following are among the many questions answered by the IBTC staff:

- Which screen-access programs support cursor routing (the ability to move the system cursor or insertion caret to a position corresponding to a specific cell in the braille display)?

- Which screen-access programs convert information on the screen into grade 2 braille before sending it to the braille display?

- Which screen-access programs are particularly useful for deaf-blind individuals and others who rely exclusively on the braille display for their computer access?

- How do the screen-access programs facilitate control of application programs from function keys on the braille display?

- The IBTC also publishes a Computer Resource List, a document containing information about all manner of blindness-specific technology. This document is available on request from the IBTC or on the World Wide Web at http://www.nfb.org.

The Code That Makes It All Possible

Braille embossers and displays operating in the United States adhere to a de facto standard variously referred to as the North American ASCII Braille Code, the US-ASCII Braille Code, or the MIT Braille Code. Lay persons often refer to the code simply as computer braille, which should not be confused with the official Computer Braille Code, used to reproduce computer notation in braille computer textbooks and other publications.

Whatever the code is called, it represents the foundation upon which all braille embossers and displays in the United States operate. Essentially, ASCII (electronically coded text) characters are paired with a braille dot pattern that is more or less related in meaning to the character. For example, the ASCII character X (or x) is paired with the braille dot combination 1-3-4-6, which is the braille letter x (not X). Other letters of the alphabet are treated similarly—that is, the ASCII characters A through Z, regardless of the case, are paired with the dot patterns that correspond to the lowercase letters of the alphabet in braille.

An understanding of this code is important if you are using braille to read information stored in a computer—particularly if that information has not been translated into grade 2 braille. Fortunately, the number of dot combinations to remember is relatively small (see Appendix).

Eight-Dot Braille

When reading certain kinds of information stored in a computer (e.g., the text of a computer program or the unmodified text of a document before conversion to grade 2 braille), it is often the case that there is a one-to-one correspondence between each character and its braille representation. Sometimes, though, it is highly desirable to know if the character being displayed is written in uppercase or whether there is a cursor under the character when it is displayed on the computer screen.

Figure 1. The typical braille cell, consisting of six dots.

```
1 * * 4
2 * * 5
3 * * 6
```

A refreshable braille cell, using eight dots.

```
1 * * 4
2 * * 5
3 * * 6
7 * * 8
```

Refreshable braille displays and braille embossers, on the other hand, have the ability to generate braille using eight dots, as shown in Figure 1. Dots seven and eight, singly or in combination, are used to provide information about the character being displayed that cannot otherwise be displayed with the normal six dots. For example, it is a fairly common practice to raise dot seven on a refreshable braille display to show that a letter is capitalized and to raise dots seven and eight to indicate that the character is highlighted. Sometimes, in order to indicate the presence of the cursor, dots seven and eight are raised and lowered together, once every few seconds.

Although braille embossers can be configured to produce eight-dot braille, the common practice is to use six-dot braille, on the theory that embossing will be done using the grade 2 literary braille code in most situations.

The High Cost of Refreshable Braille Displays

Braille displays are very costly compared with speech output. Whereas a speech synthesizer can cost as little as three hundred dollars (software synthesizers are half as much), a small braille display with eighteen cells can cost as much as three thousand four hundred dollars. Most computer users will need a braille display with at least forty braille cells, which will cost just under five thousand dollars.

Clearly, a braille display is not something that an individual computer user will choose to purchase at the drop of a hat. Although good braille readers might prefer communicating with the computer using a refreshable braille display, they most often compromise and acquire speech output instead—strictly because of cost. Attempts have been made to construct refreshable braille displays that are less expensive than the current piezoelectrically driven technology. Braille displays using memory metal and pneumatic air pressure have been tried, and some thought has been given to using electricity to generate virtual braille dots. None of these alternative approaches, however, has yet resulted in a commercially viable product.

So unless somebody comes up with a radically innovative idea, refreshable braille displays as a way to talk with the computer will continue to be highly priced, highly prized, and used only when absolutely necessary.

Suppliers of Refreshable Braille Displays in the United States

In the United States, refreshable braille displays and devices equipped with refreshable braille output can be obtained from the following companies:

Alva Access Group, Inc.
5801 Christie Avenue
Suite 475
Emeryville, CA 94608
Telephone: (510) 923-6280
World Wide Web: http://www.aagi.com

Blazie Engineering
109 East Jarrettsville Road
Forest Hill, MD 21050
Telephone: (410) 893-9333
World Wide Web: http://www.blazie.com

HumanWare, Inc.
6245 King Road
Loomis, CA 95650
Telephone: (916) 652-7253 or (800) 722-3393
World Wide Web: http://www.humanware.com

Sighted Electronics
464 Tappan Road
Northvale, NJ 07647
Telephone: (201) 767-3977
World Wide Web: http://www.sighted.com

REFRESHABLE BRAILLE DISPLAYS: THEIR ORIGINS AND EVOLUTION

by Judith M. Dixon

Introduction

Refreshable braille displays provide braille access to the information on a computer screen by converting standard ASCII text (electronically coded text) into braille characters. In response to output from the computer, braille is produced on the display by pins that are raised and lowered (refreshed) in combinations that form braille characters.

All refreshable braille displays available in the United States today can show only one line of braille at a time and are commonly available in twenty-, forty-, or eighty-character braille-cell configurations of six or eight dots. Some displays are portable and battery powered, while others are larger desktop units that typically sit under the computer keyboard (McNulty and Suvino 1993; Bower et al. 1997).

When used with screen-access programs, braille displays allow blind users to access any portion of the computer's screen. For a good braille reader, the use of a braille display can offer many benefits over other access modalities. A braille display allows the user to move quickly from one point on the screen to another; to skip large blank spaces easily; to "watch" an item on the screen change rather than having to query the screen for the latest update; to read at a personal, often variable, rate; to discern many specifics about the text, such as spelling, punctuation, and format; and to be keenly aware of items on the screen and their relative position to one another.

Braille output via a refreshable braille display has both a hardware and a software component. For more than thirty years, researchers and developers have focused their attention on the hardware that produces the braille—the braille display itself. Because of their relative expense—from three thousand four hundred to fifteen thousand dollars—efforts have centered on designing lower-cost cells that are both reliable and efficient in their use of power. To date, however, that effort continues.

The software component of refreshable braille displays, on the other hand, has steadily matured. In order for the display to function, a screen-reading software program must be running and sending information to the braille display. Early braille- display software programs provided few features, but more and more sophisticated software programs have evolved through the years. Today it is common for the programs to enable the user to view various forms of screen highlighting; direct the display to a variety of screen locations (a fixed position, a position relative to the cursor or other screen element, or a user-definable screen location); split the display to show several screen locations on one line; and, of course, provide output for Windows and other graphically based environments.

Eight-Dot Braille

Before going to a thorough review of hardware developments, a brief review of the braille cell as it is displayed seems in order. Because it is necessary for the braille display to accurately represent what is being shown on the computer's screen, the displayed text is usually in uncontracted braille and written in what is called "ASCII braille." This one-for-one code (that is, one ASCII character to one braille character) forms the basis for the Computer Braille Code (CBC) defined by the Braille Authority of North America (BANA). In general, CBC differs from ASCII braille primarily in that CBC uses dots four, five, and six of the braille cell as a prefix to other characters rather than simply to indicate underscoring, as it does in ASCII braille. The ASCII braille code was developed in the 1960s at the Massachusetts Institute of Technology (MIT) so that computer-generated symbols, such as the backslash or vertical bar, that are not normally found in braille could be represented.

Because even simple print text uses more characters than can be represented with the traditional six-dot braille cell, braille displays often have eight dots per cell and use a special eight-dot braille code instead of the usual six-dot code. When only six dots are in use, the ASCII values between 96 and 127 (lowercase letters and a few punctuation marks) are mapped to the corresponding symbols between 64 and 95 (uppercase letters and a few more punctuation marks), making upper- and lowercase letters and several pairs of punctuation marks indistinguishable. When eight dots are available, combinations of dots seven and eight provide a braille symbol for all ASCII values from zero to 255. In this way, additional cells are not needed to represent uppercase letters and the full array of punctuation marks and ASCII symbols that are not usually representable in braille. The uppercase letters retain the essential nature of their original form and are structured, for most displays, with an additional dot at the bottom of the cell.

In addition, depending on the driving software's capability, the presence of the additional two dots per cell allows the display to show highlighted or otherwise enhanced items. This strategy generally works well because it does not require the user to learn a completely new braille code. There is, however, no standard for eight-dot braille in the United States.

Recent advances in computer technology may negate the need for an eight-dot braille standard. Eight-dot braille developed because it could provide a one-to-one representation of the computer world as viewed on a screen, particularly in the 1980s and early 1990s, as refreshable braille devices became common in the professional world. But the computer world that was being modeled by eight-dot braille devices was itself characterized by a regular grid of eight-bit characters on a screen or printer, where the characters were evenly spaced on evenly spaced lines. Once the eight-dot braille symbols were mastered, the user could deal with a full eight-bit character set, including spacial formatting, through the braille display.

Currently, the development of proportional fonts, the graphical user interface, and numerous character sets that are not limited to eight bits means that much of the benefit of the eight-dot braille concept has been lost. It is conceivable that braille displays of the future may return to the use of six-dot cells, reducing cost and complexity.

Early Efforts

Efforts to present braille in a mechanical display were reported as early as the 1960s. These devices were mostly solenoid-driven—that is, an electromagnetic coil of wire (a solenoid) around a tiny rod of iron. When an electrical current is passed through the coil, it creates a magnetic field that forces the rod to push or pull an actuator to raise and lower the pins of a braille cell. Pins were latched in the up position so no power was needed to keep them raised. A major disadvantage of this technology, besides the expense, was that the user could not touch the pin while it was refreshing or it would not latch.

As early as 1966, Argonne National Laboratory described a "braille reading machine" in an article in Science magazine (Grunwald 1966). A patent application for the device was filed in 1969, and the first prototype was completed that same year. In 1971, the construction of thirty machines was authorized, but these were not delivered until late 1975.

In the Argonne Reading Machine, miniature solenoids embossed characters onto a "reading belt," a plastic belt that had bubbles molded into its surface. The bubbles were stable in their up or down position. The speed of playback could be controlled by the user or set at a fixed rate, with the maximum speed being twenty-two characters per second. The braille reading material was stored on magnetic tape, similar to that used by a tape recorder. The machine also included a braille keyboard that allowed users to input text. The machine was extensively tested, primarily in educational institutions. While test results were moderately favorable, it was not pursued (Grunwald 1977).

In 1974, Dalrymple described an effort to develop a four-dot solenoid-driven display for presenting numbers. Its application was to help a blind broadcaster access an electronic voltage meter. In 1977, Dalrymple reported on another solenoid-driven braille display that was specifically developed for a vocational application. This one was a twelve-cell display with numerous built-in functions, and it allowed a blind person to perform the functions of a telephone operator.

In the late 1970s, a company in the United Kingdom, Clarke and Smith Manufacturing Company Ltd., produced a commercially viable device called the Braillink. It was a self-contained, portable device that stored information on microcassette, with forty-eight solenoid-driven cells and both braille and alphanumeric keyboards.

The Next Generation

Efforts to develop a better braille display proliferated in the late 1970s and early 1980s. At first these were tape-based devices, but they were quickly replaced by devices with floppy-disk storage and, soon after, devices that connected directly to a computer.

A number of braille displays came onto the market in the United States at more or less the same time—Elinfa's Digicassette and Telesensory's VersaBraille generated enormous enthusiasm among both professionals in libraries for blind people and the consumers themselves. The primary reason for this sudden proliferation was the use of the piezoelectric braille cell.

A piezoelectric braille cell uses a piezocrystal, which changes its shape when electrical voltage is applied to its opposite faces. As the crystal bends upward or downward, the pin is raised or lowered. The force applied by the piezocrystal can reliably withstand the weight of a finger, so the dots can be read while they are refreshing. When the voltage is stopped, the strip returns to its normal shape and the pin is no longer raised. The advantages of a piezocrystal are low power consumption and low noise emission, which make it a very suitable technology for this purpose (Weber 1994).

Hinton (1992) suggested that five factors have led to the dominance of piezoelectric displays:

1. Very low power requirements (piezoelectric cells lock themselves, requiring no power to maintain their position except to cancel leakage currents, and they can be used with a battery).

2. Few moving parts (just benders and pin, no friction-based locking mechanism).

3. Fast display updates, because they are energy-efficient.

4. Low noise output.

5. Close packing of dots.

Between 1978 and 1981, the National Library Service for the Blind and Physically Handicapped of the Library of Congress (NLS) conducted a full-scale test of braille display technology as a possible way to distribute braille reading materials. It purchased fifty Telesensory VersaBrailles and fifty Elinfa Digicassettes and distributed them to braille readers in five cities who volunteered to participate in the study. Five popular magazines were placed on cassette in formats suitable for each machine. While 72 percent of the users found the technology to be acceptable, cassette braille technology was ultimately not pursued as a reading medium because of inadequate display design, poor display reliability, and relatively high display cost (VSE Corporation 1981).

By 1983, refreshable braille displays had reached a point where they were being tested in schools. Doorlag and Doorlag (1983) tested students in the San Diego Unified School District on their use of "cassette braille" and compared reading speed between refreshable braille and paper braille. They found that the majority of students in their tests were able to achieve slightly higher reading speeds with the refreshable braille device than with paper braille.

In 1984, Goodrich reported that refreshable braille appeared to be the most effective means for blind persons to gain access to computers, but that the devices "have not yet reached their potential." He suggested that their limitations were the slow storage and retrieval rates on devices using tape cassettes, the offer of only a single-line display, the need for multiple keystrokes to review information, the need to take one's hand off the keyboard to read, the difficulty of converting between grades of braille, and the inability to deal effectively with graphic and some tabular materials. The benefits, he said, were the quick reading of information, the immediate feedback of text entered or modified, the portability, the minimal reading of unwanted material, and the fact that it could be used by deaf-blind persons. He posited that full-page displays were at least two to three years in the future.

The Pursuit of a Full-Page Display

Interest in a larger, full-page display was evident early in the evolution of braille display technology. Users and manufacturers have generally agreed that for devices intended as reading machines, larger displays are needed. But many factors—size, weight, power, reliability, and cost—have caused such a development to be a daunting prospect. The full-page display would need to provide efficient navigational strategies and very quick display updates, and would have to be small and light enough to move, reasonably low in cost, and extremely reliable.

Many manufacturers believed that a full-page display would not only facilitate the reading of text material but could also permit the display of graphics. An early example of this effort was the Rose Reader. While this device never got beyond the prototype stage, its developer, Leonard Rose (1979), endeavored to create a full-page display designed for the purpose of reading text. The idea was that books could be distributed on cassette tape, eliminating the expense of embossing paper braille.

The Rose Reader used bimetallic strips, which bend when heated, to produce braille dots. The shaft of each braille dot had a grooved ring around it; the shaft would be pushed up by a spring, but a hook on the end of the bimetallic strip caught the groove around the ring and restrained the dot. When heat bent the bimetallic strip away from the ring, the spring raised the dot. But this technology was slow, raising only two hundred dots per second, which meant that an average braille page took about ten seconds to refresh.

The Rose Reader was patented in 1981. Thermostatic metals used in the device were less expensive than piezo-electric elements and could be designed in modular units for easier repair. The number of moving parts per dot, the direct use of heat and friction, and the use of a mechanical reset mechanism, however, all caused reliability problems.

In the early 1980s, the American Foundation for the Blind (AFB) in New York developed a prototype braille display that was also capable of displaying tactile graphics (Random Access 1985). This device was developed by Doug Maure with a grant from the National Science Foundation and consisted of a sixty-by-sixty square matrix of pins. The pins were driven by bimetallic strips as in the Rose Reader. With interlocking latch and lift bars, pins were raised and locked. The design was modular, with the idea that larger displays could be assembled from smaller sections. Dots were evenly spaced to enable the display of tactile graphics, but this made the correct display of traditional braille cells impossible. The advantages of this development were that the pins were latched into position so the power consumption was moderately low; but again, the refresh rate was very slow, and the system was expensive.

As larger displays were attempted, reliability became a greater problem. Hinton (1992) pointed out that if every dot in an eight-dot, eighty-character braille display (480 dots) worked 99 percent of the time, the display would be error-free only once in 125 displays. If the dots were 99.99-percent reliable, the eighty eight-dot cells would be error-free only 95 percent of the time, and the full-page display would be error-free only 55 percent of the time. At 99.9999-percent reliability, the one-line display would have an error every two thousand lines, but a full-page display would still have an error once in every 165 displays. The conclusion was that moving parts tend to make a display unreliable.

Virtual Displays

By the mid-1980s, there was still strong interest in a full-page braille display, but attempts by several developers to create a device with numerous rows and columns were meeting with little success. These devices were all proving to be extremely expensive, unreliable, and time-consuming to refresh. Researchers observed, however, that any cell that was not directly under the fingertip was not actually being used. So rather than have a large quantity of cells, they reasoned, why not allow manipulation of a small quantity of cells to simulate a full page of cells?

Several approaches have been attempted for simulating a full page of braille in a virtual—a sort of implied—manner. A virtual braille display can use only one braille cell in combination with a traditional pointing device, such as a mouse with one braille cell built into it. Another approach for a virtual braille display is to put one or more braille cells into a small carriage that can be moved horizontally and vertically, and, whenever it reaches a new position, would be detected by the computer and a new character displayed. Or a single-line braille display can be structured in such a way that it can physically move over the virtual page under the user's control. Many researchers believe that the movement of hands and arms in roughly the same manner as reading paper braille would be the best way to simulate the reading of a full page of braille.

In the mid-1980s, researchers at the IBM facility in Yorktown Heights, New York (Oshann 1987), developed a braille mouse that consisted of a single braille cell mounted on top of a traditional computer mouse. It refreshed itself in a static manner, one complete character at a time. The researchers found that it was not satisfactory to attach a single refreshable braille character to a computer mouse for two reasons: 1. Blind users had difficulty navigating the mouse on the screen because of the free movement allowed over the entire computer screen. 2. Blind users had difficulty reading the characters formed by multiple pins that moved vertically under one fingertip.

Lederman (1982) described the phenomenon of lateralization, or the need for the finger to be moving laterally for it to perceive surface texture. Braille dots can be thought of as surface irregularities, and thus for their pattern to be perceived accurately, the finger or the dots must be moving laterally. Lederman found that vibration of the skin, created by movement, is crucial for perceiving texture because it keeps the touch receptors from adapting to the stimulation and turning off, or not working anymore, which they do very quickly with no movement. Craig and Sherrick (1982) reviewed a considerable body of research on moving versus static displays (when all the elements are turned on and off together) and affirmed that subjects were better able to recognize elements when the finger or the elements were moving.

The concept of the virtual full-page display was taken even further by David Johnson of TiNi Alloy Company, in San Leandro, California, in 1990. He proposed a special kind of single-character display that placed one dot under each finger. Each dot protruded through the surface of each of the eight keys on a braille keyboard. The keyboard would be moved by the user's hands so that rows and columns of text were presented. To aid in navigation, a mechanical guide would be provided so that motion in the horizontal direction (along a line) is separate from vertical motion on the virtual page. A prototype was produced and, with very limited trials, the technology showed some promise (Johnson 1990b).

Two methods of navigation on the page were proposed by Johnson. In the first method, rows and columns of text were accessed in a way that used the same arm motions employed in reading embossed paper braille, with the user's proprioceptive sense enabling movement from place to place on a virtual page of text.

In the second method, a version of the device was proposed called the "Isopoint." Positioned close to the keyboard so it could be operated with the user's thumbs, the Isopoint was a small horizontal cylinder that could be rotated to indicate vertical movement and moved along a rod to indicate horizontal movement. Its advantages over a

mouse or trackball were that it took up less room, it separated horizontal from vertical movement so that operation
by a blind person is easier, and it could easily be made to
indicate absolute instead of relative position. Johnson's first
method more nearly simulates the process of reading
embossed braille, while the Isopoint method is less tiring
to the arms and usable in portable devices.

Johnson demonstrated that providing a fixed track as
a reference line for vertical movement of a forty-column
display yielded a greatly enhanced perception of layout.
Because most users read braille sequentially with one finger, reducing the virtual screen window to a few characters
may not greatly reduce reading speed or comprehension.

Johnson also proposed a compromise device that contained a line of forty refreshable braille cells that could be
moved vertically. The proprioceptive sense of arm position
is combined with the tactile sense for character detection.
Finger motion along the display would provide tactile
input similar to that of an embossed page. The display
would provide a feel similar to a true full-page format display at a fraction of the cost.

Orloski and Gilden (1992) discussed the advantages of
electronic braille and the limitations of single-line displays.
They suggested that because the traditional single-line
display must be moved in an incremental fashion, the blind
user loses the overall feel of the screen format. Dismissing
the idea of a full-page display as prohibitively expensive,
they reviewed the idea of a virtual display. The display they
envisioned could be moved on rails, which would allow
vertical movement.

In another attempt to reduce both cost and size of a braille display, Parreno and Magallon (1994) at the Organication Nacional pro Ciegos de Espania in Madrid, Spain, developed a prototype device called the Teresa 80. Using a concept called "the sliding cell approach," the device employed one refreshable braille cell that was mounted on a rail and could be moved along the eighty positions of a DOS-based screen line. The length of the rail was short, only fifteen inches, because the prototype reduced the travel distance required for a new character to appear. But this device also refreshed its cell in a static manner under one stationary finger, so the haptic abilities of the user's tactile perception were not optimized.

A particularly interesting project is being conducted by Jeorg Fricke at the Department of Computer Science, University of Hagen in Germany (Fricke and Baehring 1994). The project is investigating the feasibility of a movable, dynamic tactile display to present information to one or several fingertips resting on the display. A prototype was developed which displayed the virtual line or plane of information read using the same perceptual and cognitive resources as with real objects, such as paper braille or tactile graphics.

The device did not have traditional braille cells; it had a regular grid of pins, four rows of eighteen pins each. The display refreshed itself in the direction of movement in a continuous manner rather than the whole cell refreshing at once, which was similar to the method used by the Optacon (Bliss et al 1970), a direct inkprint reading aid consisting of a small hand-held camera that is moved across the material to be read. The Optacon was developed by Telesensory Inc. in the early 1970s. Within the camera is an array of photosensitive elements six columns wide and twenty-four rows high; the photosensitive elements register the pattern of light and dark passing beneath the camera. The pattern is transferred to an array of vibrating, tactile pins. Moving the camera causes the pattern to move across the fingertip, similar to the method used by electric signs such as the headlines at Times Square in New York City.

Such a refresh method is consistent with what is known about the psychophysiology of touch (Craig and Sherrick 1982). There is lateralization with enhanced vibration to aid identification by the skin's ability to make fine temporal discriminations.

The latest virtual display to appear is the VirTouch, or Virtual Touch System (VTS), from VirTouch Ltd. in Israel (http://www.virtouch.co.il). It is a sophisticated mouse-like device designed for viewing graphics and text both in tactile print and braille. The VTS contains three tactile displays, each incorporating thirty-two rounded pins arranged in a four-by-eight matrix. These pins can represent computer graphics, pixel by pixel. Using three fingers, the blind user can understand the curvature and shading of scanned screen pixels presented through the structure of pin height. Each pin moves up and down on several height levels that represent four shades: white, light gray, dark gray, and black. Six buttons on the top and side of the VTS device provide user interaction with the computer through screen navigation, the sending of commands, and the changing of device settings.

While virtual braille displays may be more cost-effective, traditional displays with navigation buttons are still the norm today. To date, only the VirTouch is close to becoming a commercially viable product.

Seeking a Better Cell

By 1990, the number and variety of braille displays had matured considerably. Large desktop units, battery-powered units, some hardware-only or hardware/software combinations, and stand-alone units with displays built with note-taking capabilities were all being marketed (SAF Technology Update 1990; Sriskanthan and Subramanian 1990). But during this period, efforts to develop less expensive cells continued.

In the early 1990s, TiNi Alloy Company created a prototype display with three lines of twenty cells using a shape memory alloy. Shape memory alloys are nickel-titanium alloys that forcefully return to a preset shape when heated. The nickel-titanium alloy used in this case is called Nitinol. The pin in this prototype was pulled down when activated and would spring back up when released. Because the metal needed to be heated, the display required a considerable amount of power. To reduce power, a latch was tried to hold the pin down and allow it to spring up when released. It was the latching mechanism in such a small space that proved to be difficult (Johnson 1990a).

During this same time, Blazie Engineering did initial development work on a pneumatic display that used puffs of air to raise pins that would automatically lock themselves into the up position. The air was routed to individual pins by layers of metal with channels in them. When a column was selected, each of the eight dots in that row or column could be activated at once, which required an air valve for each row and each column. The display required larger dot spacing than standard braille, but power requirements were low.

Several efforts have examined the use of various chemicals with specific properties of expansion and contraction to form braille dots directly. MIT worked with gels that release a large portion of their liquid content when exposed to intense light. The disadvantages of this technology were that the collapsed gel had to be immersed in the liquid to reabsorb the liquid and the refresh rates were greater than one second.

In 1994, the National Aeronautics and Space Administration (NASA) did some development work with electrorheological fluids. These are fluids where the viscosity (resistance to flow) of the fluid increases in a strong electrostatic field (NASA Tech Brief 1994). Cornstarch in corn oil, zelolite in silicon oil, and aluminum dihydrotripolyphosphate in mineral oil are among the materials that exhibit this effect.

In 1997, Marvin Cowens, a polymer chemist at Texas Instruments Inc., together with Alan Gilkes and Larry Taylor, received a patent for a braille cell technology concept. Their idea consisted of a matrix of small cavities, each containing a positive and negative electrode and filled with a small quantity of polar organic gel that is responsive to electric fields. A taut film would be spread over the matrix to seal the cavities and keep each one flat. Each cavity could then individually be addressed by electronic means. When voltage was applied to the electrodes in a cavity, the gel in that cavity would expand sufficiently to raise a dimple in the elastomeric film. The cavities would be cylindrical, with metal electrodes embedded on the floor and on one side (Chartrand, Sabra. Patents: Creating Braille Electronically. *New York Times,* April 7, 1997).

The researchers anticipated that dots could be produced in the standard braille size and could be adjusted to other sizes, such as larger dots for those with less sensitive fingertips. The circuitry that delivers electricity to the gel could also cause the dots to vibrate, so letters or words could be highlighted. The computer connected to the display could detect when dots had been touched, so it would know when a word had been read or when to turn a page. The researchers created a few oversized cells to illustrate the concept, but, while this technology may have promise, the project was abandoned in 1999.

Even electrodes were briefly tried as a method to make a better braille cell. A tiny electric shock would indicate the presence of a braille dot. While such a technology had many advantages—low cost, high speed, small size, and reliability—no design was put forth that was acceptable to end users.

Why hasn't one of these ideas evolved into a product that meets the reading and working needs of blind persons? In most cases, the simple answer to that question is lack of funding. Funding has often been available for innovative research, but when additional funding has been needed for development, usability testing, and assembly, monies have not been available.

More Recent Efforts

Several additional efforts to develop better, lower cost, and more efficient braille displays are under way as of this writing. Dan Hinton of Tactilics in Arlington, Virginia, has developed prototype mechanical cells stamped from aluminum with a silicon core that holds the cells up or down; a moving carriage with a very small solenoid is used to push the pins. Further support for his effort is being sought.

Another recent effort has come from Piezo Systems, Inc., of Cambridge, Massachusetts, which attempted to use a comb-shaped structure to hold piezoelectric rods in a sheet. The idea was that it would be easier to fabricate than six or eight individual reeds for each cell that must be positioned independently. Unexpected resonances in the sheet that affect the operation of the pins has proved to be a problem.

Another effort is under way, directed by Fred Lisy of Orbital Technology in Cleveland, Ohio, using microelectromechanical technology, which is reported to be very small, require very little power, and be easily mass produced.

Conclusion

The notion of what a braille display needs to incorporate in order to be a usable, viable device has changed considerably in the past thirty years. Where once developers were attempting to create a braille reading machine, later efforts focused more on the interactive capabilities of accessing a computer screen with a braille display, allowing a blind person to work in a fluid, flexible manner in a braille medium. User requirements for a reading machine are quite different than those for an interactive display designed for the input/output needs of a work environment. Interactive user requirements include a paper-like texture, height, spacing, and firmness of the braille dots an extremely fast refresh rate of all dots simultaneously; extremely reliable braille cells; and, of course, full-featured software that allows the user flexible navigation and the ability to view all available screen attributes and characteristics.

The perfect solution to the hardware development for a braille display has probably not been found. Braille display technology has evolved to the point where it is a viable, efficient means to perform work (Leventhal, Schreier and Usland 1990). From early prototype units used to convey less structured text, such as those used for telephone operator displays or for personal note taking, braille displays have evolved into sophisticated devices allowing access to personal computers with random access to the screen, cursor-routing capabilities, and facilities for adaptation to nonstandard application programs.

But the hardware for manufacturing a cost-effective braille display continues to be the subject of research and development. The goal is to raise and lower a braille-like dot quickly and reliably. The challenge is to do this inexpensively and using very little power. Meanwhile, blind persons are able to perform real work using the available refreshable braille displays of the day.

References

Bliss, J. C., M. H. Katcher, C. H. Rogers, R. P. Shepard. 1970. "Optical-to-Tactile Image Conversion for the Blind." *IEEE Transactions on Man–Machine Systems,* Vol. MMS-11 (1), 58–65.

Bower, R., J. Kaull, N. Aheikh and G. Vanderheiden eds. 1997. "Braille and Tactile Output Systems." In *Trace Resourcebook: Assistive Technologies for Communication, Control, and Computer Access.* 1998/99 edition. Edited by R. Bower, J. Kaull, N. Aheikh and G. Vanderheiden. Madison, WI: Trace Research and Development Center.

Chartrand, Sabra. Patents: Creating Braille Electronically. *New York Times,* April 7, 1997.

Craig, J. C., and C. E. Sherrick. 1982. "Dynamic Tactile Displays." In *Tactual Perception: A Sourcebook,* edited by W. Schiff and E. Foulke. New York, Cambridge University Press.

Dalrymple, G. F. 1974. "An Electromechanical Numeric Braille Display: A Familiar Tactile Representation of Electrically Encoded Digital Signals." In *Proceedings of the 1974 Conference on Engineering Devices in Rehabilitation,* edited by R. Foulds and B. Lund. Boston, MA: New England Medical Center Hospital.

Dalrymple, G. F. 1977. "TSPS Braille Display." *Braille Research Newsletter,* (October), no. 6: 78–81.

Doorlag, D. M., and D. H. Doorlag. 1983. "Cassette Braille: A New Communication Tool for Blind People." *Journal of Visual Impairment and Blindness,* 77, April, 158–161.

Evaluation of Cassette Braille. 1981. Report prepared for the Library of Congress, National Library Service for the Blind and Physically Handicapped. Alexandria, VA: VSE Corporation.

Fricke, J., and H. Baehring. "Displaying Laterally Moving Tactile Information." In Zagler W. L., G. Busby, and R. R. Wagner, eds. 1994. *Computers for Handicapped Persons.* Proceedings of the 4th International Conference, ICCHP '94, in Vienna, Austria, September 14–16.

Gill, J. M. 1981. "Paperless Braille Devices." *Braille Research Newsletter,* (September), no. 12: 26–33.

Goodrich, G. L. 1984. "Applications of Microcomputers by Visually Impaired Persons." *Journal of Visual Impairment and Blindness* 78 (November), 9, 408-414.

Grunwald, A. P. 1966. "A Braille-Reading Machine." *Science,* 154, October 7, no. 3745, 144–146.

Grunwald, A. P. 1977. *The Argonne Braille Project.* Argonne, IL: Argonne National Laboratory.

Hinton, D. E., and C. Connolly. 1992. *Braille Devices and Techniques to Allow Media Access.* Arlington, VA: Science Applications International Corporation.

Johnson, D. 1990a. Electronic Braille Output Device Using Nitinol. Final Report, NIH SBIR Phase II Grant Number 2 R44 EY0651202.

Johnson, D. A. 1990b. Multiple Character Refreshable Braille X-Y Scanner. Final Report, NIH Grant Number 1 R43 Y0763301A1.

Lederman, S. J. 1982. "The Perception of Texture by Touch." In *Tactual Perception: A Sourcebook,* edited by W. Schiff and E. Foulke. New York, Cambridge University Press.

Leventhal, J. D., E. M. Schreier, and M. M. Uslan. 1990. "Electronic Braille Displays for Personal Computers." *Journal of Visual Impairment and Blindness* 84 (October), 8, 423–427.

McNulty, T., and D. M. Suvino. 1993. "Tactile Reading Methods and Materials." In *Access to Information: Materials, Technologies, and Services for Print-impaired Readers,* edited by T. McNulty and D. M. Suvino. LITA Monographs 2. Chicago, IL: American Library Association.

Ohsann, J. T. 1987. "New Role for 'Mice': Experimental Braille Monitor Reader Helps Blind Read PC Screens." *IBM Research Magazine* 25 (Spring) no. 1: 22.

Orlosky, S., and D. Gilden. 1992. "Simulating a Full Screen of Braille." *Journal of Microcomputer Applications* 15, 47–56.

Parreno, A., and P. J. Magallon. 1994. "Teresa 80: A Braille Line With 80 Characters in One Cell." In *Proceedings of the Ninth Annual Conference on Technology for Persons with Disabilities,* edited by H. Murphy. Los Angeles: California State University at Northridge.

Random Access. 1985. "Tactile Graphics Display Now Under Evaluation." *Journal of Visual Impairment and Blindness* 79, (March), 126.

Reconfigurable Full-Page Braille Display. 1994. NASA Tech Briefs 18 (July), no. 7: 5.

Rose, L. 1979. "Full-Page Paperless Braille Display." *Braille Research Newsletter* (July), no. 10: 59–60.

Sriskanthan, N., and K. R. Subramanian. 1990. "Braille Display Terminal for Personal Computers." *IEEE Transactions on Consumer Electronics* 36 (May), no. 2: 121–128.

Weber, G. 1994. "Braille Displays." *Information Technology and Disabilities* 1 (July), no. 3.

Widening Range of Braille Displays. 1990. *SAF Technology Update* (June), 513.

TACTILE
GRAPHICS

by Jane M. Corcoran

Sighted children are exposed from infancy to a vast array of visual graphics—picture books and signs are before them constantly. Techniques of shading and color make the transition from observing a three-dimensional object to recognizing a two-dimensional representation of that object a seamless process. When sighted children begin school, pictures are used to aid in the teaching of reading and phonics. They are shown a picture along with a word, or asked to name the sound that a pictured object starts with. Their ability to recognize the two-dimensional representation of animals and objects in their world is already highly developed.

Blind children gain knowledge of their world mainly through touch. Unless they are given detailed descriptions, they know only those objects that they have physically handled. The transition of that experience to tactile, two-dimensional representations of real-life objects is difficult indeed. Consider the objects pictured in classroom kindergarten and first grade books. Blind children are unlikely to have physically handled the variety of animals and objects seen in the counting and matching exercises in those books. They may be very familiar with the interior of their homes, but, without some explanation, a two-dimensional representation of a house showing the outlines of the building, the windows, and the doors is baffling to a blind child.

As all students go through school, they are confronted with graphics in every subject: pie graphs, bar graphs, line graphs, maps, geometric figures, electrical circuits, to name just a few. It is obvious that for blind students to learn along with sighted students, they need to become adept at reading these graphics when they are presented in tactile form. How is this to be accomplished? There are two components to the solution of this problem: teaching blind children how to read tactile graphics and producing good tactile graphics.

Teaching Blind Children How to Read Tactile Graphics

By the Parent

Blind children should be exposed very early to books containing tactiles. There are story books containing tactiles available that parents can read to their children. As they read, they can help their children understand the tactile pictures. Books of this kind for preschool children are available from Seedlings Braille Books for Children and from The American Printing House for the Blind (APH). (See List of Resources at the end of this chapter for addresses.)

A drawing board in the home makes it possible for children to make their own drawings. Parents can use the board to illustrate concepts to a child. The drawing board consists of a thin rubber sheet attached to a firm plastic or wooden board. A removable and disposable sheet of plastic can be fastened on top of the rubber sheet, and a ballpoint pen, pencil, or stylus produces a raised line when pulled across the plastic sheet. Such a drawing board is available from Howe Press. Simple tactile figures can be made by using a glue stick on paper and attaching string, felt, sandpaper, balsa, etc. Tactiles for and by children are discussed in great detail by Polly K. Edman in her book *Tactile Graphics*.

By the Teacher

There is a considerable body of research on how students read and comprehend tactile graphics. An overview of the significant research up to 1982 is summarized in *Tactual Perception, a sourcebook*. Much of the material in this book is the result of a workshop and symposium on tactual perception held at the University of Louisville, Louisville, Kentucky in 1979. In the book, there is a recommendation: "There should be formal training of visually impaired children and adults in the use of tangible graphics.... [Participants in the symposium] were concerned that little or no instruction is given in such a useful skill....There was a definite mandate favoring the development and implementation of training programs for blind students and their teachers."

Ongoing studies relating to the subject can be found in professional publications for educators such as the *Journal of Visual Impairment and Blindness.*

APH has many aids for teachers: shape boards, geographic land forms, a set of three-dimensional blocks along with flat shapes to illustrate the transition from three- to two-dimensional representation, etc. They have a program called *Tangible Graphs* for teaching a student how to read various types of graphs. It consists of a teacher's guidebook and a student book containing the tactile graphs. The teacher's guide gives instructions on how to teach the student the best way to scan lines, maps, and graphs. The *Tactile Graphics Guidebook* that comes with the Tactile Graphics Kit has a section on introducing blind students to reading tactile maps. Specific directions are given for teaching the student techniques to determine the size and extent of a display, to determine the nature of the symbols used (lines, point symbols, areal symbols), and to trace lines.

The Chang Mobility Kit from APH consists of a Velcro board with a variety of blocks and shapes backed with Velcro that attach to the board. It is useful for showing the orientation of furniture in a room, or buildings and streets in a neighborhood. It also has a manual that gives helpful instruction on teaching students to read graphics.

The above mentioned products and many others suitable for use by both parents and teachers are described in the *APH Products Catalog,* which is available from APH.

Before blind students can be expected to extract any meaningful information from maps presented in textbooks, they should be introduced to maps that relate to their everyday life. The New Mexico School for the Visually Handicapped has developed a program for their third and fourth grade students that begins with a plot of a child's room, moves then to a floor plan of a home, and then to a neighborhood with houses and streets. A program such as this ensures that the child recognizes that maps have a real purpose and may give him or her more motivation to study other tactile maps.

Production of Good Tactiles

Producing a tactile drawing involves many steps, the first of which is to determine if the inclusion of the tactile figure is necessary. Print books often include figures or pictures merely for decoration, or photographs simply to accompany incidental information given in a caption—such as an auto assembly line or a city skyline. Three critical questions to ask in determining whether a tactile drawing is necessary are:

- Does the print figure illustrate an author's concept?

- Is the reader supposed to extract some information from it?

- Is the reader to perform some operation prescribed by the text, such as measuring an angle or the length of a line?

If the answer to all of these questions is "no," then the figure should be omitted and not mentioned, or it should be described in words and its caption given if the caption contains information not included in the text. However, if the answer to any of these questions is "yes," then the tactile drawing should be produced in such a manner as to make it easy for the reader to grasp the concept, extract the information, or perform the operation.

Making a tactile drawing involves two operations: layout (design) and embossing.

Layout (Design) of the Tactile

There are many methods for obtaining an embossed figure, but the principles of layout are the same for all of them. First, it is important to remember that the pattern-resolving capability of the fingers is not as good as that of the eye. The eye can see not only all of a graph or map at a glance, but often the entire surrounding page. The eye can sort out crossing and intersecting lines with little difficulty. Blind readers, however, "see" only what is under their fingers at the moment. Second, unless the reader is to measure the length of a line or the perimeter of a polygon, print figures generally should be enlarged when they are being converted to tactile drawings. Third, the amount of detail may need to be reduced. Print figures often include extraneous lines, information that can be placed elsewhere, or more information than can be included in one tactile figure. It is not enough just to run a print figure through an enlarging copier and then emboss it. A tactile figure should be as "spare" as possible. The print figure should be simplified.

Simplify. In order to simplify a figure, it is necessary to know what is important in the figure and what is not. Print producers often have, for example, standard cartesian axes and grids that they use for all graphs in an algebra book. Sometimes the grids are necessary, but sometimes they are not. If the student is being shown how $y=x^2$ is graphed, it is important to show the grid. If the student is being shown the difference in shape among, say, linear, quadratic, polynomial, and exponential curves, the grid should be omitted. A social studies book about one of the states in the United States may have a standard map of that state that is used for all sections of the book, even though the different sections of the book are concentrating on different aspects of the state's geography. Each time the map of the state is laid out for the tactile presentation, irrelevant portions of the print map should be omitted so that the necessary information for that section of text is tactually readable. When a student is asked to determine the distance between two cities on a map, the print producer may include a portion of a standard road map for that area. The extraneous material on that map should be omitted from the tactile map. In kindergarten and first grade books, simple geometric shapes should be substituted for the print pictures used as counting symbols. These examples illustrate why it is impossible to write firm rules for the production of tactile graphics. Each tactile graphic has to be designed in the context of the narrative text to which it applies.

Avoid clutter. A cluttered tactile diagram has lines too close together, point symbols too close to lines, unnecessary "lead lines," and other elements that will interfere with the ability of the reader to comprehend the diagram. Ideally, lines should be no closer than 0.25 in. ($^1/_4$") to each other. Space for braille labels must be provided. These labels should be placed so that there is no confusion about what they are identifying, but the label should be no closer than 0.125 in. ($^1/_8$") from the item it identifies. "Lead lines" are a common source of clutter. Print figures often have labels with lead lines identifying regions in the interior of a figure. There are often completely unnecessary lead lines in print going from an equation to its graph line. Such lines can be omitted simply by placing the equation near its graph line. If a print lead line goes into the interior of a figure, eliminate it by using a key at the spot being identified. A "key" is a number, or one or two letters used in place of a print label that would be too bulky in braille for use in the tactile diagram. If a figure has many labeled lines or areas, a texture key is an effective method of taking clutter from the display. A texture key shows small sections of areal textures or line textures along with the print labels of the textures or lines. When either a number, letter, or texture key is used, the keys and the print labels they stand for should precede the tactile drawing as a transcriber's note. In graphs with multiple lines, as well as in some maps, it is often necessary to make more than one tactile drawing—each showing a part of the whole. A composite diagram should be presented afterward, omitting, if possible, the small details that made the separate displays necessary.

There was general agreement at the University of Louisville workshop and symposium that a verbal description, either recorded or written, accompanying a tactile display was beneficial. Such a verbal description, however, should be written only by someone with knowledge in the subject matter being illustrated. When Recording for the Blind (now Recording for the Blind and Dyslexic) provided tactile illustrations to accompany their recorded texts, the texts were read by experts in the field of the book being recorded. This ensured that figures were competently described. On the other hand, the braille code for mathematics and science (*The Nemeth Braille Code for Mathematics and Science Notation, 1972 Revision*) is designed to enable a transcriber to reproduce even the most complicated mathematics without the necessity of understanding the mathematics involved. Although in the course of transcribing a scientific book the transcriber may get a general sense of what is important in a figure, it would not be a good idea for the transcriber with limited knowledge of the subject matter to attempt a written description, except to explain in a transcriber's note how the tactile figure has been modified or what has been omitted from the print figure.

The examples at the end of this chapter illustrate some of the principles involved in the design of a tactile diagram.

Embossing the Diagram

Among guidelines available for the production of tactile graphics are: *Guidelines for Mathematical Diagrams,* published by The Braille Authority of North America, available from the National Braille Association, Inc.; Polly K. Edman's book *Tactile Graphics; Tactual Perception: a sourcebook;* and the manual that accompanies the APH Tactile Graphics Kit.

We will not here consider methods used by braille printing houses, but will confine ourselves to methods used by small producers such as transcribing groups, or individual transcribers working at home, or in schools and universities. Advances in modern technology are becoming helpful and those techniques will be described, but currently, those methods do not lend themselves to the variety of discriminable elements available using hand embossing. There are two widely used methods of hand embossing: tooling the back of the page and/or pasting collage on the front of the page. *Tooling* is done on paper or aluminum by the use of toothed wheels or styluses. A toothed wheel produces a rough-textured line; a stylus produces a smooth-textured line. The figure is first transferred as a reverse image to the back of the paper or aluminum, either directly, or by drawing on the front of the page with carbon paper placed face-up on the underside of the page. The paper or aluminum is then placed face down on a rubber mat and tooled. The image will appear as the proper image on the front of the paper or aluminum. *Collage* is used on paper. This involves gluing string or textured areas on the front side of the paper. Often, both tooling and collage are used at the same time on paper. When this technique is used, the part of the image that is to have the collage must be shown as the finished image on the front side of the paper, while the tooled parts of the image will be in reverse on the back side of the paper. Collage technique is not used with aluminum because it is possible to produce all the different kinds of lines on aluminum by tooling.

When the tooling and/or collage is complete and the raised figure shows on the front of the page, this is the master drawing from which a vacuum-formed copy is made and given to the reader. *The Thermoform machine:* This machine from American Thermoform Corporation makes it possible to produce multiple plastic (Brailon) copies of a paper or aluminum master. The master is placed on a perforated grid; a sheet of plastic is placed over the master; a hot oven is drawn over the two sheets; and after a few seconds, a vacuum pulls the plastic tight and molds it over the master. The plastic sheet is taken off and any number of other copies can be made from the master.

Print figures employ shading, dotted lines, dashed lines, bold lines, and colored lines. In an embossed tactile diagram, texture, height, and width are varied to make distinctions among the elements of a diagram. By what means is this accomplished?

Use contrast. There are many bad tactiles produced by transcribers who have no tool other than one toothed (spur) wheel. In a graph, the line representing the equation should be more prominent than the axes; the axes should be more prominent than the grid; and if two equation lines on a graph intersect, they should be of different textures.

When all of the elements of a figure are tooled using only one spur wheel, it is impossible to produce contrast. The figure produced with just one tool may look clear to the eye, but to the fingers it will feel like a patch of sandpaper. For a map, areas of water should have a different texture than areas of land; the lines separating countries should be different from those separating the states or provinces of a country. One method of providing a textured region for oceans and lakes is to emboss the figure on paper, cut out the water areas with a sharp razor or knife, and place the remaining land area on top of a textured sheet, such as a paper place mat or some cloth. When thermoformed, the textures will show up very well.

A transcriber should keep on hand a reference sheet with an example of all of the different lines, point symbols, and areal symbols available to him or her. This reference sheet should be a thermoformed (plastic) copy of the symbols. Rough lines are generally more discriminable than smooth lines, although a high smooth line can make up in height what a rough line accomplishes by its texture. In a graph showing intersecting equation lines of equal importance, choose from your reference sheet a spurred line and a smooth line of equal prominence. Make this choice by feeling the lines. Smooth lines should be sharply defined and have steep sides. On paper, carpet thread accomplishes this.

Proofread the embossed figure with your own fingers—eyes closed! It is wishful thinking on the part of many transcribers that blind readers have extraordinary powers of touch. The truth is that they do not "feel" what they touch any better than anyone else. When you finish your tactile diagram and have the final thermoformed copy, examine it with your fingers; you may be surprised at the result. Many items such as sandpaper, non-slip bathtub liner, or pin-pricked paper, used on one map as separate areal symbols, will look very different from each other on your master page, but feel identical on the plastic page. A line made with a single layer of chart tape will look very prominent on your master, but be virtually inconspicuous in the plastic copy. Choosing your symbols by feeling your plastic reference sheet before embossing your drawing will ensure that this mistake is not made.

Embossing Mediums

Paper. Manila paper (100 weight) is available from Howe Press or American Printing House for the Blind. It may also be purchased locally, from any paper company and cut to order. The common size for tactile graphics is 11 × 11½". A variety of toothed (spur) wheels should be kept on hand to produce a variety of discriminable lines. One type of wheel is available from Howe Press; the APH Tactile Graphics Kit has four different wheels. Spur wheels are also available from fabric shops and art and/or drafting supply stores. Point symbols can be made from cardboard cutouts or punches. Areal symbols can be made of buckram, sandpaper, paper table mats, needlepoint backing, etc. Smooth lines can be achieved by gluing carpet thread, extruding acrylic paint from a syringe, or by using fabric paint. Smooth lines of varying widths can also be made using chart tape. In this case, it is important to build up the line by using several layers.

Aluminum. Aluminum sheeting, especially prepared for tactile illustrations, is available from APH. It has a white backing so that the transcriber can place the reversed image of the figure on the back side. Eleven- by eleven-inch sheets are available as well as a roll eleven inches wide by about 150 feet long. If using the roll, only the amount of foil needed for a diagram is used. That piece can then be attached to a manila sheet for thermoforming. The aluminum must be aerated before thermoforming in order for the effect of the vacuum to reach the plastic sheet covering it. This is done by piercing the aluminum with a fine needle, from the front side, around the embossed lines and the braille labels. The same tools used for paper are suitable for aluminum. The APH Tactile Graphics Kit is designed to be used with aluminum and has six point symbols and three areal symbols in addition to the spur wheels mentioned above. It is possible to use the point symbols with the manila paper if the paper is moistened slightly; otherwise, the paper fractures. Aluminum has the great advantage of making a variety of smooth lines easy to produce.

Microcapsule paper. This is white paper that has been coated with microscopic plastic capsules. When a figure is photocopied onto it, or drawn onto it with alcohol and carbon based pens, black wax crayons, or lead pencils, and the paper is run through a special heating machine (called a stereo copier or an image enhancer), the black lines absorb more heat than the white portions of the paper and become raised to produce a discriminable line. The special machines and paper for this technique are available from American Thermoform Corporation; Repro-tronics, Inc.; Humanware, Inc.; and J.P. Trading. This technique is useful for partially sighted readers who also use tactile aids because the raised lines remain black. While there is little or no variation in height of lines, lines can be made narrow or wide, solid, dotted, or dashed. The most important line in a display should be the widest line. In other words, width of lines in this technique takes the place of differences in texture and height in hand-embossed material. Areal portions of the graph can be produced by different arrangements of parallel lines, dots, and so on. Transfer designs can be cut out and used for textured areas, but be sure to test the final product with your fingers, because patterns that look very different to the eye may not feel different under the fingers. There are braille fonts available that make it possible to make simulated braille labels to import into the drawing, if done on a computer, or to print and cut out and paste on the page before running it through a photocopier. The black dots of the simulated braille label come up in readable form with the rest of the figure. With the capsule paper from American Thermoform, Humanware, Inc., and J.P. Trading, it is also possible to place the completed embossed page into a braille writer or slate and braille the labels directly onto the page. This is not possible with the Flexi-paper from Repro-tronics.

The finished product produced on the capsule paper is not as durable as plastic copies, and it cannot be thermoformed. Each copy needed must be produced by photocopying the original drawing onto the capsule paper and running it through the image enhancer. The capsule paper is quite expensive, running over $1.00/page for the 11 × 11½" size. The Flexi-paper is more durable than the others and can be crumpled and folded without destroying the embossed figure. Use of capsule paper is becoming commonplace in schools and universities.

Braille embosser. Computer-driven braille embossers ordinarily used for standard braille can be set in a "graphics" mode for use in embossing graphs and figures. This technique is acceptable for simple geometric shapes and simple graphs, such as one showing axes and one graph line. Because the figure is embossed solely with standard braille dots, little subtlety is possible. Advances are being made, however, in developing embossers that will make a lower relief, continuous line.

In Summary

Tactile graphics are an essential component of a blind student's education. Besides being an aid in learning, a familiarity with graphs of all descriptions will be important to the blind student or professional in preparing, on his or her computer, reports and papers to be read by sighted peers or the general public.

There have been moves to establish organizations that would have a bank of tactiles, especially in such areas as maps, biological, and anatomical figures, that would be available to schools and individuals. Unfortunately, most figures and diagrams are specific to a particular book or especially to problems in the book. There is much duplication of effort in this area and there are no adequate means of informing readers and transcribers what tactiles are available. APH has sets of outline maps of the United States and its regions at very reasonable prices. These come on 17 × 15" paper pages and are very useful in the classroom. The transcriber or teacher can add whatever features are needed for the particular lesson involved. The Princeton Braillists have thermoform copies of maps of some of the states of the United States, North and South America, Middle East, Russia and its Former Republics, and Morocco. They also have basic human anatomy drawings.

There is a need to develop more tools for use with manila paper. Currently, there is no way to tool a smooth line on paper. Some transcribers have had friends with machine shops produce templates that will do this, but they are not available to the general public.

Most tactile graphics accompanying textbooks are produced by volunteers. There has never been any systematic program of study or instruction in the production of tactiles. Results of all the research in the field seldom reaches the transcriber. There are workshops given at meetings and conferences of the National Braille Association, Inc. and the California Transcribers and Educators of the Visually Handicapped, plus articles in their respective journals, but no systematic training. Some school systems in need of transcribers are arranging for community college courses to train braille transcribers, but this training does not extend to tactile illustrations. If there were such training sessions, the results of research in this field could be incorporated in the training and proper tools provided, which would result in transcribers well equipped to make effective tactile graphics. In short, someone or some organization should step forward to take on this task. Just as there are classes and correspondence courses to teach the various braille codes, so should there be classes to teach the making of tactile graphics.

Example 1

This map illustrates many of the principles set forth: simplify, reduce clutter, use contrast, and emphasize what is important. The map comes from a 5th grade workbook about California. Examine the text and problems that accompany this map. The task for the student is to find the correct latitude and longitude for each city. Therefore, the latitude and longitude lines have the greatest importance. The following features of the map are unimportant and are omitted:

- the rivers and lakes

- the islands off the coast

- the distance indicator

- the fact that Sacramento is the state capital.

A transcriber's key (not shown here) precedes the map. Each city is identified by two lowercase letters and listed in alphabetic order in the key. Even with maximum enlargement, there is not enough space between the longitude lines to use the entire braille label showing the number with the degree sign and the letter W. Therefore,

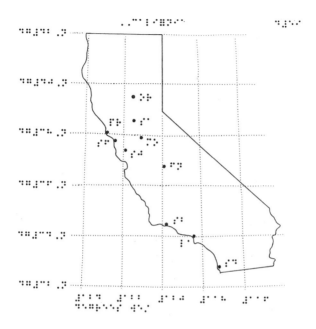

only the numbers are placed at the longitude lines and the words "degrees west" are placed on the braille line below them. [There is a print error that is corrected for the braille edition. The latitude line labeled 45°N in print should read 42°N.]

Among the outcomes at the workshop and symposium on haptic perception at the University of Louisville was a goal that there be consistency in the placement of braille labels—right or left, above or below. This is not always possible. In this display, labels are placed as often as possible to the right of the point being identified. It would be undesirable, however, to have the braille labels interfere with any of the latitude or longitude lines. That consideration takes precedence over consistency in placement of the labels.

The map is rotated slightly in order to make the longitude and latitude lines more vertical and horizontal rather than on a diagonal as they are in print. Longitude and latitude lines constitute a grid.

In print, the lines dividing California from Oregon, Nevada, Arizona, and Mexico are heavier than the coastline. Because this is unimportant for our purposes, this feature of the print map is ignored.

Two textures of lines are used: the state is outlined with a smooth line and the latitude and longitude lines are made using a spur wheel. The point symbols for the cities are punched out from cardboard using a one-eighth inch punch.

Example 2

One way of reducing clutter and achieving a clean tactile is to use a texture key. Rather than labeling the graph lines with key numbers or letters, each line is embossed with a different texture. The textures are listed in the key with the equations that identify them.

Braille labels are ordinarily placed below scale marks on the horizontal axis of a graph and to the left of the vertical axis. In this case, the labels for the horizontal axis would interfere with the graph lines if placed below. Therefore, they are placed above. There is no space available to place a label for #1 on the vertical axis. This figure is taken from a precalculus book and we may assume that the reader can locate the position of #1 by inference.

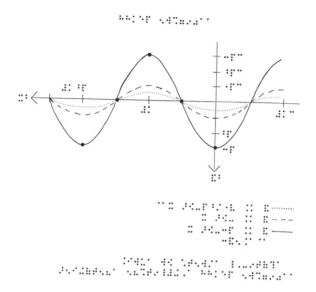

In this print figure, one of the graph lines is dashed. In many figures of this type, all print lines are the same. The eye would have no problem with that, but if all the lines in the braille edition were of the same texture, readers tracing a particular line with their fingers would have no means of knowing which line to follow beyond a point of intersection. If a print graph has several graph lines identical in color and intensity and they intersect, the braille edition should make each line of a different texture.

It is a requirement of *Guidelines for Mathematical Diagrams* that a sequentially numbered figure have its label centered on line 25 (the last line) of any braille page on which any part of the figure appears.

List of Resources

American Printing House for the Blind
    P.O. Box 6085
    Louisville, KY 40206-0085
    Telephone: (800) 223-1839 or (502) 895-2405
    FAX: (502) 899-2274
    e-mail: info@aph.org
    Web site: www.aph.org

American Thermoform Corporation
    2311 Travers Avenue
    City of Commerce, CA 90040
    Telephone: (800) 331-3676 or (323) 723-9021
    FAX: (323) 728-8877
    Web site: www.atcbrleqp.com

California Transcribers and Educators of the Visually
    Handicapped
    741 N. Vermont Avenue
    Los Angeles, CA 90029

Guidelines for Mathematical Diagrams
    Published by The Braille Authority of North America
    Available National Braille Association, Inc.
    3 Townline Circle
    Rochester, NY 14623-2513
    Telephone: (716) 427-8260
    FAX: (716) 427-0263
    e-mail: nbaoffice@compuserve.com

Howe Press of Perkins School for the Blind
175 North Beacon Street
Watertown, MA 02172
Telephone: (910) 240-9886
FAX: (617) 926-2027

Humanware, Inc.
6245 King Road
Loomis, CA 95650
Telephone: (800) 722-3393
FAX: (916) 652-7296
e-mail: info@humanware.com
Web site: www.humanware.com

Journal of Visual Impairment and Blindness
Published by American Foundation for the Blind
11 Penn Plaza, Suite 300
New York, NY 10001
Telephone: (212) 502-7655

J.P. Trading
400 Forbes
South San Francisco, CA 94080
Telephone: (650) 871-3940

National Braille Association, Inc.
3 Townline Circle
Rochester, NY 14623-2513
Telephone: (716) 427-8260
FAX: (716) 427-0263
e-mail: nbaoffice@compuserve.com

Princeton Braillists
   28-B Portsmouth Street
   Whiting, NJ 08759
   Telephone: (732) 350-3708 or (609) 924-5207

Repro-tronics, Inc.
   75 Carver Avenue
   Westwood, NJ 07675
   Telephone: (201) 722-1880
   e-mail: info@repro-tronics.com
   Web site: www.repro-tronics.com

Seedlings Braille Books for Children
   P.O. Box 51924
   Livonia, MI 48151-5924
   Telephone: (800) 777-8552
   e-mail: seedlink@aol.com
   Web site: www.seedlings.org

Tactile Graphics
   by Polly K. Edman
   Copyright 1992
   Published by American Foundation for the Blind
   15 West 16th Street
   New York, NY 10011
   Telephone: (212) 620-2155
   FAX: (212) 620-2105

Tactual Perception: A sourcebook
   Edited by William Schiff and Emerson Foulke
   Copyright 1982
   Published by the Press Syndicate of the
   University of Cambridge
   32 East 57th Street
   New York, NY 10022

THE ART OF MARKETING BRAILLE: THE NATIONAL BRAILLE PRESS EXPERIENCE

by William M. Raeder and Diane L. Croft

People say marketing is as unpredictable as the weather, but our experience marketing braille publications has been more like a steady breeze. Braille readers are perhaps among the most enthusiastic book lovers of our time. No sooner does our braille catalog of new publications go out then we hear back, "What's next?" Lately, our customers have been complaining about the lack of space in their office or home for any more braille books, but still they buy. And buy. And buy. Reading braille is their passion, and producing it is ours.

For decades, doomsayers have heralded the demise of braille: no one's reading it anymore; tapes will replace braille; disks will replace braille; the Internet will replace braille. Our experience, substantiated by steadily increasing sales, tells us that among those who prefer it, braille remains as vital and engaging as any of the alternative formats available today.

The passion our readers have for braille motivates what we do. "I want that book in braille," a customer says. We smile. Even if we don't have it in braille, or plan to, we appreciate the sentiment. Reading by touch is an art form worth keeping. The beauty of someone lightly touching a line of braille, gently sailing across the page, absorbing the language through touch, is something close to art. Or, as John M. Kennedy remarked in his book *Drawing & the Blind,* "There may be music in touch."

In 1982, we at the National Braille Press revitalized our publishing activity by hiring a new manager and by establishing three marketing principles:

1. Develop relationships with our customers to understand their unmet needs.

2. Produce products responsive to those needs.

3. Promote those products aggressively.

If we were now, almost two decades later, to ask the question "How do you market braille publications at the turn of the century?" the answer could be reduced to the simple statement of these three principles.

The key words are "relationships" and "needs." Our customers might like us, but if we try to sell them something they don't think they need, they aren't going to buy it. Similarly, we may produce terrific books that braille readers want, but if our customers don't feel good about us as a company, they will be less apt to buy from us. If, however, we are responsive to individual needs, our customers will reward us with their business. All the practices and techniques we will present in this chapter stem from that basic principle.

What Are We Selling?

We're not just selling books. Although the core of our business philosophy is based on access to the printed word, that's not enough in the end. Telling our customers we put this or that book into braille won't move it off our shelves and onto theirs, especially because their shelves are already sagging from the strain of multivolume braille books.

As important as braille access is, what we're actually selling to a blind individual, as one would in selling to a sighted individual, is a product that meets a particular need. In the case of children's print/braille storybooks, for instance, the need is for parents to be able to snuggle together with their children and participate in the age-old tradition of storytelling, albeit under the lofty banner of education (if a child can learn while snuggling and hearing a good story, all the better). From a child's perspective, books mean more than education. Books can soothe and calm, or they can scare, tickle, and invigorate. The sentiments and images in a book also help a child make connections, such as, "This grandfather clock is just like the one at Nana's."

Later, when children begin to read books by themselves, books meet a different need. Now, mastering the same skills as their peers (namely, the ability to decipher letters and words into meaningful language) takes precedence. We are society's children, and wanting to do what everyone else is doing motivates us to learn to read.

So what we're selling when we promote our Children's Braille Book Club aren't just books, but the experience of sharing the adventures of a favorite character, such as

Winnie-the-Pooh, in an intimate setting with loved ones and, eventually, learning to read like everyone else.

In that sense, successful marketing strategies for children's braille books are no different from the strategies employed by print publishers, such as Random House or Penguin Putnam. We engage the potential buyer in the story; if the author or series is famous, we splash the name across the marquee; and we state the price. Most of the time, our children's book flyers read verbatim from the dust jacket cover of the print edition.

Sometimes, though, a book deals with a subject or issue in a way that benefits a blind youngster in particular, and we then slant the promotion in that direction. Once we produced a book on manners narrated by a comedy cast of pigs. Because we felt there was extra value for the blind child who cannot see certain social customs, we plugged that additional benefit in the flyer. The book quickly sold out. Another time we offered a book on baseball that so beautifully described the field, what the players wore, where the bleachers were located in relation to first base, and so on, that we mentioned how useful it would be to read this book to a blind youngster before heading out to the game. The book disappeared from our third-floor warehouse. It may have sold anyway, but this was a chance to remind a busy parent that there's more to a book than reading words—there's the shared experience of a baseball game, and all for just $6.95.

Sometimes we don't really understand what we're selling until we hear from our customers. For several years now, we have published The Blind Community E-mail Directory, which contains hundreds of e-mail addresses of blind individuals and blindness-related organizations. Our purpose, or so we thought, was to build community, a phrase we used to promote the directory. Our thinking was that communicating via e-mail is so blissfully easy—especially for a group of people who must rely on speech or braille feedback to edit what they write—that if we put everyone's addresses in one directory, it would further stimulate communication. Besides, blind people have never experienced the luxury of a phone book.

The directory worked exactly as we had envisioned it. We received letters (actually, e-mails) from customers who reconnected with old friends and lovers on the Net. We thought, after a few directories, we could put this idea to bed. What we had not foreseen, however, was the who's who value of the directory. People who had made it into the directory had "made it" on the Internet, and that, as it turned out, was something to shout about. People would call and say, "I just got a computer and a hookup; can I be in?" Inclusion in the directory meant inclusion in a greater sense; it carried a measure of status.

So a good question to ask when promoting a braille product is What are the customers really buying? Are they buying entertainment, instruction, literacy, status? If you know what you're selling, you can tell your customers what they're buying.

Selling Promises

It's an old marketing adage that regardless of what you're selling, you're really selling a promise. Your product or service promises to clean teeth, make money, educate your children, or guarantee safe sex. And customers, like kids, never forget a promise.

We're careful about what we promise. When we produced a beginner's tutorial for Microsoft Word for Windows, for example, we discouraged proficient Word users from buying it. Here is a verbatim excerpt from the catalog: "If you are comfortably using Word, you will be bored with this book. You don't need it. This book starts off telling you to turn the computer on."

Or another time, when we published a book on the Internet, we wrote the promise as follows:

> Before you read this book, we want to tell you what this book is and is not. This book is not a tutorial, nor is it a manual or handbook. It doesn't replace mainstream books about the Internet. *Captured by the Net* covers issues and aspects of the Internet specific to blind users. Like most books published by National Braille Press, it is intended for first-time users of the Net, covering such issues as…and the like. This book attempts to fill in the gaps between mainstream books on the Internet and specialized Internet tutorials for the blind—both of which already exist.

At the end of the book, we even published a list of mainstream books on the Internet and specialized Internet tutorials for blind people that were available from other sources. Our purpose here was service, not sales.

If the customer expects ABC and you send them XYZ—especially if you have oversold the promise—you will eventually, if not immediately, lose the faith of the customer. If there are too many broken promises, the relationship suffers irrevocable damage.

Buying from Someone You Like

Customers like to buy products from companies they like; few of us buy products from people we don't like. If we do, it's generally because the company has a monopoly, an unbeatable price, or convenience—three factors that can change overnight.

At NBP, we have found that likability is a huge factor in the marketing and promotion of braille books. How do we know this? Because our customers tell us so. "You folks at NBP are great," is a comment we hear a lot, followed by, "So what new books do you have?" We're not saying NBP is the greatest, but we are saying that likability adds value to our product. There are many fine companies in the field, like Ann Morris Enterprises and Duxbury Systems, that benefit from being liked by their customers. Our experience tells us that this seemingly intangible quality translates into sales.

Turning Mistakes Around

Errors are inevitable in the printing, or brailling, business, and we've had our share. One thing we never do is cover them up. As soon as we discover that we have erred, we admit it and make amends.

One of the nicest calls we ever received about a mistake we made was from an eleven-year-old braille reader. In a high-pitched but forceful voice she told us that we had made a mistake in our *Braille Spelling Dictionary* (of all things). She told us exactly on which page and line we could find it. Her mother then got on the phone and said that her daughter had read the entire speller front to back and was pleased as punch to discover an error and call up the National Braille Press. We corrected the error and then made it public by featuring her discovery in our next newsletter.

Another time we messed up the braille translation of the best-selling book *Don't Sweat the Small Stuff...and it's all small stuff* (an irony not lost on us). Headlined in *USA Today* as the number-one book in the country that year, it seemed destined for success. We pressed a first run of two hundred copies, our standard. Not long after the initial one hundred copies had shipped, we heard from the first customer, "There are a number of strange errors in the book." This is a heart-sinking moment for a book publisher, because so much goes into the production of a book.

Production-wise, it had looked like an ordinary book: basic prose broken into small chapters. We had scanned it and foreseen no difficulties. To make a long story short, the type font that was used in the print book had a quirky little twist that confounded the scanner. Words like "learn" became "team" and "feel" became "feet"—not a trivial substitution for an inspirational book with a great deal of feeling in it. This was a "Jiffy-Braille" book, meaning it did not go through the standard proofreading, thus the errors were not caught in production.

The dilemma for us, which is similar to that of the car manufacturer who must recall and fix a costly problem, was how to minimize the financial impact while still serving the customer. There were one hundred copies in the field and another hundred on the third floor of our building. The cost to have the first hundred returned, record the data entry, run another label, and reship them, as well as to destroy the other hundred copies upstairs, would be painful.

Lucky for us, a savvy customer helped us devise our own quirky recall. She said the mistakes didn't impede readability, that she still got a lot from the book. And then she said this: "It's sort of like buying an irregular piece of clothing, like a markdown." And there was our answer.

We sent out a braille letter to the first one hundred buyers, giving them a choice: they could either return their copy for a corrected one or keep their irregular copy and earn a credit toward the purchase of a future book at NBP. The majority kept their books. New customers were also given a choice: they could buy the irregular edition at half price or a corrected one for full price. We moved the remaining one hundred books.

Free-flowing communication with our customers and a willingness to admit mistakes help us turn mistakes around and forge stronger relationships.

Offer Something Extra

When it works, we like to offer more than what the customer expects. A good example of this was a print/braille children's book we offered called *Your First Garden Book*. The idea of cultivating future gardeners inspired us to contact a seed company in Maine and ask for donated seed packets to sell along with the book. It was a huge success. We selected sunflower seeds, so the child could grow something really big, and some green beans, so the child could get a sense of farming or growing what you eat. Several families sent pictures of their children standing next to their harvest, which we ran in our company newsletter.

Just as often, we conceive of a good idea that never gets hatched. Once we produced a children's book called *Underwear,* which featured a slew of forest animals all sporting colorful underwear. We desperately wanted to package the book with a pair of really wild underwear— we could see young kids prancing around the house, like the animals in the book—but we couldn't inspire an underwear company to match our imagination with a donation.

For the holidays this year, we are brailling a book called *Grandmother's Dreamcatcher,* a perfect opportunity to offer something extra. On the Internet, we discovered a woman who custom-designs dreamcatcher kits, and she is working with us to design one that a blind child can construct independently, using braille instructions. This will make a nice holiday gift.

You Have the Best Braille

For years customers have been telling us, "You folks have the best braille." Eager for the compliment, we accepted this as a reflection of the quality of our work. Deep down, though, we knew there was something more. After all, each of the major braille houses uses the same basic equipment, translation software, personal computers, and trained personnel.

Gradually it dawned on us: it was our paper. Several decades ago, we spent some years researching the best type of paper for braille embossing. The paper we use is expensive, but we believe it elevates and holds the braille better than most, and it feels good under the fingers. From time to time, when the budget is tight, we ask ourselves, Should we use less expensive paper? So far we've held the line, and that is good news for the marketing of our braille.

The feel-good quality of our braille paper translates into enormous goodwill among our customers. In fact, we used this point when we were marketing our braille services to ADA-compliant companies, such as airlines, hotels, restaurants, and so on. It gave us an opportunity to distinguish ourselves from other braille-producing organizations. On a promotional flyer, right under the header "It Feels Right," we explained the importance of using quality paper for embossing braille:

> To maintain the integrity of the dots requires a special blend of softwood and hardwood craft. Our quality braille paper provides both the flexibility necessary to elevate the braille, and the durability to withstand sustained finger reading.
>
> It's acid-free, so it won't disintegrate. Our paper is our best-kept secret.

To Market, to Market

Although people speak of marketing and selling in the same breath, they are actually separate functions. Marketing covers four basic tasks:

1. The development of the product or service.

2. The pricing of the product or service.

3. The promotion of the product or service.

4. The distribution of the product or service.

Sales are the result of successful marketing. If we pick the right books, price them reasonably, promote them like crazy, and ship them to the right people quickly, sales flourish.

There are times when a third-quarter sales report doesn't match projections, and the temptation is to think, How can we push this product? Sometimes pushing the product does result in an additional mailing and a boost in sales, but that method of thinking only provides a quick fix for a monthly report, not a long-term strategy. A steady record of long-term sales growth comes from building a successful relationship with customers through the four functions of marketing: selection, pricing, promotion, and distribution.

That may be especially true for nonprofit organizations. When we measure our success, we don't look at sales but at the number of people served and the number of books shipped. If we aren't serving a purpose—meeting individual needs through access to information in braille—then we shouldn't be in business. Even if we weren't so downright righteous about our raison d'être, our funders keep us honest. Foundations, corporations, and individual donors want to know that we are spending their money wisely and meeting people's needs.

One last comment about sales for a nonprofit, such as ours. The more we sell, the more it costs us. Publication sales cover significantly less than half of our costs. The rest we subsidize through fund-raising. As sales go up, costs go up, and therefore fund-raising must go up, too. It's a circle. We must produce books that people want in order to justify our case to funders, as well as to serve braille readers (as a nonprofit, we serve two constituencies).

Staying Focused

One of the difficulties NBP faces in its quest to raise ever-increasing amounts of money to subsidize braille books is the small number of people served. Blindness is a low-incidence population, and only 12 percent of the blind population reads braille.

Regardless of the importance of braille literacy and access to information, the bottom line for foundations is, How many people will you serve? From their point of view, our low numbers imply limited need. We know otherwise, and the trick is to find a way to convey that to potential donors.

We have debated over the years whether we should venture into other accessible formats, like large print or books on disk, but in the end our deep commitment and passion for braille helps us stay focused on our mission. We believe this single focus is a strength in marketing our publications.

The late 1980s and early 1990s were a time of frenzied merger activity in this country. One fish swallowed another fish, and then a whale swallowed them both. Companies that made suitcases bought companies that made muffins, under the misguided assumption that selling is selling and bigger is better. The latter part of the 1990s, however, saw companies selling off unprofitable units, one by one, as they discovered the business advantage of staying focused and building on their core competency.

Selling low-cost braille publications to such a small group of people can be a tough sell to potential funders, but it keeps our own passion and the passion of our customers alive and well.

Even More Focus

People always want to know how we select the publications we braille. There is no magic to it. It's mostly a combination of selecting popular mainstream books to reprint, responding to customer suggestions, and working with blind authors with expertise in particular areas to publish books written especially for blind people.

The ideal goal is "equal access to information," but the reality is much more limited. The world is drowning in print, but braille is still a mere puddle. Recognizing that we can't be all things to all people, we focus our selection in three major subject categories: (1) braille literacy, (2) computer technology, and (3) self-help.

Braille literacy, a focus from our founding mission statement of 1929, remains a driving force in our publishing activities. Examples include our Children's Braille Book Club; our braille primer for sighted parents, titled *Just Enough to Know Better* (more than twelve thousand sold); *A Braille Spelling Dictionary;* some of our tactile graphics books, such as *Touch the Stars, Shapely-CAL,* and *Humpty Dumpty;* best-selling titles, such as *Harry Potter and the Sorcerer's Stone;* and our long-standing print/braille Winnie-the-Pooh calendar.

We chose computer technology and self-help books as two other categories to focus on because they feed our natural desire to be independent. When the world moved from DOS to Windows, so did our publications. When the Internet entered our workplaces and homes, we responded with *Shop Online the Lazy Way* and *Captured by the Net.* The category of self-help covers anything that one can learn to do for oneself, such as cooking, child care, and self-defense. Many of the books in the computer technology and self-help area are written especially by and for blind people, and who better?

Avoiding Redundancy

Whenever we conceive of a new publication idea, the first thing we do is check around to see if it's available elsewhere. Redundancy does not make sense in a field where there is so much to be done.

When we think about doing a children's print/braille book, for example, we first check the catalog from Seedlings of Livonia, Michigan. Seedlings has carved out a dynamic and important niche, namely, producing low-cost children's braille books. Unlike NBP's storybooks that combine the illustrated print book with braille overlays, Seedlings primarily prints the text from popular storybooks on a sheet of paper, and then brailles the identical text below each printed word. In that way, parent and child can follow along, each in their respective medium, word for word.

The founder and director of Seedlings, Debra Bonde, ships as many, or perhaps even more, children's books than NBP does. Bonde conceived of a need that was not being met—a word-for-word match between print and braille—and founded Seedlings. Our posture is to support her business, as she does ours, rather than to compete. Neither of us can meet all of the needs for children's books.

On one occasion, a generous donor approached us with some money if we would produce some of his favorite books from childhood. Researching the field, we found that these particular titles were already available from a number of other agencies. We explained our policy of nonredundancy and he graciously supported a different book.

Attractive Packaging

Even though our customers don't benefit directly from the attractive covers we put on our books, we believe braille books should look as appealing as print books. Whenever possible, we ask the print book publisher for a cover mechanical, or, if that's not possible, we scan in the print book cover and produce a similar one for the braille edition.

We've had customers tell us that someone on a bus or in their office was impressed to see they were reading a technical book—a fact that could only have been deduced from the printed cover. Attractive covers often draw sighted parents and teachers to our table at conventions. And these covers are especially important for children's braille books, because a familiar cover brings the braille book into the realm of the ordinary for parents and classroom teachers.

Pricing Products

It's been said that price is king, and we certainly find ours to be a price-sensitive market. The cornerstone of our publishing program is our pricing policy, which most of our customers can recite by heart. Our standard policy (unless contractual agreements specify otherwise) is to charge the same price for a book in braille as its print equivalent.

As the relationship between blind people and society has moved from one of charity to one of support, so have our services. For seventy years, since its inception in 1930, we have offered a women's magazine, *Our Special,* free to blind women around the world. Even though we charged a fair price for our other publications, we were reluctant to change seventy years of tradition in this case. Finally, however, we did, instituting a fifteen-dollar subscription price.

Whereas we no longer believe braille publications should be free (unless the print edition is), neither do we believe braille readers should have to pay more than sighted readers do. We raise the difference, as mentioned before, through ongoing fund-raising activities, which distinguishes us from for-profit publishers.

The fairness of this pricing policy is hard to dispute, and whenever we have the opportunity to point out this policy in our promotional pieces, we do. At the bottom of many of our flyers, after we mention the price, we often add, "same price as print book," to let customers know they are being treated equally. This has been a powerful marketing tool for us.

Book Discounting

We never offer discounts on our braille books (with the one exception we mentioned earlier, as part of a product recall). Discounting is an American marketing standard, but we don't use it. Not only is it not fair to those who paid full price, but once you start discounting, people wait for the sale. Furthermore, we already subsidize every book we produce.

The Direct Hit

Of all the marketing techniques we have used over the years, none works better for us than direct mail. The catalogs or flyers go out and the phones start ringing.

Rather than produce one large catalog to send to all of our constituents, we produce several smaller catalogs, each geared to a specific market. We have our braille minicatalog for adult braille readers, a print *Back-to-School Braille Backpack* for teachers and parents, a print catalog for general purposes, and various print and braille flyers specific to individual publications.

Likewise, in marketing our children's print/braille books, we don't publish one large catalog of storybooks. Instead, every other month we mail two flyers that feature that month's and the next month's book selections. That way, families, schools, and libraries are constantly being reminded of the Children's Book Club. Also, by only mailing a couple of flyers at a time, it's easy for customers to quickly scan and make a decision. Everyone is busy, but working parents and itinerant teachers are the busiest of the busy.

The disadvantages of direct mail are many, including managing all these catalogs and the additional design costs, but nothing has been more effective in promoting our publications. People want to see exactly what you have for them that will make their lives easier, and you'd better be quick about it because people don't have much time. Once we put together a catalog of just our computer-related publications and it was a huge success. Only cost and time keep us from expanding upon this model.

That's not to say that full-fledged catalogs don't have a place; they do. Increasingly, we have been referring people to our Web site—www.nbp.org or www.braille.com— where everything is in one place. The beauty of the Web, of course, is the ability to keep the information current at a relatively low cost. We have a link called Hot Off the Braille Press, which gives frequent visitors a chance to quickly scan what's new.

The fact remains that keeping all this information up-to-date in all of these different formats is a challenge we haven't yet mastered.

Communicating with Your Customers

When we mail out ten thousand braille catalogs, we have the opportunity to directly communicate with ten thousand customers. Rather than mail out a laundry list of new publications, we take the time to communicate with the people who buy our products.

The style of the braille minicatalog is chatty. People tell us they run a bath or make a pot of tea when the minicatalog arrives. It's a quick read, averaging only sixteen pages. In fact, some people call just to get the catalog ("My friend told me about it..."), but don't actually buy anything from us.

Realizing that our minicatalog was an important marketing tool, we thought several years ago about ways to make it even more effective. We asked ourselves, "What would make this direct-mail piece stand out from the rest of the junk mail?" The answer was obvious: it may be the only readily accessible piece of mail in the pile—the beauty of receiving a braille catalog, or anything in braille for that matter, is the thrill of being able to read it independently any time you like. Traditionally, our braille catalog had come wrapped in a manila envelope, hiding its best features.

Redesigning the minicatalog was easy. We simply discarded the envelope, made the catalog smaller, and secured it with a small circular sticker along the side. We field-tested it by sending it to readers in California and New York (if mail can survive New York, it can survive anywhere) and asking testers to mail it back to NBP. Even we were surprised at how well it traveled. We hypothesize that even the mail carriers can now see that it's braille and handle it more carefully.

Exposed as it was, we assumed that the outside front cover might get flattened, so we decided not to put anything too important on it. Thus was born the idea of putting a tea-bag size quote on the outside cover. Some of them have been a tad over the edge, like the saucy Mae West quote, "Too much of a good thing is wonderful," or the more poetic "The fish in the sea is not thirsty." We've had customers ask for the catalog by saying, "I'm looking for the one with the Chinese character on the front." Not everyone appreciates the humor, but the general consensus is that it stands out.

Selling Harry Potter

As we mentioned earlier in this chapter, we promote needs rather than publications. The first thing we ask ourselves when we promote a book is, What need does this publication meet? Once we think we have a handle on that, the next step is communicating that to the customer.

A publication may meet many needs, but we try to keep the message simple. Most people don't remember more than one or two features of a product or service. Take the promotion of *Harry Potter and the Sorcerer's Stone,* a children's book for ages eight to twelve. The year we transcribed the book, Harry Potter was the best-selling children's book of all time, even surpassing Charlotte's Web. That would seem to be a pretty big point to drive home to customers, but we decided it was secondary.

The more important need, as we saw it, was the fact that blind children in this age group often fall off the braille wagon. They are too old for print/braille storybooks, and other age-appropriate books, like trade books or textbooks, may not be readily available to them in braille. As Ruby Ryles of Louisiana Tech demonstrated in her important study on the lifelong benefits of early learning of braille, if a blind child isn't actively engaged in reading braille by the fourth grade, that child will probably not become a proficient braille reader as an adult (see Ryles' study in Chapter 21). This was something we cared about deeply and hoped parents and teachers did, too.

On the outside flap of the promotional flyer, we did feature Harry Potter flying on his broom—a familiar image by now, showing up in bookstore windows and tabloid book reviews everywhere—but we chose to stimulate interest in this book by posing this question to parents and teachers: "Is Your Child Getting The Very Best In Braille?" This put Harry (a beckoning image) right next to the words "In Braille?"

The inside message read, "If You Want Your Child To Read Braille And Enjoy It, Pick The Best Books To Read." The idea being, if your child has stopped reading braille, maybe one way you could renew his or her interest would be through this book. The fact that Harry Potter has "reached a level of bestsellerdom never before achieved by a children's book in the United States" followed that message.

Another example involved the promotion of a book called *The Bridge to Braille*, a dandy resource guide written by the parent of a blind child and a teacher of blind students. We distributed the book, published by the National Federation of the Blind, because we found it to be the most concise, one-stop shopping guide for braille resources anywhere.

We could have filled several pages talking about the important resource information in this book (and later on in the flyer, we did), but the most important need it filled was the benefit of buying just one book that covered it all. And that's how we promoted it: "Parents & Teachers: If You Buy One Book This Year, Buy This One." A busy teacher or parent could take one action and be done. It's a comforting statement, especially when the whole business of teaching a child braille feels overwhelming.

Promoting Like Mainstream Publishers

The actual nuts and bolts of marketing braille publications are no different from what Random House or Scholastic do. They mail out catalogs that describe their new books and list backtitles. They strive to get favorable book reviews in national tabloids, and they run appealing ads in magazines and newspapers. We do the same things.

One big advantage major print publishers have over braille publishers are bookstores. Our experience at conventions for blind people demonstrates that browsing results in buying—an experience blind people have lived without. The fact is, though, it's just not practical for mainstream bookstores to stock braille books when there are so few braille readers nationwide. We actually tried it once, with a unique bookstore called Learningsmith, but it didn't pan out. That's why we're excited about the possibilities for browsing that the Internet offers, when we get that far.

Book Reviews

Book reviews are garnered by sending advance copies of newly published books to blindness-related publications, like the *Journal of Visual Impairment & Blindness* (*JVIB*), *Dialogue* magazine, *TACTIC*, and so forth. Like print book publishers, you take your chances that the review will be positive.

Purchasing Ads

We seldom purchase ad space in blindness-related magazines because of cost, but there have been exceptions. If we know a book of ours is being reviewed in *JVIB*, for instance, we might take out an accompanying ad. Notices work better for us. Most blindness-related publications have a "Notices" section where you can get your product announced for free. We have a mailing list of more than two hundred tape and braille publications to which we mail press releases announcing new publications.

The disadvantage of relying on your own database of readers and blindness-related publications is that you keep reaching the same people. Blind individuals who do not belong to organizations of blind people or read specialized publications—in other words, who aren't connected to the blind community—are less likely to be reached.

Tapping Mainstream Media

To recruit new readers, we have found that mainstream media are the best venue. Radio, television, mainstream magazines, and newspapers give you exposure beyond the confines of your general readership. Of course, it also means that you compete for space or air time with a multitude of other issues and events, but braille is a "sexy" subject, and overall we have found a receptive audience within mainstream media.

A relatively easy way to get into mainstream magazines, for instance, is to call up the advertising manager and ask for a rate sheet with ad sizes. You can design several different ads that match their size specifications and mail them to the ad manager, asking for a free spot if and when they have room.

This worked extremely well for us with a new CD-ROM magazine (back when CD-ROMs were the rage) that had plenty of empty space because they were just getting started. For more than a year, they ran our ads for a book we published, *The CD-ROM Advantage for Blind Users.*

Our flashiest media moment was a spot on The Young and the Restless, a popular daytime soap opera. A regular character on the show was a single, blind mother with a young son. We pitched the idea to CBS (via their Web page) to use NBP's print/braille children's books for the blind character to read to her son, just like other blind parents do. They jumped on the idea and built an entire plot around it. On the show, the woman was dating a man who happened to drop by with a surprise for the little boy. The surprise, of course, was one of our print/braille books. The mother and son immediately sat down on the sofa to read together for the first time. It was a highly charged moment, the very essence of daytime soaps.

The man even mentioned that more books could be purchased from a braille press in Boston. At the end, CBS flashed an information card with details on how to obtain books from National Braille Press's Children's Braille Book Club. The next morning, the switchboard lit up with callers, many of whom were public school teachers who wanted books to share with their students under the banner of "handicapped awareness." Of course, we also recruited some new members to the Club.

Book authors, if they are excited about having their book available in braille, can also be tapped for promotion. Harley Hahn, the author of a best-selling book about the Internet, was frequently interviewed on the radio, and made a point to mention on the air that people could get a copy of his book in braille from National Braille Press. He even put a notice up on his Web site, including a solicitation for donations to support the transcription.

Publishers' Advertising Departments

Sometimes you can lean on the advertising departments of print book publishers if they are excited about the fact that you have transcribed one of their books into braille. When we brailled the *Area Code Handbook,* published by AT&T at the time, they ran several articles in their house organ, which went out to tens of thousands of people. General Mills was so excited about our braille edition of *Betty Crocker & Gold Medal Product Preparation Directions & Recipes* that they flew several NBP staff members to Minneapolis for a day-long exhibit and luncheon that reached three thousand of their employees.

Other organizations, such as Kraft Foods, Scholastic, and the North American Menopause Society, have all put their marketing muscle behind the braille editions of their books. These organizations have nurtured their own media relationships, which are so important when you compete for news coverage.

Mainstream media work because they reach the general public, many of whom know someone who is blind. These people then pass along the information.

Staying on Track

No matter how good you are today, tomorrow is a new day. Customer preferences can change gradually or seemingly overnight. For example, we used to hear that the size of the braille publication didn't matter, as long as the information was timely and the price was right. Over time that perspective has changed. Baby boomers—long-time readers of braille—have filled up their bookshelves with braille volumes and they want relief! These days they might ask for the same publication on disk in a braille file format for reading on a refreshable braille display.

Handling Customer Service Calls

We find the best way to determine whether you are on track is to handle customer service calls for a few days or weeks. The best, most reliable source of information about how your organization is doing comes from talking directly and informally with the people who buy your products. Inviting the company president, director of marketing, or even board members to come in and handle phones for a day can tell you whether you are on or off course.

Talking with customers can tell you about things that need to be fixed that you didn't even know were broken. Once a customer who had called to order a children's book mentioned a particular problem she had had with a previous children's counting book of ours. It was a small, offhand remark that turned out to be huge from our perspective.

In this counting book, there were assorted animals that entered and exited a pond. The idea was to keep track, mentally, of the count. The repeated refrain on each page was, "How many animals are left in the pond?" What we had failed to do, in the braille edition, was tell the reader how many animals were in the pond to begin with (such an explanation wasn't necessary in the print edition because of the pictures). This rendered the book useless for its stated purpose: counting. Not a soul had called to complain, and we would never had known if it weren't for this customer's remark.

Talking with customers not only tells us if things aren't working, but inevitably, when customers sense a listening ear, they will tell you what else they think you should be doing. Some of our best ideas for braille products come from our customers.

Written Surveys

We have found written surveys less effective in telling us what people want, although they do serve other purposes. The editor of *Our Special* magazine occasionally surveys readers to better understand the demographics of her readership, and this works quite well. She might discover there are many more working mothers than she thought and increase her selection of articles pertaining to employment and parenting. Such demographic information is also important to funding sources.

We once undertook an ambitious survey to determine why certain readers had not been buying from us. We didn't want to delete them from the database, but we didn't want to continue to send them catalogs if they weren't interested in our products. We cleverly titled the survey, "Who Are You?" We got back as many different answers as there were respondents. In the end, we still didn't have a clue what to do with them.

We had asked on the survey, "What could we publish in braille that you would want to buy?" Here again, there were as many answers as there were respondents; it did not give us the direction we were looking for. Even worse, we did not have the staff to enter in all the responses, and the survey collected dust in a corner of the room until we dumped it into a filing cabinet out of sight.

Looking back, we should have enlisted the services of a professional company that knows how to tailor questionnaires to obtain specific results. That could make a difference in whether a survey is effective.

Who Are Our Competitors?

Our competition in selling braille books to individuals has not been, for the most part, other braille-producing organizations. Few companies seem eager to subsidize braille publications. Our greater competition comes from mainstream information sources, such as audio books and Walkmans, inexpensive speech and scanning technology, the Internet, Newsline, and so forth. We believe these mainstream options will continue to affect the nature of what we do, which means we must be ever-vigilant to changes in our readers' preferences.

Recently, for example, we decided to move away from the production of large multivolume braille computer tutorials. We heard from users that they prefer taped tutorials so they can follow along while seated at their computer performing the required functions. Taking their hands off the keys to reference a braille tutorial doesn't work as well. We won't abandon all hard-copy braille computer guides, but we will reconsider our investment in braille tutorials.

One area where we cannot envision a decline in the need for braille products is in children's literature. Braille must be taught early and often if the blind child is to become a proficient braille-reading adult. One of our deepest commitments is to braille literacy, a commitment we have strengthened considerably over the years in spite of, or even because of, the decline in braille instruction nation-wide. Braille remains the only means of reading and writing for a child who cannot see well enough to read print effectively. Recent studies prove that blind people who learn braille at an early age have generally been found to complete more years of school, have higher incomes and employment rates, and read more in adulthood than do blind people who do not learn braille in childhood. Promoting braille literacy by enticing families, schools, and libraries to buy braille books is a major part of our marketing strategy.

Timing, Timing, Timing

Way back in the 1980s, we thought people would like to read books on a refreshable braille display. We produced two books for what was then the leading refreshable braille device, the VersaBraille. Actually, the books were a personal organizer and a speller: two seemingly practical applications for this method of access. Sales were dismal. We quietly moved away from the idea and hoped no one would notice. They didn't.

Ironically, fourteen years later, we are re-introducing the same type of product line, called PortaBooks (books on disk in a braille file format for reading on a portable, refreshable braille display). So far, sales have been modest. This time, though, rather than quietly abandoning the project, we plan to stay with the idea until we have successfully communicated the benefits of reading a braille book in this way. (Rather than carry a four-volume edition of Shop Online the Lazy Way, you can read it on a two-pound portable braille device. Plus, you can search for particular items, and generally skip around at will.)

This time also, we will offer more than just the books. We have written a user's guide to loading a PortaBook; we will provide some customer assistance over the phone; and we are designing a marketing campaign that promotes the benefits of using this new technology.

Partnership Marketing

A few years back, a braille-reading customer who also happened to work for Kraft Foods called with a proposition, Would we like to work with Kraft to produce a compilation of all of the product package directions from their food lines? Thus was launched what we call "partnership marketing."

It's a simple concept. Find a company who makes a product or sells a service, work with them to make their product or service accessible to braille readers, and ask them to underwrite the cost to produce the original. You fund reprints from sales, and you and the company and your customers all benefit.

The product was so successful with Kraft that we pitched the same idea to General Mills, and this is our third year with them. They were so excited about blind men and women having access to their products that two representatives from the company attended one of the summer conventions of blind people in Atlanta, Georgia.

This concept can be applied to almost anything. Just this year, we approached the North American Menopause Society (NAMS) to underwrite a braille edition of their guidebook, and they were delighted to do so. The other benefit of working with a company in this fashion is that you can piggyback on their advertising expertise and contacts. NAMS promptly put out a press release to their media contacts announcing the availability of their guidebook in braille.

Improving the Product

There is a yellowed cartoon posted on the wall in the marketing department of NBP that best wraps up this chapter. The cartoon shows a group of managers seated around a conference table listening to a presentation by the marketing manager, who is pointing to a falling line on a chart. The marketing manager is saying, "…and if all else fails, we could always improve the product."

We try to stay focused on improving our product, which, in our case, is not braille books, but rather meeting the needs of braille readers and promoting braille literacy. Tricks and gimmicks, and especially grand pronouncements of new products, will never stand the time test of meeting customer needs.

BRAILLE
LITERACY

by Susan Jay Spungin and Frances Mary D'Andrea

Introduction

Braille represents information and education, the currency of the future. All of us recognize that being able to manage and manipulate information is vital to our success economically as well as to our dignity and perceived self-worth. It is therefore important that whatever educational system we have, we ensure that there is choice in learning and in access to information now and in the future.

Braille always has been and always will be more than a tool or means of literacy for those blind individuals who use it. Fred Schroeder, United States commissioner of rehabilitation, points out, "Braille for some represents competency, independence, and equality." Unfortunately, for some blind people, issues of self-identity, such as the desire not to be considered or "look" blind, rather than actual need, affect their decision on whether to use braille. Therefore, the "braille problem"—the fact that it is not as widely used as it should be—is not only a literacy issue, but also a reflection of society's attitudes toward blindness.

In 1989, the American Foundation for the Blind published a booklet titled *Braille Literacy: Issues for Blind Persons, Families, Professionals and Producers of Braille* (Spungin 1989) that detailed the reasons why increasing numbers of blind children and adults were not braille literate and suggested some possible strategies to improve the situation. This chapter will discuss both the issues involved and the strategies for change and will analyze how those in the field of service to blind people have been able to successfully promote the need for braille as the primary literacy tool for all blind people in the past decade.

Issues and Consequences

The most frequent explanations of why we have increased numbers of illiterate blind people seem to fall into six categories:

1. Change in demographics and lack of accurate statistics.

2. Increased emphasis on the use of residual vision.

3. Negative attitudes about braille.

4. The complexity of the braille code.

5. Increased use of technology, especially devices with speech.

6. The need for legislation and mandates.

We will explore each of these rationales in more detail.

Change in and Lack of Demographics and Accurate Statistics

Medical advances have saved many infants who previously would not have survived. Many of these children have lower birth weights, or may not be fully developed at birth. Premature babies are at risk of having not only visual disabilities, but also cognitive, physical, and sensory impairments, or of being medically fragile. The multiply handicapped population has grown tremendously since the 1950s as a result of high levels of oxygen in incubators, which can cause retrolental fibroplasia (RLF), now known as retinopathy of prematurity (ROP), and as a result of the rubella epidemic in the 1950s and 1960s. In the 1990s, these children, who make up an estimated 60 percent of the total population of visually handicapped children, still aren't getting proper services. Many of these children have cognitive and learning disabilities that hinder their ability to learn to read and write, or they may be nonreaders entirely. Because of that, the number of potential braille users who learn with traditional methods has diminished.

Our field of service to blind people needs to examine what literacy means to children with multiple disabilities and find new methods of ensuring that all children become literate to the fullest extent possible. Our greatest concern is the federal definition of "visually handicapped children"; under that definition, there are many multiply handicapped/visually handicapped children we do not serve, because they have not been identified as being visually impaired.

The most tragic error we made as a field was to agree to primary versus secondary handicapped labels to define our population on the annual federal requirement of child count in the federal reporting system.

Of greatest concern is the different ways visually handicapped children are being counted, making accuracy in child count requirements impossible to attain. Every year the Individual with Disabilities Education Act (IDEA) and American Printing House (APH) require annual counts of children who are blind or visually impaired. The major difference is that APH uses the restricted definition of legal blindness of 20/200 or less, etc., and IDEA requires the broader functional definition that can include those children that are totally blind/legally blind as well as those who are children who see as well as 20/60 or 20/70, frequently referred to as low vision. In summary, the APH federal quota registration requires legal blindness for eligibility, a more restrictive requirement than IDEA's requirement for a visual impairment that affects the ability to learn. Yet the annual count of students with visual impairment served under IDEA has totaled less than the federal quota registration since 1977.

Why is this? Why is it that since the implementation of IDEA in 1976, IDEA's numbers have gone down, with the broader definition, compared to APH's count, in the same time period going up. Some blind children are often misclassified as another disability, i.e. learning disabled because the district has no teacher for blind children and/or doesn't wish to spend the money, or no teachers are available. Often multiply impaired blind children are not classified as primarily blind but as some other disability therefore they cannot be counted twice. A child with a physical handicap and blindness is seen as a child only with a physical handicap. Even with the multiply handicapped population, including the deaf-blind categories first reported in 1978, the numbers still make no sense. Unfortunately, we live by the numbers in order to justify funding for training programs, for teachers, vocational rehabilitation, social security benefits, to mention just a few. We cannot continue to accept or ignore the lottery-like approach we have when describing the demographics of our field.

Because of this mismatch of data, generic models of special education service are increasing, and that affects the quality of service in general to all children. As numbers of identified blind children appear to decline, so does our justification for funding programs and training teachers to teach special skills such as braille reading and writing. We are losing children to the cracks found in a system that supposedly espouses the need for the development of unique programs for individuals.

The lack of accurate numbers affects services to blind adults as well. Recently, the North American Caribbean Region of the World Blind Union (WBU) funded a project to determine how best to ensure the gathering and use of accurate demographic data on blindness. It found that no two research studies seemed to ask the question, "Are you blind?" the same way. The lack of consistent definitions of blindness makes comparisons of data sets impossible, and not having access to consistent, accurate numbers limits funding, policy development, and maintenance of existing programs, as well as growth of resources.

The people involved in the study attempted to learn how differences in the wording of two similar questions in two major federal surveys could create differences in the estimated number of people who cannot see well enough to read ordinary print, even with glasses on.

The study concluded that respondents were affected by the context of the print-reading question. In one survey, the context is health issues, while in the other, it is employment and other socioeconomic issues; respondents were less likely to report their visual impairment in the health context, apparently because it seemed minor compared to the many serious conditions about which they were asked. The study supported using, if possible, a two-part question that first asks about less severe visual impairment before asking if respondents are unable to see print at all.

Realistically, the WBU study could not provide a "magic bullet" to solve the complex challenge of using surveys to measure the prevalence of print-reading disability throughout the nation. It has, however, helped the field go a significant way toward improving future measurement, and given new insights about why and how estimates from different surveys vary.

There has been some progress in this area of demographics and accurate statistics, but much more work needs to be done. Because of the difficulties of collecting data on low-incidence populations such as the blind population, a national database for the collection of numbers and information on blind people needs to be developed with ongoing funding, similar to what the deaf and hard-of-hearing have at Gallaudet University, in Washington, D.C.

Use of Residual Vision

The work of Dr. Natalie Barraga and others in improving the use of residual vision since the 1970s has encouraged educators and parents to strive for visual efficiency and utilization when possible instead of accepting the more historically common practice of teaching braille to all visually impaired students, regardless of individual need or visual acuity. Consequently, there are fewer braille users now than in years past.

For too long, this country has been looking for a quick fix to solve problems—yes or no, right or wrong, sighted or blind. Dr. Barraga and her colleagues certainly never intended her work in vision stimulation and vision efficiency to be unilaterally applied to all visually handicapped children with some remaining sight. But that's what has been and still is done, which sends the message to the educational system and to the children in that system that a child who sees is better than one who doesn't see. It encourages visually handicapped children to use their remaining vision at all costs even when they are unable to complete their work assignments in a timely fashion. This bandwagon mentality for the quick fix—to be more like sighted than like blind people—has short-changed many visually handicapped children and adults in this country.

Fortunately, the pendulum, which had swung too far from using vision at all costs, is beginning to swing back toward the center. "One size fits all" does not work for making literacy decisions, whether print or braille. Several new functional visual and learning media assessments have been developed to assist in determining the most appropriate reading media for an individual, be it print, braille, or, as is often the case, both. Such considerations as the working distance from the page, the portability of reading skills, reading rates and accuracy, visual fatigue, and other elements are being factored into the equation of what is best for each student.

In 1994, a proposed Braille Literacy Amendment to IDEA was signed by five organizations—the American Foundation for the Blind (AFB), the National Federation of the Blind (NFB), the National Library Service for the Blind and Physically Handicapped (NLS), the Canadian Institute for the Blind (CNIB), and the American Council of the Blind (ACB)—to guarantee that braille is viewed not as a second-class communication tool but as an equal and viable option to print and as the key to literacy for blind people in the United States and Canada. These advocacy efforts of the blindness field created important changes in the re-authorization of IDEA that put a greater emphasis on braille. This would not have been possible if consumers and providers of services, represented by those five organizations, hadn't worked together.

Negative Attitudes toward Braille

Negative attitudes toward blind people and the communication skills they need do exist, although they are truly unintended. That's what makes them so insidious. We may not realize it, but how we as educators of blind children and adults perform and interact with our students or clients and other professionals demonstrates what our attitudes are toward blindness. By depriving visually impaired students of the right to read braille and instead teaching them only to read large print, when it is clear they read at a less-than-functional speed with large print, we deny them equal access to life. This approach can't help but suggest that perhaps braille is inferior and, therefore, reading print or having sight is superior. Do we positively reinforce blind children in learning braille with the same enthusiasm as we reinforce them in learning print? Or do we instead think of braille as a problem, one more headache to be attended to during our too-busy days? We need to be careful to present braille instruction not as a code to be deciphered, not as something that sets children apart, but as a method of reading and writing that is equal in value to print. We need to make sure that administrators recognize this and support the need for adequate time and money for planning, production, and purchase of appropriate learning materials.

Another problem that creates negative attitudes toward blind people and braille communication is a lack of full knowledge about the subject. That kind of negative attitude is more a function of human frailty than of any conscious decision, but the result is that if a teacher of children who are visually impaired is not comfortable in the knowledge and teaching of braille codes, the importance of teaching those braille codes becomes minimized. The popular idea, however, that negative attitudes on the part of teachers is a major cause of the decline in braille literacy is challenged by some studies done earlier in this decade. Wittenstein (1993, 1994, 1996) surveyed more than a thousand teachers of visually impaired children about their attitudes toward braille, their preparation to teach braille, and other aspects of braille literacy. Results of these surveys indicated that teachers overwhelmingly believe that braille is important and strongly support its use. The teachers in the studies were also confident in their ability to teach braille to their students, especially as their experience increased over time. There was, however, a strong correlation to confidence in teaching ability and the type and scope of preservice training they received.

The inadequate knowledge of braille by some teachers of the visually handicapped is not all their fault. The attitude and support for braille instruction at the university or college preparation level is uneven, to say the least. Some programs are truly strong and place emphasis on the understanding of braille codes and learning the appropriate teaching methods. Others give the knowledge and teaching of braille only lip service, believing it should be a prerequisite to college or graduate course work and thinking it can be covered adequately through an independent or correspondence course. Other programs reduce braille instruction to the level of typing or to a transcriber's knowledge, omitting anything specific to methods of reading or the teaching of mathematics and music. Wittenstein's work indicates that teachers who received training in methods of teaching braille reading retained their braille skills and positive attitudes about braille. Wittenstein writes:

> The implications for teacher preparation programs seems clear. Braille training programs must do more than just turn out proficient braillists. The study of the available research in tactual perception and braille reading methodology is crucial to braille training. Training teachers only in the braille code is analogous to training teachers of print reading by teaching them the alphabet and expecting that minimal competence will prepare them for the complex task of teaching reading. (p. 524)

It is sad to note that the teachers with the most preservice training made up the smallest proportion of respondents in this study. It is clear from the results of these studies that we as a field must do more to improve and expand preservice teacher training programs in the areas of braille reading and writing as well as the Nemeth math code and music code.

At the request of a number of organizations of and for the blind, the National Library Service for the Blind and Physically Handicapped of the Library of Congress (NLS) developed a National Literary Braille Competency Test (NLBCT), a three-part test of literary braille knowledge. Test administration began in 1994, and a total of 102 people took the exam. Only nineteen people passed, raising the need for a validation study of the NLBCT. A new test that more clearly represents the knowledge and skills needed by a teacher of children with visual impairments is currently being developed. Study materials published by AFB, NFB, the National Braille Press (NBP), and other organizations have been developed for individual preparation for the new NLBCT when it is completed in the year 2000. Many braille bills at the state level plan to use the NLBCT for teacher certification or have created their own test. There is the potential for disaster, considering the less than 20 percent who passed the test in 1994.

Although results of the 1994 tests clearly indicate the lack of braille skills of some teachers, the results should only be used as a mandate for the need for better training programs and instructional material development at both the preservice and in-service levels. We hope the quality of instruction will greatly improve with new materials, braille mentor programs, and the use of distance education on the Internet.

The Complexity of the Braille Code

Some continue to attribute the illiteracy of blind people to the complexity of the braille codes and to believe it should be simplified in one way or another. No research supports this notion and many students continue to learn braille reading and writing in the traditional manner.

As stated earlier, however, a large proportion of today's students with visual impairments have additional learning difficulties, which calls not for a new braille code, but for another look at the teaching methods and materials we use. Would some students benefit from learning uncontracted braille (grade 1) before fully contracted braille (grade 2)? Would students who learn only grade 1, but use it functionally and efficiently, be considered literate? The fastest growing population of people with visual impairments is older than 65. Do we have the systems in place to teach braille grade 2 to all adults who wish to learn it? Some older adults choose to learn braille grade 1 only, and use it for labeling, making lists, and other personal needs. Are they considered braille users and fully literate? Research in the area of literacy strongly suggests, over and over, that there is not just one way to teach reading and writing to children and adults, whether blind or sighted; multiple approaches are useful for individual needs. Perhaps the issue is not so much with the complexity of the code as with our definition of literacy and how people use braille.

The standard-setting body of the Braille Authority of North America (BANA) is part of a research study on the creation of a Unified Braille Code (UBC), potentially for use in the United States and all English-speaking countries. As of this writing, the results of the research are being tallied and disseminated to members of the International Council on English Braille (ICEB) in Australia, Canada, Japan, New Zealand, Nigeria, the United Kingdom, the United States, and South Africa. Workgroups, consisting of consumers, transcribers, and educators, have been established to examine, research, and make recommendations about various aspects of the code. And surveys have been distributed to numerous braille users and teachers around the English-speaking world for their input and suggestions.

The creators of UBC are striving for one complete code that would eliminate the necessity of learning separate codes for literary works, mathematics, and computer notation. Since one feature of the UBC is to be as unambiguous as possible, all contractions will have only one meaning. That means that certain contractions may be eliminated (such as "com," "ble," "dd," "by," and "into") so as not to conflict with punctuation and lower-cell signs. The creators of the UBC also recommend that braille words be written spaced from each other, as in print, so contractions that touch the following word (such as "by") could be dropped. Overall, the workgroups have attempted to make as few major changes to the current braille code as possible. The examples given here are just some of the current discussions; until the results of the study are collated and all data are analyzed, the completed code is still a work in progress.

Once the UBC is in its final form, BANA and the braille authorities of each participating country will have to approve it for use in each country. If the UBC is approved and adopted in the United States, a schedule and plan for phasing the new code into books, magazines, and other materials would be created, as well as for devising new training materials for teachers and transcribers of braille. The dream of the creators of the UBC is that all English-speaking countries will share braille materials and that braille will be easier to learn and produce. Will they reach that goal? Currently there is some strong opposition to aspects of the code and major concerns about dropping the Nemeth code in favor of the mathematics portion of the UBC. While change is always difficult, we need to remember that braille reflects a living language—in this case, English—that is also changing. The braille code we now use in the United States is relatively current (less than seventy years old) and is continually being evaluated and worked on through BANA's technical committees. We should keep an open mind about and a watchful eye on the progress of the UBC, and we should encourage the workgroups and members of ICEB to keep up their important work.

Technology

Concerns that technology in any form will diminish the need for and use of braille go back to the first half of this century, to the beginning of the Talking Book Program.

This "either/or" attitude seems to continue to plague the field of service to the blind. Throughout the years of technological development—ranging from talking books to records, cassettes, and compact disc players to computer and speech technology—I have never met a proficient braille user who has rejected braille because of these new communication skills. Most proficient braille users treat these advances in print accessibility simply as options that are available to them and that complement each other. In fact, the ability to do word processing in braille, to edit braille text accurately, and to convert it to hard-copy represents one of the most significant advances in communication available to blind persons in this century. It is ironic that the technology now in existence—such as braille translation software and electronic braille embossers—allows hard-copy braille to be produced more easily and cheaply than ever before, and yet it is also seen as a threat to braille literacy.

There does remain realistic concern that competing technologies, in particular speech output, will diminish the availability of braille. Speech output is both low cost and universal in its design, which means it can meet the needs and desires of a greater number of people, not just those who are blind or visually impaired. Once again, both the freedom to choose braille and its availability could be threatened. As we move toward the promotion and distribution of electronic books for all, we must caution that such materials are no substitute for refreshable or hard-copy braille, even though at this point in time they are less expensive and more easily produced.

As wonderful as the information superhighway is, the reality is that blind people are being left in the back seat. Now more than ever we must ensure the access of information in braille.

We need to work together with present and future programmers and technologists to ensure that gains we have made in braille literacy for blind people will not be run over in the name of access to information for all, or, more specifically, in the name of speech output at the expense of braille. Issues of computer accessibility along with the problems of graphical user interfaces (GUIs) cannot wait to be solved by someone else. Displays that rely on graphics and mouse clicks are obviously not helpful to blind people.

As a field, we cannot afford to take a reactive stance; rather, we should work with and assist the technologists and information brokers of today and tomorrow. This one area alone can change for better or for worse the future of literacy for the blind. Progress for one at the expense of the other is not acceptable.

Another problem is the lack of a central source for information on the availability of braille textbooks. The proliferation of braille textbooks, coupled with the problems of locating and producing titles with no central source of information, creates a proportion of blind students who are waiting for braille texts in school that is unconscionable. If we believe in equal access to print (in this case, via braille), and we now have the technology to accomplish it easily, why do braille users have to wait for and receive books halfway through the school year? How many books are not transcribed, and how many books are unknowingly transcribed more than once or twice? The AFB Textbooks and Instructional Materials Solutions Forum, an outgrowth of *The National Agenda,* (a publication that articulates a vision and plan of action for the future of the education of blind or visually impaired, as well as those who have additional disabilities) is a collaborative national effort to address this issue and is represented by agencies and organizations involved in the production and distribution of textbooks and instructional materials. Textbook publishers, producers of specialized media, assistive technology specialists, educators, Instructional Materials Resource Centers, parents, consumers, and others are examining the multifaceted process of producing and delivering educational materials in accessible media to students who are blind or visually impaired. The goal of the AFB Solutions Forum is to develop a coordinated action plan for ensuring equality of access to instructional materials for students who are blind or visually impaired. Five workgroups (Electronic Files, Legislation, Production, Training and Other Needs, and Communication and Collaboration) have taken the initiative to try to improve the delivery of textbooks in the appropriate media.

The blindness field is working on many fronts in this area of timely access. Textbook publishers, braille production houses, and technologists in the field of electronic data transfer are all working together to develop a national depository for textbook electronic files that can easily be translated into braille. In the not-too-distant future, blind students will receive the correct edition of their textbook at the same time as their sighted classmates. Thanks to both state and federal legislation, equality of access will soon become a reality for all.

Legislation and Mandates

The spirit and original intention of the Individuals with Disabilities Education Act has the potential to make the greatest impact on equality of access of any piece of legislation ever passed. However, its perceived strength—which is its goal to treat all children, including those with disabilities, as equals—is its greatest weakness. One size does not fit all. Children with a variety of disabilities represent 12 percent of the school-age population. Those who are blind or visually impaired represent only 1 percent, or approximately 100,000 children. Because of the multiplicity of possible problems and the very nature of this low-incidence population, the standard operating guidelines found in the Individual Education Plan (IEP) process, the concepts of Least Restricted Environment (LRE) and Free Appropriate Public Education (FAPE), and the service delivery models (special schools, special classrooms, resource rooms, itinerant programs) do not work effectively.

The IEP is a process in which experts, parents, and, when appropriate, students come together to chart the academic course of the visually handicapped student for the year. This process is so critical that its application to all school-age children, handicapped or not, seems obvious. However, it falls short in that it relies on the following assumptions:

- All members of the IEP team are equally able and willing to assess the visually handicapped child's needs and plan a program accordingly.

- All parents are committed to the process and work hand in hand with the school district and the professionals who work with their children.

- The school district has the desire, access, and money to hire trained visually handicapped teachers as well as orientation and mobility instructors and to purchase any necessary equipment.

- The IEP team and parents will work toward solving problems and use due process as a last resort.

- All people involved agree on the definition of free appropriate public education in the least restrictive environment.

There are some situations in which these assumptions are valid, and children and programs flourish. There are many more instances, however, in which limitations of resources, not needs and expectations, shape the results. To ensure the efficiency of this process, consumers and providers of services must join forces to insist that trained teachers—who have taken more than the two or three courses required by some states for certification—be present, along with informed parents. We need to recruit future teachers from our respective friends and colleagues to ensure adequate personnel. Thanks to braille bills in the majority of states, the need for and benefits of braille have become more accepted. Now more than ever, school districts are begging for teachers who can teach braille to blind or visually handicapped students but, as is true in general education, there is a teacher shortage of crisis proportions. In addition, teacher training programs in vision are closing down because of low student enrollment and lack of funding. Currently, university programs in vision have been asked by the Office of Special Education Programs in Washington, D.C., to develop a strategic plan that will ensure an increased quality and quantity of vision teachers. The continued closing down of teacher training programs in vision has profound implications for our efforts to ensure braille literacy and the quality of braille instruction. At the present time it is estimated that there are 93,600 students with educationally significant visual impairments in special education. According to Kirchner and Diament's analysis there are currently 6,700 full time equivalent (FTE) teachers. National Plan for Training Personnel to Serve Children with Blindness and Low Vision (January 2000, p. 28). Based on a recommended caseload ratio of eight students to one educator, a total of 11,700 FTE teachers (both teachers of the visually impaired and teachers of the deaf-blind) are needed. This will require hiring an additional 5000 FTE teachers of the visually impaired immediately, a major crisis when in 1998-1999 an average of 4.9 teachers were prepared for each state (p. 30).

There is one movement in the field of special education that poses the greatest threat to the education of children who are blind or visually impaired: the promotion of the "full inclusion" model as the best possible placement for all children with disabilities. Full inclusion, a philosophical concept currently advanced by a number of parents and educators, is not a federal requirement of special education. Proponents of full inclusion nevertheless take the position that all students with disabilities must receive their total instruction in the regular public school classroom, regardless of individual needs. Full inclusion works well for some students, especially in schools where a great deal of support is available to the student and the classroom teacher. Unfortunately, however, full inclusion would eliminate all special placements, including pull-out services, resource rooms, and specialized schools. Such an arrangement would be detrimental to the educational development of many students with disabilities. IDEA reiterates the need for school systems to offer the full array of placement options for all students based on individual need.

The field of service to blind people does not support full inclusion or any policies that mandate the same placement, instruction, or treatment for all students who are blind or visually impaired. Many of these children benefit from being served in the regular classroom; however, the regular education classroom is not the appropriate placement for a number of children who are blind or visually impaired because they may need alternative instructional environments, teaching strategies, or materials that cannot be provided in the context of a regular classroom placement.

We face three immediate tasks:

1. Keeping the issue of educational placement in perspective.

2. Choosing idea over image.

3. Avoiding fanaticism.

If we follow the principle of inclusion religiously and disregard the differences among the students who are blind or visually impaired, and if we continue to insist that the least restrictive environment is some absolute standard rather than a continuum of service delivery models, we will continue to lose some of the most valuable and creative students in our community.

Our allies in increased options and support for our students and in opposing across-the-board inclusive education are none other than the regular classroom teachers, the parents, and the teachers' unions, which do not mince words. These groups justifiably believe that inclusion could threaten the academic achievements of all children. They are concerned about the growing insensitivity to the unique needs of exceptional children. Inclusion is main-streaming with a vengeance—in the name of integration, it increases the likelihood of failure for students and teachers alike. The blindness field's position paper on inclusion states it well:

> We strongly urge that decision makers carefully consider and be sensitive to the impact of reform initiatives on the education of students with visual disabilities. Caution must be exercised to ensure that educational philosophy and trends such as full inclusion do not seriously endanger appropriate and specialized services for students who are blind or visually impaired. If properly

implemented, IDEA can provide legal safe-
guards to ensure that all individual children can
realize their full potential for independence and
success.

The American Foundation for the Blind's brochure, *Every
Seven Minutes,* further states:

Eliminating specialized services is a dangerous
and costly idea. Specialized services are the key
to dignity, productivity, and independence for
people who are blind or visually impaired. In an
age of cost cutting and budget slashing, blind
and visually impaired people are increasingly
concerned that the services that best serve their
needs will be eliminated, and that the only
option will be large all-purpose disability and
health service organizations—where some blind
people have already fallen through the cracks
(03).

The issue of service delivery models and their effect on
braille instruction is crucial. We have so encouraged the
placement in schools of visually handicapped children in
the community that many states have restricted the alternative of placement in residential schools, where special
skills, including braille, are often taught best. Public school
programs, such as resource programs, special classes, and
itinerant programs, would also work well if reasonable
caseloads were developed that permitted teachers trained
in working with visually handicapped children to have the
time to provide adequate services. In a recent meeting on

the development of a national plan for training personnel, Reston, Virginia, July 1999, caseload size of university programs was finally agreed on: one teacher to eight students with blindness or visual impairment was considered optimum. That is far below the national average and further dramatizes the teacher shortages. In the case of braille instruction, the main issue is to have a sufficient number of trained teachers available to provide the daily instruction that is necessary for our students to succeed.

In more cases than not, although special education for blind children promotes the outward appearance of a mainstream/inclusive setting as in keeping with IDEA, inclusion often represents the most restrictive learning environment. What we all need to do is to ensure the most enabling learning environment for visually handicapped students with appropriate teacher/student ratios according to individual needs and not administrative mandates. No child can learn anything in any academic area from a teacher who comes to a school only once a week.

Conclusion

The need to define disability as an overarching, generic condition for purposes of program design, administration, and funding is the main issue we will still be fighting as we enter the twenty-first century. It is an issue for all blind people: for children, it is inclusion and lack of specially trained teachers; for adults, it is the fight for identifiable agencies. So the importance of braille has become a symbol for much more than literacy; it is a symbol for the freedom to reach one's potential as an equal, contributing member of society, which is the right of all children.

Fred Schroeder summarized this issue succinctly: "Braille has been proven time and time again to be the way to literacy for blind people. It can be produced more easily and more cheaply than ever before in history. With braille and the other skills of blindness, we as blind people can fulfill our potential and take our true place as contributing, participating, taxpaying members of society. To achieve this goal will take concerted and collective actions."

References

American Foundation for the Blind. 1997. *Every Seven Minutes.* New York: AFB Press.

Bealty, P., and W. Davis. 1998. Evaluating Discrepancies in Print Reading Disabilities Statistics: Cognitive Methods Staff Working Paper Series No. 25. Center for Disease Control and Prevention; National Center for Health Statistics, U.S. Department of Health and Human Services.

Corn, A. L., Phil Hatlen, Kathleen M. Huebner, Frank Ryan, and Mary Ann Siller. 1995. *The National Agenda for the Education of Children and Youths with Visual Impairments, Including Those with Multiple Disabilities.* New York: AFB Press.

Spungin, S. J. 1989. *Braille Literacy: Issues for Blind Persons, Families, Professionals and Producers of Braille.* New York: AFB Press.

Wittenstein, S. H. 1993. "Braille Training and Teacher Attitudes: Implications for Personnel Preparation." *Review* 25, no. 3: 103–110.

Wittenstein, S. H. 1994. "Braille Literacy: Preservice Training and Teacher's Attitudes." *Journal of Visual Impairment & Blindness* 88, no. 6: 516–524.

Wittenstein, S. H. 1996. "Teacher's Voices: Comments on Braille and Literacy from the Field." *Journal of Visual Impairment & Blindness* 90, no. 3: 201–209.

BRAILLE AS A PREDICTOR OF SUCCESS

by Ruby Ryles

We have experienced a generation of children who are blind struggling to use print when clearly print was not the appropriate medium. The real tragedy is not so much diminished functioning, as damaged self-esteem. Children who are blind are already subjected to a society that expects little from them. If the tools and strategies available to them are ineffective, then they will logically internalize society's diminished view. There has been much written about the recent decline in braille literacy. Yet, its full impact can only be understood if we recognize that with the loss of literacy comes the loss of hope and self-confidence.

—Fredric K. Schroeder, commissioner of the Rehabilitation Services Administration, United States Department of Education, Washington, D.C. (Cited in Caton, 1994)

From 1963 to 1998, the number of students in the United States identified as legally blind more than tripled. During those three and a half decades, however, legally blind students classified as nonreaders rose from slightly more than one-tenth of one percent in 1963 to more than 45 percent in 1998. During the same time span, students who were taught to read braille declined from 57 percent in 1963 to less than 9.5 percent in 1998 (see Figure 1), while the numbers of legally blind students taught to read using print continued to rise (American Printing House for the Blind 1998).

The pedagogical move away from the use of braille and toward the use of print is well documented in the field of education and rehabilitation of the blind. There is little research, however, to either support or refute the declining use of braille and address the more vital issue: the impact of braille usage on literacy skills and employment rates.

Figure 1. American Printing House for the Blind (APH) quota registrants by reading medium

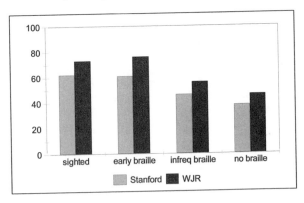

Annual American Printing House for the Blind (APH) quota registrations confirm the apparent impending obsolescence of braille usage among students. In 1963, 57 percent of all visually impaired students registered with APH used braille as a means of reading and written communication. Only slightly more than one-tenth of one percent (0.012%) of the population of visually impaired students registered thirty-six years ago were registered as having no reading medium. According to the 1993 federal quota registration, more than 44 percent of blind or visually impaired students, first grade and older were registered as auditory readers (an individual who reads neither print nor braille, but uses readers and audiotapes), nonreaders or prereaders, while only 10 percent of students who were visually impaired possessed the skill of reading in braille.

The trend of decreasing braille usage and increasing numbers of blind students with no reading medium continued as the APH quota registration figures indicated the numbers of braille readers decreased from 10.32 percent in 1993 to 9.45 percent in 1994. The numbers of blind students who could read neither print nor braille also continued to rise—from 44 percent in 1993 to 46.2 percent in 1994 (APH 1991, 1992, 1993, 1994).

Factors Contributing to the Decreased Use of Braille

There is no clear consensus among professionals regarding causes for the decline of braille readers. Explanations include an increase in numbers of multihandicapped children who are visually impaired (Rex 1989); questions surrounding the utility of the braille code (Thurlow 1988); teachers' lack of knowledge of braille and teaching methodology (Stephens 1989; Schroeder 1989); negative attitudes regarding braille (Holbrook and Koenig, 1989; Rex 1989); an ineffective Individualized Education Plan (IEP) system that encourages the use of readily available resources, such as print or recorded materials, rather than what the visually impaired child actually needs (Spungin 1990, 4); and an overreliance on the use of technology, such as speech output and print magnification technology (Paul 1993).

Emphasis on Residual Vision: Vision Stimulation

Natalie Barraga's work, published in the 1960s, established new pedagogical ground, teaching that seriously visually impaired children could "learn to see" (Barraga 1964, 85). Barraga's philosophy, which came to be known as "vision stimulation" instructed teachers of children who were visually impaired that those children could literally be taught to see and to construct clear pictures in the mind from blurred or distorted impressions (Barraga 1972).

Barraga's theories of low vision underlie a great deal of contemporary instructional practices in the field of blindness. Common adaptations designed to encourage visually impaired children to read print include increasing "visual efficiency" with vision stimulation training lessons from the itinerant teacher of the visually impaired. Educators are encouraged to customize print for legally blind students using a plethora of enlarging and other altering techniques. The research on the effectiveness of low-vision adaptations, however, is meager (Koenig et al. 1992). Unfortunately, even less research is available on the literacy skills of legally blind children who were taught to read using these limited visual abilities.

This new philosophy ushered in an era that discouraged the use of tactile methods of exploration and reading and reversed earlier accepted practices of teaching legally blind children with residual vision to read in braille. If one accepted that children with serious visual impairments could learn to see, it followed that teachers would need to teach the "skill" of seeing, rather than teaching the skill of reading in braille. A number of administrators and educators view this shift in pedagogy as a propelling force in the decline of braille usage and teacher competency in braille instruction (Schroeder 1994; Willoughby and Duffy 1989). According to Susan Spungin, associate executive director of program services for the American Foundation for the Blind (AFB), said in an address delivered to the national convention of the National Federation of the Blind (NFB):

> I truly believe that Dr. Barraga and her colleagues never intended work in vision stimulation and vision efficiency to be unilaterally applied to all visually handicapped children with some remaining sight. But that is what we did and [still] do—suggesting to the system and the child that to see is better than not to see, to encourage the visually impaired child to use remaining vision at all costs. This bandwagon mentality for the quick fix (to be more like seeing than blind) has shortchanged many visually handicapped children and adults in our country who are to be added to the twenty-five million Americans who cannot read or write. The pendulum has swung too far. It must be brought back. (Spungin 1989)

Overemphasis on Technology as an Alternative to Braille Reading

Today's technology, which offers limited access to printed material for children and adults with visual impairments, has proven to be immensely beneficial. Visually impaired children taught to read using various magnification devices, however, often find reading slow and laborious. Blind consumers stress these and other drawbacks of reading print and have tended to view the problem of decreased braille literacy as being yoked to negative attitudes and stereotypes about blindness (Schroeder 1989).

The opening sentence of an article of one federally funded study of a low-vision device illustrates the flawed logic on which the author's assumptions are based. The article begins, "Most people with low vision are handicapped in reading" (Legge et al. 1988). The author's attitude is unmistakable: Sight is required to read well. Braille is never mentioned in the study as a method of reading. Regardless of adaptations made to the print, the page, the environment, or the reader, reading by sight is typically a tedious process for legally blind individuals. Individuals with low vision are not handicapped in reading when the visual component of the act of reading is removed. Braille reading makes sense to consumer groups and classroom teachers weary of tutoring visually impaired children in subjects requiring heavy reading. If the author's opening sentence was corrected, it would express a fundamental principal regarding low vision. Corrected, the sentence would read: "Most people with low vision are handicapped in reading print."

Lack of Teacher Competency in the Reading and Teaching of Braille

Currently in university teacher education programs, no quality standards exist for teaching either the braille code itself or methods of teaching reading in braille—nor are refresher courses typically available for teachers after graduation (Caton 1991). Teacher education programs have tended to de-emphasize braille in favor of stressing the use of magnification to encourage visual reading. Many teachers of the visually impaired have limited knowledge of braille, and are uncomfortable in recommending the medium, especially for low-vision children (Rex 1989). As indicated by Carl Augusto, executive director of the AFB:

> There is a serious shortage of people qualified to teach braille. Furthermore, although the mainstreaming of blind children into regular classrooms is in many ways beneficial, these children are increasingly being taught by teachers who are not competent braille instructors. Therefore braille, the primary literacy tool for the blind, is being taught either poorly or not at all to blind and visually impaired students. (cited in Willson 1993, 15)

Under pressure from consumers and advocacy groups, thirty-five states have adopted legislation mandating that children who are legally blind be given the opportunity to receive braille instruction, thus creating further controversy in the field (Schroeder 1994; Virginia State Department for the Visually Handicapped 1991; Rex 1989). While some professional groups, such as CEARSVH (Council of Executives of American Residential Schools for the Visually Handicapped), call for renewed emphasis on the teaching of braille (CEARSVH position paper 1990), others stress that braille is only one of many options available (Paul 1993).

The Lack of Research in the Field and the Need for this Study

Although figures exist that confirm the decreased use of braille (Kirchner et al. 1988; APH 1993) and the rise in numbers of nonreaders who are visually impaired, no research currently exists that studies the literacy skills of those visually impaired students who are able to read—either in print or braille. It is reasonable to expect that the paucity of quantitative data indicating the value of braille in employment would affect the business of rehabilitation as well as education.

How literate are visually impaired students? What is the impact of braille reading skills on the employability of visually impaired adults? Is braille's impending slide toward quasi-obsolescence justifiable cause for concern? What is the role of braille in the acquisition of literacy skills and employment? The answers to these and other questions concerning the role of braille in the acquisition of literacy skills of visually impaired children and adults are unclear in the current literature. Research in the field of education and rehabilitation of the visually impaired is woefully scant compared with the plethora of studies in other domains.

In *Foundations of Braille Literacy* (1994, 131–132), Rex, Koenig, Wormsley, and Baker discuss the lack of research and its impact on the field of education of children who are visually impaired:

> Relatively little is known about braille as a literacy medium or about the teaching of reading and writing braille...The research base in braille literacy, and to a great extent the theoretical base, is fragmented and in dire need of sustained focus....The efficacy of teaching reading in braille to students who are legally blind [partially sighted] has never been empirically established, nor has it been empirically disputed.

It is reasonable to assume that the influence of a meager research base has had, and continues to have, a deleterious effect on contemporary pedagogy in the field of education and rehabilitation of blind people. Studies that speak to the current braille literacy issue are rare, and no contemporary studies address the questions that should be the essence of concern: Does a literacy problem actually exist in the population of visually impaired students? Are braille reading skills an important factor in "beating the odds" and obtaining employment in adulthood? If so, does a link exist between inferior literacy skills and the decline in the use of braille, as consumers and some professionals believe? What is the relationship between braille reading skills and employment?

Unemployment and Braille Readers

The unemployment rate among adults who are visually impaired is extraordinarily high—70 percent or greater (Kirchner, et al. 1988). Recent research, however, indicates that among those visually impaired adults who are employed, a large majority are braille readers. The Careers and Technology Information Bank (CTIB), developed and operated by the AFB, lists one thousand jobs held by visually impaired adults. A study of CTIB undertaken by the AFB indicates that 850 (85%) of those employed visually impaired adults use braille as their primary method of reading (Spungin 1989). Similar findings indicate that blind adults who received their education using braille as their learning medium tended not only to be employed but also to be better educated and to have higher self-esteem than those who did not learn to read using braille as their primary reading medium (Schroeder 1994; Ryles 1996).

In any study of braille reading, confounding variables exist that, if not controlled for, seriously affect validity. Even though causal relationships between employment or literacy and reading medium alone are difficult to establish, emerging associations between proficiency in braille and literacy and employment appear to be just cause to question pedagogy that minimizes or disregards the teaching of braille reading and writing.

This chapter summarizes two of the author's studies on braille usage and reflects on the implication of the results on the lives of visually impaired individuals. The first study was designed to examine the association between adult visually impaired subjects' original reading medium (print or braille) and their current employment rates, reading habits, income, and education status. The second, more in-depth project investigates the relationship of early instruction in braille or print to the literacy skills of high visually impaired students and their ability to read and write on a level commensurate with sighted peers.

Study of Employment Rates and Braille Reading in Washington State

Although much is written about the abysmal unemployment rates among blind adults in the United States, it seems far more informative to study the approximately 30 percent of blind adults who are employed to search for commonalities. That was the purpose of this study.

Seventy-four legally blind adults ages eighteen to fifty-five participated in a study of reading medium (print or braille) and its implications on their lives. The subjects, forty-two women and thirty-two men, were congenitally legally blind, had no concomitant disabilities, and resided in the state of Washington at the time of the study. The investigation involved personal interviews that consisted of thirty-five to forty questions designed to elicit information regarding visual status and history, current and past reading medium, education, employment, income, occupation, and current reading habits.

Of the seventy-four adults in the study, thirty-one were taught to read using print when they entered school as first-graders and forty-three were taught to read using braille as their reading medium. The reading medium used by the subjects when they learned to read as young children is referred to as their "original reading medium." The individuals in the study whose original reading medium was braille are designated as braille readers (BR) and those who were taught to read using print are designated as print readers (PR). These designations are irrespective of the reading medium (braille or print) used by the subject at the time of the study.

Figure 2. Employment breakdown by original reading medium

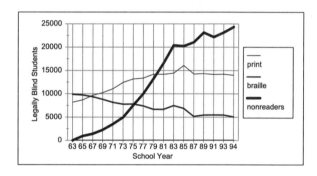

As indicated in Figure 2, 44 percent of the BR and 77 percent of the PR group were unemployed at the time of the interviews. Sixteen percent of the BR group and none of the PR group were employed in unskilled positions; 23 percent of the BR group and 10 percent of the PR group were employed in skilled positions; and 16 percent of the BR group and 13 percent of the PR group were employed as professionals. (One BR subject read print as well as braille and was employed. Five individuals in the PR group learned braille later in childhood or as adults; none of those five was employed at the time of the study.) Having learned or not learned to read braille as a young child was decidedly an important factor in obtaining employment for all seventy-four subjects in the study, but employed members of the BR group shared another critical common variable—their extensive use of braille. Without exception, all subjects in the BR group who were employed reported that they used braille extensively. Although not all members of the BR group who used braille extensively were employed, all who did not report extensive use of braille were unemployed. Extensive use of braille requires proficiency. Subjects in the study who appeared to have the level of proficiency necessary for extensive use were those who learned to read braille as young children.

In addition to employment, three indicators of reading habits were examined: hours per week spent reading, books read in the twelve months preceding the interview, and magazines subscribed to. The BR group spent significantly more time reading, reported reading more books, and subscribed to a greater number of magazines than the PR group. (This study measured only active reading—print or braille. "Reading" books or other material by using audiotapes was not noted as active reading.)

The overall difference between the educational levels of the two groups was slight, with the major distinction at the upper levels of education. Thirty percent of the BR group obtained graduate degrees, while 13 percent of the PR group completed a similar level of education.

Individuals in the study reported yearly incomes that fell into one of three categories: high ($25,000 to $70,000), middle ($7,000 to $25,000) or low (less than $7,000). Both BR and PR groups are similarly represented in the middle income range. The BR group, however, is overrepresented in the highest range (25% of BR and 7% of PR), while the PR group has a greater percentage of members in the lowest range (47% of BR and 62% of PR). Additionally, 49 percent of the BR group and 74 percent of the PR group reported regular participation in public entitlement programs, such as Supplemental Security Insurance (SSI), Social Security Disability Insurance (SSDI), public assistance, and food stamps.

Stereotypically, less sight is synonymous with lower employment possibilities. In this study, however, visual acuity was not positively correlated with employment. Subjects who were totally blind and subjects with an acuity of light perception only demonstrated an unemployment rate of 52 percent, whereas subjects with the greatest degree of vision (20/200–20/300) demonstrated an unemployment rate of 67 percent. This finding is not surprising when the trend of the study is considered: subjects who learned to read using braille tended to be employed in higher numbers. Subjects with little or no residual vision in their early childhood were taught to read braille while legally blind subjects with more residual vision tended to be taught to read using print.

Study of the Literacy Skills of High School Visually Impaired Students

The purpose of this study was to examine relationships that may exist between early braille reading experience and the ability to read. Braille reading experience is a composite term that encompasses multiple variables such as frequency of instruction in braille reading in the first three grades of elementary school; age at which instruction in reading braille was initiated; and the importance accorded to reading braille in the child's education.

Because the investigation was not designed to produce changes in independent variables under controlled conditions, it must be considered a descriptive or observational study rather than an experimental study. For obvious ethical (and legal) considerations, most studies in the field of education of children who are visually impaired cannot impose experimental controls nor compose groups that meet the requirements for true experimental comparison. In a study such as this, for instance, it would be unconscionable and illegal to assign students to experimental groups to receive more, less, or no instruction in braille reading. Because, therefore, there was no practical way to subject the variables of interest to the necessary experimental manipulation under controlled conditions, they cannot, in the strictest sense, be considered independent variables. The design of the study should therefore be considered a retrospective descriptive study rather than an experimental one.

Subjects and Criteria

Sixty teenagers participated in the study. One group of fifteen fully sighted high school students served as a comparison group, while three groups of subjects (fifteen per group) were high school students who had been diagnosed as legally blind before eighteen months of age. Subjects resided in forty-five various towns, cities or rural areas in eleven states and represented widely diverse socioeconomic and cultural backgrounds. With the exception of the sighted comparison group who did not conform to the measures of blindness, all subjects qualifying for the study strictly adhered to the following criteria:

1. Subjects were legally blind (20/200 in the better eye with correction).

2. Subjects' blindness was based on acuity (central vision rather than restricted fields).

3. Diagnosis of legal blindness in subjects was made prior to eighteen months of age (designed to minimize the possibility of significant normal visual memory).

4. Subjects were enrolled in public school in grades 9, 10, 11, or 12 at the time of the study.

5. Subjects had no history or diagnosis of cognitive or physical impairment other than visual.

6. English was the primary language of the subject and the subject's parents.

The fifteen sighted students' scores on reading tests were used as a basis for comparison with the three groups of legally blind students. All sixty subjects were tested in their homes, schools, or other sites that were able to afford necessary accommodations. Students were encouraged to use any adaptions they normally used to read, such as large print, magnifiers, closed-circuit televisions, reading stands, and adapted lighting.

The study included four groups:

1. the sighted comparison group

2. the early braille group

3. the Infrequent braille group

4. the no-braille group

The early braille group met the general study criteria with the additional variable of having had instruction in braille reading four to five days a week in the first three grades of elementary school. All members of this group were braille readers at the time of the study.

Like the early braille group members, all of the infrequent braille group members received formal instruction in braille reading, but they did not receive it with equal frequency. Subjects in this group received braille reading instruction one to three days a week in the first, second, and third grades or braille reading instruction was delayed until third grade or later. Approximately half of the infrequent braille group used braille as their primary reading medium at the time of the study. The remaining members of the group used braille with less regularity.

The no-braille group consisted of fifteen legally blind high school students who received daily reading instruction in print in first, second, and third grades, but had received no formal instruction in braille reading. This group used print exclusively and had little or no knowledge of or experience with the braille code.

Testing and Testing Instruments

All sixty subjects were administered eight sections of two well-known standardized reading tests—the Woodcock Johnson R (WJR) and the Stanford Achievement Test. Data analysis was obtained from the scores of the following tests:

1. Stanford reading comprehension test

2. Woodcock Johnson reading comprehension test

3. Stanford vocabulary test

4. Woodcock Johnson vocabulary test

5. Woodcock Johnson spelling test

6. Woodcock Johnson capitalization and punctuation test

7. Woodcock Johnson grammar test

Subjects were also required to write a one-page essay, which was scored by twelve English teachers representing three high schools in different states. Students and parents were also interviewed to ascertain the subjects' current reading habits and early experience with reading.

Figure 3. Reading comprehension mean scores

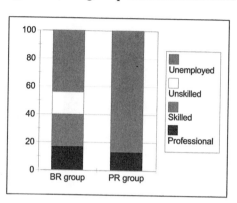

Figure 3 indicates the mean percentile scores of each group for the Stanford reading comprehension test and the Woodcock Johnson reading comprehension test. On both reading comprehension tests, an analysis of variance revealed no significant difference between the mean comprehension scores of the sighted group (Stanford 62%, WJR 73%) and early braille group (Stanford 61%, WJR 76%). Nor was there a significant difference between the scores of the infrequent group (Stanford 46%, WJR 56%) and the no-braille groups (Stanford 38%, WJR 46%). There was, however, a significant difference between the scores of the first two groups (the sighted and early braille groups) and the last two groups (the infrequent and the no-braille groups).

Figure 4 illustrates that the mean Stanford and WJR vocabulary test scores for the four study groups exhibited a

Figure 4. Vocabulary mean scores

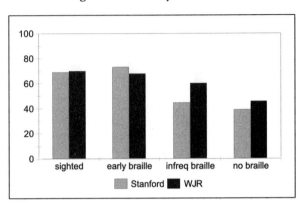

pattern similar to that of the reading comprehension scores. An analysis of variance revealed no significant difference between the mean comprehension scores of the sighted group (Stanford 62%, WJR 73%) and the early braille group (Stanford 61%, WJR 76%). Nor was there a significant difference between the scores of the infrequent group (Stanford 46%, WJR 56%) and the no-braille group (Stanford 38%, WJR 46%).

Because of the use of braille contractions, it is often assumed that individuals who use braille spell poorly. This was not true of students in the early braille group, whose mean scores were slightly higher than the scores of their sighted peers and significantly higher than the mean scores of the infrequent and no-braille groups. Mean spelling scores for the infrequent and no-braille groups indicated that students from these groups had a significant spelling deficiency.

Figure 5. WJR spelling, capitalization, and punctuation mean scores

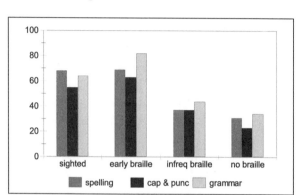

Spelling scores for the study were derived from items on two separate WJR tests—the dictation test and the proofing test—for a total of thirty-nine spelling items. The sighted comparison group's mean spelling score of 68 percent was one percentage point below that of the early braille group (69%). As they did on the comprehension and vocabulary tests, the infrequent braille group (37%) and the no-braille group (31%) produced significantly lower mean spelling scores than did the sighted group and the early braille groups.

Twelve English teachers representing three high schools scored the subjects' essay writing ability. When spelling in this arena was considered, teachers rated the sighted subjects' spelling ability highest of the four groups and the early braille group next. The spelling abilities of the infrequent and no-braille groups were again rated lowest by all teachers at the three participating high schools.

Capitalization and punctuation scores were derived in the same method as the spelling scores. Specific items on the WJR dictation and proofing tests combined to yield a total of twenty-six items on which the capitalization and punctuation scores are based. The sighted comparison group obtained a mean percentile score of 55 percent, while the early braille group attained a 63 percent, the highest mean score. The means of the infrequent braille group (37%) and the no-braille group (23%) were the lowest of the four groups.

The study explored the literacy skills of visually impaired high school students by comparing the results of testing and composition writing with those of fully sighted high school students. On the seven reading ability tests, no significant differences were found between the means of the sighted group and the early braille group. The mean scores from both the early braille and the comparison sighted group were consistently higher than the mean scores of both the infrequent and the no-braille groups and, in most all cases, the differences were statistically significant. In this study, it was clear that the legally blind students who received early, frequent instruction in braille demonstrated literacy skills superior to those of visually impaired students who did not receive such instruction.

Inordinately slower reading speed is thought to be inherent in the use of braille. Duckworth and Garrett's *Directions for Administering the Braille Edition of the Stanford Achievement Test* (1989) suggests that if time limits are used for braille readers, limits should be extended by 2.5 times. Members of the early braille group did not need time limits extended by 2.5 times, but completed the test in 1.6 times the speed of the sighted group. Rather, it was the students who received later or less instruction in braille reading who required almost 2.5 times (2.4) more time than the sighted group to read the comprehension and vocabulary tests.

When compared with the sighted group's mean essay scores, two of the three participating high schools consistently scored the early braille group's essays higher than the sighted group's. The better writing ability of the early braille group is also apparent in the fact that the group's essay scores in all areas were consistently superior to the mean scores of both the infrequent and the no-braille group as rated by the teachers of all three high schools.

During interviews, subjects of the early braille group reported a significantly stronger preference for leisure reading than the infrequent braille group and no-braille group reported. Members of the infrequent braille group expressed the least affinity for reading and supported their aversion to reading with reports of significant numbers of group members who rarely or never read for pleasure.

Conclusions

In today's era of technology, print can be accessed via computers with speech capabilities and scanners. It can be quickly enlarged with closed-circuit televisions and relatively inexpensive standard copiers. Personal computers have seemingly infinite capabilities to enlarge, darken, and change types of fonts. Most libraries have shelves of books with enlarged type, and the array of prisms, monoculars, and magnifiers to expand and darken print seems endless. So why teach braille to children, particularly those with partial sight? Despite the protestations of the adult blind community, why not allow braille to continue its more than thirty-year slide into oblivion? Is braille really worth the trouble, when enlarged print is easier than ever to access?

Chronic unemployment is a problem of catastrophic proportions among the nation's legally blind adults. The results of recent studies indicate that braille readers are employed in significantly greater numbers than visually impaired adults who do not read braille. While the national unemployment rate for the general public is currently 4 to 7 percent, this author's study in Washington state, discussed earlier, revealed a 67 percent unemployment rate among congenitally blind adults, which approaches the national figure of 70 percent unemployment for blind adults.

It is a basic tenet of our nation's education system that literacy is fundamental to employment. The visually impaired teenagers in the second study who were clearly more literate were those whose schools had provided them the opportunity to become proficient in braille by providing early daily instruction in braille. Because earlier studies of visually impaired adults indicate that proficient adult braille readers have substantially higher employment rates than visually impaired adults who read print, the link between high school literacy and adult employment is a simple one to make.

In the two studies discussed, early braille training emerged as the skill that provides the golden ring of literacy for legally blind teenagers. Why teach braille to partially sighted children? The results of this study indicate that it enables legally blind students to compete with sighted peers. Evidence from emerging studies indicates that the early braille readers will also be better equipped to compete for employment as adults.

Why not disregard the voice of experience, the adult blind community, and allow the teaching of braille to disappear? Laws prohibiting discrimination against the disabled exist today that did not exist in the past, making opportunities for employment for today's generation of visually impaired children far greater than at any time in history. Vocabulary, comprehension of written material, and written communication skills, such as spelling, organization of ideas, content, and sentence construction are all crucial skills—skills of literacy—that are necessary for employment in the information-rich environments of today's job market. In the high school literacy study, it was the early braille readers who possessed these crucial skills to an equivalent degree with their sighted peers. These are the same peers with whom visually impaired graduates will compete in the job market.

Is braille really worth the trouble it will take for the education system to bring it back to a position of prominence? Literacy is crucial to opportunities for the future, and the second study strongly supported the hypothesis that braille is crucial to literacy. The answer to whether or not instruction in braille is worth the trouble comes ultimately from two blind individuals. The first, an adult, is the current commissioner of the Rehabilitation Services Administration in Washington, D.C. His statement introduced this chapter and bears repeating:

> We have experienced a generation of children who are blind struggling to use print when clearly print was not the appropriate medium. The real tragedy is not so much diminished functioning, as damaged self-esteem....Yet, [the] full impact can only be understood if we recognize that with the loss of literacy comes the loss of hope and self-confidence.

The second blind individual is Eli, a bright high school junior who wished to participate in the high school literacy study. Eli, like a number of other visually impaired high school students who qualified as subjects, had not been provided enough instruction in braille to be proficient, but did not have the vision to endure several hours of testing required of participants. His poignant comment punctuates the sentiments of the commissioner and should haunt all professionals who work with visually impaired children: "Aren't I pitiful?"

References

American Printing House for the Blind. 1963–1998. *Distribution of Federal Quota Based on Registration of Eligible Students.* Louisville, KY: American Printing House for the Blind.

Barraga, N. 1964. *Increased Visual Behavior in Low Vision Children.* Research series No. 13 New York: American Foundation for the Blind.

Barraga, N. 1972. Increase in Visual Learning Efficiency in "Borderliners" and Low Vision Persons. Paper presented to the International Council on Education of Blind Youth in Madrid.

Caton, H., (ed.) 1994. *TOOLS for Selecting Appropriate Learning Media.* Louisville, KY: American Printing House for the Blind.

Caton, H., ed. 1991. *Braille Literacy Issues. Print and Braille Literacy.* (p 42) Louisville, KY: American Printing House for the Blind.

Duckworth, B. & Garrett (1989). *Stanford Achievement Test Form J: Directions for Administering Braille Edition.* Louisville, KY: American Printing House for the Blind.

Kirchner, C.; R. Peterson; and C. Suhr, 1988. "Trends in School Enrollment and Reading Methods Among Legally Blind School Children, 1963–1978." In *Data on Blindness and Visual Impairment in the U.S.: A Resource Manual on Social Demographic Characteristics, Education, Employment and Income, and Service Delivery.* 2nd ed. New York: American Foundation for the Blind.

Holbrook, M.C.; A. J. Koenig. 1992. "Teaching Braille Reading to Students with Low Vision." *Journal of Visual Impairment and Blindness* 86: 44–48.

Legge, G. E.; G. S. Rubin; D. G. Peli; M. M. Schleske; A. Luebker; and J. A. Ross. "Understanding Low Vision Reading." *Journal of Visual Impairment and Blindness* 82: 54–58.

Paul, B. J. 1993. "'Low Tech' Braille Vital to High-Level Literacy." *Counterpoint* (spring): 3.

Council of Executives of American Residential Schools for the Visually Handicapped. (1990) Literacy for Blind and School-Age Students: A Position Paper of CEARSVH. *Review.* Alexandria, VA: AER.

Rex, E.; A. Koenig; D. Wormsley; and Baker. 1994. Epilogue to *Foundations of Braille Literacy.* New York: American Foundation for the Blind.

Rex, E. 1989. Issues Related to Literacy of Legally Blind Learners. *Journal of Visual Impairment and Blindness* 83: 306

Ryles, R. 1996. "The Impact of Braille Reading Skills on Employment Rates, Reading Habits, Education Levels and Financial Self-Sufficiency of Visually Impaired Adults." *Journal of Visual Impairment and Blindness* 90: 219–226.

Schroeder, F. 1994. Braille Usage: Perspectives of Legally Blind Adults and Policy Implications for School Administrators. PhD. diss., University of New Mexico, Albuquerque.

Schroeder, F. 1989. "Literacy: The Key to Opportunity." *Journal of Visual Impairment and Blindness* 83: 290–294.

Spungin, S. 1989. Literacy: Issues for Consumers and Providers. Paper presented at the National Convention of the National Federation of the Blind in Denver, Colorado.

Spungin, S. 1990. *Braille Literacy: Issues for Blind Persons, Families, Professionals, and Producers of Braille.* New York: American Foundation for the Blind.

Stephens, O. 1989. "Braille—Implications for Living." *Journal of Visual Impairment and Blindness* 83: 88–89.

Thurlow, W.R. 1988. "An Alternative to Braille." *Journal of Visual Impairment and Blindness* 82: 387.

Virginia State Department for the Visually Handicapped. 1991. *A Study of Braille Literacy in Virginia's Public Schools.* Senate Document #31. Richmond, VA: Virginia State Department for the Visually Handicapped.

Willoughby, D., and S. Duffy. 1989. *Handbook for Itinerant and Resource Teachers of Blind and Visually Impaired Students.* Baltimore: National Federation of the Blind.

Willson, N. 1993. "Braille: Bridging the Gap Between Literacy and Illiteracy." *The Braille Forum* 31: 14–16.

ELECTRONIC DISTRIBUTION OF BRAILLE

by Jim Allan

The Not Too Distant Future

An individual goes to the computer and downloads the daily newspaper. The newspaper file comes complete with a table of contents, all headings, all character attributes (bold, italic, and so on), all stories, all sections, and the want ads. Transmitting the file to a portable braille reader with a push of a button, the individual is now ready to read the file at a time and place of choice.

How Do We Get to the Future?

Conceptually, the above scenario of distributing information electronically makes sense and appears easy to implement. The scenario is in fact already occurring. People who read print are able to download electronic text—with formatting, table of contents, and the complete text—to a portable visual device, such as a laptop or palm-top computer. With somewhat more effort, braille readers are also able to download their morning newspaper to read on a refreshable braille display but this document is not formatted or translated for braille reading. It has not been specifically created for braille readers by the distributor.

How can this be made easier for braille readers? This chapter will explore the questions involved in making the electronic distribution of braille universal, such as How is a braille file for electronic distribution created? What would an individual need to receive and read electronically distributed braille? What are the advantages and disadvantages of electronically delivered braille?

Throughout this discussion, the term "electronic distribution of braille" or "electronically distributed braille" is used rather than "electronic braille," because the phrase "electronic braille" is often used to mean the braille displayed on refreshable braille displays in their various forms. Electronic distribution of braille means computer files containing information translated into braille and distributed via electronic media.

Electronic Distribution of Braille: Today

Today almost all braille material is distributed using embossed paper media. Paper braille, however, has two main disadvantages:

1. It is bulky, making shipping and storage expensive and difficult. The "free matter for the blind and

handicapped" postal classification amendment to the postal regulations in 1904 (http://www.nfb.org/freemat2.htm) removed the cost burden of shipping embossed materials from the user, but did nothing to remove the bulk.

2. It has a relatively short life span in nonclimate-controlled storage.

Creation and distribution of braille in an electronic medium would minimize storage and shipping costs. To date, the electronic distribution of braille has evolved through two generations of implementation.

The middle to late 1970s heralded the beginning of the first generation of electronic distribution of braille. This innovation employed the use of computers, braille translators, and electronic braille embossers for braille production. Rather than distributing large volumes of paper braille, it was now possible to create the braille documents on a computer and send an electronic version (via floppy disk) of the documents to the destination site for embossing.

The process of distributing braille electronically in this first generation was as follows:

1. The originator produces a document on a computer using a word processor or a special-purpose braille editor.

2. The originator formats and translates the text into grade 2 braille for embossing using braille translation software.

3. The originator saves the file to a diskette.

4. The originator sends the diskette with the braille file through the postal service to the appropriate person or organization for embossing.

5. The receiver loads the file onto a computer and prints it out on a braille embosser.

6. If the receiver was not the end-user, which was usually the case, the receiver sends the paper braille document to the end-user for reading.

The use of computer diskettes to deliver a file physically through the mail and full (grade 2) translation of the information at the distribution site characterized the first generation of the electronic distribution of braille. Electronic (nondiskette) distribution of braille rarely occurred during the first generation.

The Second Generation of Electronic Distribution of Braille

A second generation of electronic distribution of braille began in the early to middle 1990s, when inexpensive personal computers became widely available. By the latter part of the 1990s, the Internet, e-mail for the non-expert computer user, and the World Wide Web (WWW) were being used at an increasing rate for the electronic distribution of information (http://www.wbri.com/history. htm, http://www.ucmb.ulb.ac.be/documents/email_FAQ/ email.history.html), which allowed for faster and wider electronic distribution of braille files. Electronic delivery media (e-mail, the Web) and grade 2 braille translation of documents at the sending site characterized the second generation of electronic distribution of braille.

The first and second generations of electronic distribution of braille shared one common factor: grade 2 braille translation of documents at the sending site, which will be discussed at the end of this chapter. The following sections will explore in detail the creation and electronic distribution of braille files.

Creating a Braille File for Electronic Distribution

The basic steps for creating a braille file for electronic distribution are as follows:

1. Acquire an electronic file or scan the original paper document using optical character recognition (OCR) software.

2. Proofread and correct any errors.

3. Import the file into a braille translation program (assuming the braille translation program can import the original file type, otherwise additional conversion is required).

4. Format the file for braille, checking for characters that do not exist in Grade 2 braille (for example, the plus sign, the at symbol, the cent sign, etc., and deal with headers, footers, sidebars, and other structural information as necessary.

5. Translate the file into grade 2 braille.

6. Save the file as an embosser-ready file.

The originating, or source, file format determines the quality of the resulting braille file. A rich source file—one with structural information (such as headings, fonts, bold, lists, and tables) rather than just plain text—results in a more accurate electronic braille file. In addition, using an information-rich file means less time and effort are required for correcting or adding format and structure for a usable braille file for electronic distribution.

Types of Braille Files Used for Electronic Distribution

The braille file type determines the output medium of the contents. Typically, two types of file formats are used for the distribution of electronic braille:

1. A braille-formatted file, also known as an ASCII (American Standard Code for Information Interchange) braille file, which contains the exact characters necessary for an embosser to produce a paper braille document. This file type may be embossed for the creation of paper braille or it may be read with a refreshable braille display; it is the most commonly used file format for electronic distribution of braille.

2. A linear braille format file, which contains a set of codes embedded in the text that display formatting information (for example, line breaks and paragraph

breaks) on a refreshable braille display or device. This file type is not suitable for embossing, because the formatting characters would be embossed along with the text rather than controlling the embosser. Linear braille formatted files are only rarely used for the electronic distribution of braille.

Both braille file types, which are created using braille translation software, contain braille-translated characters, document format, and sometimes other information relevant to the documents, such as ink print and braille page numbering.

Braille translation software uses specific rules to convert printed text into the appropriate braille code and formatting based on language (such as English, Spanish, and so on) and subject matter (such as math, literary, and so on).

While there is no accepted formal standard format for an electronically distributed braille file, the most popular file format in current usage, as mentioned, is the ASCII braille file. ASCII braille files, such as the .BRF files created with the Duxbury Braille Translator and the .BFM files created with the Megadots Braille Translator, are embosser-ready, which means they contain hard-coded braille code (almost entirely grade 2), margins, character and line spacing, page numbers, and other information.

Because of the hard coding, ASCII braille files produce acceptable, well-formatted braille only if embossed on the same paper size for which the file was originally created. For example, a common standard for ASCII braille files has a line length of forty characters and a page length of twenty-five lines in grade 2 braille. A file of this type produces properly formatted grade 2 braille when using an embosser with 11-by-11½–inch braille paper.

Embossing the same file with narrow braille paper (8½ by 11 inches) results in alternating full and partial lines of braille. The braille file was created to emboss a line forty characters long and move to the next line. An embosser using the narrower paper will only accept up to thirty-two characters before moving to a new line. On the new line, the embosser brailles up to eight additional characters before the braille file, having sent forty characters, now instructs the embosser to move to a new line.

It is clear that this nonflexible format poses many problems for those using other paper sizes or requiring grade 1 braille or some variation of braille translation. The burden of creating alternative versions (different line length, line spacing, or degree of translation) of the same file to meet the various printing needs falls on the braille file producer.

Source Material Used to Produce Electronically Distributed Braille Files

Two sources of information are used to easily produce electronic braille files:

1. An electronic version of a document obtained from a word-processor, the Internet, or similar source.

2. A paper document that is scanned using modern OCR technology.

Electronic Documents

The most common file format or file type for creating electronic braille is a plain text or ASCII file which unlike the ASCII braille file contains no character or other document formatting information. Limited formatting, such as paragraph indentation, centering of titles, and so on, is rendered using only spaces and carriage returns for page layout. Plain text files require additional work to remove unnecessary carriage returns, and convert multiple spaces into meaningful formatting before being translated into braille.

Other file formats used to create electronic braille include word processor files, such as Word Perfect and Microsoft Word, desktop publisher files, such as QuarkXpress and PageMaker, and HyperText Markup Language (HTML) files. These file formats provide rich character and page formatting information, thus improving the quality of the electronic braille document. In rare instances, printer composite files, which control a printing press on large-production books, are used to create electronic braille files. Typically, extraneous printing press commands must be converted to meaningful formatting or removed, rendering printer composite files less useful for braille file creation.

Electronic versions of nonbraille translated documents or complete books are easily obtainable on the WWW. For example, Project Gutenberg (http://www.promo.net/pg/) has more than one thousand two hundred books available for downloading. The "Electronic Texts and Publishing Resources," an Internet resource provided by the Library of Congress (http://lcweb.loc.gov/global/etext/etext.html), contains a large listing of archive sites with electronic documents and books for downloading.)

Some documents available on the Web are difficult, if not impossible, to use for the production of electronic braille files. These include images of documents (typically, scanned images of historical documents) and documents in formats that do not allow the easy extraction of text. For example, some documents created in Adobe's Portable Document Format (http://access.adobe.com/access_whitepaper.html) do not allow the extraction of text for braille production.

Paper Documents

Paper documents are also a source for the creation of braille files. Converting paper documents into braille requires the use of a scanner and OCR software. Once the paper document is scanned and converted into text, the process of cleanup begins. OCR is not perfect; it depends heavily on the quality of the original document. At its best, OCR recognition approaches 98 percent accuracy.

After a paper document is scanned, unrecognized or misrecognized characters must be corrected. Also, lost document structure (for example, headings) may have to be separated from the main document. After corrections are made, the electronic document is ready for importing into a braille translation program. Additional corrections and braille-specific formatting complete the creation of a braille file.

After a Braille File Is Received Electronically

The consumer, having received a braille file, now has the choice of reading the material using a refreshable braille display or embossing the file and reading the paper braille. Public schools are choosing to use electronic braille files to produce paper books for students. For example, most middle school students read *Huckleberry Finn*. A state library may have only one or two copies of the book in braille for loan to students, so if ten students request the book simultaneously, most students cannot borrow the book. Access to electronic braille files of the book allows the local school to provide an embossed copy on demand for the student. If students have access to a refreshable braille display on a computer or portable device, the same file used for embossing could be used for reading on the display.

Electronically distributed braille may pose problems for economically disadvantaged people, because receiving and using electronic braille assumes owning or having access to the following:

- The Web or other delivery system (of course, this is not necessary for postal delivery of a diskette).

- A computer or portable device with a refreshable braille display.

- A braille embosser and paper.

Paper braille does not impose these equipment demands on consumers.

Devices for Reading Electronically Distributed Braille

One of the first devices for reading electronic braille was the Versabraille. The original version used cassette tapes as a storage and distribution medium; it was later upgraded to use floppy disks. The Versabraille used a proprietary file format, which means that if the file was needed in another device or computer, it had to be exported to ASCII or a text file. Exporting the file caused a loss of character formatting and other structural information, which had to be added back into the file later.

Currently, any computer or portable device with a refreshable braille display can be used to read electronically distributed braille. Portable devices allow electronic braille books to be read much like paperback books, at the reader's convenience. Examples of portable devices that can read electronically distributed braille files (specifically ASCII braille) are the following:

- Laptop computers with braille displays attached.

- Laptop computers with built-in braille displays, such as the David from Baum Electronics (http://www.baum.de/).

- The BrailleLite family of products from Blazie Engineering (http://www.blazie.com/).

- The Bookworm from Handy Tech (http://www.handytech.de/produkte/wurm/ep_wurm.htm).

All these devices have internal grade 2 translation capabilities.

Who Is Currently Distributing Braille Electronically?

Distributing braille electronically has occurred sporadical-
ly, although increasingly, in the United States and around
the world, such distribution methods are more and more
frequently being employed. For example, the Texas School
for the Blind and Visually Impaired (TSBVI) (http://
www.tsbvi.edu/braille/) distributes kindergarten through
twelfth-grade library books in ASCII braille and other
formats via the Web (TSBVI has a limited number of
books in grade 1 braille); the American Printing House
for the Blind (APH) distributes the Readers Digest on
disk translated into ASCII braille (http://www.aph.org/
magsubsc.htm); the Electronic Braille Book Library
(http://www.braille.org/braille_books/), a project of the
International Braille Research Center, distributes literary
and other books in ASCII braille format via the Web; the
National Library for the Blind in the United Kingdom
(http://www.nlbuk.org/download/dload.html) also distributes ASCII braille books via the Web; and the
National Library Service for the Blind and Physically
Handicapped of the Library of Congress (NLS) has
launched Web-Braille with nearly three thousand titles in
ASCII braille that are available for download via the Web
(http://www.loc.gov/nls/braille). Users of the NLS service
will need to register with their state library for the blind
and physically handicapped to download the books. All of
the braille book resources listed above offer grade 2 braille
translated files unless otherwise noted.

Summary

The second generation of braille files distributed electronically contain a fixed line length, hard-coded structural information, and grade 2 braille translation. It is difficult to return the braille file to its original format with flexible margins that can be edited, page numbering, character formatting, and structural information. The current file format will not meet the demands of the future.

Electronic Distribution of Braille: The Future

The third generation of electronic distribution of braille is on the horizon. Moving from physical to electronic distribution signaled the passing of first generation and the ascension of the second generation of electronically distributed braille files. Braille file format will determine the third generation of electronic distribution. Braille file format becomes a critical issue as technology continues its rapid changes, braille reading devices become more portable, and embossers or paper formats change. The current ASCII braille file (grade 2) will not meet the needs of the future.

One question, however, needs asking: Why must the braille translation occur at the producer level? If braille translation occurs at the receiving point, a nontranslated file becomes the distributed file type. That is obvious, but it must be stated, because the implications are profound.

The use of a nontranslated file could mean the use of one file format that is capable of the following:

- Retaining structural and character formatting.

- Having flexible margins.

- Being transformed to other file formats.

- Being translated to different grades of braille.

- Being used by all braille translation software.

- Being embossed on a range of paper sizes.

- Being read by portable devices.

Many file types exist now, each with advantages and disadvantages. See Figure 1 (next page) for a look at the file types discussed so far.

Figure 1. File types and their benefits and problems

Document Type: Text File
Benefits: • Usable by any software
Problems: • no character formatting
• must add structural information
• must translate
• copyright problems

Document Type: Word Processor File
Benefits: • easy editing
• easy reformatting
• can edit markup
• most can be transformed for braille translators
Problems: • proprietary—must own the software to make changes
• must translate and usually reformat for appropriate braille structure
• many cannot be imported by some braille translation software
• copyright problems

Document Type: ASCII Braille File
Benefits: • easily transported
• few, if any, copyright problems
Problems: • difficult to edit
• difficult to reformat
• contains hard-coded spacing and carriage returns
• hard-coded braille translation

Figure 1. File types and their benefits and problems (continued)

Document Type: Braille Word Processor File

Benefits:
- easy editing
- easy reformatting
- can edit markup
- can be transformed for word processors
- few, if any, copyright problems

Problems:
- proprietary—must own the software to make changes
- no conversion between braille word processor file formats

Document Type: HTML File

Benefits:
- easy editing
- easy reformatting
- can edit markup
- can be transformed for word processors
- easy braille translation

Problems:
- copyright problems

A New File Format

The migration from analog to digital media for audio books (talking books) and the adoption of an international standard structured file format for digital talking books (DTBs) may signal the beginning of the third generation of electronically distributed braille. The National Information Standards Organization (NISO) states that a "DTB is envisioned to be, in its fullest implementation, a group of digitally encoded files containing an audio portion recorded in human speech; the full text of the work in electronic form, marked with the tags of a descriptive markup language; and a linking file that synchronizes the text and audio portions" (http://www.niso.org/talkbookdraft.html).

Kersher (1999, http://www.dinf.org/csun_99/session0183.html), in a presentation, finds that the file format for DTB "is perfectly suitable as input to braille translation software." Braille translation software companies are currently working on translation and formatting algorithms for the new DTB file format (Kersher 1999, http://www.dinf.org/csun_99/session0182.html). Kersher (1999) also states that the "speed and accuracy of this translation process should be better than the braille production community has ever seen. There will always be those extremely difficult braille-formatting issues that a trained braillist needs to address, but the mundane activities and even some of the tricky items should be handled by the braille translation software. We can make these statements, because of the high quality of the data moving into the braille translation process" (http://www.dinf.org/csun_99/session0182.html). Furthermore, the file format is designed to be a conversion step between the complex formatting requirements of book and other publishers and relatively basic formatting necessary for braille file production (http://www.dinf.org/csun_99/session0182.html). (See Figure 2.)

Figure 2. The benefits and problems of DTB files

Document Type:	Digital Talking Book File
Benefits:	• easy editing
	• easy reformatting
	• can edit markup
	• can be transformed for word processors
	• easy braille translation
	• intermediate file format between publishers and braille producers
	• international standard
Problems:	• copyright problems
	• translation algorithms still being developed
	• portable devices may not support the file format

Although the DTB file format seems ideal for the distribution of nontranslated files, it is prudent to look at the advantages and disadvantages. There are several advantages to using a nontranslated format for distribution:

- It is usable by all braille translation software.

- It can be embossed on a range of paper sizes.

- It may be read by portable devices.

- It retains structural and character formatting.

- It transforms easily to and from other file formats.

- It can be translated to any grade of braille (perhaps reaching a larger braille reading audience).

There are also several disadvantages of using a non-translated format for distribution:

- The reader must own or have access to braille translation software.

- The reading device used by the reader must have braille translation capabilities.

- The reading device used by the reader may not be able to read the file format.

- There may be copyright problems in the United States because the files are "distributed in a format other than a specialized format, i.e., translated braille files, exclusively for use by blind or other persons with disabilities" (http://www.loc.gov/nls/reference/facts-cop.html).

Some readers may be able to translate documents without owning braille translation software by using Web-based braille translation. There is one functioning Web-based translation service available—Braille It! from the Royal National Institute for the Blind (RNIB) (http://www.rnib.org.uk/braille/letter.htm) that allows the user to input text and simple formatting for translation. The translated file is then displayed onscreen for viewing, saving, or embossing, with choices for line and page length and contracted or uncontracted translation.

Questions

Many questions still need to be resolved before the third generation of the electronic distribution of braille becomes reality, assuming the third generation file type is a non-translated file:

1. Given the trials associated with unifying the braille code (see chapter 8 which group or groups will determine a standard file format for distribution of braille?

2. Will graphics be included in the distributed files? If so, what is the mechanism for making the graphic meaningful?

3. What encryption/copyright mechanisms must be created so the files used for the delivery of braille move electronically unhindered?

4. What copyright agreements must be established to allow distribution of files across international boundaries between countries using the same language?

5. What will be done to provide equal access to information for economically disadvantaged individuals who are not able to benefit from electronic distribution of braille?

6. When will the third generation begin?

7. What will the next generation of electronically distributed braille bring?

FUTURE BRAILLE CODES AND FONTS

by John A. Gardner

Introduction

C reated as a way for blind people to read, braille is adequate for most common literature consisting only of words, but standard braille is inadequate to convey more complex information, such as is used in mathematics, as well as the many symbols used in scientific literature. As the need for information beyond the scope of standard braille became evident, other braille codes were developed, first for math, and later for computer notation. One problem with having these new codes is that blind people who want or need to read or write scientific or mathematic formulas or computer software need to learn additional braille codes that differ radically from standard braille. Also, a problem with the braille codes in general is that preparation of braille documents requires either a great deal of human labor or complex, expensive computer translation software.

In order to reduce the difficulties of access to general information, the Braille Authority of North America (BANA) began a project in 1992 to develop a Unified Braille Code (UBC; http://world.std.com/~iceb/ubc.html). The project was subsequently adopted as an international project by the International Council on English Braille and is discussed in chapter 8.

The implicit philosophy of braille, as well as of the UBC, is that it is a method of coding print in tactile form. I hold the fundamentally different view that braille and print should be merely different methods for presenting information, and neither should be a precursor to the other.

The advent of the electronic information age and structured electronic documents makes this distinction more than just semantics. Virtually every document is now produced on a computer, and, increasingly, electronic information is transmitted directly to the user to be either read on a computer or printed by the end user. Structured formats using markup languages (World Wide Web Consortium information on markup languages can be found at http://www.w3.org/wai), such as HTML (Graham 1996), SGML (Goldfarb 1990; Cover 1999, The SGML/XML Web Page, http://www.oasis-open.org/ cover/), and XML (DuCharme 1999), are becoming increasingly popular because they permit information to be defined precisely and not simply inferred from visual formatting. Structured formats are also particularly desirable for information that is to be transmitted electronically by such networks as the World Wide Web (WWW). It is almost inevitable that much information of the future will be authored, transmitted, and stored in structured formats.

Well-structured documents will permit easy alteration by users or editors of an author's display or print style. Among the many reasons that this is desirable is that it allows a user to display or print documents in ways that are most convenient for that user to read and use. This flexibility is particularly advantageous to people with poor vision, dyslexia, and other print disabilities, because they can choose to display information in larger print, simpler fonts, higher contrast, different colors, different formatting, and so on. It is clear that one must now look at a printed page merely as one method for displaying information.

In principle, there is no reason why well-structured information cannot be displayed or printed in a tactile form just as easily. In practice, this task is made difficult, because text must first be translated to braille. If any non-standard information (such as nontext symbols and math expressions) occurs, the translator must have the ability to switch codes. Also, there are currently many common symbols and scientific expressions for which there are no acceptable braille equivalents in any code. If braille were better structured and more complete, displaying or printing braille from well-structured electronic documents would be no more difficult—in fact, it would often be easier—than displaying print.

There are two possible approaches to improving tactile printing capabilities:

1. Developing an adequate unified braille code that permits general information to be presented linearly on a conventional refreshable braille display or embossed on a braille printer.

2. Using a more general tactile font that need not be linear, so that spatial formatting can convey information similarly to the way spatial formatting conveys information in print.

In this chapter, we will consider the different requirements of these two approaches and the advantages and disadvantages of both.

Unified Braille

Standard English braille (grade 2) uses a number of contractions and shorthand conventions to reduce the dot density and the length of braille documents from what it would be in uncontracted (grade 1) braille. Unified braille proponents generally agree that it is best to develop unified braille through a major revision and expansion of grade 1 braille, because, for practical reasons, it is desirable to alter grade 2 braille as little as is reasonably possible so that it can continue to be used for common literature without imposing great burdens on current braille readers. The expanded grade 1 braille could then be used either instead of or in addition to grade 2 braille for literature that includes more complex expressions. The proposed UBC follows this philosophy.

Braille has two fundamental differences from print:

1. It uses cells having a fixed grid of only six dots or, in the case of eight-dot braille, eight dots. In addition to the space character (an empty cell), there are only sixty-three unique dot patterns possible for a six-dot braille cell. This is far too few to permit single-cell representations for all ninety-five characters on a standard English computer keyboard, much less the hundreds of characters common in basic math and science.

   Computer keyboard symbols are represented by single-cell symbols in Computer Braille Code (CBC), but it is possible to represent all ninety-five by single cells only in eight-dot braille (which permits 255 unique dot patterns). Representation of the thousands of less common symbols used in English literature requires that most be represented by multiple cells.

2. It is always read linearly. It is possible to convey information in both braille and print from spatial formatting, but braille is much more limited. For example, one may indicate titles in braille by centering, paragraphs by indentation, and small tables by spatial organization, but one cannot use raised symbols as superscripts in braille or show fractions with the numerator over the denominator separated by a horizontal line. That information is representable most

efficiently through braille markup symbols, which are not a new concept. Even standard braille has markup symbols, such as the italic word and phrase indicators, the capital word indicator, and the letter and number indicators.

If a good unified braille code were available, it would actually be much easier to display and print braille from structured files than it is to display and print information to be read visually because information in structured formats is linearly organized much like braille. Print displays should require relatively simple processing to convert the source file to grade 1 braille and little more than a set of lookup tables to convert to grade 2.

A unified braille code adequate to fulfill this promise needs to have a reasonably complete and unique font set and an adequate set of markup symbols. Unfortunately, it is not possible to create an adequate unified braille code by extending current braille without making some changes that many people consider too radical.

The font set of current English literary braille includes unique single-cell representations for lowercase letters and most punctuation marks and double-cell representations for capital letters. Most other symbols either have no representation (for example, the plus sign, the at symbol, the equals sign); are representable only in the most common context (for example, the dollar sign, the question mark, italic letters); or are represented by a code (for example, numbers).

One can add braille symbols for characters that are not currently included without changing current braille symbols. One cannot, however, remove ambiguities or create symbols for numbers without making some fundamental change. The present UBC proposal does make changes to remove ambiguities, but it does not resolve the dilemma of not having numbers as part of the font set.

In standard braille, numbers are represented by a braille number symbol followed by a string of letters in the range of a through j. In that string, a represents one, b is two, and so on up to j, which is zero. This number convention, which is retained in the current UBC proposal, makes mathematics extremely clumsy and cannot be used in a braille font such as CBC.

In the United States, Canada, and New Zealand, math and computer codes use Nemeth "dropped characters," which take advantage of the fact that the braille symbols for a through j have no dot in the bottom row. Nemeth numbers have the advantage of being intuitive to learn and remember, but have the disadvantage of being, for the most part, punctuation marks in regular braille. Consequently, Nemeth numbers could be used in unified braille only if most punctuation marks are redefined.

European computer braille fonts have adopted the "dot-six" braille numbers. The numbers one through nine are formed by adding a dot on the bottom right (the dot-six position) to the letters a through I, respectively. These symbols are undefined in grade 1 braille and therefore conflict with no letter, punctuation mark, or other fundamental symbol. The symbol for zero is an exception to this rule because it would conflict with the letter w (which was not in the French alphabet when Louis Braille developed letter symbols). The most common choice for zero in European computer braille is dots three, four, six.

Norberto Salinas and I have proposed the alternate GS (Gardner Salinas) unified braille code (Gardner 1999a) that adopts the European dot-six numbers in its font set. The fundamental prefix-root structure for braille symbols and many of the most common symbols are adopted from the UBC. The symbols include all the letters and all uniquely defined punctuation marks of grade 1 braille.

In developing GS, we imposed a fundamental new requirement on symbols to ensure uniformity between the regular six-dot version (GS6) and a compact eight-dot braille version (GS8). All single cells of GS6 are the same in GS8, but the more common multiple-cell GS6 symbols are single cells in GS8. For example, capital letters and Greek letters are double cells in GS6 and single cells in GS8. A straightforward set of transformation rules defines a unique GS8 symbol for any GS6 symbol.

Currently, GS8 is displayed by the TRIANGLE computer program (Gardner 1999b), but otherwise GS braille has not been anything other than a subject of academic interest.

Beyond Braille

In 1993, I proposed DotsPlus™ a new concept for tactile printing (Gardner 1993). The DotsPlus tactile font set is an extension of braille for which every symbol is meaning-

ful, even if it is standing alone. The font set has been tested and improved since its creation. Current DotsPlus
(Gardner 1998) includes standard braille lower- and
uppercase letters and graphic symbols for common punctuation marks that are shaped like braille punctuation
marks. These punctuation marks are not identical to braille
punctuation symbols, because they must be distinguishable
from letters when out of context, but in normal text the
similarity is so strong that DotsPlus reads like grade 1
braille.

The major departure from grade 1 braille is the set of
number symbols. DotsPlus uses the European computer
braille (dot-six) numbers described in the previous section.
The zero is represented as dots three, four, six. Braille is
used for Greek letters and a small number of other common symbols, but nearly all other symbols are tactile
graphic symbols shaped like the print equivalent. Users
may choose two variations of DotsPlus: the standard
(DP6) DotsPlus font uses standard double-cell capital letters and the double-cell Greek letters of both the
American and English math braille codes; the more compact DP8 version replaces these by single eight-dot braille
cells. All other DP8 symbols are the same as DP6. All
braille symbols of DP6 and DP8 are identical to those
used respectively in the GS6 and GS8 codes that were
described in the previous section.

Small-scale tests by a panel of blind scientists and educators were used in initial development of DotsPlus
(Gardner 1993). DotsPlus tests have subsequently been
conducted on middle school, high school, and university

students in Oregon. Large-scale tests and general use of DotsPlus have not been feasible until recently because of the lack of an adequate printing technology.

DotsPlus is expected to have two major advantages over braille:

1. Less common symbols need not be constructed from long strings of braille cells that are often not entirely intuitive and therefore are hard to learn and remember. Most print symbols have distinct shapes that can be recognized tactually as readily as visually, so the learning and remembering process for less common symbols should therefore be reasonably equivalent for blind and sighted readers. Perhaps even more important, these DotsPlus symbols, unlike braille, can be easily recognized by sighted people, which should greatly improve communication between blind and sighted readers with the consequent improvement of educational and professional opportunity.

2. A true graphics printer for blind people becomes possible with DotsPlus. With an adequate resolution tactile printing technology, DotsPlus documents can be printed from virtually any computer application using the same spatial formatting as the visual document. The only requirement of the computer application is that it can use fonts having the correct size and shape needed by the DotsPlus printout. Nearly all modern computer programs have this property. With a DotsPlus tactile graphics printer, one could print tactile documents containing graphics, charts, tables,

diagrams, maps, normally formatted math, and other nontextual information in addition to any text in the document.

The TIGER (TactIle Graphics Embosser) was invented and initially developed in my laboratory (Sahyun 1998, http://www.dinf.org/csun_98/csun98_103.htm, and Langner 1997, http://dots.physics.orst.edu/tiger_project.html) in order to make such a computer printer a reality. The TIGER Advantage™ was introduced commercially in March 1999 at the Technology for Persons with Disabilities conference, sponsored by the California State University at Northridge. TIGER is manufactured by ViewPlus Technologies, Inc. (http://www.viewplustech.com).

TIGER can be used as a standard braille embosser, but, unlike braille embossers, it has a standard Windows printer driver. Users can choose screen fonts with the correct size and shape for either standard DotsPlus or DP8 fonts or any computer braille font. The characters are large and some may have unusual shapes (for example, DotsPlus capital letters are twice as wide as lowercase letters), but otherwise they are just normal screen characters. TIGER converts them automatically to the appropriate dot pattern. Line and block graphics made with good graphics applications (for example, CorelDraw, MS Word, Excel, and Mathematica) are embossed along with any text (see Figures 1 and 2). The graphics resolution is twenty dots per inch.

Although DotsPlus has the great advantage of having made the TIGER printer possible, it has the disadvantage of not being able to be produced by a braille embosser.

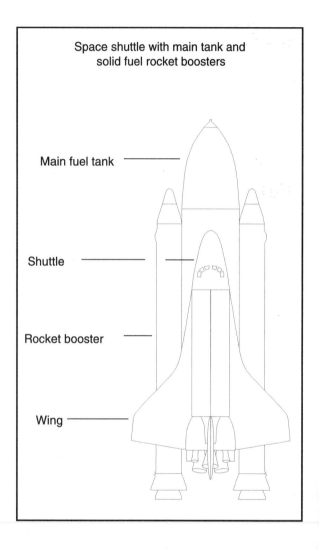

Space shuttle with main tank and
solid fuel rocket boosters

Main fuel tank

Shuttle

Rocket booster

Wing

Figure 1: Diagram of the space shuttle imported into MS Word from the CorelDraw clip art file. Labels were added, and the picture at left printed on a standard printer. The picture below shows the dots that are embossed when the same file is printed on the TIGER Advantage printer. The DP6 font is used.

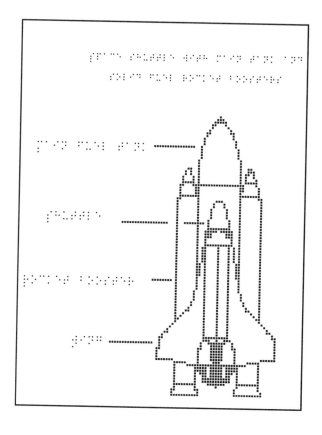

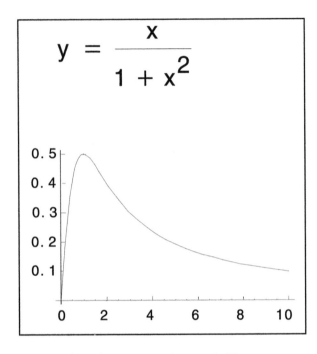

Figure 2: A math equation and its graph. The equation was created in MS Word using the MathType math editor that is bundled with that program. The graph was created using Mathematica and

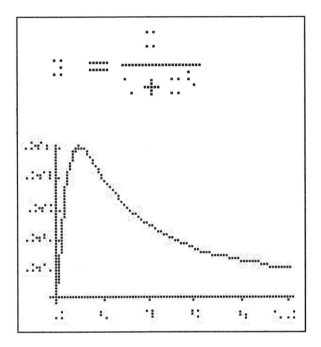

imported into the MS Word file. The picture to the left is printed on a standard printer, and the one above shows the dots embossed when printed on the TIGER Advantage.

There is also currently no technology permitting online display of DotsPlus and no DotsPlus equivalent to a simple braille slate. Development of an online technology with good enough resolution for DotsPlus is a formidable challenge, but one that must be solved before tactile readers can have truly full access to online information. A simple hand-held DotsPlus slate is not a particularly difficult challenge, and such a slate could be made commercially available if enough demand develops.

As a final note of particular interest to blind scientists, it is worthwhile to realize that one could write equations in a very compact form by using linearly formatted DotsPlus with a few markup indicators. DotsPlus symbols are generally more compact than braille, but common formatting of math is not very spatially efficient. By formatting math equations linearly but with DotsPlus symbols, one can create equations with very good spatial efficiency. This could be an important consideration for people who need to use a great deal of tactile hard-copy scientific literature. A set of markup symbols intended for such use with DotsPlus will be tested as part of a linear display routine being developed for the new mathML (math markup language) (http://www.w3.org).

DotsPlus is a trademark of Oregon State University
TIGER Advantage is a trademark of
    ViewPlus Technologies, Inc.
MS Word is a trademark of Microsoft, Inc.
CorelDraw is a trademark of Corel, Inc.
MathType is a trademark of Design Science, Inc.
Mathematica is a trademark of Wolfram, Inc.

References

DuCharme, Bob. 1999. *XML: The Annotated Specification.* Upper Saddle River, NJ: Prentice Hall.

Gardner, J. 1993. "DotsPlus, Better than Braille?" Paper presented at the 1993 Technology for Persons with Disabilities conference in Los Angeles, March 17–30, 1993.

Gardner, J. 1998. "The DotsPlus Tactile Font Set." *Journal of Visual Impairment and Blindness* 92, no. 12: 836–840.

Gardner, J. 1999a. "Introduction to the GS Braille Code." Article found at http://dots.physics.orst.edu/gs.html.

Gardner, J. 1999b. "Overview of TRIANGLE." Article found at http://dots.physics.orst.edu/triangle.html.

Goldfarb, C. 1990. *The SGML Handbook,* edited by Y. Rubinsky. Oxford University Press, New York.

Graham, I. S. 1996. *The HTML Sourcebook: A Complete Guide to HTML 3.0.* 2d edition. New York: John Wiley & Sons.

Sahyun, S., Bulatov, V., Gardner, J., and Preddy, M. 1998. "A How-to Demonstration for Making Tactile Graphics and Formatted Math Using the Tactile Graphics Embosser." Paper presented at the 1998 Technology for Persons with Disabilities conference in Los Angeles, March 17–30, 1998.

APPENDIX

ASCII Braille Characters

The following is the table of ASCII braille equivalents, commonly implemented in North American braille devices.

This one-for-one code also forms the basis for the Computer Braille Code (CBC) adopted by the Braille Authority of North America [BANA 1987]. CBC differs from this code primarily in that CBC uses the dots 4-5-6 braille cell as a prefix rather than simply to mean underscore, as it does here. The cell consisting of no dots corresponds to the space character. The other 63 possible cells correspond to characters as listed. The print equivalent is named and/or given after the braille character for which it stands. Lower and upper case letters are interchangeable in the print; that is, both b and B represent the same braille character, dots 1-2.

⠁	a
⠃	b
⠉	c
⠙	d
⠑	e
⠋	f
⠛	g
⠓	h
⠊	i
⠚	j
⠅	k
⠇	l
⠍	m
⠝	n
⠕	o
⠏	p

APPENDIX: ASCII BRAILLE CHARACTERS

Braille	Character
⠟	q
⠗	r
⠎	s
⠞	t
⠥	u
⠧	v
⠺	w
⠭	x
⠽	y
⠵	z
⠯	ampersand (&)
⠿	equality sign (=)
⠷	left parenthesis [(]
⠮	exclamation mark (!)
⠾	right parenthesis [)]
⠡	asterisk (*)

Braille	Meaning
⠰	left angle bracket (**)
⠆	percent (%)
⠦	question mark (?)
⠒	colon (:)
⠲	dollar sign ($)
⠶	right bracket (])
⠳	backslash (\)
⠪	left bracket ([)
⠄	1
⠆	2
⠒	3
⠲	4
⠢	5
⠖	6
⠶	7
⠦	8

⠂	9
⠆	0
⠳	slash (/)
⠖	addition sign (+)
⠩	crosshatch (#)
⠒⠒	right angle bracket (***)
⠄	apostrophe (')
⠤	hyphen (-)
⠈	at-sign ((a))
⠐	up-tick (^)
⠨⠨	underscore (_)
⠦	double-quote (")
⠲	period (.)
⠰	semicolon (;)
⠠	comma (,)
Adapted with permission of Duxbury Systems, Westford, MA	

LIST OF
CONTRIBUTORS

Dr. James Allan

Statewide Technical Support Specialist
Texas School for the Blind & Visually Impaired
Austin, Texas
B.A., University of Texas at Austin
M.A., University of Texas at Austin
Ph.D., University of Texas at Austin

> Dr. Allan has been a teacher of the visually
> impaired for ten years, working with transcription
> software, textbook production, and braille file
> structures.

Mrs. Darleen E. Bogart

National Braille Convenor
Canadian National Institute for the Blind
Toronto, Ontario, Canada
B.A., McMaster University

> Mrs. Bogart is a certified braille transcriber;
> co-author of *Mastering Literary Braille:
> a Comprehensive Course;* director, Unified
> Braille Code Research Project; president of the
> Canadian Braille Authority; and secretary of
> the International Council on English Braille.

Mr. Geoffrey L. Bull, MBE

President
Braille International, Inc.
Stuart, Florida
B.S., North London School of Physical Therapy

> Mr. Bull was production director of the Royal
> National Institute for the Blind in the United
> Kingdom. He oversaw production of braille, moon,
> and recorded materials. He has been president of
> Braille International, Inc., for more than eight years.

Ms. Kim L. Charlson

Assistant Director/Service Management Librarian
Massachusetts Braille and Talking Book Library
Perkins School for the Blind
Watertown, Massachusetts
B.S., Willamette University
M.L.S., University of Northern Texas

> Ms. Charlson has served as the representative for
> the American Council of the Blind to the Braille
> Authority of North America, has chaired the
> Massachusetts Braille Literacy Advisory Council,
> and is past president of the Braille Revival League.

Mr. Curtis Chong

Director of Technology
National Federation of the Blind
Baltimore, Maryland

> Mr. Chong has been a user of braille since age five.
> He has been involved with evaluating and testing
> braille hardware and software since 1984. He cur-
> rently teaches classes in braille and nonvisual access
> technology.

Ms. Jane M. Corcoran

Braille Transcription Project of Santa Clara County
Los Altos, California
B.S., University of Nevada
M.A., University of Texas

> Ms. Corcoran served twenty-five years as tactile
> illustration specialist for the California Transcribers
> and Educators of the Visually Handicapped. She
> was a member of the Braille Authority of North
> America's Mathematics Technical Committee from
> 1988 to 1998. She was employed as a school tran-
> scriber from 1973 to 1980.

Mr. T. V. (Tim) Cranmer

President
International Braille Research Center
Louisville, Kentucky
Doctor of Applied Sciences, University of Louisville
    (honoris causa)

    Dr. Cranmer is a member of the design committee
of the Unified Braille Code Project and past chair
of the Computer Braille Code Committee of the
Braille Authority of North America.

Ms. Diane L. Croft

Director of Marketing and Publishing
National Braille Press
Boston, Massachusetts
B.A., Wittenberg University
Ed.M., Harvard University

    Ms. Croft has been marketing manager at
National Braille Press since 1982 and is the author
of several books related to blindness.

Mr. Frank Kurt Cylke

Director
National Library Service for the Blind and
    Physically Handicapped
Library of Congress
Washington, D.C.
B.A., University of Connecticut
M.L.S., Pratt Institute

    Mr. Cylke has been director of the National
Library Service for the Blind and Physically
Handicapped since 1973. His previous library
experience includes school, academic, and public
settings.

Ms. Frances Mary D'Andrea

Director
National Literacy Center
American Foundation for the Blind
Atlanta, Georgia
B.S., George Peabody College for Teachers
M.Ed., Georgia State University

Ms. D'Andrea is co-author/editor of *Instructional Strategies for Braille Literacy;* editor of *DOTS for Braille Literacy,* a newsletter for braille professionals; and coordinator of AFB's national braille literacy mentor project.

Dr. Judith M. Dixon

Consumer Relations Officer
National Library Service for the Blind and
  Physically Handicapped
Library of Congress
Washington, D.C.
B.A., Stetson University
M.A., Adelphi University
Ph.D., Adelphi University

Dr. Dixon has been a user of braille since age five. Since 1981 she has been responsible for consumer relations at the National Library Service for the Blind and Physically Handicapped, where she has lectured extensively on the topic of braille. She has written numerous articles, served as editor for *World Braille Usage,* and participated in many braille-related projects, including the development of Web-Braille.

Dr. John A. Gardner

Professor and Director, Science Access Project
Department of Physics
Oregon State University
Corvallis, Oregon
B.A., Rice University
M.S., University of Illinois
Ph.D., University of Illinois

> When he lost his sight in 1988, Dr. Gardner learned braille but found it unnecessarily complicated and limiting. This inspired him to develop the DotsPlus font and, in collaboration with Dr. Norberto Salinas, the GS Unified Braille Code.

Mrs. Dolores Ferrara-Godzieba

Director, Braille Division
Associated Services for the Blind
Philadelphia, Pennsylvania
B.A., Immaculata College
M.Ed., University of Virginia

> Mrs. Ferrara-Godzieba taught blind children at St. Lucy Day School, Philadelphia, from 1966 to 1977. She is a former chairperson of the Braille Authority of North America (1995-1998).

Mr. Euclid J. Herie

President and CEO
Canadian National Institute for the Blind
Toronto, Ontario, Canada
C.M., University of Manitoba
M.S.W., University of Manitoba
Ll.D., University of Manitoba (honoris causa)

> Dr. Herie is president and CEO of the Canadian National Institute for the Blind.

Mr. Kenneth Jernigan

President Emeritus (deceased)
National Federation of the Blind
Baltimore, Maryland
B.A., Tennessee Polytechnic Institute
M.A., Peabody College
Doctor of Humanities, Coe College (honoris causa)
Doctor of Law, Seton Hall University (honoris causa)
Doctor of Humanities Drake University (honoris causa)

> Dr. Jernigan served many years as president, then president emeritus, of the National Federation of the Blind, where he led numerous organizational initiatives to promote braille.

Dr. Pamela Lorimer

Project Coordinator (retired)
University of Birmingham
Birmingham, United Kingdom
Ph.D., University of Birmingham

> Dr. Lorimer has been a teacher of young children and a team member on the Birmingham/Warwick Universities' Study of Braille Contractions project. Her doctoral thesis is on braille history, the psychology of touch perception, and the constraints of braille. She presently has a book and bibliography on early codes in process.

Dr. Marc Maurer

President
National Federation of the Blind
Baltimore, Maryland
B.A., University of Notre Dame
J.D., University of Indiana
Doctor of Humane Letters, Menlo College
(honoris causa)
Doctor of Laws and Letters, University of Louisville
(honoris causa)

As president of the National Federation of the
Blind, Dr. Maurer directs numerous advocacy
efforts on behalf of braille users, many of which
involve the legislative process.

Mr. Harvey H. Miller

Professor of Music Emeritus
Brevard College
Brevard, North Carolina
B.A., University of North Carolina at Chapel Hill
M.A., University of North Carolina at Chapel Hill
M.Mus., Indiana University

Mr. Miller is a member of BANA's music committee and serves as a music proofreader for the
American Printing House for the Blind.

Dr. Abraham Nemeth

Professor Emeritus
University of Detroit
Detroit, Michigan
B.A., Brooklyn College
M.A., Columbia University
Ph.D., Wayne State University

> Dr. Nemeth is a user of numerous braille and other raised-type codes. He created the Nemeth Braille Code for Mathematics and Science Notation, which has become a standard in the United States.

Ms. Freddie L. Peaco

Government Information and Volunteer Specialist
National Library Service for the Blind and Physically
    Handicapped
Library of Congress
Washington, D.C.
B.A., Howard University
M.A., American University

> Ms. Peaco has been an avid braille user since child-hood. In her position in the NLS Reference Section, she maintains an awareness of braille products and services available to blind persons.

Mr. William M. Raeder

President
National Braille Press
Boston, Massachusetts
B.A., Boston University
M.A., Boston University

> Mr. Raeder has been CEO of NBP since 1975. During this time, he initiated automation of braille transcription, including software development, and initiated Information Services, which became the Braille Publishing and Marketing Division.

Mrs. Linda C. Redmond

Head, Reference Section
National Library Service for the Blind and Physically Handicapped
Library of Congress
Washington, D.C.
B.A., Virginia State University
M.L.S., University of Maryland

> Mrs. Redmond has been a librarian at NLS since 1971 and head of the NLS Reference Section since 1992.

Dr. Ruby N. Ryles

Coordinator of Louisiana Tech University/Louisiana Center for the Blind Master's Degree Program
Louisiana Center for the Blind
Ruston, Louisiana
B.S., University of Arkansas
M.Ed., University of Arkansas
Ph.D., University of Washington

> Dr. Ryles, who has a blind son, began teaching blind children in the late 1970s and now teaches teacher preparation classes at the college level.

Dr. Fredric K. Schroeder

Commissioner
Rehabilitation Services Administration
Department of Education
Washington, D.C.
B.A., San Francisco State University
M.A., San Francisco State University
Ph.D., University of New Mexico

Dr. Schroeder is totally blind and has been a braille reader since the age of sixteen. His master's degree is in special education for the visually impaired, and upon graduation he taught braille in the public schools. Subsequently, he administered districtwide programs for visually impaired students in the Albuquerque public schools, creating a model program that stressed the critical importance of early braille instruction. Dr. Schroeder's doctoral dissertation was a qualitative research project studying braille usage from the perspective of legally blind adults. Dr. Schroeder served as a member of the Board of Directors of the Braille Authority of North America from 1982 to 1994 and was the first president of the International Council on English Braille (ICEB) from 1991 to 1994. He also was a member of the Literacy Committee of the World Blind Union from 1993 to 1994.

Dr. Susan Jay Spungin

Vice President of Educational and International
  Programs
American Foundation for the Blind
New York, New York
B.S., Skidmore College
M.A., San Francisco State University
Ed.D., Teachers College, Columbia University

> For ten years, Dr. Spungin was a teacher of blind
> children in California and New Jersey. She wrote a
> groundbreaking pamphlet on braille literacy for
> blind consumers and those providing educational
> and vocational services to blind persons.

Mrs. Mary Lou Stark

Head, Braille Development Section
National Library Service for the Blind and Physically
  Handicapped
Library of Congress
Washington, D.C.
B.S., Washburn University
M.S., Illinois State University

> Before coming to the Library of Congress in 1991,
> Mrs. Stark taught braille to newly blinded adults as
> a communications instructor and a rehabilitation
> teacher.

Ms. Carol A. Strauss

Reference Librarian
National Library Service for the Blind and
    Physically Handicapped
Library of Congress
Washington, D.C.
B.A., Syracuse University
M.L.S., University of Pittsburgh

> Ms. Strauss has been a reference librarian at NLS
> since 1989.

Mr. Joseph E. Sullivan

President
Duxbury Systems, Inc.
Westford, Massachusetts
A.B., Boston College
M.S., Northeastern University

> Mr. Sullivan has been a primary developer of
> braille translation software since 1969 and has
> chaired the Unified Braille Code Design
> Committee since 1992.

Ms. Carol B. Tobe

Director
Marie and Eugene Callahan Museum
American Printing House for the Blind
Louisville, Kentucky
B.S., University of Louisville

Ms. Tobe has been director of the museum at APH since 1990. She organized the museum and has conducted extensive research on all phases of the educational history of blind people, particularly embossed reading material and educational aids.

BIBLIOGRAPHY

The references in this bibliography complement the references in chapters throughout the book. It includes many, but not all, of the references given at the end of each chapter.

Origins/History

American Council for the Blind. "Braille: History, Use and Current Research." Article found at http://acb.org/Resources/braille.html, n.d.

Bell, Donald. "Reading by Touch." *Braille Monitor* (June 1972): 291–300.

Best, Harry. "Use of Raised Print by Blind." In *Blindness and the Blind in the United States*. New York: Macmillan Company, 1934.

Burns, Jim. "Braille: A Birthday Look at its Past, Present, and Future." *Braille Monitor* (July–August 1991): 391–394. First printed in *Braille Monitor* (March 1975): 117–120.

Farrell, Gabriel. "Battle of the Types." In *The Story of Blindness*. Cambridge: Harvard University Press, 1956.

Harris, Elizabeth M. "Inventing Printing for the Blind." *Printing History* 8, no. 2 (1986): 15–25.

Hooper, Marjorie S. "Braille." In *Encyclopedia of Library and Information Science*. Vol. 3. Edited by Allen Kent and Harold Lancour. New York: Marcel Dekker, 1970.

How Braille Began. Jensen Beach, Fla.: Enabling Technologies, 1999. http://www.brailler.com/braillehx.htm.

Irwin, Robert B. "The War of the Dots." In *As I Saw It*. New York: American Foundation for the Blind, 1955.

Koestler, Frances A. "The Language of the Fingers." In *The Unseen Minority: A Social History of Blindness in America*. New York: David McKay Company, 1976.

Maley, Tom. "Moon à la Mode." *New Beacon* 71 (April 1987): 109–113.

The Moon System of Embossed Reading. London: Royal National Institute for the Blind, 1968.

National Library Service for the Blind and Physically Handicapped of the Library of Congress. *Facts: About Braille*. Washington, D.C.: Library of Congress, 1987.

The New York Institute for Special Education. "The History of Reading Codes for the Blind." Article found at http://www.nyise.org/blind/barbier2.htm (June 1999).

Rodenberg, Lewis W. "The Story of Books for the Blind." In *What of the Blind? A Survey of the Development and Scope of Present-day Work with the Blind,* edited by Helga Lende. New York: American Foundation for the Blind, 1938. Reprinted as *The Story of Embossed Books for the Blind.* New York: American Foundation for the Blind, 1955.

Rutherfurd, John. *William Moon and His Work for the Blind.* London: Hodder and Stoughton, 1898.

Truquet, Monique. "The Blind, From Braille to the Present." *Impact of Science on Society* 30 (April–June 1980): 133–141.

Louis Braille

Bryant, Jennifer Fisher. *Louis Braille: Inventor.* New York: Chelsea House, 1994.

Coon, Nelson. "New Light on Louis Braille." *International Journal of the Education of the Blind* 4 (December 1954): 41–42.

DeGering, Etta. *Seeing Fingers: The Story of Louis Braille.* New York: David McKay Company, 1962.

Henri, Pierre. *The Life and Work of Louis Braille, 1809–1852.* Pretoria: South African National Council for the Blind, 1987.

Herie, Euclid J. "The Dawn of the Information Age for the Blind of the World: Reflections on the Eighteenth-Century Memorial to Louis Braille at Coupvray, France." In *International Yearbook of Library Service for Blind and Physically Handicapped Individuals.* Vol. 1. Compiled by Friends of Libraries for Blind and

Physically Handicapped Individuals in North America, Inc. New Providence, NJ: K.G. Saur, 1993.

Kugelmass, J. Alvin. *Louis Braille: Windows for the Blind.* New York: Julian Messner, 1951.

Mellor, Michael. "Louis Braille—Boy and Man." *Dialogue* 37 (winter 1998): 42–48.

Roblin, Jean. *Louise Braille.* London, England: Royal National Institute for the Blind, n.d.

Roblin, Jean. *The Reading Fingers: Life of Louis Braille, 1809–1852.* New York: American Foundation for the Blind, 1955.

Legal Standard

"Braille Bill Update." *Braille Monitor* (June 1982): 311–316.

"Braille Literacy, Braille Texts, and Braille Bills." *Braille Monitor* (August–September 1995): 481–489.

Gardner, Bruce A. "Arizona: Another Strong Braille Bill." *Braille Monitor* (July 1997): 447–448.

Grubb, Debbie. "Maryland's Braille Bill, The Law of the State." *Braille Forum* 31 (July–August 1992): 12–16.

Kaizer, Marjorie. "Braille Bill and Beyond: A Report from South Dakota." *Future Reflections* 11 (fall 1992): 26–27.

McQuillan, Carla. "The Oregon Braille Bill: An Exercise in Cooperation." *Braille Monitor* (February 1994): 93–94.

National Federation of the Blind. "Background on Braille Literacy Legislation." Article found at http://www.nfb.org/brltlaw.htm (July 1999).

Pierce, Barbara. "More Braille Bills Become Law." *Braille Monitor* (May 1994): 282–284.

Schroeder, Fredric K. "Braille Bills: What Are They and What Do They Mean?" *Braille Monitor* (June 1992): 308–311.

"Texas Braille Bill Becomes a Model Law." *Braille Monitor* (July–August 1991): 376–377.

Turco, Dawn. "Braille Bill Update." *Journal of Visual Impairment and Blindness* 87 (May 1993): 131–132.

Workplace

Boulter, Eric T. "The Increasing Need for Braille for Vocational Purposes." *Journal of Visual Impairment and Blindness* 73 (October 1979): 335–337.

Livingston, Rita, and Laurel Tucker. "Literacy, Employment, and Mode of Access to Printed Information." In *Increasing Literacy Levels: Final Report,* prepared by the Pennsylvania College of Optometry for the Mississippi State University, Rehabilitation Research and Training Center on Blindness and Low Vision (RRTC). Mississippi State: Mississippi State University, RRTC, 1997.

Ryles, Ruby. "The Impact of Braille Reading Skills on Employment, Income, Education, and Reading Habits." *Journal of Visual Impairment and Blindness* 90 (May–June 1996): 219–226.

Schopper, Hans. "The Electro-Brailler: A Communications Device and Teaching Aid for the Blind and Visually Impaired at Work and in School." *AFB Research Bulletin,* no. 23 (June 1971): 47–49.

Zambone, Alana M., and Mary Jean Sanspree. "The Relationship Between Literacy and Employment for Persons with Visual Impairments: A Review of the Literature." In *Increasing Literacy Levels: Final Report,* prepared by the Pennsylvania College of Optometry for the Mississippi State University, Rehabilitation Research and Training Center on Blindness and Low Vision (RRTC). Mississippi State: Mississippi State University, RRTC, 1997.

Library Service

Bell, Lori, and Valerie Brandon. "Braille/Large Print Reference Service." *Illinois Libraries* 75 (fall 1993): 307–309.

Braille Book Review. Bimonthly; free. Library of Congress, National Library Service for the Blind and Physically Handicapped, Washington, D.C. 20542. Also published on http://www.loc.gov/nls/bbr/bbr.html.

Bray, Robert S. "Blind and Physically Handicapped, Library Service." In *Encyclopedia of Library and Information Science.* Vol. 2. Edited by Allen Kent and Harold Lancour. New York: Marcel Dekker, 1969.

Clark, Leslie L., Dina N. Bedi, and John M. Gill, eds. *A Guide to Developing Braille and Talking-Book Services.* IFLA publication no. 30. New York: K.G. Saur, 1984.

Cunningham, Carmela, and Norman Coombs. "Creating Accessible Libraries." In *Information Access and Adaptive Technology*. Phoenix: American Council on Education and Oryx Press, 1997.

Cylke, Frank Kurt. "The Future of Braille." *Matilda Ziegler Magazine for the Blind* (February 1979).

Cylke, Frank Kurt. "Library Services for the Blind and Physically Handicapped: Yesterday—Today—Tomorrow." *Illinois Libraries* 57 (September 1975): 447–450.

Cylke, Frank Kurt. "National Library Service for the Blind and Physically Handicapped." In *Management of Federally Sponsored Libraries: Case Studies and Analysis,* edited by Charles D. Missar. New York: Haworth Press, 1995.

Cylke, Frank Kurt. "National Library Service for the Blind and Physically Handicapped, Library of Congress." Testimony prepared for presentation by Carolyn Hoover Sung to the United States National Commission on Libraries and Information Science on July 8, 1999. Washington, D.C. 1999.

Cylke, Frank Kurt, and Alfred D. Hagle. "Library Services for the Blind and Physically Handicapped." In *ALA Yearbook of Library and Information Services.* Vol. 10. Edited by Robert Wedgeworth. Chicago: American Library Association, 1985.

Cylke, Frank Kurt, and Alfred D. Hagle. "Services for Users with Disabilities." In *World Encyclopedia of Library and Information Services,* 3d ed. Edited by Robert Wedgeworth. Chicago: American Library Association, 1993.

Cylke, Frank Kurt, and others. "Blind and Physically Handicapped, Library Services." In *Encyclopedia of Library and Information Science.* Vol. 44, suppl. 9, 27-64. Edited by Allen Kent. New York: Marcel Dekker, 1989.

Cylke, Frank Kurt, and others. "Research to Develop Information Service Aids and Programs for Handicapped Individuals." *Drexel Library Quarterly* 16 (April 1980): 59-72.

Deines-Jones, Courtney. "Access to Library Internet Services for Patrons with Disabilities: Pragmatic Considerations for Developers." *Library Hi Tech* 14, no. 1 (1996): 57-64.

Dixon, Judith M. "Levelling the Road Ahead: Guidelines for the Creation of WWW Pages Accessible to Blind and Visually Handicapped Users." *Library Hi Tech* 14, no. 1 (1996): 65-68.

Epp, Mary Anne. "Library Services to Canadian College Students with Print Disabilities." *Library Hi Tech* 17, no. 2: 189-196.

Friends of Libraries for Blind and Physically Handicapped Individuals in North America, Inc., comp. *International Yearbook of Library Service for Blind and Physically Handicapped Individuals.* Vol 1. New Providence, NJ: K.G. Saur, 1993.

Goldthwaite, Lucy Armistead. "Some Comments on the Library Service for the Blind." In *What of the Blind? A Survey of the Development and Scope of Present-Day Work with the Blind,* edited by Helga Lende. New York: American Foundation for the Blind, 1938.

IFLA Standing Committee of the Section of Libraries for the Blind. "Guidelines for Library Service to Braille

Users." Prepared for the meeting in September 1997 in Copenhagen, Denmark, February 10, 1998. The Hague, Netherlands: International Federation of Library Associations, 1998.

Long, Carol A. "Making Information Available to Partially Sighted and Blind Clients." *The Electronic Library* 11 (December 1993): 373–384.

Mates, Barbara T. *Adaptive Technology for the Internet: Making Electronic Resources Accessible.* Chicago: American Library Association, 1999.

Mates, Barbara T. "Braille Access." In *Library Technology for Visually and Physically Impaired Patrons.* Westport, CT: Meckler, 1991.

McNulty, Tom. "Reference Service for Students with Disabilities: Desktop Braille Publishing in the Academic Library." *RSR: Reference Services Review* 21 (spring 1993): 37–43.

McNulty, Tom, and Dawn M. Suvino. "Tactile Reading Methods and Materials." In *Access to Information: Materials, Technologies, and Services for Print-Impaired Readers.* LITA monographs 2. Chicago: American Library Association, 1993.

Roatch, Mary A. "High Tech and Library Access for People with Disabilities." *Public Libraries* 31 (March–April 1992): 88–98.

Strauss, Carol, comp. *Sources of Braille Reading Materials.* Reference circular 96–02. Washington, D.C.: Library of Congress, National Library Service for the Blind and Physically Handicapped, 1996.

That All May Read: Library Service for Blind and Physically Handicapped People. Washington, D.C.: Library of

Congress, National Library Service for the Blind and Physically Handicapped, 1983.

Willoughby, Edith L. "Library Services in a School for the Blind." *Future Reflections* 9 (summer 1990): 14–17.

Music

Beryk, Sophia V. "Resources for Blind Students and Their Teachers." *Music Educators Journal* (November–December 1965): 75–77.

Boyer, Alison S. "Identification of Characters with Shared Representations: Decoding Musical and Literary Braille." *Journal of Visual Impairment and Blindness* 91 (January–February 1997): 77–86.

Braille Authority of North America, comp. *Manual of Braille Music Notation: American Edition, 1988.* Louisville, Ky.: American Printing House for the Blind, 1991.

Braille Authority of North America, comp. *Manual of Braille Music Notation: American Edition, 1988, 1993 International Supplement.* Louisville, Ky.: American Printing House for the Blind, 1993.

De Garmo, Mary Turner. *Introduction to Braille Music Transcription with 1974 Addenda A-C.* Washington, D.C.: Library of Congress, National Library Service for the Blind and Physically Handicapped, 1988.

Eldridge, C. "The Braille Choral Music and 'Ensemble' Score." *Braille Research Newsletter*, no. 12 (September 1981): 23–25.

Gillies, S.G., and S.J. Goldsack. "Computer Coding of Music Scores Using an On-line Organ Keyboard." *Braille Automation Newsletter* (August 1976): 62–64.

Harrison, Lois N. "Braille Music for the Blind Musician." *Oregon Music Educator* (winter 1977–1978): 18–19.

Humphreys, J. "Automatic Translation by Computer of Music Notation to Braille." *Braille Research Newsletter,* no. 5 (July 1977): 5–12.

Humphreys, J. "A Computer-Based System for Production of Braille Music." In *Computerised Braille Production: Today and Tomorrow,* edited by Derrick W. Crosidale, Hermann Kamp, and Helmut Werner. New York: Springer-Verlag, 1983.

Humphreys, J. "Computerised Braille Music Production Using CIMBAL." *Braille Research Newsletter,* no. 10 (July 1979): 6–15.

Jackson, Michael. "The Moon System Adapted for Musical Notation." *British Journal of Visual Impairment* 5 (autumn 1987): 93–97.

Jenkins, Edward W., comp. *Primer of Braille Music.* Louisville, Ky.: American Printing House for the Blind, 1960.

Jenkins, Edward W., comp. *Primer of Braille Music, 1971 Addendum.* Louisville, Ky.: American Printing House for the Blind, 1971.

"John Henry—Harpsichordist and Author of 'Braille Music: An International Survey.'" *British Journal of Visual Impairment* 3 (summer 1985): 55–56.

Krolick, Bettye. *Dictionary of Braille Music Signs.* Washington, D.C.: Library of Congress, National

Library Service for the Blind and Physically Handicapped, 1979.

Krolick, Bettye. *How to Read Braille Music.* 2d ed. San Diego: Opus Technologies, 1998.

McCann, Bill. "Automating Braille Music Transcription with the GOODFEEL Braille Music Translator." *Tactic* 13 (spring 1997): 4–8.

McLean, B. "Translating DARMS into Musical Braille. *Braille Automation Newsletter* (August 1976): 65–67.

Patrick, P. Howard, and Rosalind E. Patrick. "Computers and Braille Music." *Braille Automation Newsletter* (August 1976): 52–61.

Smaligo, Mary A. "Resources for Helping Blind Music Students." *Music Educators Journal* 85 (September 1998): 23–26, 45.

Watkins, W., and J. Siems. "SAMBA and RUMBA: Systems for Computer Assisted Translation of Braille Music." *Braille Automation Newsletter* (August 1976): 47–51.

Wilkinson, Sally. "Computer-Assisted Transcription of Braille Music." *Braille Automation Newsletter* (August 1976): 68–72.

World Blind Union, Braille Music Subcommittee. *New International Manual of Braille Music Notation.* Compiled by Bettye Krolick. Amsterdam: SVB, 1997. Available from Opus Technologies in San Diego.

Mathematics

Castellano, Carol. "Doing Math in Braille." In *The Bridge to Braille: Reading and School Success for the Young Blind Child*, edited by Carol Castellano and Dawn Kosman. Baltimore: National Organization of Parents of Blind Children, 1997.

Craig, Ruth H. *Learning the Nemeth Code: A Manual for Teachers and Students*. Louisville, Ky.: American Printing House for the Blind, 1987.

Hooper, Marjorie S. "The Nemeth Code—How and Why." *Education of the Blind* 7 (December 1957): 56–60.

Kapperman, Gaylen, and Jodi Sticken. "The Braillewriter as a Calculation Tool." *Review* 30 (summer 1998): 65–83.

Nemeth, Abraham. "Braille: The Agony and The Ecstasy." *Braille Monitor* (July 1988): 324–328.

Nemeth, Abraham. "Teaching Meaningful Mathematics to Blind and Partially Sighted Children." *New Outlook for the Blind* 53 (November 1959): 318–321.

The Nemeth Braille Code for Mathematics and Science Notation, 1972. Revision. With *Addendum 1,* adopted by the Braille Authority of North America, June 1988. Compiled under the authority of the American Association of Workers for the Blind, Association for Education of the Visually Handicapped, and the National Braille Association. Louisville, Ky.: American Printing House for the Blind, n.d.

Ostad, Snorre A. *Mathematics Through the Fingertips*. Oslo, Norway: Norwegian Institute of Special Education, 1989.

Roberts, Helen, Bernard M. Krebs, and Barbara Taffet. *An Introduction to Braille Mathematics. Based on The Nemeth Braille Code for Mathematics and Science Notation, 1972.* Washington, D.C.: Library of Congress, National Library Service for the Blind and Physically Handicapped, 1978.

Willoughby, Doris M., and Sharon L.M. Duffy. "Mathematics." In *Handbook for Itinerant and Resource Teachers of Blind and Visually Impaired Students,* edited by Doris M. Willoughby and Sharon L. M. Duffy. Baltimore: National Federation of the Blind, 1989.

Unification

Black, Keith. "Comment on UBC." *Dialogue* 34 (winter 1995): 53–55.

Bogart, Darleen, and others. *Views from Canada. International Conference on English Braille Grade 2: Proceedings.* Edited by Richard H. Evensen. From Conference at the National Library Service for the Blind and Physically Handicapped of the Library of Congress in Washington, D.C., September 13–17, 1982. Washington, D.C., 1982.

Braunstein, Anna Lee. "A Teacher's Perspective on the Unified Braille Code." Article found at http://edtech.sdcs.k12.ca.us/epd/ANNA.html (January 17, 1996).

Cranmer, T. V., and Abraham Nemeth. "A Uniform Braille Code." *Braille Monitor* (July–August 1991): 377–383. Also found at http://world.std.com/~iceb/cranem.html.

Downing, Winifred. "A Proposal for the Development of a Unified Braille Code." *CTEVH Journal* 36, (fall 1992): 79–80.

Downing, Winifred. "An Update on the Unified Braille Code." *Dialogue* 32 (winter 1993): 30–33. Also in CTEVH Journal 37 (winter 1993–1994): 106–107.

"International Community Accepts Research Project for Developing a Unified Braille Code for the English Speaking World." *CTEVH Journal* 37 (winter 1993–1994): 105–106.

Irwin, Robert B. "Uniform Braille for the English-Speaking World Achieved." *Outlook for the Blind* 26 (September 1932): 137–138.

Jackson, John, Darleen Bogart, and Hilda Caton. "The Unified Braille Code: Some Myths and Realities." *Journal of Visual Impairment and Blindness* 87 (December 1993): 395–396. Also in *RE:view* 25 (fall 1993): 128–130, and *CTEVH Journal* 37 (winter 1993–1994): 111–113.

Poole, Bill. "Unified Braille Code Project." *New Beacon* 78 (February 1994): 9–10.

"The Revival of Braille." *Dialogue* 32 (summer 1993): 1–8.

Schecter, Norma L. "Comments on Unified Braille Code." *CTEVH Journal* 37 (winter 1993–1994): 110–111.

Schecter, Norma L. "Toward a Unified English Braille Code: A Transcriber's View." In *International Conference on English Braille Grade 2: Proceedings,* edited by Richard H. Evensen. From Conference at the National Library Service for the Blind and Physically Handicapped of the Library of Congress in

Washington, D.C., September 13–17, 1982. Washington, D.C., 1982.

Schroeder, Fredric K. "The Place of Braille." *Braille Monitor* (August 1993): 874–879.

Small, Terry H. "Toward a Universal English Braille Grade 2." In *International Conference on English Braille Grade 2: Proceedings,* edited by Richard H. Evensen. From Conference at the National Library Service for the Blind and Physically Handicapped of the Library of Congress in Washington, D.C., September 13–17, 1982. Washington, D.C., 1982.

Sullivan, Joseph E. "A Perspective on Braille Unification." Paper delivered for the 10th World Conference, International Council for Education of People with Visual Impairment, August 1997. Found at http:// www.duxburysystems.com/icevi97a.html.

York, Edith. "Unifying the Codes for Numerals, Weights, Measures, Coinage, Mathematical and Literary Signs." In *International Conference on English Braille Grade 2: Proceedings,* edited by Richard H. Evensen. From Conference at the National Library Service for the Blind and Physically Handicapped of the Library of Congress in Washington, D.C., September 13–17, 1982. Washington, D.C., 1982.

Computer Codes and Computer Transcription

Beatty, K. O. "KOBRL Numeric Code: An Inkprint Output for Computer Transcribed Braille." *Braille Automation Newsletter* (August 1976): 39–41.

Beatty, K. O. "SNOBRL Transcription of Inkprint into KOBRL Numeric Code." *Braille Automation Newsletter* (August 1976): 42–46.

Braille Authority of North America, comp. *Computer Braille Code: Flowchart Design for Applicable Braille Codes Supplement.* Louisville, Ky.: American Printing House for the Blind, 1992.

Braille Authority of North America, comp. Code for Computer Braille Notation. Louisville, Ky.: American Printing House for the Blind, 1987.

Dixon, Judy, and Chris Gray. *Computer Braille Code Made Easy.* Boston: National Braille Press, 1998.

Durre, Ingeborg K., and Imke Durre. "Instant Print Braille Compatibility with COBRA." *Journal of Visual Impairment and Blindness* 93 (March 1999): 140–152.

Durre, Karl P., Dean W. Tuttle, and Ingeborg K. Durre. "A Universal Computer Braille Code for Literary and Scientific Texts." Paper given at the International Technology Conference, Baltimore, MD., December 1991. Baltimore, MD: International Braille Research Center, 1991. Found at http://www.braille.org/papers/unive/unive.html.

Gildea, R. A. J., and M. Berkowitz, eds. *Computerized Braille. Proceedings of a Workshop on Compliance of Computer Programs with English Braille, American Edition, New York City, June 7–8, 1976.* New York: American Foundation for the Blind, 1977.

Knowlton, Ken, and Marie Knowlton. "For Teaching the Reading of Braille: Computer Produced Variously Contracted Translations." *Closing the Gap* 14 (August–September 1995): 22–23, 40.

Literary Braille

Braille Authority of North America, comp. *English Braille: American Edition, 1994.* Louisville, Ky.: American Printing House for the Blind, 1994.

"Braille Code Recommendations Proposed by the Braille Authority of North America Technical Committee on Literary Braille." In *International Conference on English Braille Grade 2: Proceedings,* edited by Richard H. Evensen. From Conference at the National Library Service for the Blind and Physically Handicapped of the Library of Congress in Washington, D.C., September 13–17, 1982. Washington, 1982.

Buckley, John E. "The Efficiency of Braille as a Medium of Communication." *Braille Research Newsletter,* no. 6 (October 1977): 11–25.

Clark, Leslie L. "Research Perspectives on the Braille Code." *Braille Research Newsletter,* no. 7 (March 1978): 18–22.

Douce, J. L., and Michael J. Tobin. "The Braille Code, Extending the Use of Braille, and the Improvement of Reading Skills." *New Outlook for the Blind* 70 (May 1976): 215.

Gill, J. M. "A Study of Braille Contractions." *Braille Research Newsletter,* no. 11 (August 1980): 12–72.

Gill, J. M., and J. B. Humphreys. "An Analysis of Braille Contractions." *Braille Research Newsletter,* no. 5 (July 1977): 50–57.

Gore, George V. III, and Teresa A. Kauffman. *Braille Authority of North America (BANA): History, Organization and Accomplishments.* Braille Authority of North America, 1983.

Gray, Christopher. "Should We Modify the Braille Code?" *Braille Forum* 31 (January 1993): 24–27.

International Braille Research Center. Braille: A Code for Success, A Comprehensive Tutorial for the National Literary Braille Competency Test. Baltimore: National Federation of the Blind, 1999.

Lorimer, John, and Michael J. Tobin. "Experiments with Modified Grade 2 Braille Codes to Determine Their Effect on Reading Speed." *Journal of Visual Impairment and Blindness* 73 (October 1979): 324–328.

Maley, Tom. "Braille: The Wind of Change." *British Journal of Visual Impairment* 3 (autumn 1985): 87–89.

Morgan, Sara. "BAUK and Braille Capitalisation: What We Now Know." *New Beacon* 83 (July–August 1999): 16–18.

Nemeth, Abraham. "Braille: The Agony and The Ecstasy." *Braille Monitor* (July 1988): 324–328.

Nolan, Carson Y. "Thoughts on the Future of Braille." *Journal of Visual Impairment and Blindness* 73 (October 1979): 333–335.

Poole, William B. L. "The Recent BANA Code Changes." In *International Conference on English Braille Grade 2: Proceedings,* edited by Richard H. Evensen. From conference at the National Library Service for the Blind and Physically Handicapped of the Library of Congress in Washington, D.C., September 13-17, 1982. Washington, D.C., 1982.

Pye, Leslie F. "Revision of Braille Contractions with Particular Reference to Bridging Contractions." In *International Conference on English Braille Grade 2: Proceedings,* edited by Richard H. Evensen. From conference at the National Library Service for the Blind and Physically Handicapped of the Library of Congress in Washington, D.C., September 13–17, 1982. Washington, D.C., 1982.

Staack, Gerald Francis. "A Study of Braille Code Revisions." *AFB Research Bulletin,* no. 2 (December 1962): 21–37.

Troughton, Marjorie D. "Some Code Changes for Better Teaching and Learning of Braille." In *International Conference on English Braille Grade 2: Proceedings,* edited by Richard H. Evensen, 1982. Washington, D.C., 1982.

Production

Bagley, P. R. "Computer-Assisted Braille Production Capability." *Braille Automation Newsletter* (August 1976): 15–19.

Bagley, P. R. "A Guideline for the Improvement of Braille Production by Computer." *Braille Automation Newsletter* (August 1976): 31–34.

Berryman, John. "Computerized Braille Production: A Producer's Viewpoint." *Journal of Visual Impairment and Blindness* 75 (June 1981): 261–264.

Berryman, John. "Computerised Braille Production in Australia." *Braille Research Newsletter,* no. 10 (July 1979): 29–41.

Brösamle, C. "Braille Books from Compositors' Tapes." *Braille Research Newsletter,* no. 5 (July 1977): 13–18.

Brown, D. A. G. "The Introduction of Braille Produced by Computer at The Canadian National Institute for the Blind." *Braille Research Newsletter*, no. 6 (October 1977): 4–10.

Chalfen, Daniel Hilton, Jeffrey C. Senge, and Jamie Dote-Kwan. "New CSUF Braille Transcription Center Promotes Access to Postsecondary Instructional Materials for the California State University System." *Information Technology and Disabilities* 3 (March 1996): 1–2. Also found at http://www.rit.edu/~easi/itd/itdv03n1/article1.html.

Clark, Leslie L. "The Braille Press and Its Future." *Braille Research Newsletter*, no. 6 (October 1977): 26–34.

Coleman, P. W. F. "A Note on Hybrid Braille Production." *Braille Research Newsletter*, no. 5 (July 1977): 19–25.

Croisdale, Derrick W., Hermann Kamp, and Helmut Werner, eds. *Computerised Braille Production: Today and Tomorrow.* New York: Springer-Verlag, 1983.

Daily, D. J. "An Alternative Approach to Semi-Automatic Brailling." *Braille Research Newsletter*, no. 6 (October 1977): 45–61.

Douce, J. L. "Rationalisation of Braille Book Printing." *Braille Automation Newsletter* (August 1976): 25–30.

Gibbons, P. D., and E. L. Ost. "Plate Embossing Device." *Braille Research Newsletter*, no. 5 (July 1977): 32–34.

Gill, J. M. "Microprocessor Braille Translator." *Braille Research Newsletter*, no. 10 (July 1979): 25–28.

Gill, J. M. "The Use of Digitally Stored Text for Braille Production." *Braille Automation Newsletter* (August 1976): 6–10.

Hampshire, B., and S. Becker. "The Expansion of Braille Production in Sweden." *Braille Research Newsletter*, no. 5, July 1977: 26–31.

Hampshire, B., and T. Whitson. "On the Manual Transcription of Braille." *Applied Ergonomics*, 8 (September 1977): 159–163.

Harres, M. "New Production Systems in Braille Printing." *Braille Research Newsletter*, no. 10 (July 1979): 16–25.

Jones, Richard R. III, and Scott Flechsig. "Converting Text to Braille." *Library Hi Tech* 11, no. 1 (1993): 34–41.

Keeping, Don. "Computer Braille System." *AFB Research Bulletin*, no. 29 (June 1975): 213–215.

Ohlson, G. W., and Frank A. Saunders. "A Braille Letterpress for the Blind. A Final Report Submitted to the Smith-Kettlewell Eye Research Foundation." *Braille Automation Newsletter*, (August 1976): 73–79.

Schneider-Maunoury, P. "Report on Experiences About Modern Printing Techniques Under Consideration of Traditional Methods." *Braille Research Newsletter*, no. 8 (September 1978): 50–56.

Senge, Jeffrey C., and Jamie Dote-Kwan. "The CSUF Braille Transcription Center Project." *Library Hi Tech* 13 (April 1996): 5–6.

Simon, A. Maso. "From the Ink Print Book to the Braille Book: Difficulties of the Process." *Braille Research Newsletter*, no. 8 (September 1978): 36–49.

Thomsen, Paulli. "Braille Production Formats That Will Counteract Rising Costs." *Journal of Visual Impairment and Blindness* 74 (April 1980): 158–159, 161.

Thornhill, Daniel Earl. "Translation from Monotype Tape to Grade 2 Braille." *AFB Research Bulletin*, no. 5 (July 1964): 63–85.

Truquet, Monique. "The Automatic Transcription of French Ink Print into Braille. *AFB Research Bulletin*, no. 28 (October 1974): 169–174.

Werner, Helmut, Winfried Dost, and Peter Seibt. "Automatic Translation of Inkprint to Braille by Electronic Data Processing Systems." *AFB Research Bulletin*, no. 14 (March 1967): 99–108.

Westland, Ir A. N. "The Design of a Fast Braille Lineprinter." *Braille Automation Newsletter* (December 1976): 3–7.

Woodcock, Richard W. "An Electromechanical Brailling System." *AFB Research Bulletin*, no. 21 (August 1970): 101–107.

Computer Access

Bozic, Nick, and Steve McCall. "Microcomputer Software: Developing Braille Reading Skills." *British Journal of Special Education* 20 (June 1993): 58.

Foulke, Emerson. "Microcomputers, VIPs, and the Communication Network." *Braille Research Newsletter*, no. 13 (June 1982): 2–17.

Gense, D. Jay, and Marilyn H. Gense. "Using Assistive Technology in Literacy Education for Learners Who Are Blind or Visually Impaired." In *Increasing Literacy Levels: Final Report*, prepared by the Pennsylvania College of Optometry for the Mississippi State University, Rehabilitation Research and Training

Center on Blindness and Low Vision (RRTC). Mississippi State: Mississippi State University, RRTC, 1997.

Goodrich, Gregory L. "Applications of Microcomputers by Visually Impaired Persons." *Journal of Visual Impairment and Blindness* 78 (November 1984): 408–414.

Mack, Catherine. "The Impact of Technology on Braille Literacy." *Journal of Visual Impairment and Blindness* 83 (June 1989): 314.

Mellor, C. Michael. "Technical Innovations in Braille Reading, Writing, and Production." *Journal of Visual Impairment and Blindness* 73 (October 1979): 339–341.

Sullivan, Joseph E. "The Future of Braille." *NBA Bulletin* 33 (spring 1997): 16–19.

In the Environment

Emerson, Mary. "Using Braille to Write Checks." *SAF Technology Update* (February 1993): 18–21.

Foulke, Emerson. "Reading Braille." In *Tactual Perception: A Sourcebook,* edited by William Schiff and Emerson Foulke. Cambridge: Cambridge University Press, 1982.

Groff, Gerda, with Laura Gardner. *What Museum Guides Need to Know: Access for Blind and Visually Impaired Visitors.* New York: American Foundation for the Blind, 1989.

Kenny, Alice P. "A Range of Vision: Museum Accommodations for Visually Impaired People." *Journal of*

Visual Impairment and Blindness 77 (September 1983): 325–329.

Leuver, Robert J. "What About Tactile Marking of Paper Currency? Address Before the 24th Annual Convention, American Council of the Blind." *Braille Forum* (December 1985): 4–9.

Lowenfeld, Berthold, G. L. Abel, and P. H. Hatlen. *Blind Children Learn to Read.* Springfield, Ill.: Charles C. Thomas, 1969.

"Making Financial Information Accessible: A Report from RNIB's Automated Services Business Unit, Peterborough." *New Beacon* 83 (February 1999): 26–27.

Maurer, Marc. "Who Wants Braille on the Money?" *Braille Monitor* (June 1994): 345–348.

Miller, Diane D. "Reading Comes Naturally: A Mother and Her Blind Child's Experiences." *Journal of Visual Impairment and Blindness* 79 (January 1985): 1–4.

Shore, Irma. "Designing Exhibitions for the Visually Impaired." *Museum News* (November–December 1988): 62–64.

Simón, Cecilia, and Juan Antonio Huertas. "How Blind Readers Perceive and Gather Information Written in Braille." *Journal of Visual Impairment and Blindness* 92 (May 1998): 322–330.

Steiner, Charles. "Art Museums and the Visually Handicapped Consumer: Some Issues in Approach and Design." *Journal of Visual Impairment and Blindness* 77 (September 1983): 330–333.

Ungar, Simon, Mark Blades, and Christopher Spencer. "Effects of Orientation on Braille Reading by People

Who Are Visually Impaired: The Role of Context. *Journal of Visual Impairment and Blindness* 92 (July 1998): 454–463.

Graphics

Barth, John L. "The Development and Evaluation of a Tactile Graphics Kit." *Journal of Visual Impairment and Blindness* 76 (September 1982): 269–273.

Barth, John L. "Factors Affecting Line Tracing in Tactile Graphs." *Journal of Special Education* 17 (1983): 215–226.

Barth, John L. "Incised Grids: Enhancing the Readability of Tangible Graphs for the Blind." *Human Factors* 26 (February 1984): 61–70.

Barth, John L., and Edward P. Berlá. *Tangible Graphs.* Louisville, Ky.: American Printing House for the Blind, 1984.

Bentzen, Billie Louise, and Alec F. Peck. "Factors Affecting Traceability of Lines for Tactile Graphics." *Journal of Visual Impairment and Blindness* 73 (September 1979): 264–269.

Berlá, Edward P. "Behavioral Strategies and Problems in Scanning and Interpreting Tactual Displays." *New Outlook for the Blind* 66 (October 1972): 277–286.

Bliss, James C., and Hewitt D. Crane. "Tactile Perception." *AFB Research Bulletin*, no. 19 (June 1969): 205–230.

Caulfield, H. J. "Photographic Generation of Tactile Displays for the Blind." *Braille Research Newsletter,* no. 7 (March 1978): 23–24.

Coleman, P. W. F. "Tactile Displays: Their Current State and A New Approach." In *Computerised Braille Production: Today and Tomorrow,* edited by Derrick W. Croisdale, Hermann Kamp, and Helmut Werner. New York: Springer-Verlag, 1983.

Corcoran, Jane M. "Tactile Illustrations." *NBA Bulletin* (fall 1990): 23–25.

Craven, Roger W. "The Use of Aluminum Sheets in Producing Tactual Maps for Blind Persons." *New Outlook for the Blind* 66 (November 1972): 323–330. Also published as "Making Embossed Maps as a Hobby" in *New Beacon* 57 (March 1973): 58–62.

Cylke, Frank Kurt, and Judith M. Dixon, eds. *International Directory of Tactile Map Collections.* Washington, D.C.: Section of Libraries for the Blind, International Federation of Library Associations and Institutions, and National Library Service for the Blind and Physically Handicapped, Library of Congress, 1985.

Edman, Polly K. *Tactile Graphics.* New York: American Foundation for the Blind, 1992.

Eriksson, Yvonne. *Tactile Pictures: Pictorial Representations for the Blind, 1784–1940.* Göteborg, Sweden: Acta Universitatis Gothoburgensis, 1998.

Fricke, Joerg. "Displaying Laterally Moving Tactile Information." In *Computers for Handicapped Persons,* edited by Wolfgang L. Zagler, Geoffrey Busby, and Roland R. Wagner. Proceedings of the 4th International Conference, ICCHP '94 in Vienna, Austria,

September 14–16, 1994. New York: Springer-Verlag, 1994.

Gardner, John A. "Tactile Graphics: An Overview and Resource Guide." *Information Technology and Disabilities* 3 (December 1996): 1–13. Also found at http://www.rit.edu/~easi/itd/itdv03n4/article2.html.

Gill, J. M. "A Method for the Production of Tactual Maps and Diagrams." *AFB Research Bulletin,* no. 26 (June 1973): 203–204.

Gill, J. M. "Tactual Mapping." *AFB Research Bulletin,* no. 28 (October 1974): 57–80.

Gill, J. M., and G. A. James. "A Study on the Discriminability of Tactual Point Symbols." *AFB Research Bulletin,* no. 26 (June 1973): 19–34.

Hampshire, B. "The Design and Production of Tactile Graphic Material for the Visually Impaired." *Applied Ergonomics* 10 (June 1979): 87–97.

Hering, Sally. "How to Make a Simple Raised Line Drawing." *NBA Bulletin* (spring 1998): 19–20.

Hinton, Ronald. "First Introduction to Tactiles." *British Journal of Visual Impairment* 9 (November 1991): 79–82.

Hinton, Ronald. "Tactual Experience in Relation to Diagram Use." *British Journal of Visual Impairment* 6 (spring 1988): 11–14.

James, Grahame. "A Kit for Making Raised Maps." *New Beacon* 59 (April 1975): 85–90.

James, G. A., and J. M. Gill. "Mobility Maps for the Visually Handicapped: A Study of Learning and

Retention of Raised Symbols." *AFB Research Bulletin*, no. 27 (April 1974): 87–98.

James, G. A., and J. M. Gill. "A Pilot Study on the Discriminability of Tactile Areal and Line Symbols for the Blind. *AFB Research Bulletin*, no. 29 (June 1975): 23–31.

Kirkwood, Rita. "Tactile Diagrams: Their Production by Current-Day Methods and Their Relative Suitabilities in Use." *British Journal of Visual Impairment* 4 (autumn 1986): 95–99.

Kubiak-Becker, Evelyn, and Thomas P. Dick. "A Brief Historical Overview of Tactile and Auditory Aids for Visually Impaired Mathematics Educators and Students." *Information Technology and Disabilities* 3 (March 1996): 1–5. Also found at http://www.rit.edu/~easi/itd/itdv03n1/article2.html.

Kurze, Martin, Thomas Strothotte, and Doreen Kugas. "Tactile Computer Graphics." In *Graphics Interface '94: Proceedings*. Ottawa: National Research Council of Canada, 1994.

Lederman, Susan J. "Tangible Graphics." *Braille Research Newsletter*, no. 13 (June 1982): 18–21.

Lederman, Susan J., and Jamie I. Campbell. "Tangible Graphs for the Blind." *Human Factors* 24 (February 1982): 85–100.

Lederman, Susan J., and Jamie I. Campbell. "Tangible Line Graphs: An Evaluation and Some Systematic Strategies for Exploration." *Journal of Visual Impairment and Blindness* 77 (March 1983): 108–112.

Liner, Devon Skeele, ed. *Tactile Maps: A Listing of Maps in the National Library Service for the Blind and Physically*

Handicapped Collection. Washington, D.C.: Library of Congress, 1987.

Lötzsch, Jürgen. "Computer-Aided Access to Tactile Graphics for the Blind." In *Computers for Handicapped Persons,* edited by Wolfgang L. Zagler, Geoffrey Busby, and Roland R. Wagner. Proceedings of the 4th International Conference, ICCHP '94 in Vienna, Austria, September 14–16, 1994. New York: Springer-Verlag, 1994.

McGillivray, Robert, and Marlene Gast, eds. "Tactual Graphics: Research and Resources." *Aids and Appliances Review* (Carroll Center for the Blind), no. 14 (fall 1984): 1–60 (entire issue).

Merry, Ralph V., and Frieda Kiefer Merry. "The Tactual Recognition of Embossed Pictures by Blind Children." *Journal of Applied Psychology* 17 (April 1933): 148–163.

Minagawa, Hiroki, Noboru Ohnishi, and Noboru Sugie. "Tactile-Audio User Interface for Blind Persons." In *Computers for Handicapped Persons,* edited by Wolfgang L. Zagler, Geoffrey Busby, and Roland R. Wagner. Proceedings of the 4th International Conference, ICCHP '94 in Vienna, Austria, September 14–16, 1994. New York: Springer-Verlag, 1994.

Murphy, Paul. "The Microcomputer and Tactual Graphics." *Closing the Gap* 8 (August–September 1989): 15–16, 36–37.

Nissen, John C. D. "Virtual Reality Tactile System for Access to Graphics." *Information Technology and Disabilities* 4 (December 1997): 1–3. Also found at http://www.rit.edu/~easi/itd/itdv04n4/article6.html.

Nolan, Carson Y. "Relative Legibility of Raised and Incised Tactual Figures." *Education of the Visually Handicapped* 3 (May 1971): 33–36.

Schiff, William. "Research on Raised Line Drawings." *New Outlook for the Blind* 59 (April 1965): 134–137.

Schiff, William, and Emerson Foulke. *Tactual Perception: A Sourcebook.* Cambridge: Cambridge University Press, 1982.

Wiedel, Joseph W., ed. *Proceedings of the First International Symposium on Maps and Graphics for the Visually Handicapped, March 10–12, 1983, Washington, D.C.* Washington, D.C.: Association of American Geographers, 1983.

Marketing and Promotion

Clark, Leslie L. "The Future of Braille." *Braille Research Newsletter,* no. 9 (April 1979): 5–45.

Evensen, Richard H. "Braille Readership in the United States and Distribution of Braille Materials." *Braille Research Newsletter,* no. 8, (September 1978): 10–16.

Goldish, Louis Harvey. *Braille in the United States: Its Production, Distribution, and Use.* New York: American Foundation for the Blind, 1967.

International Braille Research Center. "Promoting Literacy for the Blind in the 21st Century." Article found at http://www.braille.org/ July 1999.

National Federation of the Blind. "Braille Mentoring Project." Article found at http://www.nfb.org/brlmento.htm July 1999.

World Braille Usage. Washington, D.C.: UNESCO and Library of Congress, National Library Service for the Blind and Physically Handicapped, 1990.

Instruction/Training

Allman, Carol B. "Braille Communication Skills: What Teachers Teach and Visually Impaired Adults Use." *Journal of Visual Impairment and Blindness* 92 (May 1998): 331–337.

Ashcroft, S. C., Freda Henderson, LaRhea D. Sanford, and Alan Koenig. *New Programmed Instruction in Braille.* Nashville: SCALARS Publishing, 1991.

Birns, Shayne. "Review of Literature on Braille Reading." *New Beacon* 61 (February 1977): 29–35.

Brothers, Roy J. "Classroom Use of the Braille Code Recognition Materials." *Education of the Visually Handicapped* 6 (March 1974): 6–13.

Burns, Mary F. *The Burns Braille Transcription Dictionary.* New York: American Foundation for the Blind, 1991.

Cardinale, John Frank. "Methods and Procedures of Braille Reading." *AFB Research Bulletin,* no. 26 (June 1973): 171–183.

Castellano, Carol, and Dawn Kosman. *The Bridge to Braille: Reading and School Success for the Young Blind Child.* Baltimore: National Organization of Parents of Blind Children, 1997.

Caton, Hilda. "Patterns: The Primary Braille Reading Program." *Braille Research Newsletter,* no. 12 (September 1981): 14–16.

Caton, Hilda. "A Primary Reading Program for Beginning Braille Readers." *Journal of Visual Impairment and Blindness* 73 (October 1979): 309–313.

Caton, Hilda, ed. *Print and Braille Literacy: Selecting Appropriate Learning Media.* Louisville, Ky.: American Printing House for the Blind, 1991.

Cheadle, Barbara. "A Parent's Guide to the Slate and Stylus." *Future Reflections* 13 (fall 1994): 6–14.

Cline, Carol S., and John Cardinale. "Braille Reading: A Review of Research." *Education of the Visually Handicapped* 3 (March 1971): 7–10.

Code of Braille Textbook Formats and Techniques. Compiled by the American Association of Workers for the Blind, Association of Educators of the Visually Handicapped, National Braille Association, and Braille Authority of North America. Louisville, Ky.: American Printing House for the Blind, 1977.

Craig, Ruth H. "A Personal Approach to Teaching Braille Reading to Youths and Adults." *New Outlook for the Blind* 69 (January 1975): 11–19.

Curran, Eileen P. *Just Enough to Know Better: A Braille Primer.* Boston: National Braille Press, 1988.

Curry, Rebecca Gavurin. "Using LEA to Teach Blind Children to Read." *Reading Teacher* 29 (December 1975): 272–279.

Dorf, Maxine B., and Barbara H. Tate. *Instruction Manual for Braille Transcribing.* 3d ed. Reprint, with 1987 code changes, Washington, D.C.: Library of Congress, National Library Service for the Blind and Physically Handicapped, 1987.

Erin, Jane N., and Pasinee Sumranveth. "Teaching Reading to Students Who Are Adventitiously Blind." *RE:view* 27 (fall 1995): 103–11.

Forbush, Dorothea. "Reading Readiness and the Blind Child: A Lesson for the 90's from the 50's." *Future Reflections* 15 (summer 1996): 24–30.

Franks, Julie. "To Braille, or Not to Braille? That Is the Question." *British Journal of Visual Impairment* 16 (May 1998): 57–60.

Hamp, Eric P., and Hilda Caton. "A Fresh Look at the Sign System of the Braille Code." *Journal of Visual Impairment and Blindness* 78 (May 1984): 210–214.

Hampshire, Barry. *Working with Braille: A Study of Braille as a Medium of Communication.* Paris: The UNESCO Press, 1981.

Harley, Randall K., and Rachel F. Rawls. "Comparison of Several Approaches for Teaching Braille Reading to Blind Children." *AFB Research Bulletin*, no. 23 (June 1971): 63–85.

Harley, Randall K., Freda M. Henderson, and Mila B. Truan. *The Teaching of Braille Reading.* Springfield, IL: Charles C Thomas, 1979.

Harley, Randall K., James W. Pichert, and Merrie Morrison. "Braille Instruction for Blind Diabetic Adults with Decreased Tactile Sensitivity." *Journal of Visual Impairment and Blindness* 79 (January 1985): 12–17.

Hepker, N. L., and S. Cross-Coquillette. *Braille Too: An Instructional Braille Reading and Writing Program for Secondary Students.* Cedar Rapids, Iowa: Grant Wood Area Education Agency, 1994.

Holbrook, M. Cay, and Alan J. Koenig. "Teaching Braille Reading to Students with Low Vision." *Journal of Visual Impairment and Blindness* 86 (January 1992): 44–48.

Hudson, Laurel J. "Training: Braille." In *Classroom Collaboration*. Watertown, Mass.: Perkins School for the Blind, 1997.

Kapperman, Gayle, and others. "The Computerized Braille Tutor: A Computer-Based Braille Learning Program." *Journal of Visual Impairment and Blindness* 90 (May–June 1996): 252–258.

Knowlton, Marie, and Karen Berger. "Competencies Required of Braille Teachers." *RE:view* 30 (winter 1999): 151–159.

Koenig, Alan J., and M. Cay Holbrook, comps. and eds. *The Braille Enthusiast's Dictionary*. Nashville: SCALARS Publishing, 1995.

Koenig, Alan J., and M. Cay Holbrook. "Determining the Reading Medium for Students with Visual Impairments: A Diagnostic Teaching Approach." *Journal of Visual Impairment and Blindness* 83 (June 1989): 296–302.

Koenig, Alan J., and M. Cay Holbrook. "Determining the Reading Medium for Visually Impaired Students Via Diagnostic Teaching." *Journal of Visual Impairment and Blindness* 85 (February 1991): 61–68.

Lamb, Gayle. "Beginning Braille: A Whole Language-Based Strategy." *Journal of Visual Impairment and Blindness* 90 (May–June 1996): 184–189.

Lamb, Gayle. "Dots for Tots: Emergent Literacy and Braille Reading." *British Journal of Visual Impairment* 16 (1998): 111–115.

Lorimer, John. "Improving Braille Reading Skills: The Case for Extending the Teaching of Braille Reading to Upper Primary and Lower Senior Classes." *British Journal of Visual Impairment* 8 (autumn 1990): 87–89.

Lorimer, John. "Possibilities for Stimulating Learning and Reading Braille. *Braille Research Newsletter,* no. 8 (September 1978): 57–65.

Lowenfeld, Berthold, and Georgie Lee Abel. *Methods of Teaching Braille Reading.* San Francisco: Frederic Burk Foundation for Education, performed by a contract with the Office of Education, U.S. Department of Health, Education, and Welfare, 1967.

Luxton, Lynne. "Overview of Braille Literacy for Rehabilitation Teachers. In *Increasing Literacy Levels: Final Report,* prepared by the Pennsylvania College of Optometry for the Mississippi State University, Rehabilitation Research and Training Center on Blindness and Low Vision (RRTC). Mississippi State: Mississippi State University, RRTC, 1997.

Malinski, Margaret. "Why Parents Should Learn Braille." *Future Reflections* 15 (summer 1996): 30–34.

Mangold, Phillip N. *Teaching Braille Slate and Stylus: A Manual for Mastery.* Castro Valley, Calif.: Exceptional Teaching Aids, 1985.

Mangold, Sally S. "Tactile Perception and Braille Letter Recognition: Effects of Developmental Teaching." *Journal of Visual Impairment and Blindness* 72 (September 1978): 259–266.

Mangold, Sally S., and Philip Mangold. "Selecting the Most Appropriate Primary Learning Medium for Students with Functional Vision." *Journal of Visual Impairment and Blindness* 83 (June 1989): 294–296.

McBride, Vearl G. "Explorations in Rapid Reading in Braille." *New Outlook for the Blind* 68 (January 1974): 8–12.

Millar, Susanna. *Reading by Touch*. New York: Routledge, 1997.

NBA Bulletin. Quarterly. National Braille Association, 3 Townline Circle, Rochester, NY 14623-2513.

Neer, Frances. "A Reading Teacher Learns to Read Braille." *Journal of Visual Impairment and Blindness* 79 (May 1985): 208, 210.

Newman, Slater E. "Braille Learning: First Experiments. *Braille Research Newsletter*, no. 12 (September 1981): 11–13.

Newman, Slater E., and others. "Factors Affecting the Learning of Braille." *Journal of Visual Impairment and Blindness* 76 (February 1982): 59–64.

Olson, Myrna R. "Suggestions for Working with the Remedial Braille Reader." *Journal of Visual Impairment and Blindness* 73 (October 1979): 314–317.

Olson, Myrna R., and Sally S. Mangold. *Guidelines and Games for Teaching Efficient Braille Reading*. New York: American Foundation for the Blind, 1981.

Peaco, Freddie, comp. *Braille Literacy: Resources for Instruction, Writing Equipment, and Supplies*. Reference circular 94–02. Washington, D.C.: Library of Congress,

National Library Service for the Blind and Physically Handicapped, 1994.

Pester, Eleanor. "Braille Instruction for Individuals Who Are Blind Adventitiously: Scheduling, Expectations, and Reading Interests." *Review* 25 (summer 1993): 83–87.

Ponchillia, Paul E., and Pamela A. Durant. "Teaching Behaviors and Attitudes of Braille Instructors in Adult Rehabilitation Centers. *Journal of Visual Impairment and Blindness* 89 (September–October 1995): 432–439.

Ponchillia, Paul E., and Susan V. Ponchillia. "Braille and Other Tactile Forms of Communication." In *Foundations of Rehabilitation Teaching with Persons Who Are Blind or Visually Impaired.* New York: AFB Press, 1996.

"Prebraille Readiness." *Future Reflections* 10 (winter–spring 1991): 13–16.

Reisfeld, Joanie Hineck. "Removing Blind Spots: My Reawakening to the Potential of Braille Instruction." *Review* 27 (winter 1996): 175–179.

Rex, Evelyn J., and Cheryl Richesin. "Report on a Review of Textbooks to Teach Braille to Blind Adults." *Journal of Visual Impairment and Blindness* 90 (May–June 1996): 266–268.

Rhyne, Jane Milnes. "Communication Skills." In *Curriculum for Teaching the Visually Impaired.* Springfield, Ill.: Charles C. Thomas, 1981.

Risjord, Constance, Josephine Stratton, and Susan Christensen. *Literary Braille Refresher Course for Teachers and Transcribers.* Rochester, NY: National Braille Association, 1995.

Stone, Juliet. "Has Braille Had Its Day?" *British Journal of Visual Impairment* 13 (July 1995): 80–81.

Swenson, Anna M. *Beginning with Braille: Firsthand Experiences with a Balanced Approach to Literacy.* New York: AFB Press, 1999.

Swenson, Anna M. "A Process Approach to Teaching Braille Writing at the Primary Level." *Journal of Visual Impairment and Blindness* 85 (May 1991): 217–221.

Tuttle, Dean W. "A Comparison of Three Reading Media for the Blind: Braille, Normal Recording, and Compressed Speech." *AFB Research Bulletin,* no. 27 (April 1974): 217–230.

Umsted, Richard G. "Improvement of Braille Reading Through Code Recognition Training: Review of the Literature and Bibliography. *AFB Research Bulletin,* no. 23 (June 1971): 50–62.

Ward, Marjorie, and Sandra McCormick. "Reading Instruction for Blind and Low Vision Children in the Regular Classroom." *Reading Teacher* 35 (January 1981): 434–444.

Weiss, Jeff. "Braille and Limited Language Skills." *Journal of Visual Impairment and Blindness* 74 (February 1980): 81–83.

Whitesell, Corinne. "Vox Pop: A New Look at Teaching Braille to Adults." *Dialogue* 27 (summer 1988): 49–54.

Willoughby, Doris M., and Sharon L.M. Duffy. "Teaching Braille to Young Children and Braille Reading and Writing." In *Handbook for Itinerant and Resource Teachers of Blind and Visually Impaired Students.* Baltimore: National Federation of the Blind, 1989.

Wittenstein, Stuart H. "Braille Literacy: Preservice Training and Teachers' Attitudes. *Journal of Visual Impairment and Blindness* 88 (November–December 1994): 516–524.

Wormsley, Diane P., and Frances Mary D'Andrea, eds. *Instructional Strategies for Braille Literacy.* New York: AFB Press, 1997.

Zulli, Ruth Dean. "Teaching Braille: A Creative and Practical Art. *Dialogue* 32 (summer 1993): 14–18.

Apparatus

ABLEDATA. "Braille Writers and Electronic Note-takers." Fact Sheet no. 18, July 1993. August 1999. Found at http://www.abledata.com/text2/elec_br.htm.

ABLEDATA. "Manual Braille Writing Aids." Fact Sheet no. 17, July 1993. August 1999. Found at http://www.abledata.com/text2/man_br.htm.

Anderson, Gary B., and David W. Rogers. "An Inexpensive Braille Terminal Device." *AFB Research Bulletin,* no. 22 (December 1970): 111–117.

Andrews, David. "Putting the Mountbatten Brailler in Perspective." *Braille Monitor* (June 1993): 772–775.

Barr, Ruth L. "Developing and Evaluating a Simplified Braille Writing Device." *New Outlook for the Blind* 62 (May 1968): 148–152.

Bower, Rachael, and others, eds. "Braille and Tactile Output Systems." In *Trace Resourcebook: Assistive Technologies for Communication, Control, and Computer*

Access. 1998–99 edition. Madison: Trace Research and Development Center, 1997.

Connell, Tim. "The Mountbatten Brailler: An Update." *Dialogue* 34 (winter 1995): 56–61.

Dotson, Nick. "Romeo and VersaPoint: A Comparison of Two Braille Embossers. *Tactic* 10 (winter 1994): 41–45.

Judy Dixon's Collection of Braille and Tactile-Writing Slates. Found at http://www.brailleslates.org/ Last modified August 1999.

Leventhal, Jay D. "A Review of an Inexpensive Interpoint Braille Printer. *JVIB News Service* 88 (March–April 1994): 18–20.

Leventhal, Jay D., and Julio C. Perez. "A Review of the Two Leading Braille Translation Software Packages." *JVIB News Service* 90 (March–April 1996): 13–16.

Leventhal, Jay D., Mark M. Uslan, and Elliot M. Schreier. "A Review of Braille Printers." *Journal of Visual Impairment and Blindness* 85 (October 1991): 346–350.

Marie and Eugene Callahan Museum of the American Printing House for the Blind. *Mechanical Writers for Embossed Characters and Typewriters Modified for Blind Operators,* museum exhibit. May 1999. http://www.aph.org/braillewriters/bwriter.htm.

Morrison, Ray E. "Braille Embossing and Transmission Equipment." *AFB Research Bulletin,* no. 22 (December 1970): 71–82.

Literacy

American Foundation for the Blind. National Literacy Program and Braille. Article found at http://www.afb.org/i_res.html#braille. (September 1999).

"Braille Literacy and the Individuals with Disabilities Education Act. *Braille Monitor* (April 1997): 237–238.

"Comments on Position Paper on Literacy of the Council of Executives of American Residential Schools for the Visually Handicapped." *RE:view* 23 (summer 1991): 67–74.

Connell, Tim. "The Mountbatten Brailler and Braille Literacy." *Braille Monitor* (June 1993): 768–771.

Council of Executives of American Residential Schools for the Visually Handicapped. "Literacy for Blind and Visually Impaired School-Age Students: A Position Paper." *RE:view* 22 (fall 1990): 159–163.

Craig, Christopher J. "Family Support of the Emergent Literacy of Children with Visual Impairments." *Journal of Visual Impairment and Blindness* 90 (May–June 1996): 194–200.

Croft, Diane L. "The Battle for Braille and Literacy." *Braille Monitor* (January 1988): 21–22.

Drezek, Wendy. "Emergent Braille Literacy with Move, Touch, Read." *Journal of Visual Impairment and Blindness* 93 (February 1999): 104–107.

Eldridge, Carlton. "Braille Literacy and Higher Education. *Education of the Visually Handicapped* 11 (spring 1979): 8–12.

Eldridge, Carlton. "Braille Literacy: The Best Route to Equal Education." *Journal of Visual Impairment and Blindness* 73 (October 1979): 331–333.

Ferrante, Olivia. "Why Blind Children Should Learn Braille." *Journal of Visual Impairment and Blindness* 80 (February 1986): 594.

Gashel, J. "National Convention Calls for Braille Literacy. *Future Reflections* 6 (fall 1988): 31–32.

Ianuzzi, Jody. "Braille or Print: Why the Debate?" *Braille Monitor* (May 1992): 229–233.

Jernigan, Kenneth. "Literacy, Braille, and a Formula for Action." *Braille Monitor* (January 1989): 48–50.

Jernigan, Kenneth. "Of Literacy, Braille, and the Oddities of Semantics." *Braille Monitor* (March 1990): 172–175.

Johnson, Louise. "The Braille Literacy Crisis for Children." *Journal of Visual Impairment and Blindness* 90 (May–June 1996): 276–278.

Koenig, Alan J. "A Framework for Understanding the Literacy of Individuals with Visual Impairments." *Journal of Visual Impairment and Blindness* 86 (September 1992): 277–284.

McCall, Steve, and Juliet Stone. "Literacy for Blind Children Through Moon: A Possibility?" *British Journal of Visual Impairment* 10 (July 1992): 53–54.

Mullen, Edward A. "Decreased Braille Literacy: A Symptom of a System in Need of Reassessment." *Re:view* 22 (fall 1990): 164–169.

Nicely, Betty. "Guidelines for Braille Literacy: A First Step." *Braille Monitor* (October 1991): 551–556.

Raeder, William M. "Overcoming Roadblocks to Literacy for Blind Children." *Braille Monitor* (July–August 1991): 363–365.

Reid, Juliet M.V. "Assessing the Literacy of Adults Who Are Visually Impaired: Conceptual and Measurement Issues." *Journal of Visual Impairment and Blindness* 92 (July 1998): 447–453.

Rex, Evelyn J., and others. *Foundations of Braille Literacy.* New York: AFB Press, 1994.

Rex, Evelyn J. "Issues Related to Literacy of Legally Blind Learners." *Journal of Visual Impairment and Blindness* 83 (June 1989): 306–313.

Schroeder, Fredric K. "Literacy: The Key to Opportunity." *Journal of Visual Impairment and Blindness* 83 (June 1989): 290–293.

Spungin, Susan J. "Braille and Beyond: Braille Literacy in a Larger Context." *Journal of Visual Impairment and Blindness* 90 (May–June 1996): 271–274.

Spungin, Susan J. *Braille Literacy: Issues for Blind Persons, Families, Professionals, and Producers of Braille.* New York: American Foundation for the Blind, 1990.

Spungin, Susan J. "Braille Literacy: Issues for Consumers and Providers." *Braille Monitor* (November 1989): 667–675.

Stephens, Otis. "Braille—Implications for Living." *Journal of Visual Impairment and Blindness* 83 (June 1989): 288–289.

Stone, Juliet, and Steve McCall. "Moon as a Route to Literacy Project: Summary of Findings." *British Journal of Visual Impairment* 12 (March 1994): 34–35.

Stratton, Josephine M. "Emergent Literacy: A New Perspective. *Journal of Visual Impairment and Blindness* 90 (May–June 1996): 177–183.

Stratton, Josephine M., and Suzette Wright. "On the Way to Literacy: Experiences for Young Visually Impaired Children." *Review* 23 (summer 1991): 55–62.

Wittenstein, Stuart H., and Maurine L. Pardee. "Teachers' Voices: Comments on Braille and Literacy from the Field." *Journal of Visual Impairment and Blindness* 90 (May–June 1996): 201–209.

Zago, Penelope A. "Weaving the Cloth of Literacy: The Relationship Between Braille and Reading. *Journal of Visual Impairment and Blindness* 90 (May–June 1996): 274–276.

Alternative Production

Hislop, David W., B. L. Zuber, and John L. Trimble. "Inkbraille as a Potential New Reading System for the Blind. *Journal of Rehabilitation Research and Development* 21 (1984): 54–57.

Braille Displays

Craig, James C., and Carl E. Sherrick. "Dynamic Tactile Displays." In *Tactual Perception: A Sourcebook,* edited by William Schiff and Emerson Foulke. Cambridge: Cambridge University Press, 1982.

Dalrymple, George F. "An Electromechanical Numeric Braille Display: A Familiar Tactile Representation of

Electrically Encoded Digital Signals." *AFB Research Bulletin*, no. 29 (June 1975): 149–152.

Dalrymple, George F. "TSPS Braille Display." *Braille Research Newsletter*, no. 6 (October 1977): 78–81.

Doorlag, Deanne M., and Donald H. Doorlag. "Cassette Braille: A New Communication Tool for Blind People. *Journal of Visual Impairment and Blindness* 77 (April 1983): 158–161.

Gill, J. M. "Paperless Braille Devices." *Braille Research Newsletter*, no. 12 (September 1981): 26–33.

Grunwald, Arnold. *The Argonne Braille Project.* Argonne, Ill.: Argonne National Laboratory, 1977.

Kendrick, Deborah. "A Lightweight Computer for Heavy Braille Use: A Review of Blazie Engineering's Braille Lite." *Tactic* 10 (fall 1994): 15–19.

Lazzaro, Joseph J. "Adapting the Video Monitor." In *Adapting PCs for Disabilities.* Reading: Addison-Wesley Publishing Company, 1996.

Leventhal, Jay D., and Mark M. Uslan. "A Comparison of the Two Leading Electronic Braille Notetakers." *Journal of Visual Impairment and Blindness* 86 (June 1992): 258–260.

Leventhal, Jay D., Elliot M. Schreier, and Mark M. Uslan. "Electronic Braille Displays for Personal Computers." *Journal of Visual Impairment and Blindness* 84 (October 1990): 423–427.

Papenmeier, F. H. "The BRAILLEX System." *Braille Research Newsletter*, no. 7 (March 1978): 3–17.

Rose, Leonard. "Full-Page Paperless Braille Display." *Braille Research Newsletter*, no. 10 (July 1979): 59–60.

Rose, Stanley E., and Joan B. Rose. "The Rose Braille Display Reader." In *Computerised Braille Production: Today and Tomorrow,* edited by Derrick W. Croisdale, Hermann Kamp, and Helmut Werner. New York: Springer-Verlag, 1983.

Sriskanthan, Nadarajah, and K. Regu Subramanian. "Braille Display Terminal for Personal Computers. *IEEE Transactions on Consumer Electronics* 36 (May 1990): 121–128.

Visser, Edwin. "The Browser: A Handheld Brailler." *Journal of Visual Impairment and Blindness* 88 (November–December 1994): 568.

"Widening Range of Braille Displays." *SAF Technology Update* (June 1990): 5–13.

Electronic Delivery

Nicolussi, R. "Use of Modern Equipment for Storing and Reading Braille Script as well as Establishment of National Data Courier Centres." *Braille Research Newsletter,* no. 8 (September 1978): 66–70.

Raeder, William M. "Braille Technology in the Year 2000." *Braille Monitor* (July–August 1991): 365–368.

Experimental Codes

Gardner, John. "DotsPlus: Better than Braille?" Paper presented at the 1993 CSUN International Conference on Technology and Persons with Disabilities, Los Angeles, March 1993.

Gardner, John. "The DotsPlus Tactile Font Set." *Journal of Visual Impairment and Blindness* 92 (December 1998): 836–840.

Gardner, John. "GS Braille." March 1998. Article found at http://dots.physics.orst.edu/gs.html.

Gardner, John. "TRIANGLE: A Mathematics Scratch Pad for the Blind." August 1999. Article found at http://dots.physics.orst.edu/triangle.html.

Sahyun, Steve, and others. "DotsPlus: A How-to Demonstration for Making Tactile Graphics and Formatted Math Using the Tactile Graphics Embosser." Proceedings of the 1998 CSUN International Conference on Technology and Persons with Disabilities, March 1998, can be found at http://www.dinf.org/csun_98/csun98_103.htm.